Knowledge
of the Self-Revealing God
in the Thought
of Thomas Forsyth Torrance

John Douglas Morrison

Knowledge of the Self-Revealing God in the Thought of Thomas Forsyth Torrance

Wipf & Stock
PUBLISHERS
Eugene, Oregon

Wipf and Stock Publishers
199 W 8th Ave, Suite 3
Eugene, OR 97401

Knowledge of the Self-Revealing God in the Thought of Thomas Forsyth Torrance
By Morrison, John D.
Copyright©1997 by Morrison, John Douglas
ISBN: 1-59752-085-3
Publication date 2/7/2005
Previously published by Peter Lang, 1997

With Special Thanks to

Robert P. Scharlemann
Carlos M.N. Eire
M. Jamie Ferreira
John C. Fletcher
Lee W. Hähnlen
Daniel R. Mitchell

This work is dedicated to my family without whose help and support this work would have been impossible. For that reason this has been as much their work as mine.

Ellen Marie
Heather Lee
Shawn Mark

Psalm 37:4
Isaiah 41:10
Romans 4:20-21

TABLE OF CONTENTS

PREFACE

For Thomas Forsyth Torrance theology which is truly that, a speaking of God, must be a scientific endeavor in which one seeks after knowledge of the object in the way that object has given itself to be known as it is in itself. God in Christ has made himself known objectively in the world and to humanity, and in obedience to that Word and the knowing relation established by it the theologian must serve that Word, inquiring into "the given," in order thereby to facilitate further disclosure through theological expression increasingly appropriate to the object. It is such theo-logical thinking which assents to and obeys the Word and the way of revelation that Torrance is working to uncover, and then to faithfully follow himself in order to serve the Truth of God in his creative-redemptive interactive relation with the world and humanity.

Torrance, author of some twenty books on theology, the complementary relation of theology and the physical sciences, and historical theology (plus numerous articles), has been considered by many the leading British theologian of the latter part of the twentieth century. Yet Torrance is also a theologian who is quite unique in bringing about the manifestation, correction and integration of both British and continental theological-philosophical concerns. Soren Kierkegaard's thought is very significant for Torrance's theology. Torrance is considered one of the leading neo-Barthian theologians in the world and one who is (with such "Barthian" theologians as Eberhard Jüngel and Robert Jenson) seeking to uncover some of the yet "untapped" aspects of Karl Barth's thought. In Torrance's case this is to be found in his restoration of a proper "natural theology" (versus the "natural theology" of all "scholastic" theology) and in his understanding of the nature of creation in relation to God. Torrance is also an energetic leader in the dialogue taking place between theology and the natural sciences and is one of the most prominent of a growing group of theologians engaging the physical sciences and/or physical scientists engaging in theology (e.g., A R Peacocke, Langdon Gilkey, Phillip Clayton,

John Polkinghorne, etc.). But therein Torrance is almost unique in emphasizing not simply some overt "theistic" position but maintaining an emphatically trinitarian base, a base he believes to be critical to both the theo-logical and physical sciences (cf. the relation of the Being and Act of God in "creation out of nothing"). Undoubtedly one finds here his emphases on objectivity, Barth's Christology and trinitarian theology, and his appreciation of the empirical sciences brought together. In and through all of these connected interests it will be shown that his concern is to clarify and to deepen realist scientific knowing out of the proper object of the particular science involved and the epistemological and methodological importance of such for theology. Theology's proper "domain" is first the knowledge of God as God has given himself to be known. It is only in this way that theology can again be done scientifically. Only as theology is called back to rigorous scientific thinking according to the nature, the mode of rationality, disclosed by God, its proper object (or "Object"), as exemplified by the "new physics," can theology as a science serve God's redemptive revelation. Because of Torrance's constant desire to "hear" the Word of God in Jesus Christ, and thereby to "think after" the way God has actually taken toward us in the world, (i.e., the "logic of Grace") in order to set forth faithful theological expression in ways appropriate to the Being of God, we will often use (as Torrance himself does) the hyphenated form "theo-logic" or "theo-logical." It is this crucial aspect of Thomas Torrance's theological efforts which we will examine. Yet while so often referred to and acknowledged, almost nothing has come forth on or in response to his creative theological thinking. As Professor Alasdair I.C. Heron of the University of Erlangen-Nurnberg has said, "[Torrance] is one of the most substantial (and most neglected) figures in recent Western intellectual history." It is my purpose in this work to lay bare something of the heart of that Torrancian substance, an issue which Torrance acknowledges to be at the very center of his thought. Torrance's important work needs to be given concerned critical analysis, especially at so significant a theological junction as revelation and the possibility of the knowledge of God.

    In order to properly examine this epistemologico-cosmologico-theological core of Torrance's thought it will be necessary to understand it against the background of his negative-critical response to the modern "re-entrenchment" of "dualism" in relation to the Christian faith and the realist knowledge of God in Christ.[1] As a result of the epistemological and cosmological influence of Descartes, Newton and Kant (among others), Christian theology (as exemplified by Schleiermacher, Bultmann and Protestant Orthodoxy) has again fallen into "dualist," "schismatic" or "disjunctive" thinking, i.e., any assumptions which would separate the transcendent God and direct, objective knowledge of God from the space-time world and human beings therein.

    We will find that the bases of Torrance's understanding of theo-logical thinking, theological science and hence his concern for true objectivity (versus objectivism), critical realist epistemology, the role of belief, assent to the truth, and the crucial, referential role of language appropriate to the object are important facets of Torrance's restorative purpose. In Torrance, such emphases in theology are analogically linked to the "modern revolution" in the physical sciences, especially after Albert Einstein, whereby the physical sciences (as in all true knowing) are found to have been healed of their old positivistic, empiricistic, phenomenalist (Newtonian) tendencies. The physical sciences are again recognizing the need to submit to the inherent rationality of external reality, to penetrate ever more deeply into the objective rational order, and thus to faithfully know their proper objects as they actually are. This is Torrance's understanding of true science as realist and truly objective. This "shift" back to realism and objectivity is found to be of signal importance for Torrance as its insights are "applied" to the theo-logical task from the place of God's self-givenness. Torrance's application of such insights from physics to what is called here his Christocentric-Trinitarian theology will be followed out step by step, or "level by level," to what he believes to be the basis of all knowledge and rationality, the Trinity.

But this study will not only examine and bring together the parts of Torrance's wide-ranging and sometimes "far flung" theo-logical thinking; it will seek also to ask the question of adequacy. Has Torrance fulfilled or completed his own theological intentions? Are his philosophico-theological bases proper to his task, enabling him to give theological expression appropriate to its Object, the historical, redemptive manifestness of the Word of God, God himself? Ultimately the answer will be that Torrance, against all intentions, has fallen somewhat short due to a latent "dualism," a "disjunctive" element in his own theological heritage and formulation.

Special thanks for help and encouragement in the process of research and writing are due to Gerald Fogarty, Stanley Hauerwas, John Fletcher, Vanessa Van Eaton, Michelle Ellison, and Susan Butler and especially to M. Jamie Ferreira, Carlos Eire and my *doktorvator* Robert P. Scharlemann. The book is dedicated to my wife Ellen and to my children Heather and Shawn.

NOTES

1. Torrance maintains that the Nicene Fathers were successful in overcoming the disjunctive dualism of their Greek culture. The Reformers were able to overcome the re-entrenchment of dualism which had arisen again after Augustine and became solidified in the theology of the high Scholastic theologians, e.g., Thomas Aquinas. These are paradigmatic for that theological task which Torrance desires to accomplish now in the face of renewed dualistic thinking.

ABBREVIATIONS

BSCL	*Belief in Science and the Christian Life*
CFM	*The Christian Frame of Mind*
CTSC	*Christian Theology and Scientific Culture*
DCO	*Divine and Contingent Order*
GG	*The Ground and Grammar of Theology*
GR	*God and Rationality*
HJC	*The Hermeneutics of John Calvin*
KBET	*Karl Barth: An Introduction to His Early Theology*
MC	*The Mediation of Christ*
RET	*Reality and Evangelical Theology*
RST	*Reality and Scientific Theology*
SOF	*The School of Faith*
STI	*Space, Time and Incarnation*
STR	*Space, Time and Resurrection*
TCFK	*Transformation and Convergence in the Frame of Knowledge*
TF	*The Trinitarian Faith*
TRn	*Theology in Reconciliation*
TRst	*Theology in Reconstruction*
TS	*Theological Science*

Chapter 1

Introduction To The Thought Of
Thomas Forsyth Torrance

In this introductory chapter to the larger issue of Thomas Forsyth Torrance's concern for and understanding of the realist knowledge of God in the world, objective, scientific knowledge of the triune God in Jesus Christ, we will first undertake to present the problem in the context of current discussion in a preliminary way. A biographical sketch of Torrance will further illuminate this matter in relation to the theology of Karl Barth and scientific theology. Then a brief overview of Torrance's theological heritage will be given, at least as he understands such to be. This will begin with the Church Fathers and move on through the Reformers, Scottish realism, Soren Kierkegaard and, interestingly, such modern physicists as Clerk Maxwell and Albert Einstein, as well as theologian Karl Barth and philosopher of science Michael Polanyi. Then several of Torrance's central theological concerns will be mentioned, primarily as they unfold from the objective self-revelation of the triune God who is understood to have given himself to be known in the world as he is in Jesus Christ, the incarnate Word. This is the heart of Torrance's thought and the ground for his emphasis on the realist knowledge of God. This will be connected to a brief, preliminary discussion of Torrance's strong, active desire to counteract epistemological and cosmological dualism. Why does Torrance see dualism as so harmful? Finally there will be an overview of the chapters. Issues and matters touched upon in this chapter will be shown in the ensuing chapters for their full significance in Torrance's theology.

The Historical Context and Concern of Torrance's Realist Scientific Theology

Thomas Torrance does theology not simply out of a strong conception of Christian faith which cannot be generalized in some amorphous way, but also from an understanding of faith as rational response to the being and act of God who has actually revealed himself in Jesus Christ.

> . . . I find the presence and being of God bearing upon my experience and thought so powerfully that I cannot but be convinced of His overwhelming reality and rationality. To doubt the existence of God would be an act of sheer irrationality, for it would mean that my reason had become unhinged from its bond with real being. Yet in knowing God I am deeply aware that my relation to Him has been damaged, that disorder has resulted in my mind, and that it is I who obstruct knowledge of God by getting in between Him and myself, as it were. But I am also aware that His presence presses unrelentingly upon me through the disorder of my mind, for He will not let Himself be thwarted by it, challenging and repairing it, and requiring of me on my part to yield my thoughts to His healing and controlling revelation.[1]

This faith or "intuitive knowledge"[2] of the actual, objective disclosure of God in Jesus Christ is so central a concern for Torrance because the actual knowledge of God as he is in himself, which is central to redemption, has been systematically rendered impossible for human knowledge by modern developments which have prescriptively limited knowledge to mere phenomena. These cosmological and epistemological developments have raised again problems for the gospel and Christian theology in ways that parallel earlier crises in the history of the Christian faith. As the early Church (e.g., Nicene fathers and Athanasius) was faced with Greek dualism which would nullify the truth of the redemptive movement of God for humanity in Christ; and as the Reformers (especially Calvin, in Torrance's opinion) are said to have been faced with the dualism of the medieval synthesis arising from Augustinian neo-Platonic, Aristotelian and Occamist elements, so too the modern Western perspective has fallen anew into dualist tendencies which lock out any possibility of direct knowledge of God as he is in himself. It is a dualism which allows at best oblique, indirect and existentialist-subjectivist tactics in relation to the question of God for theologizing. The outcome of this re-entrenchment of dualism has been the reduction of theology to "anthropology."[3]

God known as he is in himself in Jesus Christ is the proper focus, the proper object of the Christian faith, and ultimately the intelligible basis for knowledge as such. As this is seen to be the foundation and that which unifies knowledge in every realm and on every level, Torrance is adamant that any perspective that dualistically cuts off the knowledge of God has inevitably catastrophic effects not only upon theology but upon all claims to actual knowledge. Human life is thereby fragmented. The cognitive relationship of human beings to God is distorted, forcing one back upon the self (subjectivism).[4] Humanity then, having no other recourse, turns inward and finally reckons "reality" or the "truth" as that which is somehow formed and imposed on the external world (being) by the mind of the subject. For this reason Torrance is heartened by the objectivity (versus objectivism) of the natural sciences, especially physics, and calls theology (and all natural and social sciences) back to a "classical" objectivity arising from a critical realism which must proceed toward knowledge according to the way imposed by the proper, intelligible object of that particular science.

In the case of true theological science, that proper object which discloses itself and requires that all proper inquiry "think after" (*Nachdenken*) that self-disclosure is also personal, and more than just personal. It is the transcendent Lord who in all of our proper, objective questioning actually speaks. It is *Word* of God, the transcendent *Logos* who is of God's very Being, which "questions the questioner," as Torrance so often puts it, "down to the very root of his being."[5] Therefore, says Torrance, theology (and all proper scientific inquiry) must "move from a dualist outlook to a unitary outlook, and to the realist modes of thought that arise in such an outlook . . . "so that we may "have restored to us the unity of form and being." As the destructive "dualist" perspective affects all "intramundane relations" as well as that between God and the created universe, the two domains being affected by each other, so the unitary, realist perspective on the created universe and the doctrine of God as the "one creative Source of all order in the universe (intelligibility) are profoundly interconnected"[6] and must be emphasized. This theological science then is the

> . . . active engagement in that cognitive relation to God in obedience to the
> demands of his reality and self-giving. In it we probe into the problematic
> condition of the human mind before God and seek to bring knowledge of Him
> into clear focus, so that the truth of God may shine through to it unhindered
> by its opacity and the human mind may acquire clear and orderly forms
> through which to apprehend and conceive His reality . . . to allow God's own
> eloquent self-evidence to sound through to us in His *Logos* so that we may
> know and understand Him out of His own rationality and under the
> determination of His divine being.[7]

By true "theo-logical" response in accordance with the actual, self-disclosure of God to the world, Torrance intends to do for the redemptive knowledge of God in the modern context what the Nicene fathers and Reformers sought to do paradigmatically in their own crisis contexts in the face of destructive dualism, i.e., to restore theology to "rigor and dedicated rationality" in accord with its proper object as is found today among the work of natural scientists.[8] This scientific theology rests upon its own rational grounds and is highly relevant to science in every area of human experience, says Torrance, for without clarification of human knowledge of the Creator (the enterprise given to theology) then humanity will never come to the "overall rational unity in understanding for which the specialized sciences are grasping." It is only when theology is "pursued as a pure science for its own sake, or rather for the sake and service of God Himself, that its intellectual beauty is properly unveiled."[9]

Torrance is also seeking to do and to call others back to scientific theology, theological objectivity, in a modern context wherein there has occurred an "eclipse of God." The problem has the same ultimate root in the loss of objectivity, leading to subjectivism. Torrance says that

> An eclipse of the sun, Buber reminds us, is something that occurs between the sun and our eyes, not in the sun itself. So it is with the eclipse of God that is now taking place, for something has stepped between our existence and God to shut off the light of heaven, but that something is in fact ourselves, our own bloated selfhood. The root problem of the "new theologians" would seem to lie in the fact that they are unable to distinguish God from their own swollen subjectivity.[10]

Understanding of God's self-disclosure in Christ is said to be confused whenever it is encased within an epistemological framework whereby human knowing and what is objectively known are separated so that inquiries are "cut loose from an underlying and coherent substructure (ontology) in our apprehension of reality."[11] It ought to be recognized that the human subject has a necessary place in knowledge, for it is the subject who, in reciprocal relation to the object, knows the object. But increasingly the object is reckoned as relative to the subject, affected by the subject, so that in the subject-object relation it is the subjective pole that becomes masterful, intruding itself on the object. So while theology is personal and involves a personal relation with God, theology has often imposed the "self" between the person and God resulting in the inability to see God beyond or other than the self. Torrance agrees with Buber in asserting, ". . . when we interpret encounters with God as self-encounters man's very structure is destroyed."[12] This has affected the physical sciences whereby inquiries end up "putting into the mouth of nature the answers she is to give back to us," i.e., "we impose our own pattern of mind upon nature; the only nature we know then is the nature that is formed and shaped in our understanding of it."[13] In the modern "eclipse" of God by what Torrance sees to be the intrusion of human subjectivity, and hence "the conceptual letting go of God," there has occurred the detachment of thought and language from the reality of God and a "conceptuality arising out of our own consciousness" which "has been substituted for a conceptuality forced upon us from the side of God Himself."[14] When God becomes a reality seen only in and out of the human center, "when the question that man puts to God is finally himself, it is difficult to see how the way of 'God' can avoid the way taken by man." This "eclipse" has meant the loss of the dynamic conception of God as living Creator "actively at work in the world He has made."[15]   Loss of this perspective has meant detachment of nature from God and the creative activity of God. Nature is regarded as an "independent source of knowledge and as the sphere of man's own creative activity."[16]   Such separation of nature from God and thought of God has led to an "ever-widening gulf between God and the world, and a secularization set in" which has damaged the whole of human life and thought. Thought about God has swung to a total "disjunction between God and nature so that God's activity is banished from the world He has made and nature is sealed off from any meaning beyond itself in God."[17]   Thus Torrance's consistent concern and responsive agenda arises because of the "disastrous consequences" of such for human life in general and for Christian theology in particular, especially as the goal of theology is to express the objective, redemptive self-disclosure of God in the world in Jesus Christ with ever greater clarity and coherence-correspondence to the actual truth of God as it is in himself. This modern situation is a great concern,

> . . . for (this dualistic, disjunctive construct) cuts away from (Christian theology) any thought of the interaction of God with the world so that it makes impossible not only a doctrine of providence but any doctrine of incarnation, and it cuts away likewise any interaction between the revealing and saving activity of God and human historical existence so that God is made dumb, no real word of God breaking through to us . . . this radical dualism is something like the old pagan dichotomy between the intelligible and sensible realms, or the old deistic disjunction between an idle God and a mechanistic universe.[18]

Within this "confusion", with its destructive consequences, Torrance sees his role as one with the scientific realism of the physical sciences in being engaged in restoring human thought and life to its proper intelligibility, unitariness and objectivity which arises from the ultimate intelligibility of its ground, the transcendent Reality and Rationality of God.

Still, Torrance believes that his primary role within this larger cultural endeavor is as a scientific theologian. He desires then to be faithful to theology's Object, God, and to make theo-logical statements that arise from and actually refer to Reality external to the human knower as this will occur "under the compulsion of the realities they map out," including verification processes in thought and formulation. In the rationality of theology, ultimately the *Logos* of God, the theologian's goal is to bring thought and expression into actual, though limited, "contact" with the real nature of things, the Truth of the Supreme Being of God. Methodologically, the knowledge arising in particular sciences occurs in relation to the proper object of investigation. Torrance says that if scientific investigations of the world are understood to make real contact with the real nature of things (i.e., the truth of being), and then are able to bring our thought or knowledge into a consistent and illuminating mathematical representation which enables persons to penetrate to ever more profound levels at many points, then the inherent rationality of the objective world "imposes" itself upon the human knower. So it is, he says, with scientific theology.

> . . . in scientific inquiry into the ways and works of God we consider that our thought has made genuine contact with the divine Reality when we can bring our knowledge to an intelligible and enlightening unity through which the *Logos* of God Himself presses itself convincingly upon our minds. We direct our questions to the self-giving of God in Jesus Christ and allow our minds to fall under the power of the divine rationality that becomes revealed in Him. It is a rationality inherent in the reality of the incarnate Word before it takes shape in our apprehension of it . . . (as) it is opened out before us in an objective depth that far transcends what we can specify of it in our formulations and yet is infinitely fertile in its illuminating power, we become caught up in a compulsive affirmation of that which is rational through and through. This is what we mean by scientific theological thinking, from an objective centre in the givenness of God, rather than popular mythological thinking, from a subjective centre in ourselves.[19]

Theological objectivity or theological realism follows the actual, redemptive and dynamic movement of God in history. There arises a process of continual correction in the light of the ultimate Reality and Rationality of God. This brings corrective to the fragmented human being and human thought and to theology for its own proper task in the service of God's self-disclosure.

Within the sciences, theological science is, to Torrance, to be an active agent in restoring our "split culture," calling it back to unitary thinking and to the intrinsic rationality of the contingent world as upheld by the power and interactive relation of God with it. Contrary to the old necessitarian, deterministic notions in the sciences, the modern physical sciences (especially physics) are found to overthrow dualisms by re-establishing in a new way epistemological foundations in a "profound ontological and dynamic integration of theoretical and empirical (form and being) ingredients in human knowledge."[20] Proper place is given again to the concept of a "rationality objectively inherent in the universe independent of our perceiving and conceiving it."[21] There has been penetration into the structures of the world as it is in itself. As a part of this restored objectivity (cf. below on the "classical attitude of mind" versus false, dualistic "objectivism") integrating knowledge and thus culture as a whole, theology too must return to its proper place among the sciences before the objective disclosure of its own proper object or field, God's self-disclosure in Jesus Christ. Torrance sees it as his purpose (much like that of the church fathers)[22] to recover the doctrines of creation and incarnation in such a way that "we think through their interrelations more rigorously than ever before, and on that ground engage in constant dialogue with the new science."[23] This will benefit both of them within the world that physical and theological science share and within which they do their work in the face of the disclosure of their own proper objects. Torrance adopts an "empirical-theoretical" approach.[24] This means the unfolding and grounding of "ultimate beliefs" in God's acts to and in the world by penetrating "more deeply into the self-communication of God in the saving and revealing activity of Christ and in his Spirit." Theological science must again be set firmly upon an objective and "unitary" basis, both epistemological and ontological, which will entail the need to grasp the unity in being and intelligibility of God's self-giving and self-revealing in Jesus Christ. This is found to be a true knowledge of God as we allow our knowing to fall under the compulsion of that self-giving and self-revealing in Jesus Christ. This is possible because of the indivisible oneness between Christ the incarnate Son and God the Father *(homoousion)*.[25] As restored to its proper objectivity, theology as a science is rescued from its defensive posture in subjectivism to its proper place among the sciences, and there it may restore the split culture.[26] Thus, within the unitary (non-dualist, non-monist) way of thinking within the one "bipolar" structure of knowledge, there must occur, says Torrance, integration of the empirical and theoretical (form and being) in all sciences and preeminently in knowledge of God. This Christocentric "field" relation of epistemological structure and material content in theological science is "the science of God, and of God in his interaction with the world of space and time."[27]

Here one must properly follow Torrance's understanding of what he believes to be his own encounter with God's Truth in Christ. Implicitly or explicitly this is expressed in a number of Torrance's works.[28] In a more general sense, we have already found him to say,

> . . . I find the presence and being of God bearing upon my experience and thought so powerfully that I cannot but be convinced of his overwhelming reality and rationality. To doubt the existence of God would be an act of sheer irrationality, for it would mean that my reason had become unhinged from its bond with real being.[29]

> But also, I would claim that the heart of my theology is deeply Nicene and doxological (theology and worship going inextricably together), with its immediate focus on Jesus Christ as Mediator, and its ultimate focus on the Holy Trinity.[30]

Under the gracious impress of the Living God incarnate, Torrance says that he is moved to the task of doing theology as that which "essentially is and always ought to be *logike latreia*, rational worship of God"[31] known in and after his economy in the Word and by the Spirit to the Father and the inner trinitarian relations.

> What I have called the *homoousial anaphora* . . . is the discriminating movement of theological thought which gives the figurative and creaturely representations in the Gospel their proper place and function as transparent media through which Christ confronts us with himself, clothed in the power of his own Spirit, as the creative ground of our faith and the one place where we may meet and know the Father . . . we are not trapped in a projective movement of thought grounded in the knowing subject . . . . The all-important semantic and ontological relation between Jesus Christ, the incarnate form of God's concrete self-revelation to us in space and time, and God the Father, is activated by the Word and Spirit of God in and through Jesus Christ, for thereby the self-interpreting and self-evidencing reality of God in his own immediate being bears upon us within the communion of the faithful in such a way that there arises among us the bipolar conceptuality of faith and understanding which informs the Church.[32]

Torrance positions his theology in and for the service of the Church so that as a "scientific activity" theology "cannot be regarded merely as a science in itself, independent and self-explanatory . . . but solely in response to the total claim of God upon us."[33]   Only in this way, "as a scientific theology . . . resting upon its own rational grounds" does its relevance as a fundamental science become manifest.[34] Theological purpose and statement are rooted in the fact that theology is ultimately "inquiry, prayer and praise to God made in the name of Jesus,"[35] and is therefore servant to the Church in which it participates. Thinking out the faith scientifically, by maintaining the rigorousness of true objectivity as required by the Word of God in the world, is also linked by Torrance to the context of ministry.

Theology then must be done scientifically, i.e., must make clear the "actual knowledge of God" as reached "through his self-revelation to us in Christ and in his Spirit."   Such true or faithful thinking will question "all alien presuppositions and antecedently reached conceptual systems."[36] Above all theology ought to be a faithful pointer to and glorifier of God as self-disclosed in Jesus Christ. Therefore, theology must be engaged in the Truth, *aletheia*, which Torrance understands unitarily first as correspondence and then as coherence. Knowledge, whether of God or of the world, is that which first corresponds to or faithfully "falls under" and submits to the impress of the inherent intelligibility of the proper Object/object under investigation as it discloses itself. This is why the Nicene doctrine of the *homoousion* is so central for Torrance. Not only the possibility of theological science but the very gospel of Christ is founded upon this reality reflected in the Nicene insight. One can have true knowledge of God as he is in himself in and through Christ. All theology must begin with Christ, the revelation of God, i.e., "what God is toward us in the three-fold economic activity of his revelation and redemption, as Father, Son and Holy Spirit, he is antecedently and eternally in his own Being in the Godhead."[37] The basis for the real knowledge of God and the actual manifestation of his redemptive love for the world is then the hypostatic union, "the indissoluble union of God and man in the one Person of Christ."[38]

Thomas Forsyth Torrance: A Brief Biography

Thomas Forsyth Torrance was born in China in 1913 of missionary parents. Torrance describes his parents as godly and caring, and the piety of his mother seems especially to stand out for him.[39] In the dedication of his early work, *Calvin's Doctrine of Man*, Torrance refers to his parents as those who first taught him theology in the context of the love of God.[40] His fourteen years in China could in many ways be described as adventurous, even life-threatening at some points.[41]

Torrance pursued studies at the University of Edinburgh where he began work in philosophy (primarily under Norman Kemp Smith and A.E. Taylor) and classical languages, while doing some work in theology. He first read Schleiermacher's *The Christian Faith* as an undergraduate.[42] This he did in part to prepare for later study in the Faculty of Divinity. His response to Schleiermacher was Yes and No.

> . . . captivated by the architectonic form and beauty of Schleiermacher's method . . . . But it was clear to me that the whole concept was wrong. Due to its fundamental presuppositions Schleiermacher's approach did not match up to the nature or content of the Christian gospel, while the propositional structure he imposed upon the Christian consciousness lacked any realist scientific objectivity. Another, more adequate way of doing what Schleiermacher had attempted was needed and I was determined from then on to make it one of my primary objectives.[43]

Torrance also began probing the theology of St. Augustine where he found "an even greater beauty and symmetry of theological form."[44] Yet "the powerful neo-Platonic ingredients of St. Augustine's thought . . . (the) controlling presuppositions basically similar to those in Schleiermacher"[45] led to another No.

After receiving the Masters of Arts degree at Edinburgh, Torrance began studies in the Faculty of Divinity. He was heavily influenced by H.R. Mackintosh whose work *Types of Modern Theology* gave a significant introduction to the thought of Karl Barth for English readers. By Torrance's own admission, ". . . Mackintosh had a tremendous effect on me," particularly as his thought related to Karl Barth, introducing Torrance to Barth's thought in 1935.[46] At this time he began his long-term study of Barth's theology, just as the first volume of the *Kirchliche Dogmatik* (I/1) was being translated into English by G.T. Thomson (also of Edinburgh). Regarding this deep interest in what Barth sought to do, Torrance says,

> I was immensely exhilarated by the insight Barth gave me into the ontology and objectivity of the Word of God as God himself in his revelation, and by Barth's presentation of dogmatics as a science. But what gripped me also was his account of the Trinitarian content, structure, and dynamism of God's self-revelation as Father, Son, and Holy Spirit, expounded in terms of the biblical roots of our Christian faith and the Nicene-Constantinopolitan Creed.[47]

In contrast to the lack of realist scientific objectivity he found in Schleiermacher and the neo-Platonic thinking of St. Augustine, Torrance found something different, something "scientific," in the theology of Karl Barth, as reflected in the *Church Dogmatics*. Barth led the way for Torrance.

> I realized that any rigorous scientific approach to Christian theology must allow actual knowledge of God, reached through his self-revelation to us in Christ and in his Spirit, to call into question all alien presuppositions and antecedently reached conceptual systems. For we must not separate from each other form and subject matter, structure and material content. By this I do not imply a rejection of philosophical thinking but rather the development of a rigorous rational epistemology governed by the nature of the object, namely, God in his self-communication to us within the structures of our human and worldly existence. In other words, the Incarnation constitutes the ontological ground of our knowledge of God and must be allowed to occupy its controlling center. But if the activity of the Holy Spirit is to be taken seriously, both divine revelation and our understanding of it must be thought out in dynamic and not in static terms.[48]

Barth helped Torrance to see that both "liberalism" and "orthodoxy" are simply "rationalizing variations on the ancient adoptionist and docetic heresies that kept passing over into each other in their betrayal of the gospel."[49] Particularly stimulating for Torrance was Barth's distinctive evangelical position that made "fresh appropriation of apostolic, classical Greek and early conciliar theology, and, of course, Reformed theology which has proved to be very relevant to our own times."[50]

After receiving the Bachelor of Divinity degree, Torrance went to Basel in 1937, to study under Karl Barth and to pursue the doctoral degree. Torrance's initial thesis proposal to Barth involved the working out of a "scientific account" of Christian dogmatics "from its Christological and soteriological center and in the light of its constitutive Trinitarian structure."[51] This was too ambitious; so Barth probed Torrance by asking in what other way he might "think of the inner connection giving coherence to the whole structure of Christian theology."[52] By way of response, Torrance recalls that . . .

> When I pointed to the unique kind of connection found in grace, he suggested that I should examine the way in which grace came to be understood in the second century, in the period between the New Testament and the rise of classical theology. That certainly appealed to me because of my love for Patristics! It was thus that I came to write *The Doctrine of Grace in the Apostolic Fathers.*[53]

He spent two semesters at Basel with Barth which he says "made an immense impact on me." He heard Barth's lectures on the doctrine of God, which formed *CD* II/1 and II/2, and took part in "intense theological discussion with Barth in his public and private seminars." Torrance's studies with the Faculty of Theology, and particularly with Barth, were variously interrupted first by a year of teaching at Auburn Theological Seminary and then by the outbreak of World War Two.   Torrance was called to Auburn upon the recommendation of John Baillie of Edinburgh.[54] There he was able to think through what he was learning from Barth. The Church Fathers were also significant in the development of Torrance's lectures. Conceptually, the "inner logic of grace" in the Incarnation, God's interaction with humanity in space and time, were among the issues   central to Torrance's thinking.   Of great significance too was the fact that while at Auburn, Torrance was able to offer a course on the relation of theology and science.[55] This helped him clarify the scientific nature of theology.

> . . . to work out in some measure the interrelations between Christian theology and natural science and thus to begin to clear the ground for rigorous Christian dogmatics expressed within the contingent rational order. Since it is within the universe of space and time that God has revealed himself to us and his Word who is the creative Source of all rational order within it has become incarnate, I had to believe that there is a profound consonance between the intelligibilities of divine revelation and the intelligibilities of the created universe. Without taking that consonance into account I did not believe we could offer a faithful account of knowledge of God as He has actually made himself known to us.[56]

At the close of the 1938-39 academic year, Torrance interviewed for appointment to the Department of Religion at Princeton University and at McCormick Seminary. This was while Emil Brunner was lecturing at Princeton Theological Seminary.[57] When told that what was wanted was someone to teach theology impartially, because of the varied backgrounds of the students, and asked for reaction, Torrance said, "I would rather teach theology as a *science*".[58] Torrance was appointed to the department of Religion at Princeton, but, because of developments in Europe, both Torrance and Brunner decided to return "before the submarines start."[59] This series of events and responses reflects how committed Torrance had already become to scientific theology and to find himself completely in accord with the theology learned from Barth, including Barth's concern to cut away subjectivistic patterns of thought. The point of scientific theology was to hear God in His Word addressing us objectively and personally in our existence. Christian theology, then, must be set on a sound scientific basis, the objective truth of God in Jesus Christ.[60]

Returning to Scotland, Torrance pastored churches at Alyth and then Aberdeen and was a front line chaplain during World War Two, for which he was made a member of the Order of the British Empire (MBE). It was of this time that Torrance speaks of being increasingly influenced by John Calvin, especially his commentaries and *Institutes*.[61] He returned to Basel, after the war, for the summer semester of 1946 and submitted his doctoral dissertation.[62] Barth was in Bonn at the time and was concerned about something happening to him while in Germany. Torrance says that "through his sons Barth asked me if I would join a small team to complete the *Church Dogmatics* should anything happen to him in Germany!" Torrance did not know the seriousness of Barth's question.

Torrance then published *Calvin's Doctrine of Man*. He had several purposes for writing this study, but among them, he says, was the desire to "cut through the tangled debate between Barth and Brunner on the relation between grace and nature, for in their appeals to Calvin they appeared to be shooting past each other almost." Torrance also began the further English translation of Barth's *Kirchliche Dogmatik*, a project in which he was engaged for years with Geoffrey Bromiley. Torrance's major role in the actual process was "to ensure that all the translations were faithful to Barth's distinctive forms of thought and as far as possible to inject consistency into the English terminology employed."[63] At this time (1952) Torrance was appointed to the Chair of Christian Dogmatics at the University of Edinburgh, replacing G. T. Thomson, who had himself replaced H. R. Mackintosh. In both of his new responsibilities, teaching and translating, Torrance was continually interacting with Barth's thought.

At this time, Torrance became even more actively engaged in the study of the natural sciences, their history, methods, the modern developments. Of particular importance were Newton, whose mammoth contribution Torrance acknowledges along with the devastating effect of his cosmological dualism upon Western thought and theology, Faraday and Maxwell of the nineteenth century, and Einstein in the twentieth, as these latter were "restoring" physics to its proper objectivity, overthrowing the negative effects of Newton's dualism.

About this intense study in the physical sciences, especially physics, Torrance says, "I regret that I got my scientific training so late in life . . . . As it is, it took me fifteen years of hard work to repair that defect in my knowledge."[64] Of particular importance for Torrance's emphasis on objectivity were the development of "field theory" in the context of onto-relations and the vision of the dynamic openness and contingence of the universe as it may now (post-Newton) be understood as "open up" to the interactive and redemptive relatedness of the transcendent God.

According to Torrance, Barth approached him with the prospect of his following Barth in the Chair of Dogmatic Theology at Basel.[65] The fact of this offer has apparently been confirmed by Markus Barth, though the full nature of such an offer has not been disclosed.[66] Torrance remained at the University of Edinburgh to pursue more freely the relations between Christianity and the sciences.

Torrance was also the Moderator of the Church of Scotland in 1977. He received the Templeton Prize for the Advancement of Religion in 1978. Torrance has received a number of honorary doctorates from universities in Europe, the United States and Canada, not only of theology or literature, but of science as well. In 1979 Torrance retired from his Chair of Christian Dogmatics at Edinburgh. Until recently, Torrance was editor of the *Scottish Journal of Theology*. While still living in Edinburgh, where he is yet engaged in much writing, he travels often, fulfilling commitments to lectureships, including the 1981 Warfield Lectures at Princeton Theological Seminary, the basis for the 1988 publication of *The Trinitarian Faith*, a historico-theological analysis of the Niceno-Constantinopolitan Creed. This is the book about which Torrance is "most pleased."[67] Torrance has also been actively involved on a regular basis at the Center of Theological Inquiry at Princeton. While nothing has actually come into print, Torrance is rumored to have done much work on his own *Christian Dogmatics*.[68]

Thomas Torrance's Theological Heritage and Realist/Scientific Theology

Torrance and the Nicene Church Fathers

As we have noted, Torrance has a passion for the thought of the Church Fathers, an interest that led to his doctoral dissertation at Basel. Torrance's many works almost invariably make ample reference, use and analysis of the developing focus of the Fathers in the light of Christ the Word. Among the ante-Nicene Fathers Torrance refers much to St. Irenaeus whose understanding of Christ's accomplishment of redemption is considered to be of great importance for the development of the Church's theology, i.e., Christ's whole life as salvific and not merely the crucifixion and resurrection. In this way redemption becomes not just a mighty act of God for us, but also "man's consent to God's Word in the humble obedience of Jesus in whom God has recreated our humanity, reversing sin, estrangement . . . by Christ's obedience."[69] It is also of utmost importance to Torrance that Irenaeus, like St. Athanasius (cf. below) and unlike St. Augustine, avoided and sought to negate contemporary cultural and epistemological effects of the damaging separation (disjunction) between the "intelligible" and the "sensible" realms of reality arising from the influence of Greek thought.[70]

It is especially with the theological developments in the third century that Torrance begins to reflect his preeminent patristic concerns and what must be learned from such. It is the Alexandrian Fathers that are of greatest importance for Torrance's thinking for theological realism arising from a unitary theological paradigm or interactionism. Indeed, contrary to the opinion of many, Torrance is emphatic that his concern for scientific realism and realist theology arose from these Greek Fathers and from Nicene theology and not from modern trends in physics. The theological struggles of such Alexandrians as Clement and Alexander in the face of heresies arising from the "disjunctive thinking" of the culture (cf. Arianism) become for Torrance models for current needs to face down the re-emergence of dualist perspectives and to overcome the damage done by them. He believes that these Church Fathers were able to remake, for a time, the thinking of a culture and to establish the "classical" understanding of knowledge or what has come to be called the true scientific methodology as empirico-theoretical and faithful to its own object. This is understood to be a coming to knowledge of a thing out of itself, or as it reveals itself to be, by submission or assent to its objective self-disclosure (epistemological realism) which arises from the object's own inherent and contingent intelligibility. In Nicene theology there is the emphasis on "God's Being in his Act," which is central to scientific theology. From such a basis, arising from the Christian view of God's lordly relatedness to the world, Torrance says that Western culture, philosophy and science were reshaped.[71] Athanasius and Cyril of Alexandria are of great significance for him, especially St. Athanasius. Torrance has said, "Athanasius' books are surely some of the greatest ever written . . . combining spirituality and theology together so wonderfully."[72] With the Fathers and theologians of Nicaea, especially in the *homoousion* doctrine whereby it is shown that God is in himself as he is toward us in Jesus Christ,[73] Athanasius and Cyril are esteemed by Torrance as central to his own thought and in the development of "classical" Christian theology because they reflected upon and articulated the divine self-revelation in Jesus out of its own inherent intelligibility. The Church was then able to better understand the self-communication of God in Christ, God's own Being as self-given.[74] In light of the often Gnostic, neo-Platonic, Origenist traditions in the heritage of

Alexandrian Christianity, it is important to realize Torrance's conclusion that in Athanasius' theological outlook, "there is little if any trace of Hellenistic rationalism to be found."[75] The mature Athanasius is said to have rejected the philosophico-theological (Origenist) orientation of the Alexandrian Cathechetical School in seeking to show how the human mind must "fall under the compelling evidence of the reality of things . . . basic assent . . . of the mind to the evidence . . . sheer fidelity of the mind to" the object under investigation, above all to the revelation of God in Jesus.[76] Like the modern axiomatic thinking in physics, says Torrance, Athanasius' theology sought to "penetrate into its inner logic, not . . . from fixed premises but by laying bare the premises embedded in the intrinsic connections of the subject matter."[77] Against the dualism of the Arians who separated God from the world and from humanity, necessitating the categorizing of Jesus Christ as "creature," Athanasius emphasized the *homoousion* whereby salvation as participation in and knowledge of God in Christ arises from the fact that the Logos is internal to the eternal being of God.[78] One truly and objectively knows God "in and through the Logos . . . (whereby one) knows him in the inner reality of his own (God's) Being." The Christian doctrine of the Trinity is then not peripheral but absolutely basic to the Christian understanding of God. For Torrance, Athanasius is a model of theological, epistemological and scientific realism that successfully counteracted the ruinous effects of dualism upon the gospel of Jesus Christ.

Torrance and the Medieval "Scientific" Theologians

While the Nicene Greek Fathers and, with them, St. Athanasius and St. Cyril are Torrance's real "love",[79] he often points to St. Anselm and John Duns Scotus as two theologians who (contra Aquinas, Abelard and Ockham) sought to do scientific theology out of the actual disclosure of the Object, thereby bringing scientific realism to the theological task.

"Scientific theology in the modern sense began with Anselm" who operated theologically with two preeminent principles, i.e., "(a) the conformity of reason with the Truth, and (b) the method of inquiry in which the Truth is addressed and interrogated in order that the reason may learn to conform to it obediently."[80] Anselm's theology then has true objectivity and, importantly, it is dialogical as opposed to dialectical in form. Much medieval theology followed the path of the dialectic rather than the dialogical. Because of this dialectical way the system arose "not out of the nature of the Truth itself, but out of the nature of the dialectical method." Also, such theology, he says, operated with the principles of "the sacramental universe with its pre-established harmony between the visible and the invisible, the earthly and the heavenly"[81] which effected problematic perspectives of the God-world relatedness. There is in the sacramental view a kind of necessity. In Anselm (as Barth also found)

Torrance sees that *behind* scholastic methodology derived from Abelard's dialectic there is a way "under the influence of Biblical theology and the new mode of questioning . . . to build up a positive theology with 'new' logical forms derived from the Word of God."[82]   In Anselm one learns the "fundamental attitude to the problem of the knowledge and existence of God"[83] and proper scientific procedure arising out of "the actual knowledge of God given in and with concrete happening in space and time."   As it is the knowledge of God "who actively meets us and gives Himself to be known in Jesus Christ . . . it is essentially positive knowledge, with articulated content, mediated in concrete experience."   Beginning scientifically with the facts prescribed to the observer by the actual *Object* of investigation as positively known, theological thinking must be "from inside the area delimited by the actual knowledge of God, and does not operate at any time outside of it."[84] Thus, as with Anselm (cf. *Cur Deus Homo*), says Torrance, theology must put its interrogations from within this positive knowledge of God and therein also put the answers to the test.   The question *Cur Deus Homo?* can only be answered in response to the divine fact, the incarnation of the Word itself.[85] In accord with the Anselmic principle *fides esse nequit sine conceptione*, knowledge of God means that "conception takes place under the impact of His Word and Spirit."[86]   As truth is disclosure, *a-letheia*, that which shows itself to be what it is and not something else, i.e., the being of the thing,[87] then, says Torrance, the Anselmic principle and actual evidenced scientific theological method leads one to know the Being of God.

> Through His Word God confronts us with the inner speech of His divine being and through His Spirit He evidences Himself to us in the presence of His reality, in such a way that He creates in us the capacity to hear, recognize and apprehend Him, and evokes from us the consent and understanding of faith in His self-revelation. Knowledge of God (cf. Anselm) is thus conceptual in its essential root.[88]

Anselm's scientific theology penetrates and follows the inner logic and actual objective movement of God to lay bare the grounds within the intelligible connections of God's redemptive self-disclosure in Christ.[89]   Hence Torrance, like Heidegger, understands that the critical relation of language to being has been damaged.   Rather, language must be understood as a "transparent medium through which we allow the objective realities to show through" (cf. Wittgenstein).[90]

John Duns Scotus expressed his view of the God-world relation in the light of creation and redemption to show that God can be under no obligation, no necessity, to create.[91]   In Scotus, as advocate of the freedom of God, the contingent intelligibility of the created world and theological and epistemological realism, Torrance sees the founder of the "tradition of Scottish realist

theological and epistemological thought."[92] With Scotus there emerged again
the doctrine of creation out of nothing as distinct from God. It has God given
form and order as well as being.[93] Contrary to prevailing views in medieval
thought which tended to see "person" as formed by "assimilating the idea of
substance to the logical subject"[94] in some *a priori* way (cf. Boethius), Scotus
emphasized that "person", particularly as used of God, must be "ontologically
derived from God's own nature, and therefore from the Trinity, and not
logically worked up from general ideas we already hold on other grounds."
God is to be known out of himself as a result of his actual disclosure. Scotus'
theological science cannot be reduced to an axiomatic pattern like that of
Euclidean geometry, i.e., all on one level. God is seen to be free and as free
can only be known out of his free objective self-revelation. In God's free
creation out of nothing, there is reflection in creation both of the divine freedom
to bring into being and the contingent nature of the world as distinct from God.
It is known out of its own inherent intelligibility reflecting the inherent,
transcendent intelligibility or Rationality of the Creator and the dependence of
the creation upon the Creator. Incarnation as contingent in nature also reflects
the free, objective self-manifestation of God. Scotus took the contingence of the
world under God seriously. The world as intelligible on its own could be
known through genuinely empirical science.[95]

Torrance and Reformed Theology: John Calvin

With the Greek Church fathers, particularly St. Athanasius, stand the
Reformers, in Torrance's estimation, for they too sought to restore the Church
to its proper objectivity, to the knowledge of God *out of himself* as self-disclosed
in Christ. Yet it is John Calvin who is, among the Reformers, Torrance's true
"mentor" and *the* Reformer with regard to a more consistent theological science
before the objective Word. As Robert J. Palma has put it ". . . Torrance's
theology is clearly situated within the Reformed tradition, very much bearing the
imprint of the sixteenth century Reformation theology which gave birth to this
tradition."[96] Torrance's work is indebted to Calvin's thought and to a much
lesser extent the Scottish Reformers Knox, Craig, and Bruce. But for Torrance
Calvin's theology is the issue. He says, "Modern theology in its distinctive
form began with John Calvin's *Institutes of the Christian Religion* for in it there
emerged three primary features of modern scientific thinking."[97]

The Reformers are said to have variously put an emphasis upon "hearing
the Word of God, and letting it speak to us out of itself, and upon the obedience
of the mind in response to it."[98] This has affected the modern world, even the
natural sciences. Torrance says that Francis Bacon began empirical science by
means of the Reformation's new methods. Reformed theology allowed its own
proper object to speak out of itself (God's Word). Thus Bacon transferred

Calvin's interpretation of "the books of God" to the object of his science, "the books of nature."[99] As Calvin sought to understand "scientifically" by humbly thinking after the disclosure of God in his Word, so too has modern science sought to follow after the clues of nature "without attempting to force our own patterns upon it."[100] For modern theology, Calvin is said by Torrance to have called theology back so that it knows the One who is its own proper focus in accordance with his own proper nature. In effecting the transition from the medieval mode of thinking in theology to the modern mode Calvin placed Reformation theology "on a scientific basis in such a way that the logic inherent in the substance of the Faith was brought to light," assuming "mastery over human formulation."[101] According to Torrance, "Calvin made such a forward advance in theological thinking toward objectivity that he outstripped his contemporaries by centuries,"[102] so that most after Calvin reverted to the "old Aristotelian forms."[103] While some, including Barth, emphasize Calvin's Augustinian idealism, Torrance emphasizes Calvin's positive teaching and its indebtedness to Greek patristic theology as related to the realist knowledge of God.

It was after his turn to realist thought and in relation to his commitment to the Reformation, says Torrance, that Calvin broke from Ockham, Valla and Erasmus, concluding that "we do have direct intuitive knowledge of God in his Word."[104] Calvin became pivotal to scientific theology, and to all scientific knowledge. In Calvin, Torrance finds three emphases that have mightily influenced him personally. First, he finds that for Calvin theological knowledge had an intuitive character, i.e., it is directly apprehended coming through his Word as objectively, actually present as an "immediate experience of his personal presence."[105] Second, he shows the critical relation of human speech to the divine Being. Theological knowledge is not pictorial thinking, i.e., "theological language is not descriptive of God." Like Athanasius, says Torrance, Calvin saw the need and place for images in both biblical and theological statements, but only as pointers, figures pointing by their nature beyond themselves toward that which cannot be reproduced, knowable only by his Word. Human language about God (as about any entity) is transparent, and referential, pointing away from itself, so that by it the Word God is shown *through* language.[106] Third, Calvin points to the epistemological implications of the doctrine of the Holy Spirit to human knowledge and speaking of God. God's action and personal presence among us is the action of the Holy Spirit as the "unique causality of his Being as he presents himself to us as the object of our knowledge." The Spirit brings about the transparence necessary for all knowledge of and speaking of God in the context of personal relation and interactive mutuality between God and human beings.[107] Only in relation to God within the sphere of actual knowledge of God can there be also true knowledge of humanity.[108]

It is of the utmost significance to Torrance that Calvin, in the line from

Athanasius, Anselm, and Scotus, regarding proper method arising from the actual knowledge of God, sought to refer everything to God and not to the self, so that theology is an *a posteriori* task (science) following after the way of God's actual, gracious self-revelation in his Word.[109]   Calvin too rightly realized, says Torrance,

> We do not know God (a prioristically) in the abstract as He is in Himself, but only in the reciprocal relation which He has established through His revelation between God and us and us and God. The only God we know is the God who has made Himself known, the God of whom we human beings have experience, so that in the nature of the case we cannot construct a knowledge of God outside this God-man or man-God relationship.[110]

One knows God truly only as one is cast upon God's own transcendent Reality and in thinking "theo-logically" out of a center in the divine Reality itself and *not* out of a center in the self. In Calvin, and among the Reformers, truth as the *truth of being*, the Being of God revealed objectively in Jesus Christ, replaced the cognitive medieval thought.

Torrance and Scottish Realism

Again Torrance's "unitary" theology (the unity of form and being versus a dualist theological outlook) is also a realist theology, i.e., against *a priori* human contrivances arising out of the mind, Torrance understands theology as that which emerges by reason of fidelity to God's own unitary Being and Acts objectively given. "Realist" does not mean belief in the necessary existence of universals or some necessary relation between thought and being, though this sense is not wholly alien to Torrance's thought.[111]   Torrance's scientific commitment grows out of a sense of direct intuitive knowledge of the object, as well as "fundamental ideas." One must think in relation to the reality which presents itself as known and find its deep structures. One must have a basic belief or trust in reality as it presents itself. The Scottish realist tradition is said to have been much influenced by Christian faith and the doctrine of God's self-revealed Word.[112]   Included in this tradition, is John Major who had such an influence on both John Knox and John Calvin, the latter holding to a realist position to which Torrance has often acknowledged his debt. He also includes physicists Faraday and J. Clerk Maxwell. "As rational beings we operate instinctively with a belief in the reality of the external world independent of our perceptions."[113] While distinguishing between signs and the signified realities in a way in which he seeks to mediate realism and idealism, Torrance affirms that one normally focuses on the realities that are signified, i.e., "we interpret signs in the light of their objective reference."[114]

Torrance and Soren Kierkegaard

Torrance has long been greatly concerned with what he sees to be twentieth-century, existentialist misinterpretation of the dynamic Christian thinking of Soren Kierkegaard. While often portrayed and espoused by modern irrationalists and subjectivists (whose "distorted, destructive" thinking is said to result from the dualist loss of the knowledge of God) as an advocate of irrationalism (cf. Truth as subjectivity), Kierkegaard is adamantly defended by Torrance from such false charges. Indeed Kierkegaard is interpreted as an ardent defender of true objectivity—especially in relation to the coming, the movement of God in the incarnate Word, Jesus Christ. Misinterpretation has arisen, says Torrance, due to Kierkegaard's use of a dynamism of expression which seeks to appropriately follow the dynamism of the objective movement of God in and for the world in Christ, "the god in time." There must be a proper relation of the human subject in submission to the proper Object, God, who is ever the Truth of God. Also Kierkegaard's understanding of "contemporaneity" proves to be of signal importance as undergirding Torrance's own understanding of theo-logical realism, objectivity and faith-ful knowledge of God.

Torrance and Modern (Post-Newtonian) Physics

The impact of relativity and quantum physics, particularly the work of Albert Einstein, upon Torrance has been great for a variety of reasons, especially epistemological, methodological and analogical. Additionally, Torrance gives particular attention to the thought of J. Clerk Maxwell, and Michael Polanyi. Christian theology is found to have contributed to natural science, especially regarding the "rational unity of the universe," "the contingent rationality or intelligibility of the universe," and "the freedom (contingent freedom) of the universe."[115] Yet now theology is too often caught in split thinking or dualism. It must again heed the meaning of realism, now largely renewed and confirmed in physics.

Since the overthrow of Newton's deterministic, necessitarian and cosmologically dualistic perspectives, which could not make sense of real motion, physics has maintained and called the scientific disciplines back to a scientific, critical realism. Each seeks to know its own proper object out of itself. The natural sciences have also uncovered the "hierarchical structure or levels of order and coherence"[116] within the creation and thereby pushed their inquiries toward the boundary where the great cosmological questions regarding "ultimate origins and ultimate ends" are brought up.[117]

As theological science becomes engaged with natural science and the call to realism, Christian theologians must again realize the scientific status of theology in relation to its proper object. This is true epistemologically, for the cosmological revolution, the overturning of Newton's static, dualistic determinative perspective, means real knowledge of the world, the proper object out of itself, according to the interrelated "levels" of disclosure. This is true also methodologically because modern theology has largely lost its grip on reality, turning to the self-centered, anthropological, and existential, and thereby has fallen under the critique of Feuerbach. Scientific methodology arises out of the nature of the proper object of that particular science (no science can positivistically foist its proper method upon another). The post-relativity revolution in science is rightly calling theology back to its own proper scientific task, i.e., to do theology as it is compelled to do theology from the evidential grounds upon which the work is done. Theological science must think out its task objectively, controlled by the reality into which inquiry is made. Torrance relies much on an analogical relation he builds between theology and physics.[118] By this epistemological, methodological, dialogical and analogical relationship with the natural sciences, theology should be led to submit its own conceptions to the questioning of science in order to be rescued from pseudo-theological and pseudo-scientific thinking for positive theological knowledge founded upon its own proper ground, i.e., "God's self-revelation in the incarnation of his eternal Word in Jesus Christ."[119] As the physical sciences have advanced in knowledge of objective truth about the universe, so too, asserts Torrance, theological science must learn a lesson about realism. Rigorousness of its research, disciplined faithfulness of knowing and thinking to the actual nature of things has brought increasing clarity to the inherent intelligibility and rationality of the world independent of human observation. So too theological science must progress to a rationality, a rational assent, to objective reality, the self-given Reality of God.[120]

Maxwell, Einstein, Planck and Polanyi (among others) are referred to regularly and at length. Their insights into the dynamics and contingent intelligibility of the world as related to the interactive, unitary, "God-world-man" relatedness are very significant to Torrance's thought. It is, again, Einstein and Polanyi who stand out as especially influential to both Torrance's understanding of the scientific task and to epistemology. In opposition to prior "modern" scientific notions, which arose from cosmological (Newton) and epistemological (Descartes, Kant) dualism, scientists like Einstein began to call for a return to the "classical attitude of mind."[121] Rejecting abstractive procedures and instrumentalist conceptions about what science is, science has recently sought "reality", to approach "the universe, as it is independent of the observer, an external world that is inherently rational . . . that makes it accessible to scientific investigation."[122] Einstein, with others, brought about a fundamental alteration in the understanding of physical reality and how scientific explanation occurs. He found that mathematical and empirical elements, space and time reflect the "indissoluble integration of geometry and experience at all levels of scientific investigation and theoretical formulation."[123]   This required a four-dimensional geometry. For geometry to become useable as a physical science it could no longer operate in the abstracted, idealized (*a priori*) form of Euclidean geometry, but had to become "embodied" arising in and from the space-time coordinates of the universe (*a posteriori*).   Physics was provided, then, with its internal epistemological structure, away from dualistic toward unitary thinking. Einstein's "number" rationality of the universe (the rationality of determinate things) is used analogically by Torrance who asserts that the intelligibility dealt with in theology is the "kind that takes the rational form of *logos*, or 'word'."[124] The resulting statement is such that one is "forced" or "compelled" to make it "as our minds fall under the power of the intrinsic rationality of the field we are investigating." In opposition to statements arising subjectively, true theological rationality (as with the rationality of physics after Einstein) has its statements imposed upon it by actual, external structural relations which, as objective, must be expressed rightly for fidelity to the ontological integrity of the unity of form and being, structure and substance, that reality discloses of itself.

> Thus, *mutatis mutandis*, what holds good for our apprehension of objective intelligibility in nature, holds good also for our apprehension of objective intelligibility in the biblical revelation, which we call the Word of God (i.e., the actual, objective self-disclosure of God in and to humanity and the world in Jesus Christ).[125]

As Einstein is said to have been so central in bringing about the disintegration of the very dualism with which so much theology and biblical interpretation is bound up, the way is found to have opened up for one to engage again in the theological task in response to the objective self-revelation of God in Jesus.[126]

Einstein's work in "field-theory" (after Maxwell) is also important to Torrance. Against the old "container" notions of space with their inherent dualism, giving to time and space a static, rigid and mechanical form, "field-theory" emphasizes a dynamic and relational way of thinking whereby the "actual web of relations in which things are found" is determinative to the nature of the thing ("onto-relations").[127] This means, theologically, that God cannot be related inertially in some deistic way to the world, but that God is the Lordly One present and related to and in the world through Christ and in the Spirit. This was a "fundamental belief" of Clerk Maxwell's which manifested itself in "field-theory" and influenced Einstein and all of the natural, social and now theological sciences.[128]

This scientific advancement resulting from return to objectivity establishing science upon a "deeper basis in reality" has also restored the integrity of humanity's personal and rational inquiry into the meaning of the universe.[129] Polanyi has been of singular significance in calling for objectivity and in clarifying the personal, social aspect of the scientific task. Polanyi has shown his great concern for pure science, for the free and objective inquiry central to a free society, and that objective knowledge is not detached, impersonal and abstract, in contrast to the Newtonian and positivistic perspectives on science. To be truly objective, science needed to recognize that to exclude the person or the personal from knowledge means excluding that which alone is capable of self-criticism, the only one capable of distinguishing subjective states from what one actually knows objectively.[130]   What Polanyi recognized explicitly, according to Torrance, is that science needed a "new approach"

> . . . in which it overcomes the damaging split between subject and object, mind and matter, or thought and experience, and recovers the natural unity of knowing and being, for without the integrative way of thinking that such a rational balance brings, science can only obstruct its own attempts to grasp the finer and more delicate patterns embedded in nature.[131]

While it was not Polanyi's main intention to "make room" for faith and the knowledge of God, he was aware that this was a further result of his work. Polanyi has not only set Christian faith free from the distorting conception of a closed, static, mechanistic universe of rigid cause and effect but further established the necessity of "fundamental beliefs."[132]   All scientific activity works by an inner relation between faith and reason that parallels that in Christian theology as one moves from faith to understanding. Polanyi restored to objective, scientific activity the critical role of belief.[133]

Torrance and Karl Barth

Torrance is emphatic and effusive about his indebtedness to the thought of Karl Barth. Torrance is a "modified" Barthian. Torrance refers to Barth as ". . . perhaps the most powerful mind we've had for many centuries . . . steeped in the Bible . . . able to put things so ontologically and dynamically."[134] Within the larger Calvinist-Reformed perspective, Karl Barth has had the greatest influence on Torrance's thinking and is in so many ways Torrance's real theological mentor.

Through H. R. MacIntosh and in his own early reading of the first English translation of the *Dogmatics*, Torrance found in Barth a more rigorous, scientific approach to Christian theology. In Karl Barth, Torrance found one who did theology by following the actual way of disclosure taken by God in the world. Thus, the actual knowledge of God is reached by the way of God's gracious self-disclosure to humanity in Jesus Christ and by his Holy Spirit. This scientific methodology calls into question all presuppositions, all *a priori* conceptual systems foreign to God's actual self-revelation. Thus, in Barth, with his realist scientific objectivity and his "rigorous rational epistemology governed by the nature of the object," i.e., God in his self-communication to humanity "within the structures of our human and world existence," Torrance found one who did theology out of the priority of the actual ground of the human knowledge of God, the Incarnation, the Word made flesh. Theology is "not to engage in free thinking," but recognizes that, as a science, it must fall under (submit to) the nature of its own proper object within the field of investigation as an objective reality having intrinsic rationality.[135]

Many of Karl Barth's theological bases became and are still (however modified) Thomas Torrance's bases as well, and these must be mentioned here, while they will become more fully manifest in the ensuing chapters. After what, for Torrance, are the paradigmatic accomplishments of the Nicene fathers (cf. below, the *homoousion* doctrine) and Athanasius, and Calvin among the Reformers, along with their respective emphases on "God's Being in his Act" and "God's Act in his Being," Torrance wants to "stand upon" Barth's theological shoulders and to work out yet more fully Barth's balancing and unifying of the Nicene and Reformation insights. Following Barth, who is reckoned as a true "theo-logical" scientist, Torrance too emphasizes the absolute priority of God's grace, the necessity that true theo-logy be Christocentric in following God's actual movement in the world, theo-logical realism in proper response to God's self-objectifying in the world to be known as he is in himself, and above all (in recent years) the ultimate centrality of the Holy Trinity as the "ground and grammar" of all theology, indeed of all rationality and the truth of being. The Trinity is finally the heart of Torrance's understanding of the knowledge of God. In these central issues and so many others, Torrance's understanding of the self-given knowledge of God in the world, however modified, is rooted in Barth, and through a Barthian base, into the whole of the Christian tradition.

Torrance's Principal Theological Concerns

While Torrance's theological interests, concerns and engagements are many, they might be brought under four related headings. These are theological science and methodology (or philosophy of theology, prolegomena); ecumenism or the need to work toward Christian theological unity by bringing positions into engagement with the objective self-revelation of God in Christ; the need for dialogue between theology and the natural sciences; and the missionary task. Indeed, all of these lie under and relate to the issue of the knowledge of God in Christ.

Realist Theological Science and Theological Methodology

The whole of Torrance's purposes arise from his own encounter with

God's Truth incarnate in Jesus Christ. Jesus Christ is the incarnate presence of the living God within the space-time of human living. Christ the Word presents Himself factually to human beings here as the living, dynamic *object* of their faith. Theology then must think out of the Being and Act of God in Christ which affects all of life and cannot be abstracted from his acts in history.[136] Theology must be rational worship of God done in the service of God and scientific, i.e., it must reflect the imprint of the actual nature of God as self-revealed in Jesus Christ, for in true science "it is always the nature of the thing that must prescribe for us the specific mode of rationality that we must adopt toward it."[137] He finds then that his theology must be "Nicene," reflecting the meaning and implications of the *homoousion* doctrine. It means too that his theology is ultimately grounded in the Holy Trinity for the true knowledge of God is knowledge of God as Trinity. Theological science is actually and ultimately knowledge grounded in the ontological Trinity.[138] Scientific theology is thus also positive theology or revealed theology, by which he means again the actual knowledge of God by the proper conformity of thought to its object as self-given.[139] This is then his "theological science" or the "science of pure theology" in which one must allow "the nature and pattern of that into which we inquire to impose itself upon our minds."[140] Herein Torrance has done much work to "clear the way" for theology. This "meta-science to our direct cognitive relation with God"[141] clarifies the way or course taken in scientific activity in theology to cast human thought regarding God back upon God. In this way theology can be self-critical as a science[142] in much the way philosophy of science relates to the natural sciences. E. L. Mascall has said:

> One of the very few British theologians of recent years who have seriously inquired into the nature of the discipline to which they are committed is the Presbyterian scholar Dr. Thomas F. Torrance, who occupies the chair of Christian Dogmatics at the University of Edinburgh.[143]

In this way, Torrance has consistently tried to do dogmatic theology (versus "dogmatical" or "authoritarian") to "unfold and present the content of the Word of God within the limits of the Church prescribed for it by the Incarnation and apostolic foundation,"[144] which is given expression today through the analysis of past doctrinal decisions in the Church.

Realist Ecumenism

Torrance has long been active in the World Council of Churches. For ten years he represented the Faith and Order Commission under whose auspices he engaged in theological dialogue and lecturing. He was invited to Vatican Council Two, being involved in discussions which led to *Lumen Gentium*.[145] To Torrance, Christian theology must be reconciliation theology if it is to be faithful to the Church in which it serves.   Yet, as the divisions of the world, arising from disjunctive, dualist perspectives, have penetrated the church, both unity and the mission of reconciliation are damaged.   Divisions have appeared not usually from divergence from the revelation of God but from that assimilation of *alien* conceptualities and action which have obscured or cut off proper theo-logical thinking in relation to the objective Word of God.

> (This problem) imposes upon ecumenical theology the need to dig into the
> foundations and re-examine the connections between historical theology and
> the cultural environment of the Church in order to lay bare the *core* of basic
> beliefs . . . at the center of the Church's faith and distinguish it from the
> body of *secondary* concepts and relations (peripheral) . . . the more deeply
> we press into the material centre of the Church's faith in Christ and in the
> Holy Trinity, the greater is the pressure disposing us to reach agreement with
> one another.[146]

Reconciliation will occur, he believes, as every part of the Church is engaged in rigorous, scientific, obedient and thus unifying thought after the Truth of God unto realist knowledge of God.   Thus, scientific theology, as the "active engagement in the cognitive relation to God in obedience to the demands of His reality and self-giving"[147] in Jesus Christ, is reckoned to be central to the realization of unity as such thinking properly arises from and "under" its proper source.   Oneness is restored by the corrective effect upon doctrine and life arising from the Church's grounding in the self-revelation of God in Christ, indeed in the Trinity, in the very unity of God.[148]

Realism and Dialogue Between Theology and the Natural Sciences

Torrance is vitally concerned that theology be scientific in its method so that it allows for and faithfully thinks after the actual knowledge of God in Jesus Christ and by his Holy Spirit, i.e., no *a priori* conceptual systems.   This desire for realist scientific objectivity arose early in his thinking.   It can be seen in his criticisms of Augustine, Schleiermacher, Bultmann and others whose theological ways and conclusions were found to be controlled by distorting dualistic presuppositions which worked with an assumed separation or disjunction of God from the world, the human and thus from direct knowability.   Thus science, realist science, has long been an epistemological and methodological concern. But in addition to Torrance's own personal interest in the natural sciences, scientist Sir Bernard Lovell, cousin of his wife, has probed Torrance about scientific methodology in theology in light of general scientific methodology. This led Torrance to begin studying natural science in yet greater depth, a process of "catching up," in order "to communicate . . . over the interrelations

of science and theology."[149]   This led to his lengthy presidency of the
International Academy of Religious Sciences and to his election to the
International Academy of the Philosophy of Sciences.   Torrance's works
inevitably reflect his ongoing dialogue with those in the physical sciences
generally, though his keenest interest is clearly with objective realist knowledge
as reflected in post-quantum and relativity physics.   Such titles as *Theological
Science; Divine and Contingent Order; Transformation and Convergence in the
Frame of Knowledge; Space, Time and Incarnation; Space, Time and
Resurrection; Christian Theology and Scientific Culture* and others reflect this
relationship.   In fact, *Divine and Contingent Order* was written primarily with
the natural scientist in view.

Dialogue with the natural sciences must be a relationship of give and take
to the end that both sides benefit.   How can theology be of benefit to the natural
sciences?   According to Torrance, it is and has been in regard to three
foundational ideas, originally clarified and set forth by the Greek Christian
theologians in the light of the gospel of Christ, that Christian theology has been
of influence to the natural sciences.   These three ideas were mentioned
above.[150]   To this Torrance adds the contribution of the Reformation "to the
modern world," i.e., its "passion for the truth from the side of the object (the
Word of God) which represented a repentant readiness to re-think all
preconceptions and presuppositions."[151]   The contribution was a ". . .
masterful objectivity with its distinction between unwarranted presupposition and
proper entailment arising out of the nature of the object."   This brings one face
to face with the object to distinguish the objectively real from human subjective
states.[152]

Torrance emphasizes also the fact that the natural sciences penetrate into
and uncover the "hierarchical structure of levels of order and coherence" as
such are actually reflected in the created universe, thus pushing investigations
toward the "very boundaries of being, to the very perimeter of the creation of
matter and form."[153] This raises cosmological "questions of ultimate origins
and ultimate ends . . . we cannot pursue natural science scientifically without
engaging at the same time in meta-scientific operations."[154]   Science can and
must raise such questions but it cannot give answers to them.   "The closer to
that boundary science is thrust, the more necessary it becomes for it to engage
in serious dialogue with theology."[155]   Therein theological science must
become just that as it is called back by the natural sciences to true scientific
methodology in order to grasp more effectively the depth of "God's self-
revealing interaction with the world."   Theological science is then a "human
inquiry, operating within the contingent intelligibilities of space and time that it
shares with natural science."[156]   The theologian must respond faithfully under
the impress of theology's own proper object.   Theology uses concepts and
statements which fall short of divine realities but which can be transparent in
pointing beyond themselves "to that which is infinitely greater than we can

conceive or express." The sciences are interconnected in their understanding of the purpose of the created universe. Within this relationship Torrance wants to serve theologically the scientific community in answering these questions by "probing more deeply into the intelligible reality of the triune God." God has, by free creation of the contingent, orderly and intelligible space-time universe and by the Incarnation of his Son, revealed himself in his gracious interactive relatedness for the world. Indeed, of the Incarnation Torrance says that

> Just as within the multi-leveled structures of the universe, as they come to view through our scientific inquiries, we find that each level of reality is finally integrated not through its own operational connections but through relation to connections at a higher level, to which it is open at its own "boundary conditions," so the incarnation as a whole provides, as it were, the intersecting vertical dimension which gives the horizontal coordinates of the universe the integrative factor providing them with consistent and ultimate meaning, in a way which a merely deistic asymptotic relation between God and the universe could never do.[157]

Torrance sees his role as one of theological participant in the necessary dialogical relation to the natural scientific community, for learning, ministry and witness in order to bring about more effective complementarity in the priestly and redemptive functions which must be enacted by humanity, as represented especially among scientists, with God's creation.[158]

Why Realist Christian Theology Must Oppose Dualism

Dualism as a perspective on reality and relation has been a varied perspective in the history of Western thought, but for Torrance the outcome has always been the same. Whether ancient Greek, deistic, Newtonian, Cartesian, Kantian, or phenomenalist (to name a few) dualism is said to have a markedly "negative," even "devastating," effect on all progress in both natural and theological science. Whether epistemological or cosmological, Torrance maintains that such "disjunctive thinking" of whatever kind or source is invariably problematic to any realist science as a result of the unbridgeable separation or "gulf" that is projected or founded between intelligible realities, e.g., the sensible and intelligible realms, a distant (deistic) deity and a deterministic and mechanical universe, between absolute time and space and relative time and space, between the phenomenal and noumenal realms (worlds), between subject and object. This dualist disjunction that is thus posited, says Torrance, has also split modern culture.[159]

> . . . how the split has affected modern epistemology, in a sharp distinction
> between *explanation* and *understanding*, i.e., between what Droysen
> (following Schleiermacher), Dilthey and Weber called *Erklären* and
> *Verstehen*.   When they split apart, however, each becomes distorted:
> explanation becomes severely restricted . . . rigid, causal, and mechanical
> . . . understanding is construed as empathetic interpretation . . . transposing
> oneself imaginatively . . . if the culture of our society is so deeply split, it
> is not surprising that all our scientific activity is affected. [160]

There cannot be advance to new knowledge, something not previously assumed,
in such a situation.   The linguistic and conceptual paradigms of a culture which
reflect the dualistic perspective impose this upon all inquiring endeavors that
seek knowledge out of the objective reality itself.   So too is it in theological
science as it too is "certainly struggling in the toils of our split culture."[161]

Torrance sees the collapse to have been founded upon a number of dualist
assumptions (e.g., again, separation of God from the world, intelligible from
sensible, subject from object) which have caused the unitary and interrelated
levels, the "unitary rational order" or "the stratified structure of the universe"
or "the coordinated layers of orderly relations in reality itself,"[162] to be treated
as though cut off and alienated from one another as dichotomies.[163]   Under the
destructive influence of these dualisms there has ensued "the eclipse" of
objective, intelligible reality.   Objectivity becomes subjectivity, knowledge
becomes skepticism, clarity becomes opacity, theology becomes anthropology.

> With a shift in the centre of gravity from a theocentric to an anthropocentric
> point of view, and an identification of natural law with the law of
> autonomous reason, a rapid elimination of ontology and objectivity from the
> foundations of scientific knowledge sets in and there follows a serious lapse
> into skepticism . . . . If we are left to the uncertainties and limitations of our
> senses alone, without any reliance upon fundamental convictions (such as
> belief in God) which reach beyond sensation and observation, we can have
> no confidence in our ability to reach consistent and explicit rational
> knowledge . . . with the disappearance of God from the scientific outlook
> upon the universe the artificial dualist way of combining theoretical and
> empirical factors in knowledge . . . came to an end of its usefulness and
> became the source of serious error.[164]

The phenomenal surface of experience began to fall apart because it was
disjoined or abstracted from underlying patterns or coherence in objective
reality.   The abstract patterns that had been "imposed extrinsically" upon reality
or being distorted real meaning and purpose.   Nothing really new in the
knowledge of nature is possible within this dualist predicament because "nature
(then) inhibits itself from having anything to do with a reality beyond what is
observable or from taking into rational account connections that are

unobservable."[165]   Torrance finds, then, that there is need to penetrate to a more profound level behind sense experience to the "invisible object-object relations and dynamic field-structures which give continuity and cohesion to states of affairs in nature independent of our observations."[166]   Inevitably Torrance connects the modern problem to Martin Buber's reference to a "conceptual letting go of God".[167]   With the "eclipse" or closing off of key levels of reality from one another the phenomenal surface disintegrates for it loses contact with the objective structures that hold the appearances together in coherent and meaningful patterns.[168]   Of great concern to Torrance is the consequential application of this split to the historical Jesus, the separation of the phenomenal Jesus from the essential *Logos* which is "constitutive of his incarnate actuality."[169]   In dividing observable patterns in nature from the framework of objective structures in reality, all meaning, coherence, etc., are lost and distorted.   Truth and knowledge as such are lost.

Against this dualism and its outcomes Torrance endeavors to set forth a "unitary" or "classical" perspective.   "Dualism," as that which cuts the human knower off from the inherent order and intelligibility of external reality (whether the universe or God), is spurned in favor of a realist epistemology, an understanding of the inherent intelligibility of the world as objectively understood, i.e., intelligibility external to the knowing subject which is graspable by the subject. All intelligibility in nature, contingent intelligibility, is ultimately found to be derived from the transcendent intelligibility or Rationality of God. Torrance is seeking to do away with all aspects of modern dualism which make it difficult to "hear" the Word of God.   Torrance's involvement in re-establishing a "radically new, unitary basis" for natural science, a unitary way of knowing in place of a dualist one, is finally a clearing of the way for the gospel of Jesus Christ in this modern setting.[170]

> It is, therefore, up to us as theologians to develop theology on its own proper ground in this scientific context, if only because this is the kind of theology needed to change the foundations of modern life and culture, and the kind of theology that can support the message of the Gospel to mankind, as, in touch with the advances of natural science, theology comes closer and closer to a real understanding of the creation as it came from the hand of God.[171]

Parallels Between the Practice of Theological and Natural Science (Physics)

According to Karl Barth, to do theology as a science means to re-think the words in which God is objectively manifest, the biblical message. In every such word of "revelation" there is encounter, true meeting between humanity and the self-revealing God. This is emphatically Jesus the Word of God, the Word made flesh, who is as such *the place* where God in his personal self-disclosure encounters persons. In this is a clear shift from the earlier "dialectical" period of Barth's thought to theological objectivity or theology as science. This is basic to Torrance's thinking. Against Augustine and Schleiermacher, Torrance found that they both lacked realist scientific objectivity.

> I realized that any vigorous scientific approach to Christian theology must allow actual knowledge of God, reached through his self-revelation to us in Christ and in his Spirit to call into question all alien presuppositions and antecedently reached conceptual systems. For we must not separate from each other form and subject matter, structure and material content. . . a rigorous rational epistemology governed by the nature of the object, namely God in his self-communication to us within the structures of our human and worldly existence.[172]

In Barth, Torrance found one whose theological method made it possible to develop a "coherent and consistent account of Christian theology as an organic whole in a rigorously scientific way."[173] Christian theology must be a dogmatic science which is to be done upon the basis of its own proper ground and "in its own right."[174] It is, according to Torrance, the incarnation which is the ontological ground and controlling center of our knowledge of the triune God.[175]

In seeing the parallel between the method of the natural scientist and the scientific theologian, Torrance says first that the post-quantum, post-relativity understanding of scientific method is quite different from Newtonian science and consequent positivism. Until recently, "scientific" was understood as following a certain prescribed procedure reckoned as singular, uniform, a "methodological monism,"[176] imposing *a priori* conceptions of rationality upon the data and with the "unfortunate effect" of bringing a "sharp distinction between observation and thought". This left a tenacious legacy of dualism.[177] Methodology more conducive to only one of the sciences is accorded preeminence as *the* method whereby all must follow "this" procedure. "Masterful" or "positivistic" imposition of an alien process upon the search for objective truth has been largely cut away by the modern scientific revolution. The turn again is to the "classical" perspective of objective knowledge in the light of the inherent intelligibility of reality as it discloses itself objectively to us. Hence, Einstein could say that "science is the attempt to make the chaotic of our sense-experience correspond to a logically uniform system,"[178] i.e., a search for "elemental form in which to reduce the multiplicity of its knowledge to the basic order into which our thought is forced under the pressure of objective reality."[179] Quantum theory especially has shown the limited range of particular methods and differences in scientific approach and explanation. This is especially true of "complementarity." There are "various ways," says

Oppenheimer, "of talking about physical experience" each having validity and each necessary for explanation of the physical world while each may "yet stand in a relation of mutually exclusive relationship to each other."[180] One cannot be applied to the other necessarily.[181] The notion of some "general science" or "super-science" which is found to impose a method *a priori* on all that would claim scientific status is not real. There are, says Torrance, only particular sciences, though these have certain fundamental principles in common, for knowledge as such has a certain structural form in order to be knowledge.[182] The various sciences may only be generalized in the light of the objective intelligibility of nature as they submit thinking to the rational, objective disclosure of their own proper object. Each science can only follow after this disclosure. This, says Torrance, includes the *Geisteswissenschaften*, theological science, and philosophy. For all sciences, reason must behave in terms of the nature of the object whereby the "formal procedure appropriate to that behavior is universal in range." There is a procedure that is common to every science formally, but in every particular field modification is necessary as is appropriate to "the distinctive nature (mode of rationality) of the object or matter under investigation.[183] Thus, says Torrance,

> . . . while theological science shares with other sciences a generally recognized scientific procedure based on the principle of objectivity, theology has its own particular scientific requirements determined by the unique nature of its own particular object, just as every other special science has its own peculiarities owing to the special features of its object . . . . Thus, in theology we are concerned with our human knowing of God, i.e., with a mode of knowing appropriate to human minds and subjects, wherever there is a subject-object relationship . . . . But in theology we are concerned with God in Jesus Christ as the Truth, and therefore we are concerned with a mode of knowing appropriate to His unique nature. Hence theology must have its particular principles relevant to this unique object or field of knowledge where divine self-disclosure is involved.[184]

For a positive theology to pursue realist, scientific objectivity the primary requirement is "the utter lordship of the object, which is the one all-determining presupposition.[185] God has graciously condescended to objectify himself to and for humanity within creaturely existence taking human objectivity into union with his divine objectivity. Then as God has objectified himself here within the contingent intelligibilities of the universe, so scientific theology must be done in dialogue with other sciences with which theology shares the cosmos and wherein each pursues its own proper course.[186] This will deepen knowledge and relevance and strengthen Christian convictions.

Theology must then be pursued, says Torrance, out of a relationship. Only as one is rightly related to the proper Object of theology, the Subject of the Christian faith, can "theo-logy" be done. By faithful inquiry or obedient questioning into the proper subject matter of theology, the theologian is a true hearer of the Word so that, in the process of relevant questioning of the proper Object, the questioner actually becomes the one questioned. God is not like the proper inanimate object of geology. God's self-revelation as the proper Object of Christian theology is revelation of one who is by nature Subject and redeeming Lord, and scientific questions must be in accord with the nature of the proper object. Theology must have its own principles appropriate to its own Object and field of knowledge. Avoiding false, alien connections, theological thinking must think after the nature and pattern of the Truth of God itself to coherently and faithfully reflect it. We must, he says, "re-live (the) encounter with the Object, allowing ourselves to be re-addressed by Him, rethinking His Word to us."[187] The theologian must respond to God's action upon him and translate that action into transparent theological statements in a way that reflects the fact that the truth does not lie in the statements but in God to whom the statements refer beyond themselves. The interconnection of such statements should reflect the very order and movement of the Object, God for us.[188] The New Testament witnesses to Christ are "both reporting and thinking inside the inner movement of the Truth, yielding their thought . . . speech, to its inner compulsion."[189] In faithful submission to its own Object, theology too must penetrate into "the coherent structure or pattern of the Truth" in order to faithfully translate what is heard . . . tracing out the order reflected in the given Reality, allowing it to shine through.[190] Theology is then not merely *kerygma* but faithful, obedient thinking before the inherent rationality of its Object.[191] Scientific theology traces out "the logic of Grace"[192] as the dialogical "afterthinking" (*Nachdenken*) of the revelation of God mediated through the biblical message in the objective light of God's condescension in Jesus Christ. Scientific theology "afterthinks" the whole movement of Grace, God's inner compulsion in election.[193] Authentic theological thinking carries its call to question "into the very heart of that purpose (*prothesis*) and from that centre think out the 'had to' of Grace."[194] In this sense scientific, therefore dialogical, theology is "essentially theology of the Word" to which, in the questioning process, one rightly yields the response of faith. In the conformity of human thought with its Object, God is revealing Himself in His Word who encounters persons as Subject addressing subjects.[195]

> It proceeds by constant reference to its source in the Word of God, so that the content of theological knowledge is derived from the Word . . . which has assumed personal and historical form in the Incarnation . . . (so) we are bound unconditionally to the creaturely objectivity of God in the Incarnation of His Word in Jesus Christ.[196]

As Torrance was once asked to describe God, he responded simply that "we can do that only from our Lord Jesus Christ. He is, by his very nature, God."[197]

He is the revealed Word.

Therefore, theology is done under the impress of the objective self-revelation of God which encounters one in Jesus Christ and by the Spirit through the mediation or witness of Scripture. All occurs within the context of relation, in faith and only in faith. No mere exegesis is involved. Theo-logy must think after the inner logic of the movement of the grace of God in Jesus Christ which is necessary for a truly scientific theology that, in relation to its own proper Object, parallels the method of the natural scientist in relation to her/his proper object.[198]

The preceding discussion has presented an introduction and background to Thomas Torrance's theology and his concerns against theological dualism and for unitary, objective theological realism—the knowledge of God as he is in the way he has given himself to be known. The ensuing chapters will unfold Torrance's positive theo-logical expression or formulation of the Truth of God in Jesus Christ the Word of God. Here we will follow Torrance's positive, constructive theological efforts to set forth his "scientific theology" as it arises from and serves the self-revelation of God in Jesus Christ and the realist knowledge of the triune God by existing persons in the world. Chapter two will introduce and explain the background and basic issues, epistemological and theological, in Torrance's realist theological thinking. Chapter three will then develop Torrance's analogical and formal relationship to the modern revolution in the physical sciences, issues of the intelligibility of the universe, intuitive knowing of reality, the role of belief, the role of the person in the knowing process by way of the work of J. Clerk Maxwell, Albert Einstein and Michael Polanyi. Chapter four will then bring together the way in which Torrance applies these scientific insights for epistemology to the present theological need and task. Chapter five is the crucial or climactic chapter of constructive application of Torrance's scientific method and theological formulation. Here we will bring together Torrance's thought as he, in true Barthian fashion, "thinks after" the way God has actually taken in the world, i.e., through the Word made flesh and in the Spirit. Here Torrance's Christocentricity and, preeminently and ultimately, his Trinitarian grounding come to the fore as God is thereby known to be in himself as he is toward us through Christ and in the Spirit. For Torrance, the Trinity is *the* "ground and grammar" of all theology. Chapter six will present prominent criticisms of Torrance's theology, while chapter seven will assess these criticisms and go beyond previous discussion through analysis of Torrance's Kierkegaardian, Barthian and Calvinist bases. At that point we must question whether Torrance has actually accomplished the overthrow of dualism in a true, complete theological realism. Has Torrance effectively reflected the Truth of God theologically out of the fact of God in Christ and by the Spirit in a fully historical relation of the Word of God to concrete as is necessary for his own stated purpose?

NOTES

1. Thomas F. Torrance, *Theological Science* (Oxford: Oxford University Press, 1969), p. v. Hereafter cited as *TS*.

2. Michael Bauman, ed., *Roundtable: Conversations with European Theologians* (Grand Rapids: Baker Book House, yet unpublished manuscript excerpt), p. 1. Hereafter cited as *RCET*.

3. *cf.* Ludwig Feuerbach, *The Essence of Christianity* (New York: Harper Torchbooks/Harper and Row 1957).

4. Torrance, *TS*, vi.

5. *Note*: This is a point or assertion, variously put but consistent throughout, that is to be found in almost all of Torrance's works. This reflects his central concern regarding the nature of proper scientific inquiry or interrogation arising from the actual nature of the object, in the case the living and personal God who is both Lord and Judge as well as loving Redeemer in his active self-disclosure to humanity.

6. *TS*, vi.

7. Ibid., p. iv-vi.

8. Thomas F. Torrance, *God and Rationality* (Oxford: Oxford University Press, 1971), p. vii. Hereafter cited as *GR*.

9. Ibid.

10. Ibid, p. 29.

11. Thomas F. Torrance, *Reality and Evangelical Theology* (Philadelphia: The Westminster Press, 1982), p. 9. Hereafter cited as *RET*.

12. Torrance, *GR*, p. 40.

13. Ibid, p. 42.

14. Ibid, p. 47. An example Torrance gives is Paul Tillich of whom Torrance states: ". . . (he) has declared in a number of his works that faith-knowledge is symbolic and non-conceptual so that if we are to pursue theology we must borrow conceptualities from philosophy or science in order to rationalize faith. That is to say, ultimately Tillich worked with a romantic, non-conceptual approach to God. The rationality with which he was concerned in his theology had become detached from God, for he took it from his cultural involvement. Tillich played a very important part in providing the rapid

development of religion in the United States after the Second World War with a rational structure and respectability, but the way in which he did it involves him in some responsibility for the 'God is dead' way of thinking taken up by the small men. If the question as to God is correlated with the question as to man, and the question that man puts to God is finally himself, the questioner, it is difficult to see how the way of 'God' can avoid the way taken by man." *GR*, pp. 47-48.

15. Ibid.

16. Ibid.

17. Ibid.

18. Ibid, p. 49.

19. Ibid, pp. 45-46. cf. pp. 53-54.

20. Thomas Torrance, *The Ground and Grammar of Theology* (Charlottesville: University Press of Virginia, 1980), p. 25. Hereafter GG.

21. Ibid.

22. Ibid, p. 74.

23. Ibid.

24. Thomas F. Torrance, "Theological Realism," *The Philosophical Frontiers of Christian Theology: Essays presented to D. M. Mackinnon*, ed. Brian Hebblethwaite and Stewart Sutherland (Cambridge: Cambridge University Press, 1982), pp. 189-90. Hereafter cited as *PFCT*. cf. *RET*, pp. 39-42.

25. Ibid.

26. *Note*: For further discussion of theological science among the various sciences (cf. below in discussion following in this chapter) Cf. *TS*, pp. 281-352; *GR*, pp. 89-112; *Christian Frame of Mind*, pp. 49-63. Note also this latter entry with regard to the question of the role of scientific theology within the university setting.

27. Cf. Thomas F. Torrance, *Reality and Scientific Theology* (Edinburgh: Scottish Academic Press, 1985), pp. 64-97. Hereafter cited as *RST*. Cf. also Thomas F. Torrance, *The Christian Frame of Mind* (Colorado Springs: Helmers and Howard, 1989), pp. 49-63. Hereafter cited as *CFM*.

28. Torrance, *RET*, pp. 129-140.

29. Torrance, *TS*, p. v.

30. R. D. Kernoham, "Tom Torrance: The Man and the Reputation," *Life and Work*, vol. 32, no. 5 (May, 1976), p. 14.

31. Torrance, *PFCT*, p. 193.

32. Ibid.

33. Ibid, *TS*, pp. 55-56.

34. Ibid.

35. Torrance, *TS*, p. 160)

36. Thomas F. Torrance, "My Interaction with Karl Barth," *How Karl Barth Changed My Mind*, ed. Donald McKim (Grand Rapids: Wm. B. Eerdmans Publishing Company, 1986), p. 53. Hereafter cited as *HKB*.

37. Torrance, *GG*, p. 158.

38. Ibid., p. 160.

39. Bauman, *RCET*, p. 1.

40. Thomas F. Torrance, *Calvin's Doctrine of Man* (Grand Rapids: Wm. B. Eerdmans Publishing Company, 1948), dedication.

41. Personal conversation, A. McKelway, January 19, 1990. cf. I. John Hesselink, "A Pilgrimage in the School of Christ: An Interview with T. F. Torrance," *Reformed Review*, vol. 38, no. 1 (Autumn 1984), p. 49.

42. McKim, ed., *HKB*, p. 25; and Hesselink, "Interview," p. 51.

43. Ibid.

44. Ibid.

45. Ibid, pp. 52-53.

46. Ibid, p. 52; and Hesselink, "Interview," pp. 52-53.

47. Ibid, cf. the expanded discussion of the early effect of Barth's thought on Torrance in Hesselink, "Interview," pp. 52-53.

48. Ibid, p. 53.

49. Ibid.

50. Ibid.

51. Hesselink, "Interview," pp. 52-53.

52. Ibid, cf. McKim, *HKB*, p. 54.

53. McKim, *HKB*, p.54.

54. Ibid, p. 55, cf. Hesselink, "Interview," pp. 53-54.

55. Ibid.

56. Ibid, pp. 55-56.

57. Hesselink, "Interview," p. 54.

58. McKim, *HKB*, p. 16. in Hesselink, "Interview," p. 54, Torrance notes that in teaching theology as science, i.e. not detached, not disinterested, not from free thinking, but thinking as one is compelled to think by the evidential grounds upon which one is working (objectively). Thus "because we think in this way, I could not guarantee that no one would be converted!"

59. Ibid, cf. Hesselink, "Interview," p. 54.

60. Ibid, p. 57.

61. Torrance, *Calvin's Doctrine of Man*, preface. Cf. Torrance's emphatic reference to this in Bauman, *RCET*, p. 2. For details Hesselink, "Interview," p. 55.

62. McKim, *HKB*, p. 57.

63. Ibid.

64. Bauman, *RCET*, p. 2.

65. Ibid.

66. Dr. Kurt Richardson, personal interview, September 15, 1990.

67. Ibid.

68. Palma, "Torrance," p. 23.

69. Torrance, *TRn*, pp. 94f.

70. Ibid.

71. Torrance, *GG*, p. 60.

72. Bauman, *RCET* p. 1.

73. Torrance, *TS*, p. 343. This is an often repeated notion in Torrance: while often explicit it is also implicit.

74. Ibid.

75. Torrance, *TRn*, p. 216.

76. Ibid.

77. Torrance, *GR*, p. 100.

78. Ibid, p. 222.

79. Bauman, *RCET*, p. 1.

80. Ibid, p. xliv.

81. Ibid.

82. Ibid, p. 6.

83. Ibid, p. 26.

84. Ibid.

85. Ibid.

86. Torrance, *GR*, p. 21.

87. Torrance, *TS*, p. 141-142.

88. Torrance, *GR*, p. 21.

89. Ibid, p. 170, where Torrance says, "This then is the specific domain of the Spirit in theological knowledge, for by His power and enlightment we think and speak directly of God in and through the forms of our rational experience and articulation and we do that under the direction and control of the inner rationality of the divine Being, the eternal *Logos* and *Eidos* of Godhead. To use Anselmic language once again, here we are up against the *Suprema Veritas*, of the *Ratio Veritatis* of God Himself, which we cannot reduce to the *veritates* or *rationes* of our understanding even though it is only through them that we know God. It is only through the Spirit of Truth that such *trans-formal* experience is possible, for it is by His Power that we are enabled to know beyond ourselves and to distinguish what we know from our knowing of it, so that our knowing of Him falls under the continual informing and shaping of what He makes known of Himself. This is knowledge with a transcendence in form and an indefinite range of enlightment beyond anything else in our experience, in which our thinking becomes objectively rooted in the eternal Word in the Being of God and acquires out of that Word a basic conceptuality that does not vary with the many forms of man's self-centered and objectifying modes of thought." Cf. pp. 180-181 and Torrance, *TRn*, p. 264.

90. Thomas F. Torrance, *Theology in Reconstruction* (Grand Rapids: Wm. B. Eerdmans Publishing Company, 1965), p. 57. Hereafter cited as *TRst*.

91. John Duns Scotus, quoted in Thomas F. Torrance, *Divine and Contingent Order* (Oxford; Oxford University Press, 1981), p. vii. Hereafter cited as *DCO*.

92. Torrance, *DCO*, p. x.

93. Torrance, *GR*, p. 39.

94. Torrance, *TS*, p. 80.

95. Torrance, *DCO*, p. 87.

96. Palma, "Torrance," p. 2.

97. Torrance, *TS*, p. ix.

98. Torrance, *TRst*, pp. 14-15.

99. Ibid, p. 15.

100. Ibid.

101. Ibid, p. 76.

102. Ibid.

103. Ibid.

104. Ibid, p. 84.

105. Ibid.

106. Ibid, p. 89.

107. Ibid, p. 93.

108. Torrance, *TS*, p. 86.

109. Ibid, p. 244.

110. Torrance, *GR*, p. 31.

111. Torrance, *DCO*, p. x.

112. Thomas F. Torrance, *Transformation and Convergence in the Frame of Knowledge* (Grand Rapids: Wm. B. Eerdmans Publishing Company, 1984), p. 216. Hereafter cited as *TCFK*.

113. Torrance, *GG*, p. 169.

114. Torrance, *RET*, p. 58. cf. 63.

115. Ibid, p. 57.

116. Ibid, p. 144.

117. Torrance, *DCO*, p. 1.

118. Thomas F. Torrance, *Christian Theology and Scientific Culture* (Oxford University Press, 1981), pp. 8-9. Hereafter cited as *CTSC*.

119. Ibid, p. 9.

120. Torrance, *RET*, pp. 11-12. cf. pp. 30, 39.

121. Torrance, *RST*, p. 20.

122. Ibid.

123. Torrance, *CTSC*, pp. 53-54.

124. Torrance, *GG*, p. 31.

125. Ibid.

126. Ibid, p. 32. *Note*: Here where Torrance states that "theological structures may be developed only if they are directly grounded in, and epistemogically controlled by, the objective intelligibilities of the biblical revelation, such as the intrinsic significance of Jesus, the Word made flesh."

127. Torrance, *CTSC*, p. 22.

128. Ibid, p. 56.

129. Thomas F. Torrance, ed. *Belief in Science and in Christian Life: The Relevance of Michael Polanyi's Thought for Christian Faith and Life* (Edinburgh: The Handsel Press, 1980), p. xv. Hereafter cited as *BSCL*.

130. Torrance, *BSCL*, p. xv.

131. Ibid.

132. Ibid, p. xvi.

133. Ibid.

134. Bauman, *RCET*, p. 2.

135. Ibid.

136. Torrance, *RET*, pp. 129-140

137. Torrance, *TS*, p. viii.

138. Torrance, *GG*, p. 173. cf. Torrance, *RET*, pp. 42-44. 139-140.

139. Torrance, *SF*, pp. xlv-xlvi.

140. Torrance, *TS*, p. 341.

141. Ibid, p. v.

142. Ibid, p. xiii.

143. E. L. Mascall, *Theology and the Gospel of Christ: An Essay in Reorientation* (London: SPCK, 1977), p. 46. Herein, as Mascall discusses two ways or constructive approaches to the doing of theology, both Torrance and Lonegan are dealt with.

144. Torrance, *TRst*, p. 146.

145. Hesselink, "Interview," pp. 58-59.

146. Torrance, *TRn*, pp. 8-9.

147. Torrance, *TS*, p. v.

148. Torrance, *TRn*, p. 49.

149. Hesselink, "Interview," p. 62.

150. Torrance, *GG*, p. 52.

151. Torrance, *TRst*, p. 67.

152. Ibid.

153. Torrance, *DCO*, p. ix.

154. Ibid, p. 1.

155. Torrance, *GR*, p. vii.

156. Torrance, *GG*, p. 144.

157. Torrance, *DOC*, pp. 24-25,cf. Torrance *CTSC*, p. 39. and *GG*, p. 144.

158. Cf. Torrance, *CFM*, pp. 35-63; *GG*, pp. 1-14; *DCO*, pp. 128-140.

159. Torrance, *GG*, pp. 15-43.

160. Torrance, *GR*, pp. 104, 106.

161. Ibid, p. 110.

162. Ibid, p. 37.

163. Cf. chapter five. Cf. also particular criticisms of Rudolf Bultmann in the following works by Torrance: *TS*, p. 329; *TRst*, pp. 47, 78, 88, 277; *GR*, 4.

164. Torrance, *CTSC*, pp. 47-48.

165. Ibid, p. 48.

166. . . . what was required was a profounder way of bringing theoretical and empirical factors together, in fact a grasp of their inherence in one another both in nature and in our knowing of it. But how can that be gained if through the methods of observation we employ, the rational order of things in the universe is torn away from a frame of objective structures in reality or is made completely independent of an ultimate intelligible ground in God the Maker of all things visible or invisible? Ibid.

167. Cf. Torrance, *TS*, p. 14; *GR*, p. 106; *GG, p. 149.*

168. Torrance, *GG*, p. 32.

169. Ibid, p. 123. Cf. pp. 121-123; *CTSC*, p. 21; *DCO*, p. 25.

170. Torrance, *TRn*, p. 271. Cf. *RET*, p. 47; *GG*, p. 178.

171. Torrance, *GG*, p. 178.

172. McKim, *HKB*, p. 53.

173. Ibid, p. 54.

174. Ibid.

175. Ibid, p. 53.

176. Torrance, *TS*, p. 110.

177. Ibid.

178. Albert Einstein, *Out of My Later Years*, quoted in Torrance, *TS*, pp. 110-111.

179. Ibid, p. 116.

180. R. Oppenheimer, *Great Essays in Science*, quoted in Ibid, p. 111. Every science has its own language . . . (e)verything the chemist observes and describes can be talked about in terms of atomic mechanics, and most of it at least can be understood. Yet no one suggests that, in dealing with the complex chemical forms which are of biological interest, the language of atomic physics would be helpful. Rather it would tend to obscure the great regularities of biochemistry, as the dynamic description of gas would obscure its thermodynamic behavior.

181. R. Oppenheimer, *Science and the Common Understanding*, quoted in Ibid.

182. Ibid, p. 112.

183. Ibid.

184. Ibid, p. 113.

185. Ibid, p. 131.

186. *Note*: Torrance often makes this point that with the various natural sciences theological science shares the fact and situation in that each pursues its own scientific task or calling in response to the objectivity and intelligibility of its own proper object within the space-time universe and cannot take a viewpoint outside or it.

187. Ibid, p. 127.

188. Ibid.

189. Ibid, p. 128. Cf. Torrance refers to Luke 4:26; Matthew 1:22, 2:15; Hebrews 2:17; I Corinthians 15:14.

190. Ibid.

191. Ibid.

192. Ibid.

193. Ibid.

194. Ibid.

195. Ibid, p. 134.

196. Ibid, p. 134, 135, 137.

197. Bauman, *RCET*, p. 6.

198. Torrance, *TS*, p. 129. Cf. again where Torrance illustratively makes the assertion that, with regard to Einstein's supposed determinism, "The statement 'God does not play dice' rejects the idea of chance in favor of an objective but dynamic relatedness inherent in quanta. Far from being a determinist, Einstein was a realist, committed to belief in the objective intelligibility of the universe, which would have nothing to do with the Kantian idea that we can know only what we make and shape as objects of our understanding. The Kantian notion of the objectifying activity of the reason is a

renunciation of genuinely objective operations, and it was that relic of Kantian objectivity that Einstein detected and repudiated in the Copenhagen and Göttingen form of quantum theory." *GG*, p. 113. ". . . to *break* through the *surface to the depths* of intelligible reality and engage with orderly relations lodged in it (God the proper Object of theological science) that reach out far beyond our experience and understanding . . . with patterns that have objective depth and which cannot be identified with the surface patterns of our formal logic . . . in proper theological thinking we have to act within the boundary imposed upon us by the nature of the object, and *think within its inner compulsion*, for example arguing from the inner ground of the divine act in Christ to the possibility of knowledge and reconciliation." TS, p. 129.

Chapter 2

Background To Thomas Torrance's
Realist Theological Thought

(Reflecting Torrance's concerns in this chapter) In the progress of its philosophizing the human spirit is evermore inclined to fuse characteristically this conception, of the Absolute as object of an adequate thought, with itself, the human spirit. In the course of this process, the idea which was at first noetically contemplated finally becomes the potentiality of the spirit itself that thinks it, and it attains on the way of the spirit its actuality . . . . Until, finally, all that is over against us, everything that accosts us and takes possession of us, all partnership of existence, is dissolved in free-floating subjectivity . . . the human spirit, which adjudges to itself mastery over its work, annihilates conceptually the absoluteness of the absolute . . . it has also destroyed its own absoluteness along with absoluteness in general . . . . In this stage there first takes place the conceptual letting go of God because only now philosophy cuts off its own hands, the hands with which it was able to grasp and hold Him.

- Martin Buber, *The Eclipse of God*

But perhaps one can swim with a new stream whose source is still hidden? . . . the I-Thou relation has gone into the catacombs—who can say with how much greater power it will step forth! . . . The most important events in the history of that embodied possibility called man are the occasionally occurring beginnings of new epochs, determined by forces previously invisible or unregarded. Something is taking place in the depths that as yet needs no name. To-morrow even it may happen that it will be beckoned to from the heights, across the heads of the earthly archons. The eclipse of the light of

God is not extinction, for even to-morrow that which has stepped in between may give way.

- Martin Buber, *The Eclipse of God*

Introduction

Thomas Torrance's Criticism of Dualism

Thomas Torrance's positive theology is part of a larger criticism intended to overturn the various inroads of dualism in modern thinking that have damaged knowledge, and particularly the knowledge of God conceptually, thereby severing God from both the world and humanity. Torrance's concern is to show that the modern epistemological-cosmological dualism is an obsolete way of thinking. This dualism results from disjunctive thinking which cannot or will not "think together" unitarily or relationally form and being or the theoretical and empirical in the context of the knowledge of being and act.

This modern dualism, as Torrance perceives it, is a direct result of the influence of René Descartes, Isaac Newton and especially Immanuel Kant. Descartes' *cogito ergo sum* effected the epistemological separation of subject from object, locating truth in the subjective pole of the knowing relation. Newton's rigid, mathematical system of cause and effect brought about the separation of absolute mathematical space and time from relative space and time of ordinary experience, making God the containing mind which statically impresses rationality on the mechanistic creation while necessarily remaining deistically separate—outside the universe (disallowing *a priori* any possibility of incarnation, resurrection and objective knowledge of God). Kant's synthesis of rationalism and empiricism was effected at the cost of the disjunction, the "chasm," formed between the "knowable" phenomenal world and the noumenal world which is unknowable by pure reason. Objective knowledge of God, God's interactive relation in and for the world, God's salvific acts as actually historical and spatial, hereby become barred from possibility.

This led in its turn to "false" theological thinking whose elements fostered increasing skepticism about the possibility of the knowledge of God and brought such theological thinking to its *telos* in so-called "Neo-Protestantism" from Schleiermacher through Bultmann and beyond. Thus Schleiermacher's Kantian epistemology led him to his theological method of moving from a starting point in the human being, out of the piety or feeling of "absolute dependence" of the religious subject upon God (the "whence"). It is with Rudolf Bultmann that the "damaging" effects of dualistic theological thinking are, in Torrance's interpretation, brought to their destructive end.

As paradigmatic of false, dualistic theology for Torrance, Bultmann is found to epitomize the problems of twentieth-century theology. Bultmann's existentialist theology not only reflects obsolete Newtonian cosmology, which forces him to portray God as outside of a cause-effect, mechanistic universe wherein God cannot, by definition, make himself known objectively, but also Kantian epistemology whereby the knowledge of God as he is in himself is ruled out of possibility. Rather, in the existential decision false objectification is said to occur as human subjectivism, the authentically existing I, is projected out. In the line from Kant to Schleiermacher to Bultmann and beyond, Torrance finds the "prophetic" criticisms of Ludwig Feuerbach to be validated. Here Kantian separation of noumenal from phenomenal in knowledge, God as "wholly other" (versus God's objective manifest presence, power, love and self-disclosure in Christ) and, thus, the separation of subject from Object are found to be important for Torrance's theological "negative" endeavor ("the clearing of the ground"). He finds the outcome to be the "loss of God in the world," or the "eclipse of God" (from Buber), and the resulting mastery of "secularity". But this loss of the God "for us" and "with us" means the loss of humanity, the dissolution of culture and the Lordship of death.[1]

The reason why Torrance, as a theologian of the Word of God, is concerned with this modern, re-entrenched dualistic thinking and the severance of theology from experience that results from it is that it has caused theology to lose a critical element which derived from the Reformation, namely the willingness to submit all thinking to the Word of God in Jesus Christ heard through the apostolic witness of Scripture. Torrance characteristically emphasizes this "hearing through" Scripture. Theology which reflects this modern "schizoid" thinking, especially disjoining God from the world, fails to deal with the day-to-day experience of space-time existing persons in relation to the question of the needed objective reality wherein alone faith can be truly grounded. Dualist theology is not grounded in the real, actual understanding of faith that arises out of the person's relations with God in Jesus Christ. Such modern dualist theological expression is empty of the necessary objective content which would make it truly theo-logical. And as "empty" of the objective Word, it is then finally meaningless. Torrance firmly asserts that when theology is only the expression and extension of an enclosed, trapped subjective human state, as he finds in Schleiermacher and Bultmann, then it is not truly theo-logical. Without the independently given objective reference such "theology" then becomes an easy prey for the criticism of the logical empiricists and verificationists.

What theological problems has this false disjunctive or dualist thinking produced, in Torrance's opinion? He enumerates the problems often and at length. First, such thinking has done away with any thought of interaction by God with and in the world he has brought into being, thus also negating any thought of God's active providence. Above all, it has ruled out the possibility of the Incarnation of the Word. Having done away then with all notion of relation and interaction by the sovereign God in His self-revealing and saving activity in the world, such "dualism" has also negated any real relation of God with human existence, reckoning it as *a priori* impossible. Torrance contends then that statements about God which are made on such a "dualist" basis do not derive from a real Word from God to humanity, but are interpretations of human existence in its "over-againstness" to the unknowable God. An additional consequence is that "God" becomes merely a cipher of human relations with him. Given the asserted noumenal-phenomenal, God-world rift, theological statements cannot actually refer to God for they can come only to the "gulf" which is perceived to lie between God and mankind, mankind and God. Such statements arising from human subjectivity cannot "cross over" but only "bend back" to have their meaning only and wholly within the world and in the human self-understanding shut up unto itself. This "bending back," whereby "theology" is done wholly within the phenomenal structures, eventually leads to the outcome wherein "God" is turned into inter-human relations, thereby establishing "secular theology" in its various forms. In relation to these central concerns, Torrance often pinpoints three false theological consequences, each with wide ranging effects: first, theological statements are converted into anthropological or autobiographical statements (the problem of scientific theological expression in relation to its proper Referent); second, the meaning of "act of God" is radically altered (the question the actuality of God's space-time self-revelation as objective to the knower); and third, "Jesus" is divided from "the Christ" so that persons substitute the subjective self for Jesus (the problem of the perceived disjunction of God from the historical).[2]

This chapter will first touch briefly on Torrance's strong theological concern with the modern "eclipse of God" found to result from modern dualist thought. Then discussion will initially set forth significant groundwork for the way in which Torrance perceives the theological task and epistemology. Then we will deal with Torrance's interpretation of post-Newtonian scientific breakthroughs and the effect of such for modern thought and epistemology and the overthrow thereby of dualism in favor of unitary, realistic thinking. This will lead to modern scientific conceptions which Torrance has taken analogically into his theological science. With such important aspects of Torrance's "apparatus" in place, each successive step of Torrance's "Christological-Trinitarian" unfolding of the "given" scientific way from and in the Word of God will be set forth in detail, culminating at the eternal *perichoretic* relations within the eternal triune Godhead at which human knowledge of God in Christ and by the Spirit finally "arrives"—penetration and participation by Grace into the "ellipse of knowing and loving" between the Persons of the ontological Trinity which is the "ground and grammar of all theology." Thinking after and "upward" through the "levels" of properly scientific and faithful knowledge of God, Torrance follows the very "economic movement" of God in and from the concrete, historical self-disclosure of God in Christ and by the Spirit to the theoretical/theo-logical and finally to the meta-theological level "within" the very Being of God, the ontological Trinity. In this way, Torrance's theo-logical task, his theological realism, real knowledge of God out of theology's own proper Object, is brought to full, positive and final expression (cf. chapter four and especially chapter five).

Disjunctive Thinking and the "Eclipse of God"

As reflected in Buber's statements at the beginning of the chapter, it is ever important to keep in mind that Torrance is consistent in his contention that there are critical epistemological-cosmological issues which lie behind modern thought and theology which have engendered problems in the Western mind and culture, and this concern colors almost everything that he says. As a direct result of modern epistemological and cosmological dualism, God has been "eclipsed" as an inflated human subjectivism has "stepped" in between God and humanity and "shut off the light of heaven." God cannot now be distinguished from the self.

At the Reformation, says Torrance, the modern era in thinking, especially in theology, was brought about by four major changes in perspective. First, the Reformers (especially Calvin) made clearer than before that there is a mutual relation between the knowledge of God and the knowledge of oneself, i.e., one does not know God abstractly but only *a posteriori* in and from real God-established reciprocal relations effected by his self-revelation in which one may truly know him out of himself. There is a human coefficient in knowledge, particularly in the knowledge of God in personal relation. Still it is God's self-revelation which frees the self from its self-imprisonment for the Truth in God (not in the human subject) and "opens" one "out" for God and from the self, thereby to be cast upon the sheer Truth of God in His active self-giving.

Second, the Reformers are said to have reversed scientific questioning. Torrance explains that questioning had been or followed from the order of essence, and then possibility, and then finally questioning focused on the actual existing thing. The Reformers radically changed this by their theological method so that subsequently scientific questioning began not with essence or some *a priori* possibility, but rather with the question of what the actual nature of the existing thing to be known is. One begins with the "that-ness" of the existing object and belief in its own inherent intelligibility and order. One then allows the nature of what is known, the object, to determine how one actually knows it, not clamping down alien categories on the proper object. It was in this way that Calvin is said to have freed theology from alien assumptions and directed it away from the kind of questioning which solved a problem in knowledge which one already has, i.e., there must be interrogation to "*let* the object disclose itself" in order to reveal what was *not* previously known.[3] Only in this way is truly "new" knowledge possible.

Third, Torrance sees proper and corrective change in the relation of language to objective being for modern thought as a direct result of the Reformation. The Truth of God cannot be resolved into statements. One must not subordinate things to words which indicate them. Rather words must be subordinated to the things they are "intended" to indicate. This is of utmost importance for Torrance.

> . . . it is of the things themselves that we think rather than the words used of them. This is particularly important . . . when we come to speak of God, for we cannot describe Him in language or reduce His Truth to statements. Theological language is indicative, not descriptive, of God and it is to be understood only as we allow it to refer us beyond itself to God in His transcendent reality.[4]

In this way language is used scientifically, not as a symbolic medium of subjective human intention, but as its deliberate reference is dealt with seriously. As the father of "modern scientific biblical interpretation," Calvin rightly looked away to the reality to which the biblical writer points and then interprets in light of this reality.[5]

Fourth, there was also change with regard to theology proper in the recognition of God's interactive relatedness—as Creator and Redeemer—to the world. Medieval theology is said to have had difficulty separating God from nature and in understanding the God-world-human/God-human-world relationship in other than necessitarian terms. Knowledge of God and the world were posited together. But one cannot rise above created things and can then only construe God as necessarily related to the creation. If one begins with the eternal and immutable God and then thinks of created things as the objects of his eternal knowing and willing, then nature in some sense eternally coexists with God, at the least in the divine mind. God and nature, says Torrance, were correlative concepts. This way of thinking damaged "nature," for it gave to it a changeless character via a timeless relation to the divine causation (i.e., nature impregnated with divine causes). But renewal (primarily through Duns Scotus) of the doctrine of *creatio ex nihilo*, whereby God was understood "as creating the world by producing new ideas through which the world was given form and order as well as being, was developed yet further by the Reformers."[6] This revived the biblical idea of God who creates the world out of nothing and as something real and distinct from himself—yet which is contingent and thus dependent upon God for its being and order. This, says Torrance, freed the study of nature from philosophical preconceptions and "disenchanted" nature of secret divinity. Nature could only be understood by looking at nature, letting nature then disclose itself under proper interrogation, and not by looking at God who is the improper Object for such investigation. This point is important for Torrance's own methodology.

> God means for us to examine nature in itself, to learn about it out of itself, and not from the study of the Holy Scriptures or of theology. But it was the clear and unambiguous doctrine of God as the Creator of nature out of nothing that emancipated nature in this way for the investigations of empirical science. We know God by looking at God, by attending to the steps he has taken in manifesting himself to us and thinking of Him in accordance with His divine nature. But we know the world by looking at the world, by attending to the ways in which it becomes disclosed to us out of itself, and thinking of it in accordance with its creaturely nature. Thus scientific method began to take shape both in the field of natural science and in the field of divine science.[7]

In these four ways (i.e., knowledge of God and self, questioning the proper object, corrected relation of language to being, renewed emphasis on "creation out of nothing") there occurred a revolutionary "mutation" of thought which advanced the Western world in both theological and natural science, especially as the two sciences interacted. But something happened to these alterations, especially with regard to God's sovereign, dynamic, interactive relatedness to, for, in and with the created world and humanity. This change has produced the dualistic "eclipse" from which thinking as truly scientific is now endeavoring to wrest itself.

Regarding the first change in thought mentioned above, the mutual relation between the knowledge of God and the knowledge of ourselves, Torrance believes that one cannot have realist knowledge of God severed from that fact that it is this existing, individual person who knows. Indeed, *all* truly scientific knowledge is "personal" knowledge. The human subject has an unalterable place in knowledge. But if the proper object of knowledge is ever considered as merely relative to a subject, then how can one obtain objective knowledge as unaffected by the human subject? In the knowing relation the primary role is to be given to the object and not to the knowing subject.

Despite Calvin's insight into true scientific theology and theological objectivity and realism, there subsequently arose a way of thinking which is "represented" for Torrance by the thought of Erasmus, Schleiermacher and Bultmann. Herein Torrance finds that in the polar relation of human knowledge the subjective pole tends to become more and more masterful to the end that "self" increasingly obtrudes into the knowing process or relation, getting in the way of or cutting off the proper object.[8] While theology too is personal, personal space-time relation between the existing human being and God, this task must not be pursued so as to "place" the self as central and therefore "between" the self and God whereby God is finally lost. This intrusion detaches God from human knowledge and the human subject is "shut up within the realm of his own self-understanding, without any objective anchorage for his thought in the ultimate Reality and Truth of God."[9] When encounters with "God" are actually self-encounters, when God is deistically detached from space-time objectivities, then thinking takes the form of the mythological projection of human subjectivities into God. Theology is thus converted to anthropology and human structures are destroyed. Torrance has found this to lead to Bultmann's thought and to the "theological solipsism" of John A. T. Robinson, whom Torrance describes as having a "stuck adolescence."[10] This means scientifically the loss of real objectivity, i.e., the failure to understand things out of themselves in accordance with their own natures and an irrational departure from scientific thinking. Torrance approvingly quotes Buber.

> The soul can never legitimately make an assertion, even a physical one, out of its own creative power. It can make an assertion only out of a binding real relationship to a truth which it articulates.[11]

Torrance finds that a century earlier, Soren Kierkegaard (who he says is so "misunderstood" by existentialists) expounded the "Truth is Subjectivity" in the *Concluding Unscientific Postscript*. Torrance declares that while Kierkegaard was the sworn enemy of all objectivism, his focus upon subjectivity did *not* mean the loss or reduction of objectivity. Torrance sees that for Kierkegaard authentic human subjectivity is only possible when the person meets with the true *objectivity* of the divine *Subject*. The experience of faith then means that the human subject so meets the Truth of God as he is in himself that the person's own existence is transformed into conformity with it. Apart from this encounter with the objective Truth, the Truth is not known. But in the relation of knowledge, truth is found in the object known *and* on the side of the knower who must be in a relation of truth to the proper object in order to know it. Therefore he says, "The mode of apprehension of the truth is precisely the truth."[12] This is a subjectivity which, according to Torrance, arises from an objective ground in the divine Reality. This point was made to show that when the question of truth is raised in an objective manner the knower is directed objectively to the truth as an object to which he/she is related. But here attention is not focused upon that knowing relation. Rather, when the question of truth arises subjectively the knower is directed subjectively *to the truth* and it is then that the attention is directed to the nature of his/her relationship to the truth. It is in this case that Kierkegaard can say, "if only the mode of this relationship is in the truth, the individual is in the truth even if he should happen to be related to what is not true."

In the subject-object relation, the confronting object takes primacy even in one's own knowledge of it. But, with Buber, Torrance emphasizes this is a "dialogical relation," especially with the living God. In such real knowing there is said to be a true "anthropomorphism" which maintains the needed concrete quality in the knowing encounter where one is "confronted with something compellingly anthropomorphic, something commanding reciprocity," a primary "Thou." And here Torrance finds that the "danger" comes into being. As the human subject is given full place in this dialogical reciprocity in knowing, the human knower is "tempted" to take to the self the creative role, thereby adapting the object of one's own knowledge to modes of human subjectivity—obtruding the self into the content of knowledge. By such a replacement of objective encounter with mere self-encounter, "Neo-Protestantism" has "eclipsed God" and destroyed the human being as human. The second outcome follows from the first.[13]

In the second breakthrough in scientific questioning, i.e., to a beginning point in actuality (the existing object) before possibility, one seeks the actual nature of the thing known. The actual nature of what is known determines how one properly knows it. Torrance's analysis leads him to conclude that the modern loss of scientific objectivity arose when Bacon's view was followed up by Kant's. From Kant it was concluded that one must not only set forth the questions to be put to nature but the answers it must give as well. In fact, in prescribing the kind of question to be put, one prescribes the kind of "answers" received rather than letting the object form, revise and chastise the process of inquiry toward the actual nature of the object as it discloses itself. While many believe that humanity only imposes its patterns and mind upon nature via inquiry, this notion is false and damaging. With much illustration, especially from modern physics, Torrance asserts that in true scientific knowing basic human statements are formed by "conceptual assent to what is there or by way of recognition of an intelligibility inherent in the nature of things."[14] Apart from this objective rationality there could be no science (cf. below).

But he finds that this recognition is not widely heeded and the dualist claims of human subjectivism continue to assert that one can know only what one can fashion for oneself. Torrance often illustrates the great tensions involved by the differences which lie between "pure science" and "technology" (*not* a reference to applied science). Torrance defines his terms as follows:

> By "pure science" is meant the kind of knowledge we reach *in any field* when we know realities out of themselves and in accordance with their own interior patterns of thought (compulsion-assent). This is what was called "dogmatic science" in the seventeenth and eighteenth centuries, a term that was applied to physics before it was applied to theology. By technology is meant here . . . the way of knowing by inventing in which we are more concerned to *use* nature than to *know* it, and claim to know only what bears the imprint of our own minds.[15]

This is the same tension which Torrance finds today between "scientific" or "pure" theology and the "new" theology represented by Bultmann. The differences are marked and the effects are wide ranging. It is again the difference between knowledge objectively determined by God in His self-revelation and "knowledge" which the subject is said to create out of its own essential self-expression. That which is at stake is held to be all-important, i.e., the objectivity and reality of knowledge in which the human knower distinguishes what is known (object, Object) from the self's knowing of it. This is the "fundamental basis of rational knowledge."[16]

The subtle third change to which Torrance refers, change in the relation of language to being, also is said to concern issues of reference and intention. This question leads Torrance to conclude that biblical interpretation does not seek that which is in the soul of the writer but rather proper interpretation must think after (cf. Barth's use of Scripture after his discovery of Anselm) the author's intent as given in the text. The writers of Scripture are not pointing referentially to themselves but their writings intend and do bear reference (in real relation) to its proper Object, the Object which engendered this faithful response. Scripture bears witness to Jesus Christ, i.e., God's Being in his Act and his Act in his Being in Jesus Christ in his real interaction with space-time existence unto human redemption.

In the modern discussion after Butler and Hume, one must see the critical distinction between the relations of things and relations of ideas. The language of the natural sciences is concerned with reference to things (*correspondence*), but all true science (including theological science) is also concerned with the relations of ideas. This is true on several levels, but at the very least because scientific statements must be brought into *coherence* with one another for the scientific purpose. But the reference of scientific statements beyond themselves is not from ideas alone. This occurs by means of language as well. Referential language brings the mind of the knowing subject under the conceptual compulsion of the objective realities which such language has "mapped out."[17] In real relation, referential language is understood to be "transparent" to the disclosure of the proper object. But this "kind of rationality," as referring to determinate objects, Torrance calls "number rationality," which is similar to but distinguished from *Logos* or "*Word* rationality." The physical sciences investigate the world and thought makes real contact with the nature of things thereby bringing such knowledge to a consistent mathematical representation (i.e., a theory or "disclosure model") by which the world's rationality impresses itself upon the scientist ("number rationality"). Scientific inquiry into the objective self-disclosure of the ways and works of God, and thereby finally into the eternal Being of God, brings about realist knowledge which is not merely mathematical i.e., ("Word rationality"). Theological science as faithful response to the redemptive way of God in the world in Jesus Christ means that the theologian concludes that thought has met Reality. Thought

> . . . has made genuine contact with the divine Reality when we can bring our knowledge to an intelligible and enlightening unity through which the *Logos* of God Himself presses itself convincingly upon our minds. We direct our questions to the self-giving of God in Jesus Christ and allow our minds to fall under the power of the divine rationality that becomes revealed in Him. It is a rationality inherent in the reality of the incarnate Word before it takes shape in our apprehension of it (*a posteriori*), but as we allow it to become disclosed to us under our questions and find that it is opened out before us in an objective depth that far transcends what we can specify of it in our formulations (disclosure models) and yet is infinitely fertile in its illuminating power, we become caught up in a compulsive affirmation of it that is rational through and through.[18]

This kind of "obedient response" to the Word of God is what scientific theology is said to be by definition, and this is at the heart of Torrance's positive theological concern. God is the God whose Word is the conceptual self-disclosure or gracious unveiling of Himself to be known as He is only out of Himself.

Torrance believes that Western thought has experienced a "third re-entrenchment" of cosmological and epistemological dualism and as a result it has lost the referential, conceptual, language-to-being relation. While Torrance is troubled with the disjunction of language from being in more than one relation, his greater concern regards language when it is viewed as the self-expression of the human soul and is thereby cut off from objective, referential and conceptual relations to that which is external to the subject's soul. Torrance concludes that when religious language is reckoned in this way, theological statements lose all capacity to be theo-logically and responsively referential and conceptual, having content taken simply from contemporary culture. Like the early Barth, Torrance sees theology in Germany before and after the First World War as emptying theological statements of objective content in ways that are parallel to current problems. In such a situation, language about God is then regarded *a priori* as incapable of making actual objective reference, and is thus reduced to the subjective consciousness of the community. But Torrance says that matters cannot lie there in the rapidly advancing thought of modern culture caught within such a perspective. When this happens, says Torrance, either the historic Christian faith must acquiesce (cf. Ernst Troeltsch) as the religious expression of the culture, "or the cry goes up that 'God is dead'."[19] True theological statements cannot be given a "meaning" in terms of the self-fulfillment of the community. In such a situation the Church finds itself again in a "missionary" situation.

When language about God loses real capacity to refer and thus becomes detached from his Reality, and a "conceptuality" of subjective consciousness is exchanged for the real conceptuality forced upon the knower (assent) from the side of God, "disaster" ensues which Buber described as "the conceptual letting go of God." Faith becomes oblique, non-conceptual, symbolic, and thereby rationalized, rather than faith being understood as a true conceptual, direct and objective knowing. As Torrance explains,

> Whenever people prefer to follow a certain cultural way of life rather than the way of the Gospel . . . it is not surprising that they should find language about God rather empty and meaningless. All this lets us see how necessary a scientific theology is for the on-going life and mission of the Christian Church, for theology of this kind is the disciplined repentance to which the Church must constantly submit if its mind is not to be schematized to the patterns of this world but is to be renewed and transformed and grounded in the objective rationality of God in Jesus Christ.[20]

It is this theological task which Torrance wants to undertake and thereby to help the Church to accomplish for the renewal of the knowledge of God in the world.

The fourth major shift in modern scientific thought said to have taken place as a result of the Reformation was the change in the doctrine of God and nature as the Stoic-Latin *Deus sive natura* gave way to a more dynamic conception of God as the living Creator and Redeemer actively and personally at work in the world which He made. Nature was again consistently regarded as *created* out of nothing, *distinct* from and yet *dependent* on God in its real contingency and intelligibility. The difficulty was in maintaining the God-established tension between relation and distinction. As inquirers began to understand nature out of nature, this understanding was then wrongly detached from their thought of God and God's interactive, dynamic and creative activity. Nature came to be regarded as an independent source of knowledge, as the realm of humanity's own creative activity. As nature was divided from God unto itself, there occurred the widening "gulf" between God and the world which initiated "secularization" or "modernity" through the "Enlightenment".[21]

The doctrine of God and God's relation to the world then has moved on the spectrum from one end to the other, i.e., from the problem of the juxtapositioning of God and nature in a "necessitarian" relation to total disjunction so that God's interactive relation and working is "banished" from the world. Nature is sealed away from all meaning beyond itself in God. Again Torrance's primary concern with this dualist retrogression from scientific thinking is the effect of such upon theology. As has been observed, Torrance's analysis leads him to find only devastating consequences for Christian theology. The detachment of God from nature and humanity has cut away from theology all thought of God's real interaction with the world, making providence and pre-eminently Incarnation-Resurrection (redemption) impossible *a priori*. Such thinking severs "any interaction between the revealing and saving activity of God and human historical existence so that God is made dumb, no real Word from Him breaking through to us, and made otiose, no saving Act from Him actualizing itself in our condition of need."[22] "Deistic disjunction" means then that human expression about God springs not from the proper Object God, for no real Word has been given objectively by God to human beings in space-time. Such expressions have only this-worldly meaning and a "content" of mere self-understanding. Theological statements are converted into autobiographical utterances, which do not repose upon the objective self-disclosure of God in history from beyond the subject. "Act of God" is rejected as an objective event within space-time because of obsolete, un-scientific and disjunctive, instead of unitary, interactive, and truly scientific, ways of thinking the actual relatedness and givenness of God in the world by the incarnate Word. It is this false division of "religion" from "science," God from the world, which Torrance has set himself to overcome. From upon Barth's shoulders, and then beyond, Torrance wants to be for theology what Einstein and others have been for physics—to make theology truly scientific, to make it a servant of the redemptive mission of God through the Church whereby the real knowledge of God as He has given Himself to be known in Christ is facilitated in assenting human submission to *that* Word. One knows only, says Torrance, "in accordance with its nature, and you develop your knowledge of it and allow its nature to prescribe for you the mode of rationality appropriate to it."[23] To know God one must follow or assent to the mode of rationality prescribed by God's nature as self-disclosed in His Word.

Torrance desires that his criticisms of epistemological, cosmological and, thence, theological dualism in modern thought not be his only contribution to the restoration of this situation. While Torrance's vast criticisms are intended to give indirect expression of and make the way for his positive theological program, it is indeed his positive theological formulation which he hopes will facilitate the Gospel of Christ for the realist knowledge of God as He is. Torrance is quite optimistic about this. He sees the current situation as primarily one of turbulent epistemological-cosmological-theological transition. But in the face of the amazing and mysterious rationality of the contingent creation (cf. Einstein in chapter three), and more, before the sovereign, infinite and inherent rationality of God revealed in and by His transcendent *Logos* in space-time, all such current "reactionary flights" of irrationality must pass away. In the present renewal toward true scientific objectivity, theological science must both catch up and then keep pace. Through such renewal of objectivity theology will rightly be "thrown back" upon its own proper Object where, as a science, it will again relate properly to the inherent intelligibility of that Object of knowledge in its own infinite, profound depth. In this process of paring away, the true historico-theological foundations of the Church (e.g., the Nicene Creed) will be brought to a fuller understanding and responsive expression. Through such "disclosure models" the objective Reality of God in Jesus Christ and by the Spirit will be grasped in a depth of understanding beyond that of the time it was written and assimilated into the permanent theological advancement of the Church. Torrance wants to provide a "disciplined penetration into the inner intelligibility of the faith so that time-conditioned images and representations can be distinguished from the (objective) reality of the faith and concepts and relations that are justifiably retained."[24]

Bases of Torrance's Realist Theological Thought

Thomas Torrance's Theo-logical Task

Torrance wants to present a properly "interactionist" Christian theology, i.e., a theology "in which God is thought of as interacting closely with the world of nature and history without being confused with it".[25] Torrance will occasionally use the geometrical term "asymmetrical" as illustratively pointing to his emphasis on both unity and distinction. Torrance's modern models of theological thinking are Kierkegaard and Barth as they each penetrated the inner logic of the incarnation and thought again through Reformation theology in the light of modern philosophical and scientific developments.[26] Torrance believes such an "interactionist" theology must be enunciated afresh with even greater depth and advance, not as mere corrective, but as the commanded theological response to the way in which God has graciously come and actively revealed Himself in the world as Creator and Redeemer. Torrance obviously understands Karl Barth as an "interactionist" theologian and as one who has begun the task with effectiveness. Yet Barth is found by Torrance to have left much unfinished, implicit or inconsistent and thus problematic. Largely with Barth and against modern "theological dualism," Torrance has given himself energetically and prolifically to the interactionist theological task as responsively arising out of the Word made flesh, Jesus Christ.

Torrance also intends to bring about a renewal in theology as science, restoring it to its proper Object and objectivity in the realist knowledge of God, after the examples of St. Athanasius and Calvin. The beginning for dogmatic theology as scientific cannot be with an *a priori* possibility but from the "actuality" of God's revelation, from "faith in Jesus Christ as truly God and truly Man, and to seek to unfold our understanding of the double fact that in Jesus Christ the Word of God has become man . . . God's language to man."[27] Within the current crisis, this theology must effect critical revision of its theoretic framework, going on then to "fresh scientific construction under the pressure and determination of its own object."[28] Within the historic Christian faith, Torrance wants to advance apprehension of the objective Reality of God as He has given himself to be known. He believes that it is his task to reflect the disciplined penetration into the inner intelligibility of the faith. His understanding of the theologian-scientist is significant.

> . . . one must develop, like the physicist, his own meta-science or critical epistemological clarification of his basic concepts, if he is to give the faith compelling expression in the thought world of today with its roots secured in the permanent theological gains of the past and the ground cleared for decisive advance in the future. It is, I believe, through a sustained integration of theological reflection with its proper object and rigorous development of its own field of rational activity . . . . This is nothing else than a demand for scientific theology operating on its own ground, and engaging in active dialogue with the natural human sciences, in its own distinctiveness.[29]

Torrance repeatedly emphasizes that theological science, like the natural sciences, is done within the space-time world shared with the other sciences where one explores and penetrates into the inherent rationality of what is manifest objectively there and is to be known out of itself, whether that be created existence in its created rationality or God in His revelation in the world in His uncreated Rationality. As such, humanity is obedient to God, Creator and Redeemer. Natural sciences bring finite objects (the truth of being) to articulation. Beside the natural scientist, the theologian within the Church must be at work seeking understanding within those very structures in order to communicate that given understanding of God (the Truth of Supreme Being) in the forms of human thought and speech. It is necessarily within this world of concrete actualities "that the Church pursues its theological task, for it is not apart from them that God has made Himself known and it must be within them that theology fulfills its scientific function of clarification and explanation."[30] Theological science too operates in the world and must let its thinking serve the Reality into which it properly inquires. It has its own specific concern to take up with its own modes of rationality and verification which are determined for it by the nature of its Object as given to be known. Theology then must maintain scientific rigor demanded by the objectivity of its appropriate Object after which it must think in accord with the mode of rationality required by the Object, God in His Word, disclosed concretely within the structures of space-time. As a science, says Torrance, theology too has its own basic problems of knowledge that are crucial, i.e., in "conforming knowing to the nature of reality, in distinguishing knowing from what is known, and in reflecting self-critically upon (its) own operations."[31]

The physicist works to achieve complete and unitary penetration of natural events and must develop a logically unified conceptual representation of physical reality, not from interest in some conceptual system but from concern with the physical relatedness inherent in nature, the physical structure of reality itself (the unity of form/structure and being). Basic concepts should not arise via logical abstraction but through "intuitive apprehension" of experience which determines the actual cognitive value of the concepts. All of this undergoes continual refinements under the impress of objective physical reality. Yet one must operate with the difficulty of using words which are inevitably connected to obsolete or pre-scientific concepts and it becomes ever more difficult to correlate thought with actual experience of the real space-time world. But only in this way can a profound grasp of reality be reached.[32]

In like manner, says Torrance, theology under the Word must carry out critical revision, unification and simplification of the whole body of theological knowledge as it has grown in the thought of the Church. Torrance centers this process (like Barth) in and from Christology and the "economic" movement of God in the world "back" to the conception (or "disclosure model") of the Trinity of God, the ontological Trinity being ultimately *the* basic grammar or ground structure of all truly Christian theology. The doctrine of the Trinity is considered to be the supreme example of such a scientific "disclosure model," according to Torrance. Further, the Trinity doctrine is a prominent example, he says, of a "refined" model having a minimum of basic concepts immediately taken from revelation and the human intuitive apprehension of God in Christ. These are connected together in this "doctrinal model" whereby understanding is allowed to "come under the articulate revelation and power of God's own Reality and seek to grasp in our thought as much as we may what God communicates to us of his own unity and simplicity."[33] Realist, scientific theology cannot be concerned with any conceptual system as such, but ultimately with the immanent trinitarian relations in God as Father, Son and Holy Spirit in the interrelatedness of love and knowledge which he has sovereignly and graciously established between himself and human beings in their historical existence in the world. The theologian must then advance toward doctrinal development of the greatest possible unity and least foundational concepts. In this way "we can provide a revisable conceptual representation of the ultimate intelligible basis of our knowledge of God."[34]

Torrance points out that the difficulty with pre-scientific concepts and language will arise here too as it does when the physical sciences attempt to grasp and represent in language imperceptible realities and relations (e.g., relativity and quantum theories). Thus the need is for a more strenuous faithfulness in the constitutive elements in God's self-communication to us and in our experience and apprehension of God which fostered the concepts initially. But God has "adapted" his "Light" to human capacity and his own economic movement within the bounds of human apprehension. If human beings are to apprehend and rightly express the Truth of God in useable "disclosure models," then theology must think after the disclosive movement of God. It is Torrance's purpose to "keep pace with God's self-giving and in fact to become united to it in the course of its movement in our midst" through Jesus Christ and in the Holy Spirit. This will require a consistently *a posteriori* and kinetic ways of thinking "together" as thinking is to be obedient to or in accord with that actual movement of God, penetrating into the actual intelligible relations *in* God.[35] Torrance's task is then one which "backtracks" or reverses the actual movement of God in his Acts from the concrete to the economic to the ontological. In this way God-talk is only valid to the extent that it is faithfully correlated "with our fundamental experience of God and controlled by his self-revelation to us in Jesus Christ the incarnate Son of the Father."[36]

Torrance works with the conviction that knowledge of God is the basic act of the human mind and faith is the adaptation of the reason in its response to the compelling claims of God as he makes himself known in the world. From this Torrance formulates his understanding of the way to speak of God in submission to the Word of God. Using what he refers to as Spinoza's principle that once a thing is understood it continues to manifest itself in the power of its own truth without needing further truth (i.e., it cannot be lost, but rather unfolds its inherent truth out of its own disclosive power), Torrance asserts that in the same way once the self-revelation of God has seized the human mind, human understanding of God is borne forward by the intrinsic power of Truth which presents and impresses itself for ever fuller realization and adequation in theological thinking and expression. The theological task is not a second order work of reflection but a first-order activity of inquiry whereby one must pursue the self-given God within a deepening empirical and theoretical relation. Note Torrance's stress on the personal *and* rational or intellectual in describing what "theology" is in faithful response to the realist knowledge of God.

> . . . (It is) a form of intense intellectual communion with God in which our minds are taken captive by his Love and we come to know God more and more through himself. Even though we are found using third-personal language, theological inquiry of this kind is carried out face to face with God so that it may properly be regarded as a form of rational worship in which awe and wonder and joy give vent to themselves in prayer and praise . . . . (and yet) Constant arduous reflection is needed not only on the content of God's articulate self-revelation as it assumes doctrinal form in our understanding, but on the conceptual reconstruction and adaptation of our modes of thought and speech that must take place, if appropriate conceptual structures are to be developed both in order to help us give coherent and consistent formulation of what we have come to understand and to provide us with fresh intellectual instruments which, under the control of the realities we apprehend, may serve their disclosure to our continuing inquiry.[37]

Torrance's theological task is then to bring forth a form of faith-ful thinking with its source and goal beyond itself in God by his Word. He intends to lead the way "meta-scientifically" for scientific theology to burst modern autonomous thought while making theology again submit to its own proper subject-matter, thereby rejecting all "alien dogmatisms" which distort and cut off the real knowledge of God. To this end Torrance is concerned that theology uncover its own properly basic forms of thought as they do arise from God's self-objectification in Jesus. From such forms of thought he says that theology must formulate instruments appropriate to the Word for faithful expression. Face to face with God in his revelation, the theologian must be ready to repent of false habits of mind and to adopt modes of rationality that actually correspond with the nature of theology's objectively given reality.[38] Only then can theology be truly that and grounded upon its own foundations in Jesus Christ.

Torrance understands "theological knowledge" to be hinged then upon what is given from beyond the human, and which in no way is dependent upon human discovery. Theological knowledge is concerned with fact which has objective ontological reality, the hard objective reality apart from which no such human knowledge could exist. Thus even if one knows God in the knowing of faith, that human faith is not the subject of theology, but rather God in his self-disclosure. Knowledge of things occurs in their objective connections and never apart from a complex situation of subjective experiences and articulation. Through these transparent media one must apprehend that objectively given reality which is beyond the human subject. If that is so with creaturely things how much more it is true, Torrance asserts, that theological thinking must again be *theo*-logical, i.e., thinking from a center in *God only* so that human knowledge would be a "fulfilled meeting with objective reality."[39] Before the Truth of God thinking is changed (*metanoia*), not only transformed but, by assent, conformed to the Truth of God in "disciplined repentance." Torrance desires this so that, like Einstein in physics, he would emancipate theology from the damaging structures of modern dualism by entering the rational freedom that comes with objectivity and its detachment of thinking from arbitrary subjectivism. This objectivity in theology is like the objectivity in all true sciences, i.e., "rigorous correlation of thought with its proper object and the self-renunciation, repentance and change of mind that it involves."[40] But more, Torrance engages in epistemological analysis to test the thought and speech of the Church to see whether these match the proper content of theology on the ground of actual knowledge of God in the Word. Clearly this is a development of Barth's goal for the *Church Dogmatics*.[41] As theological science and expression must arise from and be verified out of the Word, real coordination is necessary to keep theological concepts from being severed from the real space-time structures which God has made and in which God has placed humanity and through and in which he has made himself known to humanity.[42]

Torrance's task then is to re-establish and do theology as a science, in order to clarify and unify the knowledge of God in a way that theological order can be brought to every day experience and to faith in God, and also to advance deeper understanding of God. By God's Word and Spirit human beings are enabled to know God in real measure as he is in himself. Yet theological science can never be more than the continual refinement and extension of that knowledge which has been informed by the fundamental ideas with which the knowledge of God is built up in the Church. Therefore, says Torrance, in theological science "we must take care at all levels to maintain intuitive contact with immediate experience, knowledge and worship of God, for that determines the cognitive value."[43] The theologian, like the physicist, selects a few primary convictions as close as possible to the ground of experience and faith and organizes these into a preliminary "disclosure model" by means of which one seeks to "penetrate" ever more deeply into the rational configuration of the proper field of inquiry in order to trace the inner connections (and transcendent Rationality) of it. In this way the inner logic of God's Grace is brought to light from the actual coming of God in Christ.[44] In this way theology as science generates concepts of God that are actually, though finitely, worthy of him as he is and are not mere projections of human devising out of the self-understanding. Rather these concepts are "forced" upon the mind by the nature of God's majesty disclosed in Christ.

In a larger sense, as a direct result of his understanding of God's dynamic, interactive relatedness to and in the world, Torrance desires also that theology would effect restoration on the epistemological and cultural levels. Thus, as with Athanasius and Calvin, Torrance states that this new synthesis and realist unification will increasingly advance and transcend the gulf in "popular" understanding between false antitheses, e.g., faith and reason, religion and life, theology and natural science, in the integration of all thought and culture.[45] In directing theology back to its proper Object and to proper method out of that Object it will again become truly scientific. Theology then will have its legitimate place in the world to the end that God would be known out of himself in his relation as Creator to all of human life and Redeemer by the Word of God. In this context dialogue between theology and the various sciences will have significant impact for openness to God, the source of all rational order in the world.[46]

Thomas Torrance's "Foundationalism" and Theo-logical Realism

We have begun to observe already that an important aspect of Thomas Torrance's own epistemology, and thus of his understanding of the knowledge of God, is his foundationalism. The "upper stories" of his thinking are supported by the "lower stories," or foundations which are given. This issue

in Torrance's theo-logical thinking proves to be significant to his understanding
of the nature of human knowledge of God, hence theological methodology, while
becoming too a point of possible criticism (cf. chapters six and seven).
Plantinga has explained that basically "foundationalism" is the view

> . . . that some of our beliefs are based upon others. According to the
> foundationalist a rational noetic structure will have a *foundation* — a set of
> beliefs not accepted on the basis of others; in a rational noetic structure some
> beliefs will be basic. Non-basic beliefs, of course, will be accepted on the
> basis of other beliefs, which may be accepted on the basis of still other
> beliefs, and so on until the foundations are reached. In a rational noetic
> structure, therefore, every non-basic belief is ultimately accepted on the basis
> of basic beliefs.[47]

A properly basic belief is one that belongs to the foundation of a rational noetic
structure. There is a sense of hierarchy in which every belief is either basic or
derivative. Torrance never explicitly declares himself to be a foundationalist.[48]
Torrance's explanation of the centrality of certain "ultimate beliefs",
"assumptions", "fundamental ideas", and even "foundations" to proper thought
which are not themselves verifiable have made clear that Torrance is a
foundationalist.[49]

In previous discussion of Torrance's "theological task" it was noted that
his use of foundationalist perspectives directs him when he says, "Let it be
granted, then, that the basic convictions and fundamental ideas with which our
knowledge of God is built up arise on the ground of . . . experience . . . in
response to the way God has actually taken in making himself known to
mankind."[50] While not explicit here, this model of human knowledge will be
shown to be quite important for Torrance. Torrance says that the truly basic
questions which are pressed upon persons are the ones which finally "penetrate
to the ultimate assumptions and regulative beliefs governing all knowledge in the
world, whatever the specific field of inquiry in which we are engaged."[51]
These "fundamental questions" reveal that the power of argument lies not with
reasoning processes, though these are important, but with an ultimate belief
which arises necessarily within the human thinking from the basis of one's
experience in the universe. Thus, he says that there is what Michael Polanyi has
called the "inarticulate" grasp of reality or the "tacit dimension" on which all
rational knowledge and all scientific investigation is based. While non-formal,
it is said to form the necessary basis of all knowledge in the various sciences.
This "tacit" knowing possesses capacities to underpin and guide in constructive
formalization of knowledge, and "projects" human thought "heuristically"
beyond present empirical evidence. This is so because it is founded in
"unbounded intelligibility which invites unceasing inquiry and unconditional
commitment."[52] It is in light of this, for example, that there ought to arise real

appreciation for the community structure of human life and the moral ordering of human affairs in the world which press upon thought and thereby bring deepening realization in obedience to the imperatives of ultimate reality. This ordered state of human affairs is said to necessarily raise the question of the transcendent Source of rationality and the activity of an ordering Agent.

Torrance intends to emphasize the necessary priority of belief in all true knowing, i.e., the "fundamental beliefs" which have been at the basis of the effectiveness found in modern physical sciences. But contra John Locke's attempt to discredit belief as ungrounded persuasion of the mind or subjective feeling without justification, Torrance follows recent insights into the priority of belief for true knowledge as found in Maxwell, Einstein, Polanyi and others, and from theology in Barth via Anselm (*Fides quaerens intellectum*). Within this modern renewal of ontological commitment to the inherent intelligibility of the universe, Torrance finds that fundamental beliefs, e.g., the intelligibility of the universe, are objectively founded. He means that ultimate beliefs are personal convictions but they are not merely subjective. They are convictions tied together with the elemental interactions which occur between persons and realities external to themselves. These are basic acts of acknowledgment in response to the intelligibility inherent in things.[53] Fundamental beliefs rest then upon the objective pole of the knowing relationship and cannot be reduced to subjective states.

> . . . beliefs arise in us because they are forced upon us by the nature of the reality with which we are in experimental contact, and as we allow our minds to fall under the constraint of its inherent intelligibility which we cannot rationally or in good conscience resist. Thus belief has to be understood strictly within the context of rational recognition of and willing submission to the claims of objective reality upon us and of obligation towards the truth laid upon us by the truth itself. It is this ontological anchoring of belief in reality transcendent to ourselves which prevents it from being subjective or arbitrary, for it binds belief to what is independently and universally true.[54]

Belief, he says, can only be maintained within the commitment to reality, "assent" to the universal validity of what is believed. Torrance follows Polanyi in maintaining that as belief and truth are correlated, truth is the external pole of belief and belief must be reckoned as "obedience" of the mind to the truth in the recognition of its universal claims. As belief is seen to be founded upon the objective pole of the knowing relationship, the subjective pole has its proper role as subordinate to the intelligible objective reality. The rational agent believes as one who is convinced that such is the way one ought to believe in faithfulness to the truth. Like Barth, Torrance relates faith directly to belief as real cognitive relation having conceptual content. Yet it is a cognitive relation to its Object which, like "tacit" knowledge, must then be rigorously pursued, unfolded and brought to ever greater understanding and expression. Faith is the mode of rationality taken by reason as it adapts itself to the nature of that proper Object (God in his self-disclosure) which it endeavors to understand.[55] As physics has a mode of rationality "dictated" to it by and proper to its own proper object, so too Torrance asserts that faith, or faith-knowing, is the proper mode of rationality in relation to and correlated to the nature of God in his Word, the Word made flesh. This, says Torrance, is the recovery of the epistemic process basic to historic Christian theology (*fides quaerens intellectum*).

Torrance develops this in speaking of the conviction that in the universe there is ultimately a trustworthy, reliable order grounded in the eternal, transcendent *Logos* of God which takes into account the evil, pain, error, sin, darkness, disorder and irrationality in the world. The crucial term for Torrance is the word "ultimately," i.e., the evil is taken into account, but with it there lies the "nevertheless" or the "in spite of." Theologically, Torrance asserts that evil must be accounted for face to face with God's self-revelation in Jesus Christ and thus in conflict with God's will and love. Founded upon the goodness and faithfulness of God the world must be viewed as ultimately good and orderly from beyond itself in the commanding Word of God. "In spite of" the evil there is beyond it the unrelenting faithfulness of God in which faith is put from within the devastation. There is ultimate belief in the divine order of righteousness, that order lies behind all of creation under the Word of God, though often inscrutably. This "belief" is reckoned to be "foundational" to the faith-knowing relations face to face with the Word of God.

Reflecting upon the notion of order as it applies in physical and theological science, Alastair Mackinnon's statement "There is order in the universe" in *Falsification and Belief* is said by Torrance to express that ultimate belief upon which all sciences rely. Despite events which as yet appear inscrutable and regarding which no final scientific sense can yet be made (Torrance often refers thus to quantum theory), persons remain convinced of order. It cannot be proven but must be assumed much like the laws of logic must be assumed in order to be "proved."[56] "This is an ultimate assumption of science . . . which is both unverifiable and unfalsifiable, yet we cannot give it up without plunging into irrationality."[57] Likewise tragedies bring forth the question "why?" and the sense of contradiction to belief in the God of love and order. Belief in order causes revolt against the evil or the fact of disorder to be found in the world. In this same sense, Torrance says that "God is love" cannot be either verified or falsified. Like fundamental beliefs in the physical sciences upon which all depends and from which all that we know in the universe is construed, that God is love is basic in the "ordering force behind the creation and operation in all God's providential government of created existence."[58] All is finally dependent upon it. That God is love is a conviction which one cannot give up without falling finally into irrationalism and despair, he says. Therefore one seeks by reference to the love of God to make some sense of disorder found in the world. It remains humanity's conviction that evil cannot be the ultimate, final word to human existence. Torrance, then, is contending for the rationality and the necessity, as well the crucial methodological role, of belief, or rather ultimate beliefs, in knowledge of objective reality. Belief in the intelligibility and graspability of the space-time universe is no mere subjective sense or personal prejudice, but is the truly cognitive, though "tacit", response to the impress of the world's ultimate order and intelligibility despite the disorder found in it. As yet "tacit," "inarticulate," such knowing contains within it the basis for one to move to the higher level of faithful conceptualization and expression. While the world's intelligible pattern may yet elude us in this or that event, still we continue to interrogate the event until the embedded order in the nature of that creaturely entity becomes clearer unto understanding. God the Creator is Love. This ultimate order, this immanent *logos* in the world, though, points beyond itself, beyond its created rationality to the uncreated Rationality of God from whom the creation and all that is therein receives its contingent order and intelligibility. As with belief in the physical sciences in relation to the ultimate rationality of the universe, so too faith in the God who has revealed himself to be known is a knowing, but yet a "tacit" knowing, in response to the objective Word of God. It is a knowing in relation in which theology seeks understanding of its own proper Object, God, who is Redeemer as well as the transcendent Creator of the intelligible, contingent world. Herein one notes something of Torrance's renewal and modification of "natural" theology.

While this contention may be commonly accepted, Torrance goes further. It is central to Torrance's positive theological concern to posit "the order of redemption in which everything depends upon the love of God." But Torrance finds something here which has no parallel in the natural sciences, namely the "incarnation in our world of the very *Logos* or Word of God by which all things were made, which is a movement of the ultimate love of God penetrating into our world in a creative reordering and renewing of it from within."[59] Because this is the active love of the Creator-Redeemer this is no intrusion alien to the world, as Bultmann would have it. Torrance understands the incarnation, along with creation, to be the clearest revelation of the reality of "asymmetrical" God-world relatedness. Upon the basis of God's sovereign relatedness to the world, the love of God revealed in Jesus Christ is wholly proper to it.

Thus the recognition of "ultimate" or "fundamental" beliefs and the role of such in scientific activity is derived now from renewed ontological commitment to the inherent intelligibility of the universe, especially after Einstein, that is, submission to the compulsion of objective reality in the overthrow of dualistic theories of knowledge in favor of a realist, unitary theory of knowledge wherein the empirical and theoretical inhere inseparably (cf. chapter three). In theology this has called into question many positivistic assumptions governing the nature of inquiry which have cut off belief in the interaction of God with the world in which God "makes himself known in an evidential and conceptual way."[60] Ultimate beliefs in Christian theology must be the very ones which press upon recognition from the actual ground of God's disclosural interaction. These foundations of theological knowing, he says, have not been taken over uncritically.

> . . . they have to be put to the test by reference to the evidential grounds of our deepening knowledge in theological and hermeneutical activity, so that they may really measure up to the compelling claims upon us of God's self-revelation and self-communication to mankind in his historical dialogue with the people of Israel and in the incarnation of his eternal Word in Jesus Christ . . . our ultimate beliefs have a normative function to fulfill which does not conflict with rigorous biblical and theological studies, for they direct the bearing of our inquiries upon reality and thus are essential to the establishment of knowledge.[61]

This point of the function of these foundations for scientific knowledge is significant. In all proper sciences the mind is committed to the claims of intelligible reality upon it and it is recognized that "belief," or what Torrance also terms "intuitive apprehension," is the source of knowledge in discovery, so that in the knowing relation the mind is actually understood to be in direct touch with intelligible reality beyond the knower. Then upon the ground of this ultimate belief, reason is entrusted to that rational order and reliability of the contingent world. Scientific activity in pursuit of understanding is said to require this "faith."

> . . . there is an elemental, overwhelming faith in the rational constitution of things, but faith also in the possibility of grasping the real world with our concepts . . . above all faith in the truth over which we have no control but in the service of which our human rationality stands or falls. Faith and intrinsic rationality are interlocked with one another.[62]

Torrance repeatedly points out that Polanyi has shown that no human intelligence can work outside of faith. Before objective reality there arises in thought "a regulative set of convictions or a framework of beliefs which prompts and guides our inquiries and controls our assessment of the evidence." That these preliminary convictions prompt and guide scientific inquiry into objective reality to be known out of itself is important to Torrance's understanding not only of theological science but of the "transformation of natural theology" as well. "Ultimate beliefs" are then understood to be actually based in reality and are the premises upon which all subsequent scientific endeavor relies, giving them persuasive power. Torrance thus is clear in his position that unless thinking is informed by "prior intuitive contact with reality" which impresses these basic beliefs upon the mind, then the mind struggles in useless surmises.[63] For Torrance these "ultimate beliefs" in the order and intelligibility of the universe are the basis of scientific thinking, and they are grounded beyond themselves, having their source in the created rationality of the universe and ultimately in the uncreated Rationality of God. This assertion can be observed throughout the corpus of his writing, though usually the theo-logical point is made more implicitly than explicitly. A brief reference to this *ultimate* belief, indeed *the* ultimate belief and basis of rationality in Torrance's thinking, may be found in the following interview response:

> To me, the living God is the most real thing there is. Knowledge of God is the most natural, most intuitive thing of all, especially for me . . . . Belief in God simply pervaded everything. To me, it has always seemed so natural.[64]

NOTES

1. Torrance, *GR*, p. 3.

2. Ibid., pp. 49-51.

3. Ibid., pp. 31-33f.

4. Ibid., p. 37.

5. Ibid., p. 35f.

6. Ibid., p. 39.

7. Ibid.

8. Ibid., p. 40.

9. Torrance, *CTSC*, pp. 137-138.

10. Ibid., p. 138 and *GR*, p. 40. Cf. *GR*, chapter 5 on the issue of "Ecumenism and Science."

11. Torrance, *TS*, p. 6, note 1, a pertinent quotation Torrance takes from Martin Buber's *The Eclipse of God*, p. 82. This work is often used and highly admired by Torrance.

12. Soren Kierkegaard, *Concluding Unscientific Postscript*, translated by David F. Swenson and Walter Lowrie (Princeton: Princeton University Press, 1974), p. 287, referred to in Torrance, *TS*, p. 5. This interpretation of Kierkegaard has been largely confirmed in the most recent Kierkegaard scholarship. Cf. especially M. Jamie Ferreira's excellent study of Kierkegaard, *Transforming Vision* (Oxford: Clarendon Press, 1992).

13. Torrance, *TS*, p. 330, note 3.

14. Torrance, *GR*, p. 42.

15. Ibid., p. 44.

16. Ibid.

17. Ibid., pp. 44-45. Torrance agrees with Buber, *The Eclipse of God*, p. 82, where he says "the soul can never legitimately make an assertion, even a metaphysical one, out of its own creative power. It can make an assertion only out of a binding real relationship to a truth which it articulates."

18. Ibid., p. 45.

19. Ibid., p. 47.

20. Ibid., p. 48. Cf. Torrance, *CTSC*, pp. 7-8.

21. Ibid.

22. Ibid., p. 49.

23. Ibid., p. 52-53.

24. Torrance, *TRn*, p. 284. Cf. Gray's comment on "The Church in an Era of Scientific Change," where Torrance refers with approval to D.M. MacKinnon's contribution, "'Substance' in Christology: A Crossbench View," in S.W. Sykes and J.P. Clayton eds., *Christ, Faith and History, Cambridge Studies in Christology* (Cambridge, 1972), pp. 279-300. MacKinnon traces the history of the concept, pointing out that the use of ontological categories enables us to see what it is that encounters us in the person of Jesus, and that the debate concerning the *homoousion* serves to remind us how central to the Christian theological argument is the debate concerning Christ's person. He sees the most fundamental task in Christology as "the one or reconciling the use of the category of substance in the articulation of the christological problem with the recognition that it is the notion of *kenosis* which more than any other single notion points to the deepest sense of the mystery of the incarnation," Ibid., p. 294.

25. Torrance, *TCFK*, p. 285.

26. Ibid.

27. Torrance, *TRst*, pp. 129-130.

28. Torrance, *GR*, p. 5.

29. Ibid., p. 6.

30. Ibid., p. 113.

31. Ibid.

32. Torrance, *RST*, p. 160. Cf. Torrance, *RET*, 30-38, cf. in further discussion below on the important epistemological and methodological relationship between theological science and the natural sciences. This relation is reflected in many of Torrance's works including *TS, GR, CTSC, DCO, STR, STI, TCFK*.

33. Ibid., p. 161.

34. Ibid.

35. Torrance, *CTSC*, p. 98.

36. Torrance, *RST*, p. 162. Cf. Torrance, *TS*, p. 24.

37. Torrance, *RST*, p. xii.

38. Torrance, *TRst*, pp. 74-75.

39. Torrance, *TS*, pp. 28-29.

40. Torrance, *GR*, p. 10.

41. Karl Barth, *Church Dogmatics*, vol. I/1, translated by G.T. Thomson (Edinburgh: T & T Clark, 1936), pp. 51-53.

42. Torrance, *GR*, p. 123.

43. Torrance, *RST*, p. 85.

44. Ibid., p. 86.

45. Ibid., p. x.

46. Torrance, *GG*, p. 43.

47. Alvin Plantinga, "Reason and Belief in God," in *Faith and Rationality*, ed. by Nicholas Woltersdorff and Alvin Plantinga (Notre Dame: University of Notre Dame Press, 1983), p. 52. Cf. the critical work Woltersdorff has done and has been engaged in recently on "foundationalism."

48. It is most interesting to note how both Thomas Torrance and Carl F. H. Henry, whom Torrance vigorously critiques both implicitly and explicitly (cf. chapter 5), have not only great commonality in their foundationalism (though Torrance's foundationalism is less "systematic") but consequently in their concern for the Word of God (in different ways), for proper epistemology (realist), and the critical relation of such to culture.

49. Ronald Thiemann, *Revelation and Theology: The Gospel as Narrated Promise* (Notre Dame: University of Notre Dame Press, 1985), pp. 32-45, 52, especially 39, 52. Thiemann rightly argues for Torrance's "foundationalism" and uses this fact as central to his criticism of Torrance's understanding of revelation and the Truth of God (cf. chapters six and seven in this study).

50. Torrance, *RST*, p. 85.

51. Torrance, *RET*, p. 53.

52. Torrance, *RST*, pp. 112-113.

53. Torrance, *CTSC*, pp. 67-68. Cf. Torrance's discussion of three controlling beliefs regulating the understanding of the universe in Torrance, *TCFK*, pp. 204-212.

54. Ibid., p. 68. Cf. Torrance, *TCFK*, pp.. 202-203, 220, and 149-150 on M. Polanyi's restoration of the balance of human cognitive powers versus positivism and scientism in their "depersonalization" of science. Rather he shows how science is indeed *personal* knowledge properly understood.

55. Ibid., p. 70 Cf. Torrance, RET, pp. 53-54.

56. Torrance, *RET*, pp. 54-55.

57. Ibid., pp. 131-132.

58. Ibid., p. 132. Cf. Eberhard Jüngel, *God as the Mystery of the World: On the Foundation of the Theology of the Crucified One in the Dispute between Theism and Atheism*, translated by Darrell L. Guder (Grand Rapids: Wm. B. Eerdmans Publishing Company, 1983), pp. 3-42, 226-396.

59. Ibid., pp. 132-133.

60. Torrance, *RET*, p. 56. Cf. pp. 56-59.

61. Ibid., pp. 57-58.

62. Torrance, *CTSC*, p. 64.

63. Ibid.

64. Michael Bauman, *Roundtable Talks*, p. 3.

Chapter 3

The Revolution In Epistemology: Torrance's Understanding Of The Modern Return To Objectivity And Realism

Introduction

Of signal importance for Torrance's realist theological agenda in the latter part of the twentieth century is the "restoration of true scientific thinking" that has broken the dualistic and static bonds of Newtonian science and Kantian epistemology. This restoration (sometimes he will use the term "renewal") in the sciences has, he says, resulted in the return and the deepening of scientific objectivity and thus realization of the need to know the world realistically out of its own intrinsic and contingent rationality. But, as in previous eras of scientific renewal, this transformation in the physical sciences is said to have clarified the interrelations between the physical sciences and theological science. Within the domain of the physical sciences Torrance is interested primarily in physics which is perceived to have taken leadership in this renewal of science. Torrance's interest in the physical sciences beyond theological science is itself theo-logical at several levels. He particularly believes that such inquiry along the lines reflective of the modern restoration of realist scientific knowing is mandated by the very nature of God's interactive relatedness to and in the space-time structures and creaturely rationality of the world as Creator, Sustainer, and Redeemer, and by the created nature of the human being who is capable of knowing and of bringing to "word" the inner intelligibility of creation as the "priest of creation." Beyond even this, Torrance finds in the physical sciences, particularly physics, that field of inquiry which has begun to overthrow the alien and damaging Cartesian-Newtonian-Kantian dualism which has been clamped down on modern thought, and has begun to re-establish true objectivity, acceptance and pursuit of realist knowledge of what had been reckoned as the unknowable (by pure reason), the "noumenal world." He believes that such restoration can only benefit and heal theological thinking, calling it back to rigorous, truly scientific thinking from its own and only proper object, God, the concrete self-revelation of God in Jesus Christ. We will find then that Torrance's interpretation of the seminal work of physicist J. Clerk Maxwell, especially in his "field theory," causes him to reckon Maxwell's thought as opening the way for the yet more effective work to be found especially in Albert Einstein and general relativity and quantum theory. This in turn made the way for the recognition of the dynamism and the personal element in knowledge, and the priority of belief in the thought found in Michael Polanyi. By examining what Torrance finds to be so helpful in these scientists we will find their effects are found to be primarily upon the understanding of the universe, epistemology, and language. These will be discussed as they play formative roles in the context of Torrance's own theological expression.

Epistemological Realism and J. Clerk Maxwell

It is of great importance for Torrance's analysis of the nature of true science that physicist J. Clerk Maxwell of Edinburgh, professor at Cambridge, stood within the "Scottish Realist" tradition, a tradition which Torrance has traced back at least to Duns Scotus. This is because Torrance claims to think and write (though he expresses this rarely) within the Scottish realist tradition, which is characterized by its seeking to recover the concepts of contingence and objectivity, contingent intelligibility, and to move away from false notions of necessity. One must be clear that Torrance's critical realism is not that of medieval realism. There is no automatic or necessary correlation between reality and thought. Rather he maintains that reality presents itself for the knower. To this disclosure the knower must obediently respond. The truth shines through "transparencies." There is an actual correspondence between reality and thought or language if the thinker is conformed to the mode of rationality of reality or being. In his later writings, Torrance often expresses his particular indebtedness to the Scottish realist thought of Maxwell who has made an "epoch-making contribution to the revolution in our understanding not only of physics, but of the universe itself, with which relativity, quantum and thermodynamic theory are so closely related today."[1]

Torrance finds that Maxwell's achievement, as it was carried on and greatly developed through Einstein's work, can only be understood out of the interrelationship of his life, his faith and his scientific work. Torrance sees this interrelationship, integral to the realist tradition. Maxwell's predecessor in the Scottish Realist tradition, Michael Faraday, was characterized by this same effectual interpenetration of the personal and scientific. Both, men, says Torrance, were devout Christian believers in the Reformed tradition. Maxwell himself wrote of the relation between Faraday's science and his religious belief. One of a number of examples which Torrance refers to comes from a lecture at Cambridge on experimental physics. Here Maxwell expresses how scientific understanding of the universe and faith in God were profoundly integrated.

> The habit of recognizing principles amid the endless variety of their action can never degrade our sense of the sublimity of nature, or mar our enjoyment of its beauty. On the contrary, it tends to rescue our scientific ideas from that vague condition in which we too often leave them, buried among other products of a lazy incredulity, and to raise them into their proper position among the doctrines in which our faith is so assured, that we are ready at all times to act on them.[2]

Their Christian faith and scientific experimentation affected one another through relation via their ultimate belief in the orderliness of nature. Maxwell's "belief" in the orderliness of the universe was the basis for his experimental research, namely the compatibility between a humble belief and scientific investigation. Maxwell thus shared Faraday's fundamental beliefs in the contingent rationality and intelligibility of the universe and the same experimental impulses which were grounded in his commitment to God as self-revealed in Jesus Christ. This should not be considered a prejudicial interrelation, according to Torrance.

> Far from detracting from the independence of his mind . . . Maxwell's evangelical convictions . . . fostered his scientific inquiries and urged them to break new ground in an untrammeled and reverent investigation of nature's secrets. In view of what he called 'the unsearchable riches of creation,' Clerk Maxwell had little use for mere empiricism or narrow scientific professionalism obsessed with measurements carried out in a physics laboratory. An approach of that kind which left no room for a theologically and philosophically empowered grasp of things in their natural wholeness and continuity was finally unable properly to assess analytical particulars or to come up with genuinely new ideas.[3]

Maxwell is said by Torrance to stand out as a crucial transitional and original thinker having a formative sensitivity for those "fundamental ideas" which he owed to the influence of Scottish realism. He could think independently, and, under the impact of the Christian faith upon his thought, break from mechanistic Newtonian conceptualizations and open the way toward the change in understanding of the universe now taking place.[4] Maxwell's ability to grasp things in their wholeness and in their dynamic connections was what made it possible for him to assess the meaning of those interrelated particulars.

But for Torrance, it was Maxwell's ground breaking work toward "integrated" and "relational" scientific thinking of the proper object which has been of greatest import to restored objectivity in the sciences. His development of "field theory" is of central epistemological and, analogically, theological concern. Maxwell's field theory had its roots in his earlier studies in metaphysics rooted in theology and philosophy. Maxwell drew upon this in order to formulate his field theory. This, says Torrance, is another example of proper and needed cross-fertilization at the base of some of the outstanding advances in knowledge (e.g., Athanasius and Philiponos, Calvin and Bacon). Torrance extends this principle point of integrational and rational thinking of the world.

> . . . (Maxwell's) acquisition of a deep intuitive grasp of God in relation to the world he had created and ceaselessly sustains and the relation of nature in all its harmony and intricacy to the kind of Creator he knew through Jesus Christ . . . he developed a mode of thinking in which the practical and the theoretical were held inseparably together . . . every science must have its fundamental ideas . . . by which the process of our minds is brought into complete harmony with the process of nature.[5]

The idea of God as infinite author of all contingent being gave to Maxwell the unchanging foundation of his confidence in the intelligibility of the world. It gave to him his leading ideas and thereby a "humbling insight" into the nature of created reality which is characterized throughout by "flexible structural relatedness," namely that the "relations" between things, whether objects or events, belong to what things really are because in nature all things are inseparably and ontologically interconnected in the field in which they are found. If that is so, then "relation" is the most important thing for the scientist to know. Therefore it is of greatest importance that "the determination of relations and the development of relational ways of thought be allowed to have a primary place in scientific investigation and explanation."[6]   Again, this point of Maxwell's field theory, that is, the need for relational thinking with the re-orienting integration of abstract and concrete, theoretical and practical, form and being, had its roots in his fundamental beliefs about God's interactive relation to the world in creation and incarnation/redemption.[7] Indeed, from and with Maxwell, Torrance explains that the intelligible structure of the universe is an obligation laid upon the human mind, i.e., that intuitive belief in the world's objective order. The contingent nature of that order points beyond itself to a transcendent center of order which operates a powerful but implicit role in the back of the human mind in the recognition of all empirical and rational order.

So it was for Maxwell and others, says Torrance.

> . . . Maxwell came to rely upon a basic cast of mind, shaped through intuitive apprehension of God in his relation to the creation, as a "fiducial point or standard of reference" in making discriminating scientific judgments in respect of the real modes of connection found in the created order of things and of the tenability or untenability of scientific theories. Nor is it surprising that even Albert Einstein should so often speak of "God" in this connection, in reference to the simplicity, constancy, reliability and trustworthiness of the universe in its rational order or that Werner Heisenberg should speak of his need to tune into "the Central Order," his expression for "God," if he was to succeed in disentangling the mathematical complexities and grasp the sheer beauty of quantum theory.[8]

From such "convictions" Maxwell was able to penetrate more profoundly within the subtle harmonies and symmetries of the contingent universe. This has recast human understanding of the universe from the Newtonian mechanistic, dualistic, and atomistic approach to the recognition of the universe's dynamic integrational, open and even organismic qualities, while also reforming the cognitive structures of the scientific enterprise itself in all of the sciences.

In this way Maxwell is said to have found that by means of the interaction between the mind of the scientific inquirer and the intelligibilities of objective reality "the structural kinship between human knowing and what is known"[9] becomes disclosed as well. This disclosure of the nature and kinship found in the knowing relation of subject to objects in the world is often taken by Torrance as appropriate and disclosive as an analogy for theology, that is, for created and uncreated Reality, created and uncreated Light, created and uncreated Rationality or Intelligibility, ever reflecting that interactive relatedness of God and the world. This is a relation arising only out of the free sovereignty of God. For example, modern insights into the nature of created light from physics which show it to be central to reckoning with and understanding the nature of the whole of the created universe is then used "analogically" by Torrance to point out the parallels in the "uncreated Light" of God, which is the source of the former. The point Torrance is seeking to make by means of Maxwell's thought is not only the interrelatedness of the universe, but that there is in fact a fundamental harmony between the "laws of the mind" and the "laws of nature" in the sense of an inherent harmony between how humans think and how nature manifests or discloses itself to be as independent of the mind. In that relation the mind submits to or assents to the impress of that objective reality.

Torrance believes then that in the line of thinking from Maxwell, the dualist basis for understanding the world began to be broken as he brought about this transition in the scientific understanding. This process of transition is still ongoing. Maxwell began to restore objectivity, and realization of the need to

think together unitarily the dichotomies of Newtonian science.   Newton's
mechanistic patterns began to be replaced in scientific thinking by a continuous
dynamic field in order to give a truly scientific account of the rational order as
it actually exists, pointedly as found in electromagnetism as well as in light.   In
this way Maxwell reintroduced or restored real "contingence" into the scientific
description of nature.   The Newtonian "absolute" and necessitarian perspectives
on the world gave way to the space-time metrical field of relativity theory in a
universe which is not infinite but (as Einstein later asserted) finite, though
unbounded or "open up" (to the yet higher level).[10]   Obviously then the
relational interpretation needed for the nature of the open-structured universe
requires dynamic and relational ("kinetic") thinking and new kinds of questions
for the actual field or web of relations (onto-relations) in which things are.
Maxwell brought physics and the sciences to the radical change in thinking
needed; he introduced the coherent, unified, conceptual framework necessary for
human thought to penetrate reality and to know it as it is out of itself in a
realist, unitary theory of knowledge of objective reality's intrinsic intelligible
relations.[11]   This meant transition from dualistic, necessitarian, positivistic,
abstractionist thinking in the sciences to unitary or integrated, non-positivistic,
empirical and realist science in relation to contingent states of affairs in their
singularity, within the invisible, continuous field of the created universe.   This
"led" to relativity physics.   Maxwell's unitary, non-dualist thinking of "field
relations" was concerned to reflect the inter-dependence or mutual involution of
empirical and theoretical factors in knowledge of the universe, "physical
concepts" or "embodied mathematics."   What this means is that within a context
of thought dominated by the Newtonian cosmological and Cartesian-Kantian
epistemological dualisms mathematics becomes idealized and begins to take on
an autonomous and tautological status as detached from the empirical reality
from which it was derived and which it must serve by means of expression.
This creates problems for human understanding and for the interpretation of the
contingence and the contingent intelligibility of the universe.   Mathematics is not
the problem.   The problem lies in the detached or external way in which it is
brought to and applied to relations in nature.   Rather, if understood properly,
says Torrance, mathematics is not alien to but in fact arises from the created
rationality of nature.   It is rather its elaboration into a formal system through
abstraction and generalization which brings about the problematic detachment
from nature.   These symbolic systems are meant to increase human capacity in
relation to objective reality whereby,   through mathematical structures,
penetration into the determinate relations of the world and advance in
understanding of those relations beyond ordinary thought and speech take place.
More than deductive clarification, mathematics has, as properly integrated with
the structures of the universe, heuristic power to disclose structures within the
intelligible universe.   It is thus that one is to understand Maxwell's designation
"embodied mathematics," which retains its natural bond with nature.   This

integration takes its rise from the mysterious "analogy" or "structural kinship" arising between the intellect and the external world. Mathematics is not merely a detached symbolic system. But rather Maxwell found mathematics to arise from nature itself. Mathematical formalization and physical theory are meant to be intimately related and brought together in investigation of the space-time field, for only then is mathematics the real and proper servant of scientific discovery and knowledge (cf. electromagnetic theory).[12]

Maxwell's change to unitary, relational, integrative ("field theory") thinking, as a result of the compelling nature of his ultimate belief in God the Creator and Redeemer, has also been of formative and restorative significance to theology, says Torrance. It has opened the way for recognition of the human being as creaturely, personal being along non-dualist Judeo-Christian lines, although development here is yet much in process (cf. as developing from and beyond Barth, MacKinnon, Mascall, Florovsky, Baillie, and to a lesser extent Rahner). The deep interrelations between the sciences has been applied to the interrelationship between natural science and theological science, though they are concerned in different ways with the kind of intelligible order inherent in the created universe in its contingent difference and dependent relation to God. Each is said to be truly scientific to the extent that it submits to the objective disclosure of its own proper object/Object (cf. chapter one).

> That the nature and order of the human mind and of the created universe to which it is correlated are contingent is an ultimate belief or primary conception . . . . It is a conviction, however, that has been introduced from outside into the stock of fundamental ideas with which science operates, through the Judeo-Christian doctrine of God and creation. Contingence is not a truth which natural science can reach or account for on its own, but which, nevertheless, exercises a heuristic and regulative force in the advance of scientific knowledge and in its open-structured understanding and formulation of physical law. Thus in the ultimate analysis we shall have to leave room even in our most vigorous scientific activity for the openness of the human mind to God, the creative and controlling center of all order in tangible as well as intangible reality. Without even a meta-reference to God our scientific discoveries will be finally pointless and meaningless.[13]

The finite, contingent world is "open" up to and not cut off from God as though God were the Newtonian "inertial absolute" or the divine receptacle (*divinum sensorium*). The universe is "open up" to dependently receive God interactively in his sovereign, dynamic relatedness for the world and humanity, especially in his self-presenting in the incarnate Word. By way of addition, this restoration in thinking about the world is said to transform "natural" theology from an independent "preamble to faith," to its "proper place" as now integrated in and with the actual knowledge of God in Jesus Christ (cf. chapter five).[14]

Yet Torrance also finds that Clerk Maxwell did not make the full transition in scientific thinking and epistemology generally, and was still in part partaker of "mechanistic" thinking (cf. maintenance of the "ether theory" and disinterest in Riemannian four-dimensional geometry). It was only through the subsequent thought of Albert Einstein that Maxwell's "field theory" was brought to fuller and more consistent application and effect.

Epistemological Realism and Albert Einstein (and "Relativity" Theory)

Thomas Torrance's interpretation and theological application of modern developments in scientific thinking moves from Maxwell to Albert Einstein and from there to Michael Polanyi. Yet in many ways Einstein's thought forms the real center of the epistemological-cosmological-methodological analogy which Torrance builds between physics and theology because of the way in which created reality is related to and interacts with the uncreated Reality of the triune God, which is its ground.[15]

Maxwell's field theory had formative impact upon Einstein's thought. Maxwell's partial differential equations gave rise to much scientific advance for they are said by Einstein to be the natural expression of the foundational realities of physics. But it is Einstein whom Torrance sees as responsible for the most important modern scientific achievement. Einstein's formulation of the general and special theories of relativity changed the course of physics and, Torrance adds, established it upon profounder unifying bases appropriate to a wider range of empirical data.[16] Because of the breakthrough created by Maxwell's objective, realist, relational-unitary thinking, Torrance points out that Einstein was enabled to probe into the order and intelligibility of nature and to re-form modern human understanding of the universe's intricate structures, while overthrowing the now obsolete dualist, positivistic forms of thought and inquiry. But Einstein then brought Maxwell's thought into a wider synthesis with his special and general theories of relativity.[17] In this way, Einstein was able to unify mechanics and Maxwell's theory. Indeed, Torrance finds that the change in the sciences from mechanical thinking to relational "field" thinking reached its culmination in Einstein's work. Moreover, the effect of Einstein's discoveries reached far beyond physics to the foundations of human understanding of the universe. The change in thinking that was thus brought about "imports a radical alteration in the regulative basis of knowledge, transforming not only the structure of science but of our basic ways of knowing."[18]

In his essays on science and religion, Einstein too spoke of the reciprocal relations and dependencies between them. Torrance finds that Einstein also discounted positivistic science with its false separation between "knowledge" and "belief" and the equally false notion that belief must be replaced by knowledge. Einstein found this false contrast to actually undermine true science along with the whole of ordinary daily experience. The natural sciences are limited in their own callings to the intelligibility of their own proper objects, and they cannot dictate to theological science *a priori* how it can or cannot know its own proper Object, God as objectively self-revealed to be truly known in space-time. In the following statement Torrance interprets Einstein on the limits and relations of the sciences.

> . . . (natural sciences must aim only) to determine how facts are related to, and conditioned by, each other, and in that way to attempt what Einstein called "the posterior reconstruction of existence by the process of conceptualization." Science is quite unable through demonstration of this kind to provide the basic belief in the objective rationality of the universe or the aspiration toward truth and understanding which it clearly requires. Without profound faith of this kind, which comes from religion and revelation, science would be inconceivable. However, science itself has a religious dimension in which it contributes toward "a religious spiritualization of our understanding of life," if only through the "humble attitude of mind toward the grandeur of reason incarnate in existence."[19]

Here we see again Torrance's concern for reciprocal relation between natural and theological sciences and the role of belief in all true knowledge. The last phrase in the quotation, regarding the attitude of mind, is repeated often by Torrance, particularly where he is dialoguing with physics regarding the break-through of science and the epistemological importance of it for scientific theology as it pursues the real knowledge of God by the Spirit in Jesus Christ.

But to develop the point Torrance wants to make by means of Einstein, it must again be emphasized that he finds "religion" or theology reciprocally "dependent" on the rigorous activity of the natural sciences. As the sciences help to disclose the objective rationality in the space-time universe, they help to purify theology of the "dross of its anthropomorphisms" which a truly scientific theology must ever endeavor to dispose of. Yet this is not to dispose of that which is properly "anthropomorphic" or personal in theology, namely, that there is an element of the "anthropomorphic" which must arise from the profound, personal reciprocity which God establishes with persons through his Word.[20] God is the "person constituting Person" and theology is a personal and knowing response to the Word of God. Einstein too held to much the same ultimate beliefs or foundations as Maxwell, that is, to the objectivity of the world as over against or external to the subject and to the comprehensibility of that world. Einstein likewise held that these beliefs are intuitive and religious in character. The "intuitive" character of such is tied to the mysterious, "miraculous" fact that the universe is intelligible and comprehensible to the human mind. Einstein found that there is a pre-established harmony or correlation between human thought and the independent empirical world. The human mind can grasp the relational structures actually embedded in nature. According to Einstein, it is only by means of intuition or direct (non-formal) apprehension of the world as it is that humanity can hope to reach the elementary "laws" of the universe.[21]

Torrance finds it most significant for modern thought that Einstein, like Maxwell, did not see "regulative (or "ultimate") beliefs" as mere primitive guesses, but as rational insights "pressed" upon the mind by the objective lawfulness and harmony of the universe. Indeed, the intuitive nature of these beliefs, coupled with the progressive discovery of the simplicity of nature (e.g., the general theory of relativity), elicited awe from Einstein and he was constrained, says Torrance, to attribute to them a "religious" character. Einstein asserted that

> To the sphere of religion belongs the faith that the regulations valid for the world of existence are rational, that is comprehensible to reason. I cannot conceive of a genuine scientist without that profound faith. The situation may be expressed by an image: science without religion is lame, religion without science is blind.[22]

Here Einstein's turn of the famous Kantian phrase certainly expresses Torrance's general position. The statement reflects Einstein's understanding of the "religious" nature, as well as the strength, of his intuitive beliefs. When face to face with the rational order of things independent of the self and over which one has no control, Einstein would "naturally" speak in "theistic" terms of "God" or "the Old One," referring thereby to what Torrance finds to be a clearly realist understanding of the deep intelligibility of the universe. [23]

In overturning the dualistic split between thought and experience or subject and object in order to recover the natural unity of knowing and being in the more subtle structures of reality, that is, the kinship between our knowing and the order in the universe, which is not always "on the surface" (whereby theories would be esteemed to have no actual relation to the nature of external reality), Einstein, like Maxwell, demonstrated that the epistemic relation of the human mind and reality cannot be reduced to formal relations, for this destroys true science. Such a view would deny real knowledge. Recognition must be given to the non-formal, extra-logical relation of subject and object inasmuch as what we know always outstrips our capacity to express it, for it is the objective ontological reference of thought, the truth of being, the proper object as known, which forms the basis of all empirico-theoretical science, and not subjective constructions projected out of "agent intellect." Einstein recognized that informal "extra-logical" beliefs are "profoundly rational" as they do arise in the "responsible commitment of the human mind to the compelling claims of intelligible reality upon it."[24] This is true objectivity which is in "direct" contact with the world.

Again, Torrance is quick to point out that Einstein was largely responsible for effectively bringing an end to the massive dualism that so damaged the sciences from Galileo through Newton. The deterministic dualism as "revived" cosmologically in Newton and epistemologically in Kant especially, says Torrance, has given way to the Einsteinian recovery of objective reality and the ideas of contingent intelligibility and contingent freedom (in contrast to mechanistic and noetic/subjectivistic determinism) crucial for experimental science (versus technology). In Einstein (and to an extent in Max Planck) science has reformed epistemological foundations in a "profound ontological and dynamic integration of theoretical and empirical ingredients in human knowledge, and thus restored to its proper place the concept of a rationality objectively inherent in the universe"[25] external to human perception and conception, and to which thought must submit. Through Einstein, Torrance concludes that the natural sciences have achieved a true rigorousness and more deeply penetrated into the structures of created, contingent reality. This has brought about a restored realism in epistemology and objectivity in science, along with ideas of contingency, dynamism and integration (or relation) in the world. This sloughing off of Newtonian and Kantian "absolutes," whether they be upon the universe when God is construed as "container" or in the mind's *a priori* "categories," frees nature from the alien imposition of human abstractions, thereby allowing the truth of being to disclose itself in its own intrinsic order which the inquirer cannot master by *a priori* mechanistic or idealist forms of thought. To do this Torrance says that Einstein had to use an integrative, unitary way of thinking which overcame the dualism or division of matter from its field of relations. Speaking again analogically, Torrance says that in a way analogous to the early Church's conclusions in the *homoousion* doctrine of the Nicene Creed, Einstein and physical science had to part from Newton and Kant, for it must obediently "think after" the disclosure of ontological reality or empirical understanding at the immediate level and at the theoretical level, and finally "back" into the internal relations of objective reality (see chapter five below). This then is, says Torrance,

> . . . the decisive point of Einstein's critique of the phenomenalist and Kantian approach to knowledge, when he broke through it and grounded scientific knowledge in the objective intelligibility of the universe: that is, upon an inherent relatedness that characterizes the universe independently of our perceiving and conceiving of it. This all-important point, theologically speaking, may be called the *homoousion* of physics, the basic insight that our knowledge of the universe is not cut short at appearances or what we can deduce from them, but is a grasping of reality in its ontological depth, and that we are unable to pierce through appearances and apprehend the structures of reality unless we operate with the ontological integration of form and being, or of structure and matter, which is, after all, what $E=MC^2$ entails.[26]

Nature then does not deceive because, as inherently in itself what it is disclosed to be toward the human inquirer, it is everywhere intelligible, trustworthy and reliable in its order. The Einsteinian *"homoousion of physics"* represents to Torrance a revolution in the nature of human knowing, having also far-ranging implications for theological science wherein, according to the Nicene *homoousion* doctrine, God is in himself as he is toward us in the world in Jesus Christ.

Against the Newtonian closed, inertial system with its *a priori* fixed axioms, Torrance finds in Einstein's relativity theory that premises can only be known *a posteriori* and not disjoined from the process of inquiry. Thus antecedent axioms, as a set of logical premises, gives way to a submissive faithfulness to the object. Axioms only arise from the intrinsic connections of scientific operations as they "force themselves upon us as the necessary structures of thought through which the intelligible nature of things imposes itself upon our minds"[27] from that which is given from beyond the self. Einstein's understanding of basic scientific knowledge is the grasping of objective reality in its depth and articulating such, which is amenable to mathematical representation, or "number rationality," as Torrance terms it. Then, Torrance asserts that one can see why apprehension of the order, rationality and intelligibility objectively there in the universe means that true scientists can have little to do with the philosophies of existentialism and linguistic analysis, which are still trapped within the old disjunctive dualisms of Kant and Newton. He quotes Einstein who says "science is the attempt to make the chaotic diversity of our sense-experience correspond to a logically uniform system of thought,"[28] and this was brought to pass when his work on relativity achieved its simplification of conceptions. Quantum theory, Torrance says, has done much the same. This has meant the "refinement of everyday thinking, for it respects the fundamental nature of things and seeks to understand and explain them in their own intelligibility," according to Einstein. This lets the empirical relation to the object, as grounded in the nature of the object, dictate the mode of rationality appropriate to it within a reciprocal, dialogical connection.[29] In the past, theology has followed this *a posteriori* way of axiomatic thinking in order to penetrate and faithfully "think after" (*Nachdenken*) the inner logic of the redemptive movement of God in Christ (e.g., the Nicene fathers and Reformers). Theology as truly scientific must now again repent of false thinking, assent to the compelling Truth of God, and faithfully penetrate and express the inner logic of God in Christ. This is not in accord with the "number rationality" of things, but rather in accord with the "word rationality" of God's self-disclosure in his objective Word in Christ, and not from human subjectivity.[30]

Einstein is understood to have restored science and thinking to its proper objectivity, realism, and belief in the order and apprehensible intelligibility of the world with its unitary character. He has brought Maxwell's field theory and relational thinking to final antithesis to the old disjunctive ways of thinking things in the world. The intelligibility of the universe, which Einstein found to be so awesome and wonderful, especially in its contingency and unity, and which then is not self-explanatory, points beyond itself, and demands a sufficient reason, a "higher level" of intelligibility.[31]

This relational thinking, which Maxwell opened, is not limited to some flat "horizontality" but is said to be understood metaphysically in the "vertical," for only here in the "vertical" is the "ultimate" basis of intelligibility in the former to be found. In *Physics and Reality*, Einstein accounts for different "levels" or "strata" of knowledge in a scientific system, these arising from the natural cognition of ordinary experience. Scientific theory must then be brought unto "logical" unity, and finally to a strict "higher level" of logical unity with minimum concepts and relations and greatest conceivable unity. Each level of knowledge is related to and grounded in the "higher" level, whereby thinking penetrates more and more toward the interior connections of reality which is the basis of primary, everyday cognition. Torrance describes the relation and process in the interactive levels as that of refinement and extension and continued relation whereby each level is "open up" to the next and disclosive "down." No level "below" has its truth in itself, but is true to the extent that it is open "up" to the refinement and greater consistency found in the interactive ground at the higher level, and that level is refined at the next higher, etc., all being grounded finally beyond the contingent in that sufficient reason for the contingent order of rationality and intelligibility "below" it. Torrance sees in the theory of relativity, like the Nicene *homoousion* doctrine, a pre-eminent example of such a theory which penetrates the objective data of reality in order to bring to disclosure the profounder "higher level" reality.

Why does Torrance understand knowledge to now be more firmly and profoundly based? Beyond previous discussion, Einstein's "relativity" theory, which has been falsely thought to undergird "relativism," brings forth the opposite outcome by injecting that radical change mentioned above into the regulative basis of knowledge in both the various sciences and epistemology generally.[32] This "higher-order" theory, characterized by logical simplicity and comprehensiveness, is one in which Einstein revealed the idea of "relativistic invariance" by devising a form of mathematical invariance as a useful theoretic framework or conceptual instrument to know the world's unitary nature.

> . . . to discern and grasp an inherent relatedness in the universe. This mathematical invariance is not to be identified with the objective invariance of the universe, but is relativized (in the other sense of the term) by it and is revisable in the light of it. Thus in relativity theory we have to do with one of those ultimate structures in nature and in science that constitutes a rational basis for the unification and simplification of knowledge. Regarded

in this light the stratified structure of a scientific system appears like a sort of "hierarchy of truths" . . . inquiry advances through levels of increasing logical rigor and simplicity until it reaches the ultimate set of a minimum of intelligible relations in terms of which, as its *ultimate grammar*, the whole structure is to be construed (i.e., from the "top down"), each level being reckoned the limiting case of the one above it, in reference to which, however, it reaches its own consistency and truth.[33]

The theory of relativity is a "disclosure model" to be used in order to uncover objective truth in a way that unifies knowledge and grounds it firmly as well. In overcoming dualism, with its inertial "container" or "receptacle" notions of space and time, and which dualistically disjoins the space and time unity, relativity theory transforms knowledge of reality in dynamic relational terms out of the givenness of the thing itself. In this way, Einstein is found to have restored "dogmatic realism" in scientific knowledge. The objective reality of the universe "forced" Einstein to ask the unasked question, says Torrance, to take a leap of thought, to disclose what had remained hidden under false thinking in a way matched in theology only by Karl Barth.[34]

Einstein's writings, especially some of his well known sayings (cf. endnote 26), are said to drive thinking back to the great truths of classical Christian theology, particularly the rationality of the world and its contingent interactive relation and dependence on the uncreated Rationality of God and its basis in God's self-revelation. Yet Torrance says that Einstein finally falls prey to "impersonal" thinking, losing sight of the properly personal in knowledge, which is recognized at a lower "level". When Einstein speaks of "God" or "the Old One," e.g., "God does not play dice" or "God is sophisticated but not malicious," referring to the realist understanding of natural law, the subtle reliability of nature, and penetration into the inner truth of the universe, was he dissolving God without remainder into the immanent rational order of nature? Torrance says that there is some justification for this criticism — the superior Mind which is revealed in the order of the universe Einstein associates with the "pantheistic" God in Spinoza. But the "God" of Spinoza, with the universe, actually constitutes a necessary, mechanistic, logico-deductive system which is very different from the rational order of the universe reflected in Einstein's thought. This real difference is clarified when Einstein says "God does not wear his heart on his sleeve," i.e., there is a ground of rational order hidden behind the appearance of things as transcendent or "superpersonal." Einstein's belief in "God" is essential to the invisible ultimate ground of reality and the "reason incarnate" in existence to which the mind must humbly assent. Karl Popper called Einstein's thought "theistic." Still, Spinoza's "impersonal" God was maintained in much of Einstein's thinking to the extent that it was "still constrained at this point by an impersonal model of thought." While objecting to Newton's notion of inertia, Einstein's "Judaic intuition would have rebelled, and very rightly" against any notion of "reciprocal relation in which God could be acted upon."[35] It was left then to Michael Polanyi to bring the centrality of the "personal" in the knowing relation back into the fore in scientific thought, says Torrance.

Epistemological Realism and Michael Polanyi ("Personal Knowledge")

In the writings of Michael Polanyi, Torrance has found thinking which he believes manifests the real shift of thinking back to its proper objectivity, to its proper realist position in relation to the proper object, i.e., in knowing that object out of itself. The scientific thinking which Torrance roots in the Scottish Realist tradition (Maxwell) is then seen to be brought to yet profounder depth of objectivity in Einstein. But Einstein's remainder of "impersonal" detached knowing is reckoned to be not only unscientific but thus false as a way of knowing because knowledge is the knowledge of persons. While Einstein began to recognize this, it was actually Polanyi who brought the "personal" aspect of the objective, realist knowing relation in the "new physics" to fruition. According to Torrance, this advance has great implications for the knowledge of God in Jesus Christ by the knowing of faith, and for theology as science in personal response to its proper Object who is ever lordly Subject.

Torrance wants to make it absolutely clear that Polanyi too rejected the modern dualism of Descartes, Newton and Kant, and the subsequent mechanistic (Laplacian) view of the universe, conventionalism and positivistic perceptions of science and scientific theory, as reflected in Ernst Mach and the "Vienna Circle". This also means rejection of Kant's synthetic *a priori* whereby knowledge of the phenomenal world is said to be reduced to an "order" without actual penetration into the *ding an sich*.[36]

Torrance sees in Polanyi the proper distinction (and relation) between pure science pursued for its own sake and applied science used for some social goal. The first has its home in academic contexts, and its purpose is knowledge as such; the other is used in factories and in sectors of practical life. The point is not derogation of the second, but that these operate with different kinds of knowledge determined by different *teloi*. Polanyi's concern is that "positivistic" technology replaces pure science, thereby damaging real scientific inquiry in pursuit of knowledge as such, i.e., for science to be science it must work with that *given* over which it has no control, a "transcendent reality," but also an objective given whose order calls for inquiry. He saw the distinctive order to be actually to be found in living organisms and in crystalline formations, an order having an interior power of organization which resists analytical explanation, but which is an ordering wherein human beings participate when learning or teaching. Third, Polanyi reflected at length on the organization of science within the state and the challenge of Marxism to science in a free society and in free inquiry. This "social coefficient of pure science in the pursuit of the truth for the truth's sake"[37] is related to Polanyi's profounder understanding of knowledge as "personal." Torrance sees as Polanyi's basic conviction that there is structural relation between what is known and the human subject's knowing of it.

In the development of true science then, the nature of Polanyi's rejection of the "old dualism" means that he stands firmly within the "Einsteinian revolution." He saw that following nature out of itself necessitated a new unitary outlook on nature where understanding maintains the co-inherence of space-time in the processes of nature, and where science works out from the intrinsic unity of form and being, structure and matter. This entails a change in the basic principles of knowledge. Following Maxwell and Einstein, Polanyi is said to have worked to replace the modern dualisms with the foundational conviction that the world is inherently comprehensible independent of the human knowing of it. Yet human knowing of the objective world is an activity of the mind as guided by a direct, intuitive contact with reality, thereby bringing about real penetration into the coherence and objective structures in the field of inquiry. For Polanyi too, says Torrance, the human knowing of nature involves, from the beginning, integrated processes in which the empirical and theoretical are inseparable.[38]

Thus Polanyi followed Einstein in claiming that basic to all truly scientific knowing is an "intuitive" apprehension or "in-sight" into the actual intrinsic relations in nature. "Intuitive" meaning, again, is rational, but non-logical, non-inferential knowledge, i.e., those "foundations which arise in the mind's assent under the (impress of) objective structures of nature." These fundamental relations are then brought together in theorems for the development of further ideas and relations. Then, attempt is made to provide a theoretic and logically coherent structure to bring to understanding (that is, a theory or "disclosure model") the inherent and coherent structure of nature. Yet there is no *logical* bridge between the structure of scientific theories and the inherent objective structure of the real world.[39] It is here, says Torrance, that Michael Polanyi's contribution becomes clear.

Torrance finds that when the basic question is asked: "How are our ideas related to experience?" Einstein held that nothing could be said about the way in which concepts are made and connected and then how these are coordinated with experience. Yet this relation determines the cognitive value of systems of concepts. Polanyi was not content with this and thought out the "heuristic" process whereby knowledge of the real world is reached, that is, new knowledge which is not inferred from what is already known. In this way, he is said to have far surpassed Einstein in carrying on the coordination between ideas and experience. Central to this advance is Polanyi's claim that human beings know more than they can tell. Torrance explains:

> . . . in addition to our "focal awareness" and the explicit knowledge . . . we
> always operate with a "subsidiary awareness" and an implicit knowledge on
> which we rely in all our explicit operation. It is evident in the basic activity
> of knowing as in the recognition of a problem or the intuition of a latent
> coherence without which the mind's contact with reality would be blind and
> fruitless. This is what Polanyi has called "the tacit dimension" both in the
> activity of scientific discovery through an unaccountable intuitive
> apprehension of a structure in reality, and in the development of knowledge
> through a process of integration in which largely unspecified clues are
> organized in response to the intimation of a true coherence in nature. Since
> it is "intuition" of this kind that is "the tacit coefficient" of a scientific
> theory, this seems to call for a significant modification in what we understand
> by knowledge, for knowledge cannot then be defined merely in terms of what
> is explicit, reality cannot be defined in terms of what is only correlated with
> explicit concepts and statements.[40]

Polanyi's discovery of "tacit knowledge" is a first order contribution to the
philosophy of science.

But, platonically speaking, if one knows more than can explicitly be told,
then it seems one knows before one knows, or, with regard to learning, is this
a learning of what we know or of what we do not know? Torrance's anti-
Platonic concern is to show that true inquiry leads to "new" knowledge, to that
which was not known previously. Platonically, one would say that either one
knows what is looked for, or else what one is looking for is not known and thus
one cannot expect to find anything. If Plato's doctrine of recollection is
rejected, what is to be done? Polanyi believes Plato has shown that if all
knowledge is explicit then a problem cannot be known nor solution looked for.
But learning involves a "tacit knowledge" in the intimation of a "hidden" reality
which may yet be discovered. Polanyi is said to have solved the dilemma by "a
tacit foreknowledge of yet undiscovered things."[41] This is described by
Torrance as a type of "vision" which reaches toward what is beyond what one
explicitly knows. This fore-knowing enables one to judge what things are
capable of being understood, and directs conjecture with reasonable probability.

But is this "preconception" some "*a priori* knowledge" or perhaps "what
the existentialists call 'pre-comprehension' (*Vorverständnis*)?"[42] Torrance
answers himself that it is not a preconceptuality as much as a kind of "foresight"
or "fore-knowledge" which the scientist derives by intuitive grasp of an object
in which the inquirer is not able to specify the actual structure of that reality.
But it does form the initial clue. It is "intuitive insight," informed intuitive
contact with objective reality. It is then called an "inductive insight" having a
"semantic or ontological reference which is objectively correlated to an aspect
of nature seeking realization, as it were, in the mind of the inquirer . . . what

the Greeks called *prolepsis*."[43]   Scientific inquiry operates by this incipient
knowing of the coherence of things not yet known, and which goes beyond what
can be formalized.   It is formed under the impress of the objective internal
structure of reality as it unfolds within the relatedness existing between human
knowing and what is known.   It is the all-important, though informal and
unaccountable component in true scientific activity. Polanyi insists the scientist
is helpless in the process of inquiry until the profound principles of the rational,
ordered world have disclosed themselves to her or him.   The real problem in
scientific discovery then is the "ontological reference of scientific concepts and
theories,"[44] which scientists can only deal with intuitively.

      This too is an aspect of Polanyi's thought which Torrance uses extensively
and analogically for application to theology. It is his point then to show,
through Einstein and Polanyi, that the sciences have been throwing off the
"myth of induction" for the scientific method, a way which, while advocated
theoretically (e.g., Newton), was never actually done in practice.   Such
"induction" was espoused because of lack of insight into the actual way of the
"heuristic act" of the scientific process of intuition, conjecture and the creative
power of imagination.   Theories are not derived by abstractions or
generalizations from particular observations. As Einstein said, "whether you
can observe a thing or not depends on the theory you use . . . (it) decides what
can be observed."[45]   Yet beyond even Einstein, Polanyi gave attention to the
critical epistemic process in all scientific discovery which recognizes the lack in
inductive logic, while giving room for a process in the heuristic act which is
truly rational. He brought to clarity, says Torrance, that tacit capacity of the
mind in discerning *Gestalten* or patterns in experience in the heuristic movement
from parts to a whole, the grasping of patterns of coherence, in the non-logical
but rational process of integration. The structures of scientific intuition which
move relationally from ordinary perception to scientific activity is a
"stereoscopic" awareness enabling one to apprehend the object as a
comprehensive entity in its own coherent and intrinsic structures at an objective
depth. This results in the assent of the mind to the compulsion of that objective
reality and its own structure.   This, in turn, leads to re-orientation of the
conceptual image. Scientific discovery is a process of bringing together. This
shows, says Torrance,

> . . . how the visual and the conceptual images operate inseparably together
> in our orientation to the objective structure of the world around us. It is this
> fusion of the rational and ontological elements in nature, and the empirical
> and theoretical elements in our apprehension of it . . . (which Polanyi has
> shown, pointing out that) twentieth-century physics, and Einstein's theory of
> relativity in particular, demonstrate the power of science to make contact
> with reality in nature by recognizing what is rational in nature. It is because
> nature is inherently rational that reason cannot be separated from experience

.... Since form and being are fused (unitarily) together in nature, they must be grasped together . . . (thus) the epistemic process in scientific discovery is essentially an *integrative* activity rather than analytical or an abstractive (deductive and thus disjunctive) activity.[46]

Confronted with a problem, the scientist's intuitive reasoning makes a reasonable conjecture regarding the hidden coherence of nature as clues are integrated by intuition toward new conjectures. "Verification" is taken to profounder levels in the deeper apprehension of the structures of reality. Polanyi finds that this is the actual way in which persons think, act and learn in ordinary daily life. Torrance often repeats Einstein's conclusion that scientific thinking is but ordinary, everyday thinking that is refined. Polanyi, then is said to have disclosed the organic substructure of knowledge operating by the intuitive grasp of the objective unity underlying empirical diversity. Human thinking works with its indefinable capacities and with the correlations and coherence in nature at every level. Thus the scientist is found having to make responsible judgments without explicit *a priori* criteria for discovery. There must be *personal* judgment. Polyani asserts ". . . that science (is) grounded on an act of personal judgment, and called this knowledge, therefore, a personal knowledge."[47] In scientific activity which penetrates into the coherent rationality of an objective entity, the knowledge acquired is the knowledge acquired by persons. This carries a unitary view of knowing as an activity of the whole person in correlation with external things. Therefore, there is that unalterable element of "anthropocentricity in true science." Torrance then sees that Polanyi has restored the "personal coefficient of knowledge" to rigorous scientific activity by recognizing that human reason never operates apart from basic or ultimate beliefs. Having, with Maxwell and Einstein, overthrown the mind-matter dualism which leads to an unbalanced emphasis on the phenomenal, Polanyi has brought to clarification, especially in his *Personal Knowledge*, the fact that there cannot be knowledge of tangible realities apart from the personal activity of the knower. There is a natural unity between knowing and being.[48] While the rationality of nature lays claim upon the human mind, the personal coefficient in knowledge remains as an essential element in all true objectivity. The mind's structure is correlated to the intrinsic rationality of objective reality in such a way that one is intellectually under obligation to affirm such in a personally responsible act claiming universal validity. This obedience to what is independent of the self saves personal knowledge from mere subjectivism as it fulfills an active role. As Polanyi says, "Subjective knowing is classed as passive; only knowing that bears on reality is active, personal and rightly to be called objective."[49] Also, this personal knowledge, in real relation and as correlated in structural kinship to the inherent rationality of the world, is considered to be central to the necessary restoration of ontology.

In the stratification of knowledge, awareness of particulars must go on to the integration of an entity apprehended, via tacit knowing, as having being and reality in itself. This means, says Torrance, that Polanyi has further broken through dualism and phenomenalism to science as penetration into the nature of things in their interior relations, and brought about a more fully developed theory of ontological stratification ("levels") which enables one to establish a continuous transition from the natural sciences to the study of the humanities. Earlier ways have lacked a proper ontology, and thinking about things must be ontologically grounded or else meaning is lost. At issue is, again, the relation of knowing and being, that is, whether knowledge is objectively founded on being or not, whether the truth of a proposition is to be found in its bearing on reality. Thus, in tacit knowing one has to do, says Torrance, with the "ontological reference of knowledge, in virtue of which we establish empirical contact with reality in its intrinsic coherence and rationality, and therefore with that aspect of knowing in which its content is grounded evidentially and objectively, although informally, upon the structure of experience or reality."[50] True science now finds, according to Torrance, that "the logic of tacit knowing" and "the ontological principles of stratified entities" disclose a universe having a built-in principle of transcendence and a structure of knowing wherein the human mind is left open at its boundary situations to the indeterminate reality which transcends it completely. For Polanyi, belief in such a transcendent reality independent of, yet accessible to, knowing is the "ultimate determinant" of the scientific call.

It follows, says Torrance, that while knowing God is outside of Polanyi's main argument, this conception of knowing effectively opens the way to such a relation. Natural knowing expands into actual knowledge of the supernatural. Polanyi says, "Such, I believe, is the true transition from science to the humanities and from our knowing the laws of nature to our knowing the person of God."[51] Upon this basis in Polanyi, Torrance comes to theological science in something of an *a fortiori* manner. In belief there is direct contact with reality. The mind is open to the invisible reality transcendent to the human subject. Belief or faith and rationality are found to be bound together. Indeed faith is understood to be the very mode of rationality proper to God in his objective self-givenness in Christ Jesus. In this, whereby the epistemic process is restored, there is simultaneously the way to restoration of the knowledge of God, to true theo-logical thinking, which is also at the center of historic Christian theology, *fides quaerens intellectum*. Thus, there is formal similarity in the operation or functioning of natural and theological science, though each must be faithful to and to think in accordance with the rationality of its own proper object.[52]

It is by this truly scientific activity that one may rightly know and respond to the self-revelation of reality. Each activity corresponds to the other in the "double-activity" in which reality gives itself to be known, gives the mode of rationality by which alone it can be known in its own internal structures, and the inquiring person actively responds by knowing it according to that given mode of rationality which the object has presented. In active inquiry "scientific intuition" is always a movement of thought away from the knower to reality external to and independent of the knower. This movement in knowing is personal. But it is also an element in the interaction with external reality which is ever controlled under the authority of that objective, external reality. But the natural sciences also necessarily face the question of the ultimate intelligible Ground of the universe with its contingent order, says Torrance. The universe is neither self-sufficient nor self-explanatory. Having introduced time into explanations of the dynamic, contingent states of the finite universe, the various sciences cannot get around the question of origin and end (*telos*) and the "why" of the universe if they are to retain belief in the objective reality and unitary intelligibility of the universe.[53] Though the natural sciences are not in and of themselves able to answer this rational question which must arise, they do perceive that the universe points beyond itself to an ultimate, Rational, self-sufficient Ground. Polanyi's reintroduction of personal thinking is said to move this thinking beyond the yet impersonal thinking of Einstein. Polanyi's liberation of thought from the "impersonal" has also brought to fuller understanding the "multi-leveled structure of reality" as the process of inquiry leads human thinking up the "ascending hierarchy of meaning to envisage the meaning of the universe as a whole in which natural knowledge continuously expands into knowledge of the supernatural." [54]

Maxwell, Einstein, and Polanyi are esteemed by Torrance as makers of the modern revolution and reorientation in the foundations of scientific knowledge of the universe and, in that way, also in epistemological structures generally. As these have followed the disclosure of nature with increasing profundity, there has resulted the demand that scientific thinking recognize that belief, or intuitive apprehension, is the source of knowledge from which human acts of discovery take their rise. It is in belief, rationally and conceptually understood, that the inquirer is in direct contact with reality, and, by means of belief, the mind remains properly open to the invisible realm of intelligibility in being which is not imposed by the mind but is "the given" and is independent of the knowing subject. In contrast to dualism, faith and rationality are found to be intrinsically bound together. As Polanyi has directed implicit attention, by means of natural scientific inquiry, to the theological, so Torrance, in building upon Einstein and Polanyi, advances explicitly to the "theo-logical." The natural sciences have increasingly allowed objective reality to disclose itself as it is, having penetrated level by level "upwards" toward a profounder depth of reality and development and refinement of theories as "disclosure models," which facilitate yet greater disclosure. Torrance says, "All this applies, *mutatis mutandis*, to theology and the development of disclosure models in Christological inquiry . . . intellectual structures that arise in our knowledge as we seek to let our minds and hearts fall under the self-disclosing power of Christ through his *Logos*."[55]   God's objective self-disclosure in Jesus Christ and by his Spirit unto the realist, redemptive knowledge of God by persons in the world is Torrance's concern as the center and whole of the theological task. He desires that his work, like that of the Nicene Fathers in the Creed, would form an effectual "disclosure model" bringing into redemptive clarity in modern human culture knowledge of the objective Word of God's love and actual penetration into the "perichoretic" relations between the Persons of the ontological Trinity.

Before setting forth Torrance's own Christocentric-Trinitarian theo-logical "disclosure model" as a scientific theology, a number of crucial transitional points regarding his scientific understanding and its implications for knowledge must be stated.

NOTES

1. Torrance, *DCO*, p. x. Torrance has edited the republished edition of Maxwell's thermo-dynamic theory.

2. Torrance, *TCFK*, p. 217.

3. Ibid, pp. 216-217. Here Torrance quotes Maxwell, who says that "The habit of recognizing principles amid the endless variety of their action can never degrade our sense of the sublimity of nature, or mar our enjoyment of its beauty. On the contrary, it tends to rescue our scientific ideas from that vague condition in which we too often leave them, buried among the other products of a lazy incredulity, and to raise them into their proper position among the doctrines in which our faith is so assured, that we are ready at all times to act on them. For Clerk Maxwell scientific understanding of the universe and faith in God were profoundly integrated."

4. Ibid., pp. 218-219.

5. Ibid., pp. 219-220.

6. Torrance, *CTSC*, pp. 49-50.

7. Ibid., p. 61.

8. Torrance, *CFM*, p. 41.

9. Torrance, *CTSC*, p. 75. This occurred in relation to Maxwell's theory of radiation. Torrance explains and applies the theory, saying that "Since it is through his self-revelation to us in the universe that we realize that God has established a relation of dependence and created correspondence between its contingent rationality and his own transcendent rationality, we may be allowed to use our understanding of physical or created light as a foil for articulating our understanding or divine or uncreated Light. This is not to say that the Light of God may be understood only as it depends on and is conditioned by created light as a necessary medium and carrier for its movement." Cf. *CTSC*, chapter 3, "Theology of Light."

10. Torrance, *CFM*, pp. 36-37.

11. Cf. Torrance in *RET*, pp. 32-33; *CTSC*, pp. 11-12, 17, 22, 52; *GR*, pp. 14, 132; *DCO*, pp. 76-77.

12. Cf. Torrance in *TCFK*, pp. 226-229 and *DCO*, pp. 48-49; *CTSC*, pp. 53, 129.

13. Torrance, *CFM*, pp. 41-42. Cf. *STI*, pp. 70ff. Careful note should be taken of the detailed discussion by Torrance on this crucial issue of beliefs and knowledge of the external world in *TCFK*, 221-222.

14. Torrance, *RET*, p. 33.

15. Torrance, *CTSC*, pp. 77-78. In personal correspondence with Christopher Kaiser, a physicist (Ph.D., University of Colorado) and theologian (Ph.D., University of Edinburgh under T. F. Torrance), says that in such discussion Torrance "baptizes" Einstein. Kaiser finds Niels Bohr to be better or more suited for Christian theology. See Christopher B. Kaiser, "The Logic of Complementarity in Science and Theology" (unpublished Ph.D. dissertation, University of Edinburgh, 1974.)

16. Ibid., pp. 11-12.

17. Ibid., pp. 75-76.

18. Ibid., p. 12.

19. Ibid., p. 7.

20. Ibid., p. 8.

21. Ibid., p. 58.

22. Albert Einstein, Ibid., pp. 58-59.

23. Ibid., p. 59.

24. Ibid., p. 63. cf. Torrance, *TS*, p. 184.

25. Torrance, *GG*, pp. 23, 74.

26. Ibid., p. 162. Though he makes affirmative reference to three well known sayings of Einstein (from his writings) it is in *GG*, pp. 112ff. that Torrance elucidates what he takes to be the significance and implications for knowledge in, 1.) "God does not play dice," i.e. God is not arbitrary and there is immanent order everywhere; 2.) "God does not wear his heart on his sleeve," i.e. the real secrets of nature, the reasons for the objective immanent order, cannot be read off the patterns of the phenomenal surface, one cannot deduce the depth structures of reality, 3.) "God is deep but not devious," i.e. the complexity and subtlety and yet ultimate simplicity of reliability of the universe. Cf. Torrance, *TS*, pp. 91-92, footnotes one and two, regarding Einstein's thought and the structure of thought versus Kant's "categories" and Newtonian mechanics.

27. Torrance, *GR*, p. 100.

28. Torrance, *TS*, pp. 110-111.

29. Torrance, *GG*, pp. 35, 31, and *GR*, p. 10.

30. Torrance, *GR*, p. 100 and *GG*, pp. 35, 31.

31. Torrance, *GG*, pp. 11, 105. Torrance's discussion on p. 105 is quite significant here.

32. Torrance, *CTSC*, p. 12.

33. Torrance, *GG*, p. 171-172. Cf. Torrance, *TCFK*, pp. 83-84.

34. Torrance, *GR*, p. 177. Cf. Torrance, *GG*, p. 72.

35. Torrance, *TCFK*, pp. 59-61.

36. Torrance, *TCFK*, 110-111. Cf. Torrance, *CTSC*, p. 16.

37. Ibid., pp. 108-109.

38. Ibid., p. 111.

39. Ibid., p. 112.

40. Ibid., p. 112-113. See discussion on "tacit knowledge" and relation to "personal knowledge" and to "complementarity" in Ibid., pp. 123-124.

41. Ibid., p. 113.

42. Ibid.

43. Ibid., p. 114.

44. Ibid., p. 115.

45. Ibid.

46. Ibid., p. 118-119. With regard to the nature of language and truth there is real conceptual relation here to Wittgenstein's notion of "seeing. . . as. . ."

47. Ibid., p. 123, quoting Polanyi, "Genius in Science," on p. 11.

48. Torrance, *CTSC*, pp. 62-63. Cf. Torrance, *TCFK*, pp. 88-89, and *GG*, pp. 113-114.

49. *Personal Knowledge*, p. 403, quoted in Torrance, *TCFK*, p. 154. On p. 155 he says that "Within this general framework of commitment to external reality, all responsible personal knowing appraises what it knows by a universal or objective standard which it posits for itself.   Responsibility and truth are in fact but two aspects of such a commitment: the act of judgement is its personal pole and the independent reality on which it bears is its external pole.   Thus the scientist is himself the ultimate judge of what he accepts as true or rejects as false, but this judgement implies a submission to standards of judgement independent of him which he freely accepts as the criteria for his own judgements.   This is what Polanyi calls 'the paradox of self-set standards.'   Far from doing as he pleases the scientist forces himself to act as he believes he must act under the requirements of reality and its intrinsic rationality.   He is compelled to rely throughout his inquiries on his own personal judgement, but this is objectively grounded for its functions through assent to the claim and jurisdiction of external reality over him, so that reality itself is accepted by the scientist as the ultimate judge of the truth or falsity of his conceptions and statements about it.   His own ultimate judgement is thus an echo of the ultimate judgement of reality.   Hence within the framework of commitment to reality upon which all scientific knowledge depends, the personal and the objective instead of being opposed to one another are mutually correlated." Cf. *RST*, pp. 55,77 and *GR*, pp. 96-100.

50. Ibid., p. 158.

51. In *Scientific Thought in Social Reality*, Ibid., p. 160.

52. Torrance emphasizes that ". . . belief in God calls for a mode of response in accordance with his nature as the transcendent Ground of all created being and intelligibility. . . . In theological inquiry, however, we are concerned with God himself who is not only the transcendent Creator of all contingent reality but the creative Source of all personal being in the universe, and who reveals himself to mankind through the acute personalization of all his relations with them in the incarnation of his eternal truth and love in Jesus Christ. Here, then, we have to reckon with the personal factor on both sides of the knowing relationship; we know God only through intelligible communion with him. This means that the personal character of belief in the knowledge of God is much more intense than in our knowledge of the physical world. In one sense it is also much more objective, for the objective pole of knowledge is the Lord God who by his very nature objects to the imposition of our subjective notions on him, not to speak of any misguided attempts to bring him within the range of our controlling knowledge. Now in (scientific) theological inquiry we are not able to hold apart this intensely personal understanding of God from our understanding of him as the ultimate intelligible Ground of the universe. From the perspective of theology, therefore, the ultimate intelligible ground of the universe, which is the sufficient reason for the intelligible states of affairs in the universe disclosed by natural science, is personal. Indeed, he is the one self-sufficient Person who is the Source of all personal being other than himself." Ibid.

53. Ibid., p. 71.

54. Ibid., p. 72.

55. Torrance, *GG*, pp. 125-126.

Chapter 4

Torrance's Understanding And Analogical Use Of Critical Aspects Of The Modern Scientific Reorientation

> . . . the scientist allows the reality he investigates in its own internal structures to impose itself on his apprehension, so that in his contact with it he is committed to a boundless objectivity beyond himself together with an unceasing obligation to let himself and all his preconceptions be called radically into question in face of it.
>
> Thomas Torrance
> *Transformation and Convergence*
> *in the Frame of Knowledge*

> Theology and every scientific inquiry operate with the correlation of the intelligible and the intelligent.
>
> Thomas Torrance
> *Reality and Scientific Theology*

Introduction

After observing Torrance's theo-logical concern and receptivity in relation to the thought of Maxwell, Einstein and Polanyi, several critical issues in the modern reformulation of objectivity, scientific thinking and epistemology have come forth. Those of pre-eminent concern to Torrance, as they are directly related to the objectivity and realism of the knowledge of the triune God in the world, will be discussed here in further preparation for the transition to Torrance's positive expression of theo-logical realism as scientific (chapter five).

The True Nature of Realist Science

As found in previous discussion, Torrance stands within the Scottish philosophical and theological tradition from Scotus, Major, Calvin, to John Knox. Herein one finds as well the combination of intellectual and devotional thought in Jonathan Edwards, Joseph Butler and John McLeod Campbell. Thomas Reid, A. E. Taylor, Norman Kemp Smith, John Macmurray and D. M. Mackinnon, among others, also stand within this Scottish Realist tradition which is said to have given rise to the work of Faraday and Maxwell. It is Maxwell's work which Torrance connects as formative to Einstein and Polanyi. Thomas Reid may be understood as a significant representative in the later Scottish realist tradition as it affected scientific thinking and method. Reid's basic thesis was that there are certain truths of common sense, which while perhaps clear by deductive proofs, yet have a command over human beings because of the absurdity of espousing opinions contrary to the dictates of these truths.[1] By following this sense regarding knowledge, Torrance holds that post-Newtonian or post-Einsteinian science has been shown to be nothing other than the refinement of everyday thinking or as repentant thinking before and *a posteriori* "thinking after" the objective disclosure of reality. Epistemology follows ontology. False thinking in science is said to have brought about the failure to recognize the intelligibility actually there in nature and the kinship in the human knowing capacity to the objective rationality to be known.[2] Dualist, disjunctive, positivistic science's false "objectivity" as "control" has led many to reject the idea of scientific theology and the objective knowledge of God, preferring rather to relegate theology somewhere within the sphere or domain of the non-objective. The often repeated claim is that God cannot be controlled or acted upon as though he were some kind of mere object. But that, says Torrance, is not true objectivity, but reflects the "objectifying" tendency of dualism.[3] True science in every realm of knowledge must, as Einstein did, stand in submissive awe of that mystery of the contingent intelligibility of the universe. That includes theology as the science of the Word of God, as Torrance emphasizes.

True science then, as it has been found not to be other than or against ordinary experience, but rather as that refinement of it, is the deeper penetration into the objective rational order with which human beings already operate. The goal of science in every field of inquiry is to discover the relations or to facilitate the disclosure of things and events at the different levels of complexity, and then to develop the understanding and expression of these multi-leveled relations so that their real nature in themselves becomes progressively disclosed whereby human knowledge is actually knowledge out of the things themselves, the "given."[4]

By "science," then, Torrance refers neither to the "natural" sciences necessarily nor to some single supposed "scientific" method as abstracted from one particular discipline to then be imposed upon another science. "Science" refers rather to appropriate procedures which each science has developed and must develop in relation to the rationality of its own proper object in which "it has solved its own inductive problem of how to arrive at a general conclusion from a limited set of particular observations."[5] There occurs then critical and controlled extension of ordinary ways of knowing for the goal of real, positive knowledge of the object. The outcome of true science is knowledge of the proper object which is "transcendent" to the self, but in strict accordance with the object's actual nature as it has disclosed itself to be in itself. Therefore, the appropriate mode of rationality and inquiry will be "dictated" by the object in the process of "questioning."

In seeking to know an object "out of itself" and in the order and rationality it manifests in its own inter-connections and interrelations, and thereby to penetrate down to the unitary logical basis of the understanding of experience, every science necessarily has its own distinctive way of inquiry which must be appropriate to the nature of the proper object being investigated. Determinate objects will require physical inquiries or experimentation whereby "speechless" nature is made to "answer." Such an approach cannot be used with persons where there is reciprocity. Precision requires that each science develop a method and a vocabulary in keeping with its own particular entity or field of study. Change from one field to another will mean shift in the appropriate mode of rationality involved. Such "fidelity" is said by Torrance to be the only way to avoid irrationality and to provide the appropriate modes of verification. This Torrance describes as a two-way movement of thought. The scientist penetrates to the inner rationality of the reality by discovery (not invention), imagination and insight in order to construct forms of thought and knowledge (disclosure models) through which the rationality of the object may be discerned. To the extent, says Torrance, that the scientist can reduce to "consistent and rational expression the ways in which his knowledge is related to the grounds upon which it is based . . . (he has) come to grips with the inherent rationality of things . . . the truth of his reconstructions."[6] To this end then the way of questioning must arise from a center in the object and not the knowing subject. Investigation open to truly new knowledge must allow that which is supposedly "known" to be called into question by the object. A "dialogical" relation is thus established as investigation means correlation of question to objective answer with a measure of both independence and mutual dependence, so that even the question is altered by the force or impress of the object of one's thinking. It is therefore "repentant" thinking which works to construct theories for yet further disclosure so that the ultimate rationality immanent in nature, which is transcendent to the inquirer, seizes the scientist (cf. relativity and quantum are given by Torrance as examples). Importantly, this transcendent element, this immanent rationality or *logos* inherent in the universe as created, is not God, but, says Torrance, "it does cry aloud for God if only because the immanent rationality in nature does not provide us with any explanation of itself." [7]

In the same way, *mutatis mutandis*, Torrance finds that the "restored" understanding of science and scientific thinking and knowing has pointed theology, as a "pure" science, back to its own proper bounds in relation to its own, singular, proper Object, namely God in his Word, Jesus Christ. Contra many modern thought forms and positivistic prejudices regarding "proper scientific method," theological science, says Torrance, must not allow itself to be swayed by the imposition of alien thought and methods which are applicable only to certain finite entities, and in fact become false when transposed to and imposed on another sphere of inquiry. Theology follows the objective revelation of the transcendent Word of God within history where the Word became flesh (John 1:14). And this appropriate method of theo-logical thinking out of the nature of the Rationality of the Word of God arises from the nature of God's dynamic and Lordly relation to the world (context) and humanity (subjects therein). [8]

Realism and Onto-Relations/Field Theory
(Unitary Knowledge)

As a result of Einstein's return to true objectivity and realist knowledge out of the object, Torrance believes that true science has again been shown to be objective knowledge of a particular reality as it discloses itself. Maxwell's work left him convinced that the relations between objects or events belong to what those things actually are. In nature all entities are ontologically connected or interrelated in the field in which they are found. If that is so, then "relation" is the most significant thing to know regarding an object. Therefore, to know entities as they actually are what they are in their relation "webs," then relational ways of thinking regarding an object and the determination of its actual relations must have a prominent place in all investigation. Therefore, what Torrance terms "Onto-relations" points more to the entity or reality as it is what it is as a result of its constitutive relations. "Field theory" tends to look to the larger "web" of relations wherein objects or events are constituted and are found and known. Relational thinking works to think things not only in context but to "see" wholeness and how the web of relations "makes" the thing what it is in its reciprocity.

Maxwell did not come to the relational character of the world and to the need for relational thinking merely from physics, but it is said to have come from his participation in theological and metaphysical convictions. But this relational or onto-relational way of thinking, says Torrance, was set against the disastrous "atomistic" and abstractionist thinking from Locke and Newton.[9] Maxwell found that the Newtonian mechanism was largely unworkable outside of very limited situations. His need for more profound explanation led to the theory of the electromagnetic field which used relational, non-mechanical ways of thinking. In this way, he could begin to overcome the un-natural instrumentalist, observationalist, dualist modes of knowing and interpreting reality by means of scientific, unitary understanding of the orderly universe as it is out of itself. Mechanistic thinking had destroyed understanding of actual relations. Einstein and Polanyi are said to have brought relational and "personal" thinking to fuller expression. This relational way of thinking is also more flexible and a more faithful way of thinking something within the field of its actual being.[10]

Einstein found too that these actual "onto-relations" (whereby a thing is what it is as a result of its being-constituting relations within the proper field) and the need for "field theory" implied that one must view contingent reality not as a static uniformity of causal patterns but rather, says Torrance,

> . . . as a continuous integrated manifold of fields of force in which relations between bodies are just as ontologically real as the bodies themselves, for it is in their interrelations and transformations that things are found to be what and as and when they are . . . not as abstracted from the actual fields of force in which they exist, but in accordance with their immanent relatedness in the universe and in terms of their own inherent dynamic order.[11]

Modern science has discovered then that the world as it is forces the scientist to gain an ever more adequate sense of connection. To think rightly means to connect things up with other things, thinking their constituent interrelations, and thus it is important for thinking to determine the kind of relation that exists between the realities contemplated. Pure science investigates objective realities in their inherent order or intelligibility which they reveal in their interconnections, and in this way they reveal their unitary logical basis. The world as it is, Torrance emphasizes, is found to be one in which form, being and movement are inseparably bound together. Objects and events are investigated and interpreted in terms of ontological reasons, the being-constituting web of relations making these contingent realities what they are. Penetration into entities themselves in their interior, onto-relations reveals the intrinsic rationality which is external to the knower, and thus these differentiate themselves from theories arising in response to them and require the revision of such in accordance with the ever profounder penetration into the patterns and interrelations of the thing.[12] New kinds of questions had to be asked and these have altered understanding of time and space. Post-Einsteinian questions have to do with the actual web of relations in which and by which things are in reciprocity.

Regarding the real field of relations wherein the entity is found, Torrance says that the scientist must also use an appropriate, unitary way of thinking the physico-empirical and the theoretico-mathematical together. By its own appropriate modes of thought each science engages in the process of bringing mind, concept and then expression into increasing accordance with objective nature.[13] Modern science has uncovered that the whole of physical reality is representable as a "field" whose constituent elements depend on the four space-time parameters. As science arrives at the elementary laws from which knowledge of the universe can be built up, selecting, refining and reducing concepts and their interrelations to as few as possible for the simplest possible system, then more complete, unitary penetration of events is achieved. But in developing a logically unified conceptual representation of physical reality, i.e., that is "the disclosure model," the scientist's concern is not then with the "system" but with the relatedness inherent in nature, the actual structure of objective reality. Thus, again, only those basic concepts which arise from and make actual reference to reality are useable for correlation of thought to experience of the real space-time world.[14] In this way, says Torrance,

> This means that if we seek to know things in accordance with their own interior principles and powers of signification . . . we develop objective forms of thought correlated with the ultimate openness of being and its semantic reference beyond itself . . . when we allow objective being to reveal itself to us like that out of its own inner *logos* or intelligibility, our thought is thrust up against its reality, its truth of being . . . it is sustained by an objective signification beyond itself and does not fall back into the emptiness of its own inventive, objectifying operations. Not only do we grasp the truth of intelligible being out of its own depth, but we let it interpret itself to us as we develop appropriate structures of thought under its impact upon us . . . (it) *proves itself* to us by bringing our minds under an imperative obligation that we cannot rationally resist (assent).[15]

Seeing the unity of form and being, the *logos* or intelligibility in being, the "web" or field of constituent relations, has clearly altered the way the sciences have come to regard the particulate element in nature. It was necessary, Torrance finds, to develop "unitary" theories beyond the phenomenal and observational at higher levels, all of which must be coordinated to allow penetration to ever greater depth into the real rationality of nature whereby the inner coherence of the created universe is allowed to shine through as it is.[16]

This new unitary way of thinking opened up through "field theory," in the recognition of objective ontological (onto-) relations, is said by Torrance to be of the greatest import for theological science, the realist knowledge of God's Word, God himself, in Jesus Christ. The onto-relations of field theory have shown that reality is open to explanatory interpretation in differential and functional relations. The scientist, whether physical or theological, must develop a disclosure model with axiomatic penetration occurring in response to reality/Reality which will effectively disclose the natural logical structure of the object/Object. Admittedly, says Torrance, this would seem to be more difficult in theology than in physics. For in theology (like biology) the distinctive connection is far richer, more elusive, ontological and dynamic. One must recognize here the differential conception in accord with the divine and human poles of knowledge in the active interaction which takes place, the transhistorical and historical, emphasizing the side of the object and actual relations to it in the objective field.

Torrance finds that field theory raises questions for biblical hermeneutics and theological formulation as these are tested for unwarranted presuppositions which bear little actual relation to their distinctive subject matter, God in his Word. In this way not only is ontology recovered but the way is opened for the realist reconstruction of theology similar to what has taken place in physics. In this way there results a deeper grasp of the created, contingent order within which both sciences must work, and ought to work, with "complementarity."[17] This unitary "thinking together," this knowledge of relation and in relation, as prescribed by the Object, helps theology to reject the disjunctive mistakes of modern dualism.[18]

Scientific principle requires that all proper objects of inquiry be thought in ways strictly appropriate to their own nature in the interaction of knower and known. Torrance asserts that the interpretive basis of theology as science, that is, the realist knowledge of God, necessitates that "evangelical sources for our knowledge of Jesus Christ" must "be allowed to speak to us in their own right, and Jesus Christ himself must be understood in accordance with his own intrinsic *Logos*."[19] Any other way would mean subjectivist fantasy--a modern Arianism--in opposition to the onto-relational disclosure model of the Nicene-Constantinopolitan Creed (*homoousion*). In following the redemptive movement of God in Christ, theology's thinking must be, as God's movement itself, subtle, flexible and rational, for only in this way can it have the precision and range appropriate to the interaction "between God and the world, between human and divine agency." Theology must then pay heed to objective, subject-object relations, indeed to the "invisible object-object relations" in dynamic field understanding, if it is to think of God's interaction with his creation appropriately and God's "Being-in-His-Act" and his "Act-in-His-Being" in balance (as Barth did) and ontologically, i.e., from the economic and reciprocal to the onto-logical (cf. chapter five).[20] This will carry theo-logical thinking through to the conception of the Trinity, to the onto-relational realities in God.[21] Torrance's requirement of realist, scientific thinking "up" through the "levels" of the rationality of God's objective self-revelation requires that these "levels" be explained yet more fully later.

Restored Realism and Levels of Truth/Thought

Reference has previously been made regarding "levels" of truth and thought as this has proved to be significant in modern scientific discovery and as this is used analogically for theology by Torrance. "Levels" of thought or truth refers to the "hierarchy of Being and Knowledge," that is, that the truth, rightness and propriety of the "lower" levels of reality are true, not within themselves, but in relation to, in correlation to and in openness "up" to the deeper, more profound level "above." The nature of science, and field relations must be understood, says Torrance, in the context of the "stratification of Truth" which Einstein and Polanyi have made clear. Torrance's point is that the deeper understanding effected in the natural sciences by the recognition of the inherent intelligibility and order in the world out of its own intrinsic relations and unity has clarified the need to "stratify" its thinking. True science must think after and up through the "levels" of truth of the contingent world to the sufficient Truth which is the basis of the truth of the "lower" levels.

Modern science has disclosed not only the interrelatedness and kinship of thought with reality, but that the rationality of the universe is not to be and cannot be read off of the "surface" of objective reality phenomenalistically. It is rather a rationality founded at a much deeper level. As with the false Hellenistic dichotomy between the intelligible realm ("noumenal" in Kant) and the sensible ("phenomenal") realm, modern dualistic science from Galileo to Descartes and Newton has made the radical distinction between the geometric frame and tha phenomenal surface of experience. Now while theory and experiment were brought together in some very fertile ways, yet Torrance explains how it was finally Newton who mathematically elaborated and systematically built into the structure of physics a dualism between the theoretical and the empirical aspects of reality by imposing upon the world of contingent events ("relative space and time") the rigid, "isotropic" framework of "absolute space and time in order to bring about a uniformity in scientific formalization." This absolute, which he equated with the mind of God, had to be maintained inertially as independent of empirical reality. Newton falsely separated experience from the geometry found in being (e.g., crystals) while forcing thought of a universe of bodies in motion into an idealized geometry without relation or regard for time--into an antecedently conceived (*a priori*) framework. This led to the process whereby facts were merely abstracted from surface phenomena and thereby disengaged from empirical reality and from the levels of intelligibility, the "inner *logos*" or "inner logic" of the object itself. Torrance finds that this same kind of dualistic or disjunctive abstractionist process was at the root of the Arian heresy. It too did not take hold of the inner logic or *Logos* of God in Christ. True objective thinking cannot be, then, in the "flat", on a singular level, but must itself be stratified or multi-leveled. For this reason also Torrance often points out how Einstein has emphasized that true science develops a system of stratification and relation (interaction) between levels (or "layers") of concepts or relations which are coordinated together to enable the investigator to penetrate through intermediate layers of a temporary nature "down" (or "up", depending on the metaphorical context) to the "narrowest basis of fundamental concepts or relations through which we may reach (to the level of) the greatest conceivable unity in our understanding of the world."[22] This is applicable not only to broad disclosure models but also to "levels" of rationality, the two being ultimately interrelated for human knowledge in Torrance's thinking. The rationale for this is simply that by working with the different "levels" of rationality and conceptuality one can increasingly clarify the logic of the conceptual "fields," and thereby establish the fundamental concepts which "form the basis for the illumination and organization of all our knowledge in that field."[23]

In the context of the mysterious rationality and comprehensibility of the universe which, while truly knowable, is yet finally beyond the capacity of human understanding, the scientific inquirer assents to the reason incarnate in the universe. In coming to know or "apprehend" it at its primary and even secondary levels, one is said to find that at its profoundest depth it is inaccessible to human knowing. Still, what one does know truly both points toward that "higher" level and is open to it as the ground of its truth. The ultimate reference of scientific concepts and statements, as Einstein also found it, must be understood to go back to the being of the intelligible universe as final ground of human concepts and statements about it. As elaborated at some length, Torrance explains.

> The being of the universe, reality, has an ineffable character. It manifests such an infinite depth of comprehensibility that, no matter how far we manage to penetrate into it in intelligible ways appropriate to it, "our notion of physical reality can never be final," let alone anything we might think of the reasons for the existence of this state of affairs . . . (in physics) this means that the more profoundly we penetrate into the ultimate invariances in the space-time structures of the universe, we reach objectivity in our basic description of the universe only so far as relativity is conferred upon the domain of our immediate observations. It is precisely because our thought finally comes to rest upon the objective and invariant structure of being itself, that all our notions of it (at the lower levels) are thereby relativized. This means that knowledge is gained not in the flat, as it were, or by reading it off the surface of things, but in a multi-dimensional way in which we grapple with a range of intelligible structures that spread out far beyond us. In our theoretic constructions we rise through level after level of organized concepts and statements to their ultimate ontological ground, for our concepts and statements are *true only as they rest* in the last resort *upon being itself.* Yet in so far as *they have their truth in that reference,* they are thereby revealed

by the inexhaustible intelligibility of being to be *inadequate* and *relative in themselves*.[24]

Knowledge in the sciences is then not merely a knowing of this or that field of experience or some particular entity, even in its complex of relations. Rather, knowledge is finally knowledge of things or events which partake of being. Knowledge is not some abstracted quality apart from real existence, but being as such which we cannot fully master. As one seeks to "match understanding" with the actual nature of the proper object as given or disclosed to the knower ("the truth of being," ontology), the scientific inquirer also knows that while the proper object is open to our real knowing of it, it ever exceeds our knowing of it.[25]

Thus epistemic correlation is said to occur between the mind and that which it seeks to faithfully know and a "structural kinship develops between the stratification of scientific knowledge and the actual stratification of the universe."[26] Scientific knowledge involves these "hierarchical" levels/layers of coherent comprehension which are correlated to the interrelated levels of orderly relations in objective reality. The integrated structure in reality, and, then, in the knowledge of it, forms an "ascending hierarchy" of orderly relations which, as coordinated and grounded in being itself, are found to be "open upward" in ever greater comprehensiveness and profounder ranges of intelligibility. But importantly, this cannot be "flattened downward" to a single level of reality whereby the intelligibility at the lowest level would be lost. This is because truth and coherent integration occurs from "above," says Torrance. This is quite significant and formative both epistemologically and theologically for Torrance, as it was for Einstein, as reflected in his well-known statement, "God does not play dice." Torrance explains the point by asserting that in inquiry into some field or cluster of entities, a situation or a reality is uncovered which cannot of itself be incorporated or organized into coherent relation with another. It does not "fit" previous "knowledge." In a "flat" conceptualization this would then appear to be incoherent. But in thinking the coordinated multi-dimensions or levels of reality, it is found that they reveal at a higher level(s) an intrinsic coherence in what appeared to be incoherent before. They make rational sense when it is seen that they are not of the same homogeneous level but belong to differing but coordinated levels of ever profounder interconnection and rationality. An excellent example, and one which Torrance refers to in a number of contexts, is quantum theory.[27] Torrance agrees with Waismann who said "If (classical) logic is right quantum theory must be wrong, and if quantum theory is right then classical logic must be wrong (in particular the law of excluded middle)." For this reason some are rightly endeavoring to elaborate a new kind of logic on different levels, or "quantum logic." In any two levels of order, it is by the interaction of the "higher" and more profound with the "lower" level that the lower is thereby brought to its unfolding "inchoate order." Indeed, says Torrance, the "higher" level itself, while in a different but related way relying on the "lower," interacts with a still "higher" level, and in the process a far richer form of rational order is produced and the role of the human knower in the universe becomes of signal importance for the human being as "priest of creation" (cf. below).[28] "Stratification" has been forced on scientific thinking under the constraint of the intrinsic rationality of nature. In its most basic form, Torrance speaks of Einstein's three levels, that is, the primary level of basic observation and experience, the secondary level of depth related to the fundamental concepts or ideas and their connection into a theory (disclosure model), and the tertiary or meta-scientific level. Torrance says that these three are usually sufficient for a realist, unified conceptual grasp of reality in the field of investigation.[29]

Just as the physical sciences have found the need to reckon with the "stratification" of reality, the "hierarchy" of levels of truth "up" in increasing profundity and simplicity, so too does theological science need to follow and think after the "downward" movement of the Word of God, by following it back "up," level by level, back to its ontological Source in the uncreated Truth and Rationality which is God, the "ontological Trinity" and the relations in God (cf. chapter five). The discovery of these analogical relations or levels in the physical sciences is said by Torrance to make the analogical relation in the human knowledge of God both simpler and more profound. In theology this is found to occur through the coordination of conceptual levels, by reference to which the individual concepts are defined. One must reckon again with a critical difference between the kinds of knowledge obtained in each science. God as Person discloses himself (*Logos*). In contrast to the impersonal, contingent rationality of the universe, Torrance asserts that

> . . . God opens himself up to us and informs us of himself in a way that no created thing can. Even though he retains behind a veil of ineffibility the infinite mystery of his uncreated being, he nevertheless unveils himself to us as the transcendent Source and sustaining Ground of all created being and created intelligibility, and therefore of all our knowing of him as well as of the universe he has made . . . as Subject being, not just as Object-being over against us (though that is true and necessary also) . . . . God interacts personally and intelligibly with us and communicates himself to us . . . he establishes relations of intimate reciprocity . . . our knowing of God becomes interlocked with God's knowing of us. In fact our knowledge of God thus mediated is allowed to share in God's knowledge of himself (an "ellipse of knowing") . . . it still remains the case that God confronts and interacts with us as he who is utterly transcendent over our knowing of him, infinitely inexhaustible in the Truth and Intelligibility of his own eternal being. As such the Reality of God ever remains the Source of all our authentic concepts (cf. theories, "disclosure models") of him.[30]

By way of example, one which is at the center of Torrance's movement of thought in scientifically thinking out, in a "balanced" way, the "Act and Being, Being and Act" of God in and from the Incarnation (cf. below), Torrance explains how in thinking through the "levels" of God's economic disclosure one is not concerned with direct (lowest level) analogical correspondence between the father-son concept in human relations and the Father-Son relation in God. The relation can only be determined in the coordination of whole levels of conceptual relations with one another, and through the ultimate coordination of the basic concepts with the intelligible, triune relations actually in the eternal God. God in his self-disclosure takes "cataleptic control" over all human conceiving of him. As a result, the use of "Father" and "Son" in reference to God is not a projection from the human, but derives from God as he has dynamically given himself to be known in Jesus Christ.[31]

Restored Realism and the Re-discovery of Contingency

Torrance desires to clarify the parallels which he finds to exist between the earlier overthrow of Hellenistic dualist thought about the world by means of the thinking fostered by the Nicene *homoousion* and the rejection of dualist Newtonian structures by Maxwell, Einstein, Polanyi and others. As knowledge of God is said to arise out of the God established interrelational structuring in God's Acts of Creation-Incarnation, the God-world relation is one which forces real thought of the radical contingency, intelligibility and dependency of the world. Torrance emphasizes that this issue engenders renewed emphasis on the important interrelationship between physical and theological science, reflected in the repeated impact of the doctrine of *creatio ex nihilo* by God in his freedom and sovereignty and love upon the thought of the physical sciences through the centuries (e.g., Maxwell). Einstein's "general relativity" defines the universe as a continuous whole, which Torrance finds to be a reinforcement of the creation of all things by one God. The universe is a unitary rational order, everywhere orderly, intelligible and open to consistent rational investigation and understanding. But the universe also reflects limitless variety of form and pattern. Knowledge of it is therefore not accessible to mere logico-deductive processes. The unity of form and being implied by general relativity refers to such an inherence of form in nature that it is affected by its space-time dynamic variations. "The pervasive rational order which we find in the world is multivariable in its modes as well as unitary in its character."[32]

Torrance claims that the tradition of Scottish realist epistemology and theology from Duns Scotus through Maxwell has played a key role in the modern recovery of the concept of contingence and contingent intelligibility for modern science.[33] Such thinking from God's Act of "creation out of nothing" has then been bound with the consequent view of the universe as a unitary open system, as orderly and rational, as knowable out of itself, as dependent and finally pointing beyond its own rationality (*logos*) to that which transcends it, while being also distinct from its ultimate Source in the increate Rationality or *Logos* of God, who was under no necessity to create. Again it is Maxwell who is given greatest credit in making the way for the reintroduction of the concept of the real contingence of nature back into modern thought, from which it had dropped out, along with his idea of the continuous dynamic field of rational order in electromagnetism and light. Newton's imposed absolutes have been replaced by the space-time metrical field of relativity theory. The real contingence and contingent intelligibility of the universe has become more and more accepted. In connection to the "levels" of truth referred to previously, Torrance finds that Maxwell came to realize that if our mathematical propositions are "certain they are not true and that if they are true they are not certain, and that the universe, far from being infinite, is finite though unbounded or open, as also . . . (in) Godel's incompleteness theorem (as) applied to the universe as a whole."[34] The universe has been found to manifest itself as a continuous, open system of contingent realities and events having an inherent, unified order. That being so, its internal consistency must at last depend upon a relation to an objective ground of rationality beyond the bounds of the contingent universe itself. The universe cannot explain itself. That, says Torrance, is the effect of Einstein's reconstruction of physics and science's perception of the universe as finite, open, dynamic and grounded in a "depth of objectivity and intelligibility which commands and transcends" human comprehension.[35] Working with the conviction of one intelligible, rational order pervading the universe, and with the principle of sufficient reason, rather than with the law of non-contradiction, Einstein saw that the contingence of the space-time universe must be taken seriously in its own right, with no concealed "necessity" allowed in thinking. The universe is open "up" and interrelated because no one level in the contingent order provides sufficient reason for its own contingent ordering. Torrance explains the nature of the universe's actual contingency as it must also be thought:

> . . . the universe confronts us as an open, heterogeneous contingent system characterized throughout by coordinated strata of natural coherence of orderly connections of different kinds in and through which we discover an uncircumscribed range of rationality grounded beyond the universe itself but reaching so far beyond us that with all our science we realize we may apprehend it only at its comparatively elementary levels. That is the universe to which we ourselves belong, with the structure of which we share in the distinctive structure of our own human being, so that we find our own rationality intimately connected with its rationality and as open to what is beyond us as the universe itself to the ultimate source and ground of all that is in the unlimited reality and rationality of the Creator.[36]

Here is a critical point for Torrance's discussion. The contingent nature of the universe clarifies the fact that, for the world to be what it is, it is dependent upon a non-contingent factor of intrinsic meaning beyond it. Wittgenstein claimed, "The meaning of the world must lie outside of it . . . . If there is any worth that does have worth, it must lie outside all that happens . . . . For all that happens . . . is contingent. What makes it non-contingent cannot lie in the world. It must lie outside the world."[37] The point is that what is contingent need not be. But once it is, it is what it is and can only be fully appreciated as such through its dependence upon an independent, self-sufficient reality having intrinsic rationality and worth. The Judeo-Christian tradition, and particularly "classical" (Nicene) Christian theology, is said to understand the contingency of the universe out of its relation (onto-relation) to God. As "created out of nothing," the universe thereby receives a created rationality of its own derived from (that is, not participating in) the uncreated Rationality of God. It is transcendentally grounded (not theologically grounded) in that Rationality. The world has been given a freedom of its own derived (not extended) from the self-sufficient freedom of God in which the world is again "transcendentally" and mediately (not immediately) grounded. But Torrance adds too that the universe was not only created out of nothing but continues to be maintained in its creaturely being by the constant, active and loving interaction of God with it in his faithfulness. It is therefore also stable, rational and free, under God, and thus open to investigation out of itself.[38]

In this way, Christian theology is said to have "radicalized" the idea of contingence and understanding of the contingent nature of the world. The world and its order, as contingent, are then to be understood from the constitutive relationship between God and itself which God has freely, but not without reason, created out of nothing. The universe has a contingent, dependent rationality, but yet it is a rationality of its own having its own authenticity and integrity distinct from God's own Rationality, while ever reflecting that eternal Rationality and reliability of God which is its ground. Indeed, this claim regarding the actual nature of the world as contingent is, says Torrance, the "baffling thing." By this he means that the contingent nature and rational order of the world reflect the relationality or interlocking of dependence and independence. The "independence" or "distinctness" of the universe from God wholly depends upon the free creative act of God to give being and form to it entirely differentiated from himself. But this differentiation is in a way conditioned by the dependence or anchoring the universe beyond itself in the reality and freedom, the legislative Word and unifying Rationality of God the Creator.[39]

Therefore, Torrance emphasizes the need to remember that in understanding and conceptualizing this contingence, contingent realities might not and need not have come into existence. Yet once they have come into being they must be what they are and cannot be otherwise. In knowing them one is obligated then to know them in accordance with what they truly are in their own natures and in no other way. Also, within this actual correlation which exists between the contingent rationality of the universe and the commanding intelligibility of God in his Word, the human mind receives those basic beliefs which have been found to exercise a regulative function in all scientific knowledge.[40] Theologically, Torrance's emphases directly related to the contingence of the universe are, first of all, the doctrine of the one God who is Creator of all things and who is the ultimate Source of all order and rationality. Hence, there occurs the negation of the dualism, pluralism, and polymorphism of ancient philosophy, religion and science, while also giving rise to the conception of the universe as one harmonious system which reflects throughout one pervasive, yet multi-variable, order. But secondly, the infinite difference between the being of the Creator and that of created reality must also be understood. God does not necessarily and logically belong to what he has made. Space and time belong to the created order and rationality of things. They are the "bearers of" the rationality of the universe and inseparable from human rationality. Finally, God's transcendence over all space-time implies that his interaction with the universe rests wholly upon the free, sovereign ground of his own eternal being. "God lives and acts in lordly freedom over all that is not God . . . creation of the universe out of nothing . . . far from meaning . . . necessity implies that it is given a contingent freedom of its own grounded in the transcendent freedom of God."[41] All of this is yet more deeply, indeed, preeminently grounded in God's self-disclosure in active, redemptive love in the Incarnation of the Word, as the coming and presencing of the Word discloses the precarious state of the world which God personally and sacrificially united to himself in his Son (cf. chapter five).[42]

Restored Realism and the Intrinsic Rationality and Intelligibility of the Universe

As a result of these modern insights in the physical sciences, Thomas Torrance understands the universe as created, rational and ordered, and as contingently distinct and relatedly intelligible or open to knowing ("graspable") by the human mind. This must be made explicit in order to clarify the nature and connection of such with the next section on Torrance's "correspondence theory of truth," reflecting "disclosure" of inherent "coherence" in the proper object. His findings are then applied "*mutatis mutandis*" to theology's own proper Object as self-disclosed to be known as he is.

As Newton could not take seriously the contingence of the universe nor its contingent intelligibility because of the necessitarian structures he built into his conceptualization of the universe, he cut away the foundations for a truly empirical science.   According to Torrance, Kant transferred the "inertial absolute" from the mind of God (Newton) to the mind of the human subject. Kant's denial of the knowledge of the *ding an sich* restricted knowledge to the realm of mere appearance to the human subject by means of the *a priori* categories of the mind.[43]   But scientific knowledge of objective reality cannot be the projection and imposition of the self into the "knowledge" of the object, nor can it be something non-conceptual or non-objective.   Science, says Torrance, is not the detached impersonal questioning of the *skeptikoi*, and it does not begin with doubt.   Rather, according to Torrance, true science is, in the "classical" sense of the term, "dogmatic" science (the *dogmatikoi*). This means that true science is the inductive advance to real knowledge as the mind of the knowing subject assents and submits to the truth of the objectively given subject matter in personal commitment to truth, and to the increasing attainment of positive answers to inquiry.   The new physics is described then as "dogmatic science" because inquiry is concentrated away from the knowing subject and is focused upon the subject-matter in itself in order to derive understanding of it out of its own inner connections. Epistemology is "established" *a posteriori* by or from the disclosed nature of the object to which the knower assents, given too the structural kinship between human mind and knowing and the disclosed object which one seeks to know.   Critical questioning must ever return to the objectively given realities so that science, whether physics, geology or theology, occurs as the human mind falls under the direction of the proper object's own natural pattern.   From this there results the revisable but positive "laws" or "dogmas".   Knowledge rests upon the openness, the inherent intelligibility of reality to be understood out of its own rational order.[44]

One of Torrance's central emphases which pervades his works, which was also learned, he says from, Einstein, is the avoidance of *a priori*, abstractionist impositions upon the supposed nature of knowing and the knowledge of the object, that is, upon what can and cannot be known and therefore upon scientific methodology. This is coupled to Torrance's emphasis upon rational "assent" to the compelling disclosure of the nature or being of the object. It must also be understood that "proper object" is then no addendum to his view of objective, scientific knowledge and the way in which an object is to be known out of itself. One cannot scientifically seek knowledge of the "proper object" using a method true only to the nature of some other object.   There is no *a priori* scientific method to be clamped down upon all objects.   The only scientific requirement at this level is the responsibility to "hear" or to rationally "assent" to the object's own inherent rationality, according to its actual nature, as it gives itself to be known. As Torrance's scientific "realism" means, among other things, conformity to "the given" by means of transparent media, human response must be openness to this gift.   Knowledge only occurs in relation to reality and by that "insight" or intuition of which both Einstein and Polanyi have spoken. Torrance says that this "intuition" takes shape in human understanding under the imprint of the internal structure of that reality into which one is investigating, and it develops within that "structural kinship" which arises between our knowing and that which we know as we "dwell in it and gain access to its meaning." Thus, scientific intuition is in no sense to be thought of as an *a priori* conception or preconception. The "foreknowledge" with which scientific investigation works is an "intuitive anticipation of a hitherto unknown pattern" or order in reality which arises "compellingly in our minds under the surprising disclosure and intrinsic claim of the subject matter."[45] In this way, Einstein spoke of the scientist as helpless until principles reveal themselves to him. Polanyi, as we saw (chapter three) analyzed the mind's "tacit power" to discern *Gestalten* through a "heuristic leap." This is a "personal" and "informal" integrative process whereby an insight occurs in a mind informed by that intuitive contact with its object/Object. The "insight" (or "clue") persists through the entire process of inquiry, thereby deepening awareness of the object/Object as thought moves away from the inquiring subject, and from what is held to be already "known," to that which is external, previously unknown, and independent of her or him. That object/Object has "legislative authority." The split between subject and object, noumenal and phenomenal, absolute and relative space and time in human knowledge, and then ultimately in culture, is overcome as one faith-fully or scientifically engages "in an interpretation that penetrates inductively into the genuine intelligibility of the facts or the coherent reasons of things through explanatory axioms . . . which gives unity to understanding."[46]

Coupled with the recognition of "intuition" in the restoration of the unitariness and objectivity of personal human knowledge is the nature and role of "belief" in the sciences. As observed in chapter three, belief is not found to be the equivalent of opinion. Properly understood "belief" is at the root of scientific realism. Some would respond pragmatically to the question of why reality must be as we suppose that it is and what upholds scientific activity. It works. But Torrance, following Einstein and Polanyi, maintains that the basis of all natural and theological scientific inquiry is "belief" whereby all scientific knowledge is acquired and extended. Torrance understands "belief" to be a "prescientific but fundamental act of acknowledgment" or an "epistemic awareness of the mind" regarding the nature of reality which is more "deeply grounded than any set of scientific evidence." Without such belief all scientific inquiry would be impossible.[47] Belief is essential to knowledge and not to be contrasted with it. Indeed, beliefs of this ultimate kind are irrefutable (cf. below). To put this another way, whereby Torrance's own theo-logical point is reflected, belief or faith is essential to and part of reason. Faith is found to be the very mode of rationality taken by reason in relation to what it seeks to understand, and is, hence, the most basic form of reason. Its structure is said to duplicate scientific activity because the proper object of belief commands belief. The task of science, at whatever "level" of objectivity, whether natural or theological, is to unfold this belief in a way appropriate to the truth and objectivity to which it is the response. This may be (as is prominent in Torrance's analogy) the basic scientific beliefs in the order, graspability and contingency of the universe, which ultimately point to the limits of the physical sciences. This leads finally to the question of the ultimate Source of the contingent order. Or this can be applied to God (cf. *credo ut intelligam, fides quaerens intellectum*).[48]

As Einstein switched to "embodied mathematics," and thus from Euclidean to four-dimensional geometry and physico-relational, dynamic space-time concepts actually associated with natural objects, he came to operate with ontologically grounded objectivities and intelligibilities which cannot be reduced only to mathematical formalizations. Operating under the control of one's objectively formed "ultimate beliefs" and "intuitive insights" (cf. above), the true scientist is said to thereby make intuitive contact with reality. Following out Einstein's own essay on Maxwell, Torrance explains that

> . . . (in sharp distinction from positivism and conventionalism) The (intuitive) belief in an external world independent of the perceiving subject is the basis of all natural science . . . another (is) belief in the intrinsic comprehensibility of the universe . . . . There could be no science without the belief in the inner harmony of the world or without the belief that it is possible to grasp reality with our theoretical constructions . . . . Einstein (like Maxwell) held that these fundamental beliefs are intuitive and religious in character . . . bound up with the mysterious and indeed miraculous fact which we can never understand that the universe is intelligible in itself and comprehensible to the human mind.[49]

Einstein found a pre-established harmony between thought and independent empirical reality whereby the mind can intuit, know and develop understanding of the objective, relational, ordered structure, the inherent rationality, in the universe, which strikes the scientist, like Einstein, with wonder and awe.

Thus scientific investigation is enabled again, says Torrance, to penetrate into the subtle, surprising harmonies and symmetries of nature. This has forced a recasting of the understanding of nature in its physical structuring and relations, and a recasting of the cognitive structure of the scientific enterprise by the interaction and relation occurring between the mind and the rational, harmonious, beautiful intelligibilities actually there within objective reality.[50]

This leads Torrance to assert the importance of those two basic forms of rationality, "number" rationality and "word" rationality. The universe as it is and as it is to be understood is not only rational, intelligible and objective, but Torrance's further point is that the inherent rational order of the universe must be brought to coordinate expression in mathematical and verbal forms. In the interpretive interaction of word and number, Torrance finds that in "number rationality" the physical sciences have to do with the rationality and intelligibility of the creation in its impersonal determinate and immanent forms. In scientific investigation of the determinate world significant contact with the nature of things in their depth has not truly occurred unless knowledge of them can be brought to enlightening mathematical expression. Yet these mathematical equations, these numerical expressions of the "number rationality" (immanent *logos*) objectively present in the universe, are only meaningful to the extent that they actually bear upon and refer to that objective non-mathematical reality of the world independent of such equations. By mathematical formalizations the physicist is not merely dealing with consistent sets of abstract symbols or axioms in themselves, but with the relation or connection between them and the external realities he is investigating. Torrance's point then is that the physical scientists (physicists being Torrance's focus) are concerned with the openness and referential relatedness of mathematical structures to ontological structures in the real world beyond them. In "word rationality," on the other hand, one has to do, he says, with the rationality of creation in its personal form transcending the visible, tangible and determinate levels. By interaction with word, the rational, orderly connections in nature, to which mathematical formalization is given, are found to be incomplete in themselves. But as coordinated with the orderly, wider, richer connections in "word" at the higher levels of reality they gain a meaning and consistency which they could not have in themselves. Language keeps abstract symbolic systems from pointlessness in order to serve forms and levels of rationality which transcend them. But both forms of rationality are necessary to gain understanding of the tangible and intangible levels of reality. Both come together in humanity in the interrelation or unitariness of the physical and spiritual existence in space-time and as "man's interaction with nature and as its inherent rationality is brought to coordinate expression in mathematical and verbal language . . . its inherent nature and intelligibility" are meaningfully articulated. The tangible (number) and intangible and personal (word) are not only inseparable but necessary together. Number is brought to meaning in referential word and word needs the determinate, invariable character in the referential character of number. That is the realm which supplies the reliable medium for intelligible systems of representation and the basis necessary for universality and continuity of communication. As a result, Torrance again finds, in this mutual interrelation of number and word, that natural science and theological science have much common ground. This is said to be preeminently true in the intellectual aspect of such. Beyond clear differences in relation to their particular objects, Torrance explains that it is the aim of natural science to investigate the empirical world or realm of created rationalities in its real differentiation from God as it is to be known out of its own contingent nature and intelligibility, but without taking God into account. Theological science inquires into "ways and works of God" as God is made known in his self-revelation to humanity in the world. God has given himself to be known, and such responsive inquiry leads to worship and knowledge of God in his distinctness from all he has created while avoiding the projection of creaturely images into this knowledge. Herein, though, the physical sciences must ask the question regarding the sufficient reason for this rational state of affairs as it reaches beyond the range of human scientific competence. The coordination of number and word rationality presses thought to a transcendent element. Theological science must ask about the structured objectivities of the space-time world within which the Word became flesh and wherein God continues to make himself known by his Word. Serious attention to the Word requires account of the determinate objectivities with which the Word is enwrapped and through which it is mediated to persons in the world.[51]

This discussion Torrance analogically, and at times audaciously, places in the context of "light," the "created light" of the universe. The new physics has shown that the physical universe is essentially a universe of light "for it is ordered throughout in accordance with the primacy of light and its invariant behavior."[52] Torrance deals directly with the larger significance of the physics of light and at greater length, analogously and theologically, with regard to the relation between created light and the "uncreated Light of God." What Maxwell's mathematical properties of radiation were able to do, Einstein then developed and clarified for science. It was found that light represents the most fundamental form of radiation in the electromagnetic field, and also that it behaves in a way that defies mechanical (Newtonian) explanation. Light is also found to be the most refined form of matter, thus giving to it a role akin to "mediation" within the universe. Light then has a supreme place among physical realities in the universe. In virtue of its unparalleled speed it has a unique function in linking and coordinating the realities of the universe together within its rational harmony. Light "illuminates" the rational nature of physical existence while enlightening the mind, says Torrance. The rational, intelligible universe discloses its harmony and beauty to the mind and shows itself to be structured throughout in accordance with the principle of the primacy of light.[53] This is said to point toward or reflect the modern change from abstractive truth to truth of being. Light in its constancy (or "invariance"), invisibility, and inaudibility is, in spite of the vast difference, reckoned by Torrance as surely a created reflection of both the uncreated and unlimited Light which God is in the Constancy of his Truth and Grace, and the invariant, dynamic, objective Ground of his eternal purpose in the creation. The mystery of his invisible Light, unapproachable and inaccessible, has been made visible and accessible, embodied in Jesus Christ and in his audible Light and Word. These coinhere as the transcendent creative Source of all intelligibility, and above all "as revealing himself to us through luminous Word or audible Light" when the Word became flesh.[54]

For theological science the created universe, within whose created rationality it too must work, must be regarded as having been given and as sustained in its rational order only so far as it is "open upward" toward God, the Creator of all. The rationality and unitary intelligibility of the universe is seen as finally integrated from above by the creative, redemptive and active Trinitarian relations within the Being of God (cf. chapter five).[55] Torrance agrees with physicist John Polkinghorne's conclusions.

> "Because of the intelligibility of the universe, its openness to the investigation of science, there lies the fact of the Word of God. The Word is God's agent in creation, impressing his rationality upon the world. That same Word is also the light of men, giving us thereby access to the rationality that is in the world" . . . (Torrance adds that) scientists and theologians must surely act and think together in inquiring . . . into the interrelation between the kind of order that is disclosed through the Incarnation of the Word . . . and the kind of order that nature discloses . . . . It is when this order that pervades the whole universe is correlated with the Word of God incarnate in Jesus Christ, that it becomes articulate beyond what it is capable of itself . . . a sounding-board . . . for the message of the Truth and Love of God in Jesus Christ.[56]

Only *a posteriori* through his self-revelation to humanity within the concrete intelligibilities of the space-time creation can it be known that God has established a relation of dependence and created correspondence between that contingent rationality and God's own transcendent Rationality. Torrance thus uses the modern "revolution" in natural scientific understanding in order to analogously enhance theo-logical understanding in pointing to the uncreated Truth of God. Torrance has found this to be necessary for theology which again must ask about the world's structured objectivities wherein the incarnation occurred as historical event. Therefore Torrance says that

> . . . theological inquiry is unable to give serious attention to the Word which God has addressed to man without taking into account the determinate objectivities and intelligibilities of the created order with which it is clothed and through which it always is mediated to us. Therein . . . theological inquiry bears upon the rational connections inherent in the empirical world . . . . Thus questions rising out of theological science . . . blend with questions asked in the inquiries of natural science.[57]

Theological science, much like the natural sciences, is realist knowing in correspondence with the objective coherence self-disclosed to it.

Restored Realism and Torrance's "Correspondence"
(to Inner Coherence) Understanding of Truth

The concept of truth enshrines at once the real being of things and the revelation of things as they are in reality. The truth of being comes to bear in its own light and in its own authority, constraining us by the power of what it is to assent to it and acknowledge it for what it is in itself. St. Anselm who developed that further in a more realist way held truth to be the reality of things as they actually are independent of us before God and therefore as they ought to be known and signified by us. Everything is what it actually is and not something else and cannot according to its nature be other than it is. That is what he called its inherent "necessity" or "truth."[58]

Within the Scottish Realist tradition, Torrance's understanding of realism is emphatically a critical realism or realist knowledge in opposition to naive realism. Torrance has also been found to assert the objective nature and basis of knowledge rooted as it is in the object out of itself as it discloses itself to be what it is, to which the knowing subject then assents. Yet this realism and objectivity is also a personal knowing, committed knowing, for "knowledge" is the knowledge of persons who, in relation and by assent, attempt to respond to the object appropriately so as to form reviseable "disclosure models" by which the truth of the object is clarified for understanding and brought to semantic expression (cf. "word rationality"). The methodological and epistemological underpinnings and some of their implications for Torrance's scientific theology have now begun to become clearer.

But with this goes Torrance's understanding of Truth as "correspondence" *and* "coherence," or more particularly correspondence truth whereby the proper object is known as it is in its own inherent, internal coherence. The rationality and order of the object in its internal relations is to be known unitarily. Again, the role of statement, as truly referential in relation to the object, is a critical part of this process. While Torrance often seems to give greatest emphasis to the correspondence understanding of truth, his desire is to bring forth the necessity of both simultaneously and together in real knowing. Disjunctivist or dualist notions have trapped and distorted thinking into one or the other (correspondence *or* coherence) and must be corrected. It is then within this "confused" context of epistemological dualism that various "coherence" and "correspondence" theories of truth have been continually asserted in the history of thought. Torrance links this to his concern for the restoration of ontology. Thus he states

> What is at stake is a distorting refraction in the ontological substructure of knowledge. There can be no satisfactory theory of truth within the brackets of a dualist frame of thought, for it can only yield the oscillating dialectic between coherence and correspondence. There can be no way forward except through (first) a rejection of dualist modes of thought in an integration of empirical and theoretical components and of form and being in our understanding of reality. That would restore the integrity of the semantic reference of idea and sign to reality, in which reality would have objective

priority over all our conceiving and speaking of it. Strictly speaking, the contrast, let alone the conflict, between realism and idealism would not then arise, nor would the distinction between a coherence and a correspondence view of truth which depends on a disjunction between form and being . . . the meaning of realism . . . describe(s) the orientation of thought that obtains in semantics, science or theology on the basis of a nondualist or unitary relation between the empirical and theoretical ingredients in the structure of the real world and in our knowledge of it.[59]

While what Torrance calls "the classical attitude of mind," a perspective which is said to have made human knowledge possible, had been the basis of Western thinking arising from the Christian conviction of the intelligibility of the world, there subsequently began that increasingly problematic shift from the truth of being to cognitive truth (subjectivism and "agent intellect"). The issue here for Torrance's understanding of truth is that if the immediate objects of human apprehension are not things in themselves but are "worked up (mental) representations" derived from the senses, then "it is a correspondence view of truth that seems to become necessary." But if things are not apprehended in themselves but rather as only sensible images, how does one know that the entities correspond to the objects in the mind? Some verification beyond correspondence becomes necessary. In such discussion one may well question Torrance's descriptions. But his point is that "in the lack of any transcendental reduction of the conditions under which objective knowledge can be established, there can only take place a retreat into a coherence view of truth."[60] But this "damaging" process cannot stop there, as the *via moderna* and its "new logic" meant further retreat to mere linguistic notions of truth.

While all scientific knowledge has systematic concern to order knowledge into a coherent whole, Torrance says that it is unscientific to force upon reality some "alien" "coherence" not derived from the self-revelation of the object. The nature of the object prescribes how it is to be known as the mind seeks to correspond to the internal coherence of the object. He states that "the order is in the Object (in theology) before it is in our minds, and therefore it is as we allow the Object to impose itself upon our minds that our knowledge of it gains coherence."[61] As each science advances, forms of appropriate thinking of its object are developed to penetrate even behind subjective variables so that in all sciences a critical and realist epistemology becomes possible and "physical" statements are not rejected. There is no way to establish the truth outside of the truth and by means of some alien principle. Torrance believes that the "new physics" has found and shown that there is an actual interaction of the mind and the intelligibilities external to the subject in objective reality. It is that "structural kinship" he refers to as existing between human knowing and what is known which allows thinking to be increasingly conformed to the object's particular rational nature.[62] Here one must note the nature and interrelation of "existence statements" and "coherence statements" in Torrance's thought. An "existence statement" is said to be an act of reference in which something is experienced which is other than the self, the "intuitive" apprehension of the world. The meaning of such is not to be found in the statement but in the objective thing. "Coherence statement" is a reference to single "existence statements" as they refer only to particular things or events, and thus they require the clarification of the relationships between them to manifest their proper consistency. This particular form of terminology Torrance does not use after the early 1970's, but emphasis upon the idea and the interrelationship or integration of the larger correspondence and coherence theories continues. Each is said to unitarily require the other for significance. No meaningful knowledge can occur, he says, except in correspondence, consistency and coherent integration (cf. field theory, onto-relations) in a pattern of meaning.[63] As will be seen below, within this knowledge established in relation to the object the mind's correspondence to the object is also termed "analogical." The truth in the assenting mind is not a replica of the objective structures. That would not be true correspondence as found in proper scientific knowing. But while human knowing distinguishes what is known from the knowing of it, yet there is real contact with reality and new, even surprising, knowledge of the object as it is in itself. The *a posteriori*, responsive formulation of theories or disclosure models serve heuristically to open out further relations and understanding of disclosure between being and thought as the human mind is increasingly adapted to or conformed to the objective intelligibility by means of experimental and heuristic operations of objective penetration. This re-forming of the mind is, again, said to be a "repentant" thinking.[64] This personal knowing relation is then said to be a unitary thinking that assents to the unitary rationality of the universe by thinking together form and being, correspondence and coherence, thereby un-covering the "analogies" in thought, being and relations which bear on each other in the universe and point beyond themselves.[65]

This last point is said to be the most amazing feature in the "new (post-Einsteinian) science," the role accorded to the human knower in knowledge which cannot be severed from the structure of the universe in which that knower exists. This means, says Torrance, that by human interaction with and inquiry into the universe, the deepest nature of the universe, which would otherwise remain undisclosed, now takes on expressive form by means of the human being, the "priest of creation." While having objective, immanent intelligibility independent of human perception and conception, still the universe as impersonal is not self-disclosing. It must be brought to expression. Nature must be questioned in order to be known as it is, while human rationality as well does not occur apart from the reciprocal action between knowing subject and the objective world.[66] Torrance, following Einstein and Polanyi especially, finds that the inquiring, rational human being and the universe are relative to or correlated to each other. This is something of the nature of that "structural kinship" between the human knowing subject and objective reality, and the question of the relations between human knowing and the intelligibility of the object known.[67] This is said to be reflected in the previously mentioned stratified structure of science which parallels the stratification or "levels" of reality. This kind of correspondence relation between knower and the actual disclosure of the object is found to avoid subjectivism generally and the *a priori* categories of the static subjectivity of Kant in particular (cf. the *a priori* "categories" as "absolute"). This epistemological position is said to exclude all obstructive ego-centered activity because it is thus "open" to the object. Indeed, only such a rational subject can participate in genuine objective operations, for only such a subject can distinguish what is known (object) from the knowing of it, while yet allowing the knowing to be determined by the nature of the object. Only such a knowing mind in relation to such an open reality could effect mental penetration through and into the form inherent in the object and bring such to intelligent rational expression.[68] This correspondence or correlation, which Torrance understands to be true scientific knowledge, commits the knower to a situation as bound to that which is discerned to be objectively the case.

Thus, while "abstractive procedures" are said to distort the world because the personal mind is retracted by such procedures from the object in its natural form and inherent order, and thus from experience of external reality, realist knowing or "scientific" knowing of objective reality is held to be the process in the order of human knowing which corresponds to the order of being and acting in the Truth itself whereby the elements of coherence in the given reality are grasped.[69] From this experience of the world, science seeks to know reality and the "truthful coherence" of ideas with each other. Therefore scientists are clarifying the objective nature of human knowledge in ways that "do full justice to the fact that the discoveries in these areas of existence are not inventions of our minds but correspond to the nature of things . . . into a profounder and a more massively grounded objectivity."[70] As this is coupled with "tacit knowing," Torrance concludes that one can formulate knowledge of an object because within the knowing relation, in terms of the object's particulars and their coherent relations, the whole is held unitarily together. There is found to exist then the "ontological reference" which establishes real knowing contact with reality in its own intrinsic rational being and coherence.[71]

Correspondence and coherence truth must then be understood as inseparable in relation to the objective nature of reality itself to which the mind assents, says Torrance. True scientific knowing is occupied with objectivity, real contact and real (profound versus naive) correspondence of the mind in related, committed submission to the disclosed truth of being "out there." The entity discloses the inner order of the relations of truths in the unity of the whole of its being. Therefore the mind can progressively and revisably bring thinking, and then from thinking a conceptual model or theory, into harmony with external reality. Through that disclosure model the truth pattern of the object can disclose itself yet more fully as it is thus "served."[72]   Note Torrance's emphasis on compulsion and necessity in the following:

> In the nature of the case, (the object) must be discerned and known strictly in accordance with the necessity of its being what it is or in accordance with its inherent truth of being. Thus to the truth or necessity in the object of knowledge, that a thing is what it is, there must correspond a truth or necessity in knowledge, the impossibility of conceiving the object as being other than it is. Hence all our concepts and statements must be tested through a critical inquiry in which we listen in to the truth of things, yielding our minds to their ontic necessity, for in that way we are enabled to straighten out our conceptions and statements in accordance with the nature of things as they really are and so think and speak rightly of them.[73]

At this point in the analysis of Torrance's epistemology and his understanding of truth as "correspondence" and "coherence," it becomes necessary to show how crucial Martin Heidegger's discussion or expression of "truth as disclosure" and his expression of *a-letheia* in *Being and Time* is for Torrance's own understanding of correspondence truth as disclosive truth. This apparently has gone wholly unnoticed in any analysis of Torrance. Torrance's understanding of truth as disclosure of the proper object is much influenced (in however modified a way) by Heidegger.   Yet many have understood Heidegger's own position on "truth as disclosure" to be in marked and critical contrast to the grouping of views that may be classified as "correspondence" theories of truth. James J. Dicenso's larger discussion seems to make him a proponent of this view, placing "disclosure" outside "correspondence."   He says,

> *Aletheia*, Heidegger argues, means "unhiddenness", and this tells us something essential about the nature of truth . . . . Heidegger introduces the argument for truth as disclosure by indicating the limitations of correspondence theories, which are determined by "the kind of relation that obtains between the statement and the thing." Modes of relationality, or being open, antecede any specific and determinable existential encounter or experience. That is, the open region is a necessary dimension of the human capacity to relate hermeneutically to a world and to others and hence to have any form of experience . . . . Heidegger's argument is that prior to any possible experience of truth as the correspondence of entity and idea there must be a constitutive region of disclosure that informs the specific mode of apprehension of the given . . . no judgment . . . is purely objective and context free.[74]

Dicenso's larger discussion seems to understand Heidegger as relegating the use of correspondence truth (if not negating it finally) to a place of minor usefulness because of its static and oppressive nature. But is this necessarily so? Is

Heidegger's understanding of truth finally a negation of correspondence? Torrance would appear to say that this is not so.

Torrance's response to Heidegger's thought is admittedly mixed. Negatively, Torrance believes that Heidegger, like Kant, is to be faulted for finally denying that genuine knowledge in every proper field of inquiry is established in terms of the object's actual, internal relations with real intelligibility (including theology).[75] In Heidegger, he sees again finally a dualist leap into nothing as a result of having lost the eternal-temporal interactivity. Torrance finds that despite important advances Heidegger falls back from ontology to existentialism because he works with a non-conceptual relation to being as a result of the fact that *logos* is not understood as inhering in being and therefore cannot be conceptually grasped. Heidegger can only think of letting being disclose itself through a non-conceptual leap into that nothing. In this way he is said to fall back upon himself and his own self-understanding.[76]

Yet Torrance also finds Heidegger's insights into realist thought and truth to be of great importance. Going back even to Heidegger's dissertation on Duns Scotus, Torrance contends that he rightly traced the difficulties of Western philosophy back to the false separation of thought from reality and the ascendancy of abstract formalization over nature, all of which Heidegger learned from Scotus. From Scotus he is also said to have been influenced toward a negative reaction to Aquinas and his endeavor to establish a more realist epistemology, wherein room is made for a direct relation between mind and being. Belief in the openness of nature to the empirical investigation of its intrinsic relations and rational order is said to have thus influenced Heidegger by means of Scotus' realism. It is as a result of this indirect influence that Torrance interprets Heidegger as seeking to clarify his critical realist concern regarding the separation of *logos* from *physis*.[77] In calling attention to the problem of such a false and damaging severance, Heidegger is said to have revealed appropriate concern for detachment of thought from being. Subjectivistic human thinking then develops dictatorial, legislative habits of thought which attempt to impose nomistic structures upon being.[78]

According to Torrance, Heidegger desired that thought again approach being appropriately in accord with being's own interior principles of activity and powers of communication and signification whereby propositions of meaning are true only when manifesting being's own intention. In this way, objective modes of thought are correlated with the ultimate openness of being and its semantic reference. It is here that Torrance is especially interested in Heidegger's analysis and interpretation of *aletheia*. Heidegger is found to let being itself show through in its own freedom and reality. In relating *logos* and *physis*, he is said to rightly perceive *logos* to be the natural force of being by which to manifest itself, to come out into the open and to show itself in its own light. *Logos* immanent in being is not seen to be itself the locus of truth, but "is the manifesting of the reality of things or their unconcealment *(aletheia)*."[79] Torrance finds it significant that Heidegger's thought has no need for intermediary representations, which happens whenever *logos* is separated dualistically from being. This is because the actual concern is with the showing of reality itself to the human knower, which is why Heidegger gave so much effort to the analysis of "existence" *(Dasein)* in order to destroy the false ontologies which arise by means of the verification of substitute-symbolisms. This was to the end that the entire focus of attention would be directed upon being in the full and proper sense *(Sein)*.[80] Despite perceived problems, then, Heidegger is still found by Torrance to have brought to preliminary corrective clarity the need to allow reality to unveil itself in its own inner intelligibility *(aletheia)*. Torrance says that thinking must be thrust up against the truth of being in such a way that it is "sustained by an objective signification and does not fall back into the dark whirlpool of man's self-understanding . . . we grasp the truth of intelligible being out of the depth of its own reality, but we let it interpret itself to us."[81] Building upon Heidegger, then, Torrance says that "if (these structures or modes of thought) serve the uncovering of being, let it show itself or come to view or stand out in its reality, they are true, but if they obscure being or distort its showing forth by imposing . . . an alien structure of meaning . . . they are false."[82] Heidegger's understanding of *a-letheia* or "unconcealment" of being is highly regarded by Torrance and developed in a way which reflects Torrance's own emphasis on the disclosure and the realist knowledge of objective being as correspondent as well as coherent. Only in this way, he says, can objectivity and ontology (the truth of being/Being) be recovered.

The restoration of correspondence and coherence truth by the "new science" is also seen by Torrance to have many significant implications for theological science. Here one must reckon with what has been discussed previously, especially with regard to the realism and objectivity of knowledge as well as the role of the knowing person and of ultimate beliefs in the knowing relation. Torrance has found that theological knowledge intersects the general coefficient of human knowledge "from above" and the general interpenetrates the theological "from below." The social and interactional coefficients of knowledge are operative in the tacit substructure of theological knowledge by which the theologian gains initial grasp upon invisible realities into which inquiry is made. The theologian becomes "open to the disclosure and concept-generating power of their intrinsic intelligibility."[83] Seeking the Truth of God out of God's prior self-disclosure by scientific questioning, one finds the truth of God opening with ever greater depth and the truth lays hold of thinking in its own objective force, setting up its own "laws" in the mind. At the same time the theologian is thereby questioned down to the roots of her or his being. In this way the theologian apprehends the Truth of God by the Holy Spirit in Jesus Christ, and the mind is restructured and understanding adapted to that objectively disclosed Truth.

In its most basic sense, truth is seen here to denote a state of affairs which is necessarily and ontologically prior to the truth of cognition or statement. The truth of being is basically synonymous with objective reality. As with Augustine, the truth is "what is" or "that which manifests what is . . . and manifests it as it is." The concept of truth is said to enshrine at once "the real being of things and the revelation of things as they are in reality."[84] The "new science" is said to have restored the penetration behind the subjective variables of the observer to bring about the emergence of a critical and realist epistemology where physical statements are not jettisoned for "ideal" or abstractionist statements. Thought and statement refer beyond themselves and this is said to clarify scientific activity in theology. In this, the knowledge of God as he is out of himself means that human thought of God is thrown back upon God as its direct and proper Object. Thought is brought increasingly into accord with God as he is in his personal movement of disclosure, and thereby as he is in himself. We are addressed by the compelling Word of God's openness to be known in his "unconcealedness" in Christ, and then summoned to faithful and disciplined response in the exercise of reason.[85] Torrance says that theology is called to proper scientific scrutiny of given realities in order to know God as given and thus as God is in himself.

> Thus understood theological dogmatics is not a closed, logico-deductive system of knowledge, but an open science, disciplined and controlled by a logic beyond our own minds, and therefore never relieved of the need for critical and positive reconstruction in the light of the truth as our minds become progressively open to it through appropriate inquiry.[86]

Behind all truth of knowing there stands the Truth of God, Truth as Personal Being, which has taken the form of active life in human historical existence in Jesus Christ. He is the Truth of the Father. In Jesus Christ, God "turns in Grace toward us and makes Himself open to us . . . (bearing) directly upon us with the presence and impact of ultimate Truth."[87] Theology is concerned strictly with the ultimate Objectivity of God who personally comes and impresses his Truth in openness upon our thought, which then has a corresponding conception of Truth and which is, in that sense and in that measure, not provisional but ultimate. God's Truth is his Word which is his own Person in self-communication. God's Truth is the communication of himself which is not apart from truths. But such truths must cohere in the one Person of the incarnate Word of God in dialogical relation with human knowing for faithful response. In this God-established knowing relation in Christ by the Spirit there is adaptation of human thought and human theo-logical expression in accordance with the creative, revealing and saving acts of God among human beings. This theo-logical thought and statement must have a logic of reference which does "correspond to the logic of God's self-communication to men--and correspond is here the appropriate term." In theo-logical science, Torrance is not merely concerned with human reference to divine Being, but with redemptive knowledge of the living God in Christ and by the Spirit, with the responsive correspondence of human thought and word to the divine Word, and human act with the divine Act in accord with faith-ful scientific process. Human theological statements arising responsively out of God's ultimate Truth will then not be ultimate and final. Theological statements must refer away from themselves and away from human subjectivity, beyond, to the "level" of ultimate Truth which has ontological priority.[88]   As an ongoing process of conformation, adaptation or correspondence to the Truth of God in its own objective, inner coherence, scientific clarification and progressive development ensues in theological understanding and in statement/disclosure model in the context of that faith knowing.

In theological science, Torrance advocates that correspondence and coherence be finally integrated, for to know God in a realist way means that one ("by the Spirit and through the Word") faithfully "follows" or "thinks after" the objective disclosure (*a-letheia*) of God's Word in Christ in God's "economic" coming, and finally into God's own internal rationality and coherence as it is in the eternal relations within the "ontological" Trinity (cf. chapter five).

Restored Realism and the Proper Function of Language

As with the theory of relativity, which is for Torrance a prominent example of a scientific disclosure model whereby objective truth is brought into language in order to serve that disclosure and to bring about still fuller disclosure, so too theological science must bring its revisable understanding of the Truth of God to language. Again, a preeminent example of such a theological disclosure model (as arising from and transparent to the Truth of God) is the Nicene-Constantinopolitan Creed and particularly the *homoousion* doctrine, which is the foundation upon which Torrance's own positive theological expression (disclosure model) lies.

Therefore a further critical aspect of the affects and developments of the "new science" which has been brought to light is the function of language as the person fulfills the scientific calling, in the world and before God, which is to bring the world in its own ordered being from objective disclosure to expression. Torrance obviously wants to apply these changes and their significance to Christianity and theo-logical expression at this crucial time.[89] How has natural science altered the function of language?

Torrance says that one of the outstanding features of science in this century has been the invention of symbolic systems or highly formalized "languages" which enlarge human capacities for scientific penetration, thought and expression of reality. But this is not flight into abstraction. It is rather a way to refine and develop the natural operation of the mind in its realist use of language. These "languages" are instruments of thought which aid in coping more effectively with the objective world of actual experience. These extend thought beyond what it would be capable of without them, expanding effectiveness of thought upon empirical reality, whereby one is enabled to grasp the intrinsic intelligibility of the object at a yet deeper level. But the "language" must be ever refined for all goes wrong if the language is not apposite in its referential relation with the realities upon which they are meant to bear.[90]

Torrance's discussion of the distinction and relation between number language and word language means in this context that scientific language must function in accord with the knowledge and interpretation of things as they are and not simply in an observationalist or phenomenalistic way. He sees that language has now been shown to have objective orientation which is then "use(d) as a transparent medium of representation in the process of knowing and speaking about realities in terms of their own intrinsic significance."[91] Direct intention is primary. An artificial relation between language and things brings only detachment and the obscuring of or loss of knowledge because there is no natural bearing upon reality. In this way language is emptied of significance, and the question of truth or falsity is gone. Yet total adequation in representation would mean substitution ("ultra-realism"). Therefore, "words or signs" can only accomplish their given task appropriately if there is a measure of incompleteness so that the wording can point away from itself to the intended reality. Yet Torrance asserts too that words and statements must be related to the realities of intentional signification in such a way that the realities are able to manifest themselves through them. But this cannot be in a way whereby knowledge of the realities can be read right off of the language. The objective realities are and remain independent. "Words and statements are understood only when we come to know through them what is being indicated apart from them."[92] Torrance's is, then, a consistently "realist" position wherein signs are "naturally" correlated to and ontologically controlled by the objective realities they signify. This is the relation of language to things, which the new science or new physics has brought about by its assent to the appropriate objective reality. Torrance illustrates the problem by the Gödelian theorem which can be transposed from a logico-deductive system to a grammatical system, and yet give warning that "no syntactics contains its own semantics." The referential relations of language must be given priority over syntactical relations which are open at the boundary conditions to a controlling center beyond them and which can be meaningfully understood.[93]

In grasping the rational order of the universe in its variety and unity, the sciences then have developed different "languages," in accordance with the kinds of objective reality encountered, in order to understand the realities adequately and to coordinate them in thought. Whether it be symbolic or technical languages used to convey the conceptual structures impressed upon human thought at different levels of investigation, whether physico-chemical or theological, the proper object/Object must be the "judge" of the truth or falsity of the questions put and the language used to bring the truth/Truth to light.[94] There is to be understood then a real referential relation of language to being out of the object to the end that, again, the language be transparent, actually letting the reality be known while not obtruding itself in the way of knowing. Torrance does not believe that the proof and exact nature of this relation can be expressed because then all would be resolved into statements alone. As in Torrance's emphasis on the integration of correspondence and coherence notions of truth, language too must become increasingly appropriate to the objective reality as the conceptual must be brought to expression.

Theologically this scientific reorientation regarding relation of language to objective reality is said to be of the greatest significance in the whole context of theological epistemology and theological expression. The mode of rationality appropriate to God's Word is the center of Christian theology because the concern is not only with some kind of subjectivistic relations between the human being and God but with those relations as actualized objectively and historically within the universe. Therefore theological thought and language which are faithful to the Word of God are meant to lift the human mind to where they are not bound to contingent realities or the control of such, but are made "open to the infinite objectivity and inexhaustible intelligibility of God the Creator of all things." Yet there can be "no relevance or meaning for us if they were cut adrift from the actualities of the created order through which God reveals himself to us . . . to respond to him."[95]

Mute, impersonal creation must be brought to expression if humans are to know it. It is not so with God's own self-disclosing. The Word of God does not require conversion into another form to be apprehended. This is a critical point to Torrance's theological concern, to the place of theology among the sciences after Einstein, and to his own positive theo-logical disclosure model.[96] Torrance's point is that God constitutes the ultimate objective Basis of all truth and thereby establishes the truth and referentiality of statements about God, while conferring upon such relativity. This results from the fact that the Truth itself is the objectively self-given God. Thus, while one cannot state in statements how statements are related to Being, still in authentic knowledge Being shows through the speech it engenders. It is then, as the Word subsists in the Trinitarian consubstantial relations and as human words exist in the public language of the community, that if the Word of God is to "enter the forum as speech to man through the medium of human words it must be directed to man in community, and if that Word creates reciprocity between God and man it must create a community . . . the appropriate medium of its continuing communication to man."[97]

Conclusion

It is Torrance's contention here that the modern restoration of objective, realist thinking has been potentially a great boon to the process of restoring theology and the theological task. It enables the scientific theologian to both clear the way of false dualistic modes of thought and to restore rigorous modes of rationality to theology which, he is convinced, is in desperate need of such after dualism's reintrenchment generally by means of prominently Descartes, Newton and Kant, and theologically by such as Schleiermacher and Bultmann. In assenting to its own proper object theology is to take its proper and unique place among the sciences. Its appropriate task consciously occurs before God and within and in relation to the same space-time, contingent, objective world as is the case for the other sciences as each pursues its own proper calling here. Other sciences must specifically develop understanding of the immanent rationalities of nature, being content with fields of rationality which are not in themselves ultimately self-explanatory. The contingent world as created *ex nihilo* must be investigated out of itself and not out of God. Yet the scientist engages in dedicated service to a transcendent rationality or *logos* in the world which, while not to be identified with God, does point to God and the *Logos* of God. Theology, though, is the science which by its Object and task cannot stop at the limits which must satisfy the natural science, for it is concerned above all, says Torrance, with penetration into the "transcendent and fontal rationality, the ultimate source of all that is intelligible to man and which is presupposed in the created rationalities of nature explored through natural sciences."[98] As we have observed, Brian Gray is largely correct as he expresses Torrance's position, saying, "As a science theology is only a human quest for truth in which man seeks to apprehend God as far as he is able, to understand what he apprehends, and to speak clearly and carefully about what he understands."[99] Within the context of the special sciences, theological science too must remain faithful to its ultimate reference beyond itself in God, who has revealed himself in the concrete intelligibility of the world, and not upon the grounds of other sciences.

From this modern alteration of thought, theology, he says, is being helped to bring to clarity its own proper way of objective thinking, formulating and expressing (cf. theological disclosure models) the Truth of God under God's compelling self-revelation. Theology can then engage in yet more flexible and fruitful ways of knowing that which theology seeks to know. Theology is also learning of the variety and unity of the rational order in creation, which is so critical to following the Word of God in his sovereign, interactive relatedness to this world and humanity. Theology has gained much in adhering to its own proper mode of rationality by recognizing the stratified structure of objective truth (levels) and the need to penetrate past the phenomenal "surface" in actual knowing relation to the proper Object.[100]

This restoration of the way of theology out of the Word of God in responsive accordance with its own proper Object along scientific lines also requires theological expression, the establishment of that "disclosure model," whereby further advance in the knowledge of God under the Word and by the Spirit can take place in the Church. In the process of bringing together Torrance's own bases, directions and pivotal work in the reciprocal relations (that is, "complementarity") between theology and the natural sciences, this chapter has included much already of Torrance's positive theo-logical expression. But this will now be made explicit beyond that which has already been said. Torrance's way of knowing, understanding and following the Truth of God out of God in the space-time way God has revealed himself to be known in the world in Jesus Christ, the theo-logical "heart" of Thomas Torrance, are presented in the following chapter.

NOTES

1. Cf. S. A. Grave, *The Scottish Philosophy of Common Sense* (Oxford: Oxford University Press, 1960); and especially M. Jamie Ferreira, *Skepticism and Reasonable Doubt: The British Naturalist Tradition in Wilkins, Hume, Reid and Newman* (Oxford: Oxford University Press, 1987). Note particularly herein the sections on Hume and Reid.

2. Torrance, *TS*, pp. 76-80. Cf. Torrance, *CTSC*, pp. 15-25. Herein Torrance discusses three false, problematic views rooted in thought from Galileo to Newton: first, the universe is a closed and rigidly mechanical system; second, the "container" notion of space and time; third, the severance or dualism between theoretical and empirical aspects of reality.

3. Torrance, *GR*, pp. 10-11. Cf. *GR*, pp. 89-107.

4. Torrance, *TCFK*, p. 265.

5. Torrance, *TS*, p. 106.

6. Torrance, *GR*, p. 93-94. Cf. Torrance's discussion of the nature of scientific "penetration" into the "inner rationality" of objective reality, p. 94.

7. Ibid., pp. 96-97.

8. Cf. Torrance, *TS*, pp. 100-105 and *CTSC*, pp. 17-25, 116-131, and many others.

9. Torrance, *CTSC*, pp. 50-51. Cf. Torrance, *RET*, p. 57, and *DCO*, p. 77.

10. Ibid., pp. 27-28.

11. Ibid., p. 28. Cf. references above in endnote nine.

12. Torrance, *GR*, p. 11. Cf. Torrance, *CTSC*, pp. 28-29.

13. Cf. Torrance, *TCFK*, pp. 220-231. Cf. Torrance, *RET*, p. 71.

14. Torrance, *RST*, p. 160.

15. Torrance, *GG*, p. 97, cf. pp. 95- 100, and *CTSC*, pp. 53-54.

16. Torrance, *GR*, pp. 131-132. Cf. Torrance, *CTSC*, 52-53.

17. Torrance, *GR*, pp. 131-132. Cf. Torrance, *CTSC*, 52-53.

18. Ibid., p. 29.

19. Ibid. Cf. Torrance, *GG*, p. 11.

20. Torrance, *GR*, pp. 131-132. Cf. Torrance, *CTSC*, pp. 50-51, and *RET*, pp. 42-51, 57, 71, 139.

21. Torrance, *GG*, p. 173. Cf. Torrance, RST, p. 160.

22. Torrance, *GR*, p. 24. Cf. Torrance's discussion of false, phenomenalistic thinking in *CTSC*, chapters one and two; *DCO*, chapter one; and *STI*, chapter two.

23. Ibid., cf., Torrance, *RST*, p. 131, 134.

24. Torrance, *RST*, pp. 135-136 (emphasis added).

25. Ibid., p. 136. Torrance explains this further saying that "This way of describing the stratification of truth has its considerable merit, for it sets out the different levels of truth in their cross-lever coordination with one another. Each level is found to be open to the level above it and to require that meta-level relation in order to be consistent in itself as a level on its own. Thus there becomes disclosed the organic structure of thought that characterizes out apprehending of reality in all its depth. It must be recognized, however, that this is a posteriori reconstruction of the way in which our knowing is coordinated with the reality known, and does not take into account the actual heuristic processes of inquiry or the complex systems of thought and statement which build up in the course of those processes as the hypothetical compounds through which we try to penetrate more and more deeply into the objective structures of reality. In order to understand something of the actual gradient of inquiry, however, we must consider it all from the other way round, from within the perspective of our inductive struggles to reach the truth, and thus to trace out how we build up different logico-syntactical systems in different stages in the advance of knowledge. This procedure will also serve to reveal the difficulties and problems with which we have constantly to cope in the verification and clarification of our knowing. Let us glance first at what we do in natural science, taking our cue once more from Einstein, and remembering his point that science is after all a refinement and extension of our everyday thinking." p. 146-147.

26. Torrance, *CTSC*, p. 37.

27. Ibid., p. 38. Cf. Torrance, *TCFK*, pp. 135-148.

28. Torrance, *DCO*, p. 129. For further discussion, cf. Ibid., pp 101-103. Cf. Torrance, *TCFK*, pp. 208, 265.

29. Torrance, *GG*, pp. 168-172.

30. Torrance, *RST*, pp. 138-139.

31. Torrance, *GR*, p. 25.

32. Torrance, *CTSC*, pp. 31-32. Cf. Torrance's discussion of the four modes of rational order, *DCO*, p. 17.

33. Torrance, *DCO*, p. x. Cf. Torrance's extended discussion on God, creation and the real contingence of the world in *DCO*, chapters two and three; *CTSC*, chapter four; and *GG*, chapter three.

34. Torrance, *CFM*, pp. 36-37.

35. Torrance, *DCO*, p. 11. Cf. Ibid., pp. 15-16.

36. Ibid., p. 20-21.

37. Ludwig Wittgenstein, *Tractatus Logico Philosophicus*, in Torrance, *CTSC*, p. 120.

38. Torrance, *DCO*, p. 21. Cf. Torrance, *GG*, pp. 53-57 on the important difference between Christian and Greek dualist perspectives. Herein Torrance says that "The idea of the contingent rationality or intelligibility of the universe. This registers another immense step forward, although it was considered to be even more difficult. The idea that the rationality of the universe is contingent, i.e., neither necessary nor eternal, that there is an order in the universe created--along with the universe--out of nothing, was quite impossible for Greeks and Orientals alike. Again and again when Christians taught the doctrine of creation out of nothing, they were met with accusations of "impiety." It was, they were told, a form of atheism, for it called in question the rationality of the eternal forms--and denied the necessary connection between the rationality immanent in things and its source in Deity whether Deity was conceived in a Platonic, Aristotelian, or Stoic way--and it undermined the stability of the natural principles informing all that is, without which there would be nothing to stand between cosmos and chaos. It is certainly understandable that from the Greek point of view, this Christian idea should be regarded with such horror, but nevertheless it did prevail and it took root along with the victory over Greek polytheism achieved by the monotheistic concept of God. . . . The contingence of the universe means that it might not have been, or might well have been other than it is, so that we must ask our questions of the universe itself if we are to understand it--that is the reason why we cannot do without experimental science, which is the appropriate way of questioning nature. But the contingent universe is intelligible-- endowed with a rationality of its own--so that if we are to understand the universe, we must probe into that intelligibility, which is the immanent language by means of which the universe answers our questions or experiments. Thus it becomes apparent that the doctrine of contingent intelligibility or rationality is the foundation of all empirical and theoretical factors, both in what we seek to know and in our knowing of it. Today general relativity and the singularity of the universe so astonishingly disclosed by modern

cosmology provide massive support for this masterful idea as never before in the history of science. Yet this idea, which was quite impossible for the pagan mind, is a direct product of Christian theology. It is evident from this alone that far from theology being grounded upon natural science, natural science rests for one of its most basic concepts upon Christian theology." *GG*, pp. 53-54, 56-57.

39. Torrance, *CTSC*, p. 121. Cf. Ibid., pp. 122-125.

40. Torrance, *CFM*, pp. 40-41.

41. Torrance, *DCO*, pp. 2-4, 26-61.

42. Torrance, *TF*, pp. 98-109 in an important paradeigmatic analysis and use of the thought of the Nicene Fathers on the "contingence" of the world as they "scientifically" thought out the God-world relatedness and the world's dependence and contingent being out of Creation and Redemption in Christ. Also here versus prevailing Greek dualism and the eternality of matter.

43. Torrance, *CTSC*, p. 21. Cf. Ibid., chapter four.

44. Torrance, *GR*, pp. 89-90.

45. Torrance, *TCFK*, p. 113.

46. Ibid., p. 110.

47. Ibid., pp. 133ff.

48. Ibid., pp. 194-195; Torrance, *TS*, pp. 37-43; Torrance, *TF*, p. 199.

49. Torrance, *CTSC*, pp. 57-58. Cf. here pp. 65-69 where this is developed more fully.

50. Ibid., p. 75.

51. Ibid., p. 109-113. Cf. Torrance's larger discussion of immanent word and number in Ibid., pp. 109-144; *DCO*, pp. 46-61; *TRst*, pp. 69-75; *GR*, pp. 89-111; Torrance, *RST*, pp. 138-139.

52. Ibid., pp. 109, 75-107. Cf. Torrance, *TCFK*, pp. 333-349.

53. Ibid., p. 76.

54. Ibid., pp. 99-100. Again note Ibid., pp. 75-101 and 48-49.

55. Ibid., p. 39.

56. Torrance, *CFM*, pp. 26-27. Cf. Torrance, *CTSC*, pp. 82-83, 118-119, and *TCFK*, pp. 102-105 on Nicene Fathers.

57. Torrance, *CTSC*, pp. 113-114.

58. Torrance, *RST*, p. 141.

59. Torrance, *RET*, pp. 59-60.

60. Torrance, *RST*, pp. 9-10.

61. Torrance, *TS*, p. 138.

62. Torrance, *CTSC*, p. 75.

63. Torrance, *TS*, pp. 169-172.

64. Ibid., pp. 227, 242, 265.

65. Torrance, *TCFK*, pp. 229, 224.

66. Ibid., p. 84.

67. Ibid., pp. 84-85. ". . . a real correlation between the two is implied, may be traced back to the unity of structure and matter, or form and being, which is forced upon us particularly through general relativity, for that unity demands from us a corresponding way of knowing in which knowing and being, instead of being split wide apart as in traditional modern science and philosophy, are reconciled and conjoined . . . the astounding fact that the universe is accessible to our rational inquiry, so compellingly evident in the coordination that can be achieved between its inherent comprehensibility and our rational formalisations. What confronts us is an inner correlation between the structure of human knowledge and the structure of the world known by man . . . there is (from Polanyi) 'a correspondence between the structure of comprehension and the structure of the comprehensive entity which is its object,' or 'a structural kinship between subject and object.'"

68. Ibid.

69. Torrance, *TS*, p. 129. Cf. Torrance, *RST*, pp. 140-141; and *GR*, pp. 89-90.

70. Torrance, *GR*, pp. 43-44.

71. Torrance, *TCFK*, p. 158. On p. 159 Torrance says: "Thus a theory of knowledge based on tacit knowing requires both an ontology of mind an ontology of commitment of two poles of being are involved, the being of the knowing mind and the being of what

is known. Hence, against the objectivist and positivist theory of knowledge which refuses to acknowledge the existence of comprehensive entities as distinct from their particulars, Polanyi argues, within the framework of epistemic commitment to reality that the human mind is real and indeed more real than what we know through the mind on lower and more tangible levels of existence. . . . the concept of ontological stratification in the universe comprising a sequence of rising levels each higher one controlling the boundaries of the one below it and embodying thereby the joint meaning of the particulars situated on the lower level, which implies that all meaning lies in the higher levels of reality that are not reducible to the laws by which the ultimate particulars of the universe are controlled. Putting these two notions together we find that they tell us that as we move up the hierarchy of levels of reality from the more tangible to the more intangible we penetrate to things that are increasingly real and full of meaning. Since what is most tangible, such as a stone, has least meaning, it is perverse to identify the tangible with the real. Rather we conclude that deepest reality is possessed by higher things that are least tangible. In this sense profound reality is to be attributed to intelligence or mind, which is the superior principle of governing living beings."

72. Torrance, *TS*, pp. 144, 148, 239-240. Cf. TS, pp. 164, 169-172. Brian J.A. Gray, "Theology as Science: An Examination of the Theological Methodology of Thomas F. Torrance," (unpublished doctoral dissertation, Catholic University of Louvain, 1975), p. 153.

73. Torrance, *RST*, p. 141.

74. James J. Dicenso, *Hermeneutics and the Disclosure of Truth: A Study in the Work of Heidegger, Gadamer and Ricoeur* (Charlottesville: University Press of Virginia, 1990), pp. 56-58. Cf. John D. Morrison, "Review of Hermeneutics and the Disclosure of Truth," Journal of the Evangelical Theological Society, forthcoming. Heidegger's understanding of truth/aletheia as "dis-closure" or "un-hiddenness" in Being and Time begins to be set forth in section six, but it is emphatically in section forty-four where Heidegger's discussion is fullest.

75. Torrance, *GG*, p. 42. Cf. Torrance, *STR*, p. 151. Cf. Robert P. Scharlemann, *The Being of God: Theology and the Experience of Truth* (New York: The Seabury Press, 1981), chapters two and three.

76. Torrance, *TCFK*, p. 309. Cf. Torrance, *RST*, p. 49.

77. Ibid., p. 1.

78. Torrance, *TS*, p. 252. Cf. Torrance, GG, p. 81, as he follows Heidegger and the description of how logos became separated from being and how this led to the attempt to throw a "logical bridge," natural theology (a priori) between knowledge of this world and knowledge of God.

79. Torrance, *RST*, p. 47. Cf. Torrance, *TRst*, pp. 17-18.

80. Ibid.

81. Ibid., p. 48.

82. Ibid., p. 49. Cf. Torrance, *GR*, pp. 177-178.

83. Ibid., p. 121.

84. Ibid., p. 141.

85. Torrance, *TS*, pp. xii-xiii.

86. Torrance, *GR*, p. 90.

87. Torrance, *TS*, pp. 142-143.

88. Ibid., pp. 231-232. Cf. p. 145.

89. Torrance, *CTSC*, pp. 12-13.

90. Torrance, *RET*, pp. 61-62.

91. Ibid., p. 64.

92. Ibid., p. 66.

93. Ibid., pp. 73-74.

94. Torrance, *CTSC*, pp. 32-33.

95. Torrance, *GR*, p. 42. It is epistemologically important to see how he explains. He says that "Mention must also be made of a cognate feature that characterizes all genuine knowledge, whether it be knowledge or some limited field of being or knowledge of the universe as a whole, namely, an inner ratio between objectivity and revisability. In so far as our knowledge is objectively grounded upon reality independent of ourselves, the concepts and statements we employ in expressing our knowledge function properly by referring to that reality away from themselves, even while taking shape under the compelling claims of its inherent intelligibility. But for that very reason they are continually open to revision in the light of further disclosures of that reality which may come about. In objective knowledge of this kind there come to light invariant elements which govern our basic conceptions and affirmations of the reality concerned, but in so far as that reality exceeds our capacity to master it or resists encapsulation in our forms of thought and speech, there inevitably arise tentative variable representations of it which are to be regarded as having their truth not in themselves but in that to which they refer beyond themselves. It is only in so far as we can operate with "constants" or

"invariants" in our basic apprehension of some reality that we can develop inquiry into positive knowledge and advance further by building upon foundations thus securely laid. The material content of our knowledge, what we apprehend, the objective referent, does not change, but because it is objective it transcends and relativises the conceptual and linguistic forms we develop in advancing our knowledge of it. The intelligibility inherent in the reality apprehended is unchanging, but the rational forms in which we seek to articulate our apprehension of it are variable, and must be variable in that they are inadequate to the inexhaustible nature and invariant reality of being. Their openness to revision is measured only by the depth of their objective reference." e.g. Torrance, *GR*, p. 36. Cf. Torrance, *TCFK*, pp. 130-135.

96. Ibid., p. 101. Cf. pp. 82, 118, 126.

97. Torrance, *GR*, p. 146. Cf. Torrance, *CTSC*, pp. 122-123; and significantly Torrance, *TS*, pp. 180-183. Gray, "Theology as Science," pp. 164f., 169f.

98. Ibid., p. 96. Cf. Torrance, *TS*, p. 100-101, 113.

99. Bryan Gray, "Theology as Science: A Critical Analysis of the Theological Methodology of T. F. Torrance," unpublished doctoral dissertation, University of Louvain, 1975, p. 307. Cf. Torrance, *TS*, p. 282.

100. Torrance, *CTSC*, pp. 28-39. Cf. p. 12 and Torrance, *STI*, p. 70, *DCO*, chapters two through four.

Chapter 5

The Redemptive Knowledge Of God
Out Of God: The Theo-logical
Basis For The Knowledge Of God
In Thomas Torrance's Scientific Theology

> (I have) written under the conviction that we must allow the divine realities
> to declare themselves to us, and so allow the basic forms of theological truth
> to come into view and impose themselves on our understanding. Theology
> is a positive science in which we think only in accordance with the nature of
> the given.
>
> Thomas F. Torrance
> *Theology in Reconstruction*

Introduction

In this chapter analysis and synthesis of Thomas Torrance's positive
Christological-Trinitarian "theo-logical" expression will be given in a way which
will seek to follow the very movement of thought Torrance is advocating. In
thus reversing or "thinking after" the "economic" movement of God to be
known in the world from the Father, through the Son and in the Holy Spirit, we
will endeavor to move back, as Torrance requires for theological thinking, from
the concrete to the "economic" to the "ontological," or from the Christocentric
and pneumatological back to the *telos*, indeed the *alpha* and *omega*, of a true,
faith-ful and knowing response to God, that is, into knowing participation in the

relations of knowing (or "higher theological" or "scientific") and loving within the Trinity which is, as Torrance asserts, the ultimate "ground and grammar of all theology."

The Christological Center
of Realist Knowledge of God:
A Preparatory Statement

With Barth, Torrance clearly and often asserts that the objective self-revelation of God is Jesus Christ. The Word became flesh to the end that human beings would have real, direct knowledge of God, which is life eternal. Therefore, theological science, in service to that Word, must then be done out of this concrete, objective knowledge of God, jnd necessarily in actual relation to it, in order to bring that knowledge of God to expression in and for God's Kingdom and for ministry in the Church. Now while theological statements are said to be baffling to many, stretching ordinary language within an extraordinary relation and reference, the problem is said to be unavoidable. Yet the objective intention of theological statements is the reconciliation accomplished by God. Theological statements are then said to be statements "in the mode of the Word and Truth of God as it is in Jesus Christ and in accordance with His activity of justification and reconciliation."[1] In Jesus Christ, the Truth of God actively entered human life and history and endured the contradiction of sinners. Before Jesus Christ persons repent of their untruth and are adapted to the Truth of God (cf. Kierkegaard). Human language must responsively and faith-fully express the Truth of God in a God-established relation and do so appropriately, and thereby refer beyond itself to the transcendent, ultimate level in the revelation of God. The truth of theological statement lies only in being derived from and effectively referring to the Reality to which it is the proper response. Therefore, says Torrance, theological expressions arising out of the revelation of God in Christ and by the Spirit are "true" not simply as human statements "about" God, but as "God's statements, as God's communication of His own Truth . . . as they are true from the side of God and correspondingly true from the side of man."[2] They are only "true" because they are rooted in the Mediator, the God-man.

It has been observed how theological science relates reciprocally to the "new science" as post-Einsteinian scientific advances have helped the discipline of theology to become again more faithful to itself as the science of God in Jesus Christ, and thus faithful in reckoning the interconnectedness of the creation-redemption relation of the universe to God and of God to the universe through the Word. For Torrance, then, the center of all theo-logical thinking is the fact that the "Word became flesh and dwelt among us and we beheld his glory, glory as of the only begotten of the Father full of grace and truth" (John 1:14). As developed fully below, the incarnation is absolutely central epistemologically, cosmologically and thus theologically and methodologically for Torrance, and cannot be construed in his thought as some kind of symbolic, subjectivistic representation of human experience of God. Such notions would be considered "pre-scientific."[3] Rather, the issue is realist knowledge of the objectively given "truth," here the Truth of God in Christ. Torrance has found that in every science there arises a structure of tradition and authority which is necessary for advance, clarification and the testing of human understanding toward ever greater objectivity. But these sources and issues are secondary before the actual objective disclosure of the truth or Truth, and thus are relativized by the absolute priority of that Truth. That which must be the scientific conscience of the Church of Christ and its theology directs it in service only to the One with whom it has to do, with the majesty, glory and authority of God who has given himself as Truth within the concrete objectivities of the created universe to be truly known in accord with that Truth. Genuine authorities in the Church, both theological and ecclesiastical, Torrance maintains, are appointed by God to serve and facilitate God's majesty and authority as effective instruments so that the faithful in the Church would be taught in the redemptive understanding of the Truth of God, as well as bringing about greater objectivity and universality.[4] In the Church, and thus in theology, the free, ultimate, sovereign authority of the Supreme Truth of God, God himself, must be exalted over all authorities. This in turn creates freedom in and by the Truth as it establishes the redemptive and actual human knowledge of the Truth of God. As with all truth, but especially here, Torrance emphasizes that obedience is demanded to that Truth of God's self-objectification. All ecclesiastical and theological authority serves as the way of historical mediation of the given Word of God to humanity. Only in that faithfulness and service to the Truth of God, God self-given in Jesus Christ, are secondary authorities to hold our due respect. The theo-logical task in the Church is found by following the rule of authoritative representation exhibited in New Testament teaching regarding the Spirit of Truth who speaks not from himself but speaks only what is heard from another. It is by the Holy Spirit, the Spirit of Truth, the Spirit of Christ, says Torrance, that the Church is directed away from itself to the one Word of God revealed and incarnate in Jesus Christ. All true theological formulation will assent to, think after, penetrate and faith-fully express the one ultimate place of God's self-disclosure in the space-time of human existence, the Word made flesh. Scientifically, Torrance says that this can be done only from Jesus Christ, and by the Holy Spirit, for only there is the revelation given preeminently, as it is the proper Object of theology. There is the Word.

This realist knowledge of God, as freely, sovereignly self-given in the world, is seen to be "analogical" knowledge. God has chosen to disclose himself truly, but it is true disclosure within the space-time contingencies of creation. This must be so, for "God cannot reveal himself to us in any other way than by a comparison with things (as "transparent" to the Truth of God) which we know," that is, in the God-givenness of correspondence or "analogy" of levels "up", the *analogia gratiae* (or *analogia fidei* to follow Barth).[5] In divine interaction with the world it is always grace which defines that relationship. Torrance emphasizes then that the strength of such analogy is not between the world or humanity and God but between the Word, whereby God communicates himself in the world, and the Word which God is from all eternity in himself.[6] Nothing is prior to grace, and the knowledge of God begins not with the world but in the hearing of the Word of God, the Act of God's grace in Jesus Christ by the Holy Spirit. It is the Word of God's grace, specifically the objective fact that God has given himself to and for humanity in the world as Word concretely in Jesus Christ, which is the "given" for the knowledge of God. It is that Word, Jesus Christ, which theological science must serve in order to clarify and follow in faith-ful theo-logical thinking. Torrance states that

> Theological thinking is *theo*-logical, thinking not just from our own centres, but from a centre in God from a divine ground . . . *theo*-nomous thinking . . . the fact that God has made Himself known and continues to make Himself known, that He objectifies Himself for us, so that our knowledge is a fulfilled meeting with objective reality . . . . The given fact is not a mute fact . . . . Here our fact is the living God, the active, willing and loving God, who communicates Himself to us, and it is through His . . . self-disclosure that He gives Himself to us. In other words, the given fact is the Word of God, God giving Himself to us as Word and in Word, God speaking to us in person . . . . In theology (then) we have knowledge of an objective reality in which we hear a Word, encounter a *Logos*, from beyond our subjective experience, a Word which utters itself . . . . speaks for itself . . . . Word to be heard, as Truth to be acknowledged, not just a rationality to be apprehended . . . . In Jesus Christ God has condescended to reveal Himself to us within our creaturely existence and contingency, and has assumed our humanity to meet us as man to man and to make Himself known to us within the conditions and limitations of our earthly life, within our visible, tangible, temporal flesh.[7]

God's self-givenness is to be found in the created humanity of Jesus Christ as the final basis for "analogical" knowledge and relation between God and human beings in the world. God alone can and must establish analogical knowing of himself for only then can one be sure that those human forms of thought and speech, in faith, are actually founded in the Being of God who remains sovereign over all human notions of him (*fides quaerens intellectum*). The utter lordship, personal nature, objectivity and centrality of theology's proper Object of knowledge, the self-objectification of God for humanity, are the basic God-established requirements for the realist knowledge of God and scientific theology. Torrance, like Barth, understands true faith to be a knowing wherein God remains free in being known within his own knowing of the existing person in the context of the dialogical (conversational) relation he has established in his Word. God, who is Person and Word, communicates himself to human beings in the world as the addressing Word in the form of his own personal Being. Therefore, realist, scientific theology is said to be first of all (penultimate) the recognition of the supremacy of Christology (cf. below on the supremacy of the Trinity in and via Christ). In the "twofold objectivity" of God there is, Torrance says, the primary objectivity of God's self-giving as Lord, and the secondary objectivity wherein God gives himself in human form concretely within space-time human existence. Again, for Torrance epistemology follows ontology. Thus God is only known *a posteriori* from the initiating action of God in history, only out of and after God's actual place of revelation. Any *a priori* way which would prescribe how God can or cannot make himself known must be an alien principle and can only distort. The Truth of God itself must prescribe how knowledge of God is to be ordered. Any "systematic" interests must arise from and serve the given objective knowledge of God. The order for the realist knowledge of God, and hence for theology, is therefore in the self-given Object before it is in the mind. It is as one allows the Object, the Word of God, to impose itself and its own transcendent Rationality upon the mind that knowledge of it as it is gains coherence. The knowing which is proper to God is then held to be the knowing of faith, and, in theo-logical knowledge, God, in the way he has taken, is known as he is allowed "to impose Himself upon our minds or as we allow His Word to shape our knowing dn (increasing) conformity to Him."[8] For Torrance, the real knowledge of God and thus the centrality of the "concrete" Word, Jesus Christ, is "all-determinative." It is the norm as well as the focus of human knowing of God in the actual way God has taken and given himself to be known.

In following or thinking after the "inner logic" of God in the incarnation, the faith-knowing relation and theo-logy can then only be true if each process "moves," faith-fully in relation to Jesus Christ, to Christology, in as much as Christocentricity is said to be necessary for any scientific theology. This is because Christ is found to be *the way* whereby God has objectively revealed himself in the world to existing humanity, and according to Torrance, this is also the way in which God continues to reveal himself. It is, he asserts, only through one's actual "sharing in the knowledge" of the Son by the Father and that of the Father by the Son that God in Christ by the Spirit can be known "as He has given Himself to us in Jesus Christ."[9] As Torrance's way of theo-logical thinking is (as a modified Barthian) Christo-logical or Christocentric, then for him the organic unity of theology moves back "up" the way of God by the epistemological effecting of the Spirit to Christ and in Christ to the Father and the unity of the triune Godhead. This he believes is the only way true theology can take. Theology cannot, as "scientific," try to seek the knowledge of God in a way separated from the proper object. It cannot choose a way of thought apart from Jesus Christ. Torrance finds then that scientifically it is necessary for theology to think after or to move, so to speak, from the observable or concrete, and to set all things and to show all things in relation to the preeminent revelation of God's active relatedness to the world in Jesus Christ, the place of the Word of God in the world.

Thus realist knowledge of God occurs only in the way specified by the actual disclosure of faith-knowing's proper Object, which is then the proper Object of faith-ful theo-logic in following God's movement back to the ultimate "Source." God had no need to "break through" to that which he had made and would recreate by the Word. Contra Bultmann, Creation as well as Incarnation-Redemption are said to show clearly that God is not alien to the space-time universe, but rather that the world is "open up" to and ever dependent upon God's active relatedness to and in the world. God is known under his own sheer objectivity as actively impressed on human thought. Torrance's explanation of this essential framework of theological knowledge is helpful.

> We begin with the Grace of Jesus Christ—that is, with the condescension of the Truth of God to become incarnate and freely to give Himself to us. The whole movement of the Truth of God from beginning to end is one of pure Grace even in our knowing of the Truth. This means that we must acknowledge the unconditional priority of the Truth and the irreversibility of the relation He establishes with us . . . "the Word became flesh" cannot be reversed as "the flesh became the Word" without falsification. The action of the Truth belongs to its nature as the Truth and can be truly known only in accordance with that action. When God gives Himself as the Object of our knowledge (of Him) He does not thereby cease to be Subject or hand over the control in that knowledge to the human knower—He remains throughout the Lord.[10]

The lordship of the rational Object in and over knowledge of it is necessarily foremost for Torrance. The knowledge, and thus the real knowability of God, results only from the disclosive Act of God who as Word is Lord over true knowledge of himself. As given and founded for us christologically, knowledge of God is predicated only of God in his freedom and unconditional priority. It is from that concrete place which is Jesus Christ that God's own interior logic must be thought after.

Torrance's central concern with the realist knowledge of God, then, is with the unitariness of God's lordly and sovereign interactive relatedness with the world and humanity as Creator and especially Redeemer. Contrary to "dualist" theologies (e.g., Schleiermacher and Bultmann), Torrance's concrete starting point is seen to reflect the necessity of a truly adequate theological and cosmological basis by which to think out of the Creator-creation-human being (or "God-world-man") relationship wherein God is God and thus "ontologically and maximally free to interact with his people."[11]   For Torrance's understanding, everything is founded upon God's will and initiative.   The possibility of human knowledge of God is based upon God's freedom to personally "cross" the "boundary" or difference between himself and existing persons in frail space-time existence.   Schleiermacher and Bultmann are said to have conceptually distorted and finally broken the inherent oneness of God the Giver and the self-revelatory Gift of God's Word.   God's relation to the world, must be understood in a way which facilitates personal encounter with God in his actual "Being and Act, Act and Being" in the world.   The incarnation is that ultimate basis for such encounter, given the nature and relation of the Word and humanity in Christ.   This is not an existential projection of the "divine" out of the self, but real knowing as "learning" that which is radically new to the knowing subject.   The realist knowledge of God, this ultimately Trinitarian knowing (cf. below), is knowledge of One who "freely acts upon us and addresses us in his Word."   In his Word, Torrance says that God is declaring himself to us through an articulate mode of communication.   Therefore this "discovery" of theo-logical science occurs only by God's own initiative out of God in an "articulate" and "intelligible" form which is "information-laden" and without need of decoding.   As such God's self-giving is not less than "word" but infinitely more.   God has concretely communicated not merely something *about* himself but *himself* actually, rationally and thus as knowable in the world. The knowledge of God and theological inquiry is then not only discovery, but above all it is the direct result of God's self-revelation.   It occurs by God's articulate and intelligible communication mediated in the world to persons through those very created objectivities and intelligibilities, and thus in modes of human thought and speech.   But it is God who addresses the world "from the ultimate ground and under the creative control of his transcendent Objectivity and Intelligibility"[12]   Only from the fact that God in his Word has freely objectified himself and caused his divine Objectivity to impress upon and interpenetrate created objectivity is there objective knowledge of God.

    Scientifically, then, Torrance asserts that the true question regarding knowledge of God cannot be the *a priori* abstract one, i.e., can God reveal? or can persons know?   Proper questions are only from the actuality (*a posteriori*), that is, how does God give himself to be known?   where does God reveal himself?   how does the human subject actually receive and know what has been given to be known?   Torrance emphasizes that God has condescended to reveal himself within existence, assuming real humanity to meet persons in order to reconcile humanity to himself, thereby overcoming all alienation from within existence.   But further, Torrance finds that God has also condescended "to provide from the side of man and from within man, full, adequate and perfect reception of that Truth."[13]   At once and at one place God's self-objectification and our humanity has been adapted and conformed to that revelation, Word spoken and Word heard, received, understood and faithfully actualized (cf. below).

Like the theology of the Nicene fathers and the Reformers, theology now which knows its proper Object must be a process to scientifically think after the redemptive movement of God. Any other way is said to lose Christ and to turn theology into anthropology, as observed previously (cf. Schleiermacher and Bultmann). Torrance clarifies his point doctrinally in a way which applies in every doctrinal area according to his formulation. If the "atonement" of Christ is narrowly conceived in human thought as merely and only what Christ "did" in his death upon the cross, while the incarnation and incarnate life of Christ are handled either symbolically or as simply prelude to the atonement, then the Person of Christ is lost in favor of the functional Christ, and in that way also true theology is lost. Proper Christology, for Torrance, is concerned rather with the nature and person of the Son, not simply with function. When atonement is not understood as grounded ontologically in the Person of Christ, and therefore in God, it then becomes a theology of events (*Ereignistheologie*). "Saving benefits" are then detached from Christ's Being and reduced into timeless events with no essential relation to history. But when the *kerygma* of salvific events is detached from history, the human subject is cast back upon its own subjectivity and the truth of God is cut away and lost.[14] Like the "new science," the true knowledge of God and then true speaking of God means that theology must again come to and move through and beyond the phenomenal surface into the ontological substructure of the Truth of God, the interior logic and movement of the Word of God. As with Kierkegaard, Torrance maintains vehemently that theology as theology sees that man there, that one, the teacher who is the God, who is the Truth, who can in himself put one in the Truth.[15]

If theology is concerned with the Truth of God and Truth as personal Being, and this is certainly so for Torrance, then this is Truth which has taken active life and being in the midst of human existence and is revealed in Jesus Christ.[16] Torrance sees that the Truth of God is demonstrated out of the Truth itself, and the only way for human beings to "prove" the ultimate Truth of God then is to let him be what he is before them. He is the "Truth who will not be mastered and yet will not remain closed to us, Truth who unveils himself for us and who is known only through Word and Grace on God's part and faith . . . on our part."[17]   Only therein are existing human beings released from themselves and made free and open for God.[18]

As a result, Torrance's conclusion follows that all human theo-logical statements referring to the Truth will have validity only by derivation from and correspondence to the actual revelation of God, in his Grace and reconciliation. Theological knowledge is also concerned with critical realist knowledge of objective reality known out of itself in its own inner *ratio* and according to its own mode of being. But, as scientific, theological knowledge is, above all and particularly, concerned with its own specific mode of rational activity in accordance with the actual nature of the given Reality. Out of Christ, this specific God-established mode of rational activity between inquiring human beings and the Truth of God is, again faith, which he defines along Barthian lines as "the theological reason in which our knowing is adapted to the manifold nature of the incarnate Truth as divine, personal, human, historical."[19] Faith is not meant to be an ecstatic activity or some kind of "leap" in the popular or existentialist sense. It is not one's standing outside of rational activity, but rather it is in faith that human knowing attains to inner conformity to the Truth of God in Christ, given in the Church, wherein the real knowledge of God in Jesus Christ, in direct address, is the proper center.[20]

Theological knowledge arises within a certain God-prescribed sphere where the Truth of God's self-disclosure in its historical manifestness is personally and historically received and communicated. In actual knowing (faith) relation, theological thinking is unconditionally bound to its proper Object, and in that relation it is to think in orderly correspondence with his actual nature.[21] The divine Object of theology, the incarnate Word, says Torrance, does and must have earthly, human and historical objectivity, and as a result faith-ful theological expression must share that kind of objectivity. The concern then is not with divine Truth and human truth, but with the "divine-human Truth of the Mediator, with that which is utterly unique (*deus non est in genere*).[22]

Thus Christ and Christocentric thinking are for Torrance the one place and the one way for theology to "hear" God's speaking himself, his Word, in the Spirit. In accord with that Word theology must obediently follow, think after and faith-fully speak in accord with God's Truth in order to serve the Word and effect further clarification by such responsive "disclosure models." It is the unfolding of Torrance's "disclosure model" level by level from Christ the Word that we must synthesize and analyze below.

Theological Realism and the Hebraic-Patristic-Reformational Pattern

While Torrance sees that "dualism" has variously tempted and plagued the Church and its theological calling from its earliest days, especially in its Platonic and neo-Platonic forms, Torrance emphasizes that the Augustinian "style" or form of dualism is that which again and again has distorted the Church's thinking about the "God-world-man, God-man-world" interactive relationship in creation and redemption by the Word of God. Such thinking perceives God as somehow unable to directly relate to the world, unable to create reality independent of himself, unable to act personally and objectively in the world, and as only abstractly related to it. As such, God was perceived to be cut off from objective relation and disclosure in the way of realist knowledge. Torrance's "Hebraic" emphasis is used to counter the Hellenic (the "Hebraic" often used in the sense of "Scriptural"),[23] coupled with his firm belief in the restoration of the Hebraic world-view in the Nicene Fathers. Torrance's Christological starting point is intended to use and exemplify this "unitary, non-dualistic understanding of the universe."[24] This "unitary", non-dualistic, non-monistic, or Hebraic-Patristic understanding of God's interactive, Lordly relatedness to the world and humanity, as centered ultimately in Jesus Christ, the creative and redemptive Word, must be recognized for all of its importance in Torrance's constructive thinking and theological concern.

In seeking to reflect and illustrate theo-logically the modern scientific recovery of a more integrated, unitary way of thinking or approaching the universe, Torrance speaks "anthropomorphically" (and quite ambiguously) regarding the history of the knowing relation between God and Israel, of God's desiring to make himself known to mankind. Thus one small race from all humanity was chosen, he says, and subjected by God "to intensive interaction and dialogue with himself in such a way that he might mould and shape this people in the service of his self-revelation."[25] God subjected Israel to his will personally as a father would impart distinctive characteristics to his children. In this way, God founded a covenanted kinship with Israel whereby he might imprint himself upon the generations of the nation so that it would become an instrument of his self-revelatory purpose. In Israel God established appropriate forms of understanding, worship and expression for all nations, so that the knowledge of God would "take root" in humanity. Therein a two-way movement was involved as divine revelation was adapted to the human mind, and the articulate forms of human understanding and language were adapted to divine revelation by the penetration of the Word of God into the depths of Israel's being in a way that took human shape and called for human response which was so locked to the Word that it was used as the means of further address on the part of the Word to Israel.[26]

This "ever-deepening spiral movement of God's self-revelation to Israel" Torrance describes as "painful," as the Scriptures, "the product of that process show clearly." Israel was on the "wheel of divine Providence" and made useable within the movement of God's intimate self-giving. This covenant bonding, Torrance asserts, meant that Israel would be used by God in the mediation of divine reconciliation. Through this long historico-religious encounter with the living God in Israel's entire integration of culture, religion, literature and life, this people was prepared as the "matrix" for the "Word made flesh."

> . . . And at last in the fullness of time the Word of God became man in Jesus
> . . . within the embrace of Israel's faith and worship and expectation, himself
> God and man, in whom the covenanted relationship between God and Israel
> and through Israel with all humanity was gathered up . . . . In him the
> revealing of God and the understanding of man fully coincided, the whole

Word of God and the perfect response of man were indivisibly united in one Person, the Mediator . . . . Thus as both the incarnate revelation of God and the embodied knowledge of God, Jesus Christ constitutes in himself the Way, the Truth and the Life through whom alone access to God the Father is freely open for all . . . for it is only throuhh the assimilation of our minds to the Mind of God incarnate in Christ that we are given the modes of discernment, forms . . . understanding which we need in order to grasp and articulate knowledge of God in a way worthy of him.[27]

The penetrating Word established the covenant bond in Israel and made the way for that final revelation at "the fullness of time" in Jesus. In this way the Word founded the "community of reciprocity," Israel and then the Church, to mediate God's disclosure. God's relatedness to creation in covenant bond in Jesus Christ is said to have fully and finally cut away dualist bases and ways of thinking of the world and God's relation and revelation to it. From actual meeting with the self-revelation of God, says Torrance, the resulting community of reciprocity was impressed with the concrete historicity and locality of the divine Word. This encounter, as finalized in Jesus Christ, formed in itself the proper way for human thinking as "unitary, non-dualist" and thus a new "unitary outlook on God and the universe" wherein persons can know God out of himself.[28]

It was briefly observed how this Hebraic/Scriptural way of "unitary, integrationist thinking" is said to have been restored by the Nicene Fathers and developed by Athanasius. Torrance believes they recovered the Hebraic or biblical, unitary world-view and God-world perspective out of and from (a posteriori) God's actual, historical revelation of himself in Jesus Christ, in contrast to the dualism of the time.[29] To apprehend this in full measure, Torrance maintains that the Church had to bring conceptual integration to the complementary meanings of the Jewish doctrine of creation ex nihilo with the patristic formulation of the incarnation. The Jewish doctrine of creation establishes that the Creator Word did not call the world into being out of any primordial substance, thereby granting to the cosmos a unique, contingent identity distinct from that of God himself. Then the incarnation doctrine of the Fathers first grounds the intensity and extent of the interrelatedness possible between God-world-humanity, and also clarifies the impossibilities within such a relation. Neither reality is lost in nor estranged from the other. This establishes a "field" not only of relationship but of knowing.[30]

Incarnation of the Word has then demonstrated and upheld each reality in its own "dignity," integrity, nature and proper intelligibility, but also, and fundamentally, each has been upheld in relation to the other. Creation ex nihilo and Incarnation-Redemption as God's Act pro nobis must be thought theologically together, Torrance says, for only then can the actual God-established distinction between himself and the world and the freedom God has to personally, actively interrelate with the world and humanity be held together without contradiction. Therefore it may be said that for Torrance creation and incarnation are foundational to the actuality of the real knowledge of God.

Again, Torrance is convinced that, like the patristic paradigm (which is said to have followed the Hebraic), the paradigm of the Reformation sought to restore and reappropriate the "inner logic" of the historic doctrines of the faith. The maintenance of largely proper modes of rationality in the Reformation was then possible, he says, because the Reformers too wanted to reestablish Christian thinking on the ontological difference between divine and creaturely realities which had again become confused. The Reformers are said to have moved from primarily ontic to primarily dynamic modes of thought, as evidenced in their emphasis upon the actual interaction of the living God with the world and human beings in space and time. A prominent example of this, Torrance says, was the Reformers' re-statement of the doctrine of the Fathers in identifying God's grace with the person of Christ, and the gift of his grace with God's own self-giving Act in the world.[31]

In line with his interpretation of the Fathers and the Reformers (especially Calvin), Torrance also views his own task as that of maintaining the crucial distinction between the Being of God and creation while also supporting and clarifying the reality of God's objective, personal, self-disclosive Act in his Being in ontic and ontological balance and complementarity, so as to serve the space-time knowledge of God. All of Torrance's positive theological expression is grounded in and for these. In so perceiving God and the world in this relation of unitariness or duality (or even "proper dualism" as opposed to a "radical" one[32]) the Reformers too are then seen to have concluded that the contingent world was made to tell its own story, and that likewise God's rationality, the Truth or Word of God, is only known or apprehensible from the side of God as he has disclosed himself to be known in accordance with his actual nature in Jesus Christ and by his Spirit. This explains Torrance's strong Barthian opposition to notions of a "sacramental universe" or to natural theology in the "Thomistic" or "scholastic" sense. Such inherent correspondence would leave God incomplete without the world and at best allows for a kind of synergism. Confident that he follows the Reformers here, Torrance's commitment to the "Godness of God" and to the "naturalness of (contingent) nature" means no "intrinsic" connection with or participation of creation in divinity at any level within the created order.[33] The Reformers, he says, asserted rightly that God is God and can be known only out of God by the grace of God.

Theological Realism and Covenanted Correspondence

Following what he sees as the Patristic (Being-Act) and the Reformational (Act-Being) paradigms of the self-givenness of God in the world in Jesus Christ,

Torrance makes his case for God's real interactive, interrelational involvement in the world which from God, while distinct, is yet capable of real relation to God as the direct result of God's Word, and not from necessity or some *a priori*, self-contained capacity. Thus, while Torrance will often use the terminology of early dialectical theology, e.g., God's "breaking through," he does not mean "intrusion." Out of creation and incarnation he finds that there can be no dualistic or natural barrier in creation which would hinder God's direct relation or action. But the world and its structure is also said to have no intrinsic capacity for conveying God's Word. This simply is in keeping with the way God made the world. Stamps correctly describes Torrance's consistent position saying

> God may come to man *through* nature but never *by* it. His relation with the world, particularly in his act of revelation, is not an unnatural one, i.e., not an act out of character with either his own nature or the nature of the created order. His way to man in the world is in harmony with his relationship to created reality generally. He comes to man and speaks to him only out of his eternal Word. His way and his Word are purely his own, not that of the world. Regardless of how closely God is involved with the created instrument in the revelatory act, the created element as such (i.e., the finite or human) never becomes substantially part of the content of revelation. The created intelligibility is God's servant, never his consort. God's revelation is wholly self-revelation.[34]

Making use of the Reformed doctrine of "the Covenant of Grace," Torrance refers to "covenant" or created correspondence as emphasizing that God's relations with the world are not based upon some "imagined" inherent relation of likeness (cf. *analogia entis*), but upon the free decision of God's Grace to be so related to the world. Consequently, in the "reciprocal" or, in faith and theology, "dialogical" relation between Creator and creation, that relation does not begin with the world. God in his self-giving is the sole initiator, and the relation is neither reversible nor can the created element of that relation account for its own part in the relation. The relationship must be interpreted from God's action therein.[35] Torrance's point here is this "asymmetrical" (emphasizing the Lordship of God in the relation) God-world relatedness.

At the center of Torrance's understanding and theo-logical formulation of the God-human knowing relation in the world is God's intention to redeem human beings and the world from its estrangement in fallenness back to himself and to completed relatedness, and thus completed knowing. The world is meant to redemptively serve God's covenant purposes for humanity as the divinely founded place of his self-revelation.[36] The heart of the issue for Torrance is just that God's covenant with humanity in and with the world has been fulfilled in the very particular and historical objectivity of Jesus Christ. The objective, intelligible contingent creation serves the Word of God, pointing toward God's own divine-humanity whereby God has formally disclosed himself.

> The object of theological knowledge is creaturely objectivity bound to divine
> objectivity, not just creaturely objectivity in general but that specific
> creaturely objectivity which the divine objectivity has assumed, adapted and
> bound to Himself, Jesus. Thus theological activity is concerned with that
> special creaturely objectivity in its relation to divine objectivity, and therefore
> with that creaturely objectivity as it is given ultimate objectivity over against
> all other objectivity within the created universe (viz. with the "creaturely
> objectivity of God in the Incarnation of His Word in Christ"). Thus the
> supremacy of Christology for theology.[37]

As will be shown in yet more factual, epistemological and theo-logical detail,
"the way of God" into and for the world and "the place" of the redemptive
knowing relation of God in himself is in and from the Incarnate Son by the
enablement of the Holy Spirit.

The "Logic of God" in Christ
and Torrance's Realist Theology

Robert J. Palma has rightly said that Torrance's theology is not only a
Reformed and Christocentric theology, in developmental line from Calvin
through Barth, but also a Trinitarian theology, a unitary theology, a realist
theology, a rationalist theology and, in a unique way, a natural theology.[38]
Such a characterization is almost complete. C. Baxter Kruger properly adds a
"Pneumatic" theology, and one could rightly add even "eschatological" theology
because of the crucial epistemological role of the Holy Spirit in the disclosive
"economy" of God in the world and the *telos* of that redemptive relation and the
nature of participation in it.[39]   Kruger wants Torrance's theology to be
understood as having a three-fold structure reflecting that which stands behind
the fulfillment of the redemptive purposes of God in Christ, the ontological, that
is, the Trinitarian and Christocentric (Word) elements, and the economic aspects
of the human subject's sharing in Jesus Christ (cf. below). Yet each of these
interpreters tends to flatten out Torrance's clear and emphatic beginning place
which, whether in the world or in the eternal Being of God, is never set aside.
This is because of Torrance's desire for unitary thinking into and after the actual
self-revelation of God. One must begin from and ever work as fixed upon and
within the Word of God, Jesus Christ, if one is to follow Torrance's own
emphasis, and only within that place is the integrated "co-inherence" of these
other crucial elements in the knowledge of God in the world to be reckoned.
Torrance is then first and always Christocentric in the heart of theology and
theological method, and therein ultimately Trinitarian. Everything theologically,

epistemologically, soteriologically, doxologically, and methodologically falls out
from the "dictation" of the Word made flesh. The absolute cruciality of the
Christ-established mediation of God and humanity from the "side of God" in
Torrance's theology is reflected in his statement that "the vicarious humanity of
Jesus Christ" is the cutting edge of his theology.[40] For Torrance all begins
with the historical facticity of God's Word in Jesus Christ who is thereby the
Mediator between God and humanity. Everything rises or falls from the reality
of such historicity. In this way, that is, in his incarnate Person, Jesus Christ
actively "holds together" both sides. This is the divinely given and appointed
way in which persons are called to share freely through the Holy Spirit. Jesus
Christ is

> . . . the place (*topos*) where God and man meet, where God stoops down to
> man and man draws near to God, the one place where we have access to the
> Father in the Spirit, the new and living way consecrated in the flesh of
> Christ. As such he is the one Mediator between God and man and man and
> God, the Apostle from God to man and the High Priest of man before God,
> who in and through his divine-human constitution as the incarnate Son
> mediates the Word of God to man and the word of man to God, and ministers
> the immeasurable love of God to man and the answering love of man to
> God.[41]

Torrance's Christology is meant to be neither a Christology "from below" nor
a Christology "from above." It is Christology, and thereby theology, from the
specific historical place and person, the God-man, by whom God has disclosed
himself to be known by existing persons as he is in "cognitive" union with
Christ. Jesus Christ is both human salvation and the human knowledge of God,
in Torrance's understanding.

But the knowledge of God in Christ by the Spirit unto real knowing and
redemptive participation is not only the constant center, the Object of the faith
knowing-relation, but the ever present and God-given entrance into personal
knowing communion with the Trinity, which is the basis of all theology. The
encompassing movement of God, whereby human redemption is effected, is
from the ontological (Trinity) to the economic-ontic (from the Father through the
Son, Jesus Christ, incarnate Word, and by the Spirit), and then in human
knowing back "up" to the ontological (human communion with God in God's
own Being). This is a retrogressive movement of human thought back to God
which is held to be a movement occurring in and from the person of Jesus
Christ. Jesus Christ is the center and, to put it in Torrance's terms for scientific
theology, the critical axiom of all of his thinking out of and after the Truth of
God. By actually knowing God as he is in the incarnate Christ, Torrance
understands that one meets, knows, and participates in the inner "logic" of
God's coming, a logic which can be followed into the blessed communion of the

Trinity. Torrance then wants the incarnation to decidedly affect his doctrine of God and vice versa.[42]   The incarnation as the "logic" of God's self-objectification and the "logic" of Torrance's theology therefore includes in its movement not only the relation of Father and Son and Spirit economically and ontologically (cf. the *homoousion* doctrine) but necessarily the Son's relation to humanity in the Spirit as incarnated Word/Son, as revealer of God within existing humanity, as Savior and Lord.   Thus Torrance's theology as a whole, along with his central concern for the restoration and theo-logical expression of the realist knowledge of God in Christ, is largely the outworking of the meaning and consequent implications of the "inner logic" of the incarnation, the consubstantiality and the hypostatic union of the Son of the Father with existing humanity. Herein Torrance sees the "logic" of God in the context of the space-time covenant relation of God and humanity, founded with Israel, culminating in the Person of Jesus Christ, the God-man. The Lord Jesus Christ is the actual instantiation of the Logic (*Logos*) of God, the "logic" of Grace, which is said to be the formative factor of all true theology.

> We . . . seek . . . to discern the pattern inhering in its material content, or to let it reveal itself to us as we direct our questions toward it to find out its central frame of reference. When we do that we are directed to Jesus Christ, to the Incarnation, to the hypostatic union, the unique togetherness of God and man in Christ which is normative for every other relationship between man and God . . . . It is the whole life of the incarnate Son, the historical, crucified and risen Jesus Christ that forms the core or the axis of the body of Christian theology. It is from that centre that we take our bearings as we consider the doctrine of the Trinity, of the Father and of the Holy Spirit as well as of the Son, and therefore of creation as well as of redemption . . . all have their place and their truthfulness by reference to this central point in (the incarnate) Jesus Christ . . . . It is here then in the inner life and being of Jesus Christ, in the hypostatic union, that we discern the interior logic of theological thinking, the logic of Christ.[43]

The union of God and man in Jesus Christ is then the critical point in Torrance's doctrine of God. Jesus Christ, as God-man, founds the entire hermeneutical setting for theology as this God-man union in Christ is bound finally with the inner Communion of the Trinity—but only through God's free, covenantal relations in the world. As Torrance has sought to "think after" the knowledge of God and the "logic" of Grace in Jesus Christ back to the ontological Trinity, it is necessary here to "think after" and uncover Torrance's own theological expression and to understand yet more fully the heart of his Christological (incarnational)-Trinitarian theology level by level "up" as the "faithful" outcome of the realist knowledge of the sovereign God who is free for and in the world in his Acts of Creation and Redemption.

The Freedom of God and Torrance's Realist Theology

God is to be known as he is only out of himself as freely self-given, while he yet remains Lord over that knowing relation and over knowledge of himself. How, where, or under what conditions, or to what extent God is to be revealed are not issues which one can establish *a priori*, but only, again, *a posteriori*, that is, not from the possibility but the actuality, because actuality establishes possibility. God, Torrance says, is free of all strictures humanity would place in the way of thinking theo-logically, but false human thinking can obstruct human knowledge of God. In the process of restoring thought of God again to its scientific moorings, Torrance repeatedly points out that first of all God, by his Word incarnate in Jesus Christ, has shown himself to be free and free for self-giving, free to be known as he is in himself, free for and in the world.

The "Object" of theological knowledge is the living, acting God; it is God in his action or movement to the world and human beings in the world. In this way, Torrance wants to emphasize God's loving freedom to act and in act. God is free and free "for us." Thus he finds that God's objectifying of himself never stops being his self-giving action, and the knowledge of God in Christ by the Spirit in the world is correspondingly a knowledge in responsive faith which is spontaneous, free and active—analogous to the freedom of God in his revelation. Torrance understands that freedom is to be known and understood Christologically, for, in Jesus, God has freely "stooped" or deigned to reveal himself within the contingencies of creaturely existence, within humanity, thereby meeting persons personally within the subject-object relations. So again, the possibility of human knowledge of God is not a human possibility as such, but is grounded in "his divine freedom and grace to cross the boundary between Himself and us . . . in making Himself the object of our knowledge He confronts us as the one true God who is before all but who as transcendent Saviour stoops down in boundless freedom and grace to lift us up to Himself."[44] God's transcendent freedom is such that he is free to condescend himself for humanity in order to accomplish in and of himself human reconciliation from within. But again, the knowability of God is not reversible but is totally of Grace in Jesus Christ and thus strictly speaking can only be predicated of God in his divine freedom. Only on the prior ground of the actual historical divine Grace and the reflexive self-giving of the Truth in Grace may the "knowability" of God then be predicated of human subjects in faith relation to God. In this way, Torrance reinforces the historicity of the self-disclosure of God which cannot be anticipated or made over into timeless "events" or statements (e.g., Bultmann). The knowledge of God, and thus theology, as it follows that inner logic of Grace back to the Logic of and in God, can only stand by submission to the majesty and freedom of God in his Word.[45] Hence, for Torrance, actual knowledge of God, and then theological science, is both free and un-free. Theology is not free to create idols of the mind out of human subjectivity thereby denying the freely given Truth of God. But theology is free from the bondage of false, dualistic thinking which engenders such entrapment and occurs when there is detachment from God's objectivity. The Truth of God is found in the one who, in one's relation to him, sets one free.

In light of God's freedom, the knowledge of God is, again, an act of "sheer discovery" which follows the historic actuality of Grace.[46] There was no deterministic frame in the Act of God. In and from creation and redemption (incarnation), God is said to be factually known to be open and free for the world by his Word. And that is so wholly from the free, sovereign decision and contingent act of God's Love in unconditional Grace. God's "election" flows without constraint from his ultimate purpose or reason in his constant Love, and it is not conditioned by some necessity in God whether that of being, knowledge or will. It is motivated or restrained by nothing beyond God. In God's elective, decisive freedom there is said to be nothing less than the Love of God in its sheer mystery, the Love that God himself is in his action.[47] The freedom of God is only known out of actual relation between the uncreated Rationality of God and the created rationality of the world in Christ, and hence too the mystery of the divine "reasons."

But God's elective freedom and openness for the world as the not-the-world Other has, of course, its clearest manifestation in the incarnation as understood in the context of God's freedom, that is, as his free self-projection into creaturely existence and the embodiment of his Love in an utterly unique way in Jesus Christ. Jesus reveals God's freedom to be, as transcendent Lord, active and present for us, and not dualistically held away from us in some noumenal realm or to some deistic paradoxical relation. The incarnation is the eternal decision of God in his Love not to be unto himself, so to speak, but to freely give himself in unrestricted Love in the world which he has freely made.[48] God's freedom to be open to and for humanity, freedom for historicity, is his self-objectification or projection which is found to be the very antithesis of all mythology.

The Self-Objectification of God and Torrance's Realist Theology

The "specific" freedom of God with which Torrance is concerned is the freedom of God toward the world and humanity in creation and redemption as centered epistemologically, and therefore theologically and methodologically, in the Incarnation of the Word or Son of God. In Christ, God has manifested freely his active relatedness in the world in objectifying himself here in order to be known.

Remembering that Torrance emphasizes the primacy of the proper object in all sciences, then in the realist knowledge of God, God must be self-revealed and known out of that revelation. In his encounter with persons in the world, God is understood as ever retaining his own majesty and objectivity, even in personal relation. God is understood as ever Lord over all knowing of him and against every attempt on our part to make God "submissive" to this or that form of human subjectivity. But in Torrance's understanding and formulation of the absolute primacy of the divine Object who freely objectifies himself as divine Subject, God thereby inverts the subject-object relation in that very retention of lordly control of human knowing in the faith relation. The way of God is God's Truth, which is his Person turning to mankind and freely condescending in Love to become one with humanity. God does not have to be the object of human knowledge, but he has freely or of pure Grace made himself to be Object for persons in order that they may know and think after the Truth of God, and there share in the Life of God.[49] God in sheer Grace gives himself and establishes existing persons in knowing fellowship with the Ultimate Truth from beyond the human, the conditional and the determinate. This means for Torrance, as it did for Kierkegaard, that the Truth cannot be found "within" the self for we are not in the Truth but in untruth. But in his self-objectification God has entered into existence and human life from "outside," from the point of transcendence as Creator and Redeemer of the not-God other (cf. Kierkegaard's "teacher") .

God is said to objectify himself freely, to give as he wills and even to withdraw, but then, in his self-objectification, God cannot be put, so to speak, to the test because he is ever Subject, ever himself. But Torrance also contends that in objectifying himself God gives himself to be known as personal Subject, the one Lordly Subject who "approaches us and assumes us into personal relation with Him as subjects over against His own divine majestic Subjectivity."[50] This reminds us that in emphasizing the objectivity of the Word of God and realist knowledge of God as assent and conformity of thought to divine disclosure, that the human cognitive relation to God's self-objectification is said to be dynamic and unceasingly "dialogical." Indeed, this "dialogicality" is the call to do theology responsively and openly out of the self-given Word. Torrance regularly refers to his theology as "dialogical" in vigorous, conscious opposition to dialectical and existentialist theology. Under the impress of the Word, the human subject as knower is also called to responsively "speak" and to inquire after and formulate theological expression in accordance with the nature of the Object. This is the very nature of the faith-understanding process for Torrance.[51]

All genuine knowledge of God arises from its concrete occurrence. The God who has objectified himself to be known in relation is "speaking Subject," says Torrance, the Word of God in and through creaturely (space-time) objectivities. These are the media or "bearers" of all rational communication and relationship. Unlike a stone though, God freely, personally and graciously utters himself rationally to the understanding of contingent persons whom he has made to know him, but who as Word yet ever distinguishes himself from the creaturely media and from the human knowing of him. Torrance finds that one so confronted with the self-objectification of God's Word can, by faith, increasingly grasp as well the aforementioned "Logic of God."[52]

Again it is important to recall the openness of God for the world and humanity and the world's openness to God as God's creation for the Creator in asymmetrical interactive relatedness.   Herein God addresses persons with himself and does so not with the impersonal number-rationality of creation, though Torrance affirms that this is a rationality grounded contingently in the transcendent *Logos* or Rationality of God.   But above all his address is to persons personally and articulately in the form of divine communication, the eternal Word, within the contingent and creaturely realm.   Only in this way could God address human beings as such.   But again this *Logos* is not alien to the world.   In the context of created rationality, the uncreated Rationality of God, the Word, has come unto its own (John 1: 1, 10-12, 14), while simultaneously entering into that which is creaturely and different.   This difference in relation is not left unthought, given the self-objectification of God's Word in the world.

> He encounters us as one whose Word and whose Act belong to the self-subsistence of his person. What he speaks takes place of itself, for it is filled with the power of his Person, the power by which he is what he is and by which he lives his own personal Life in absolute self-sufficiency and freedom. His power to act is none other than the power of his Person or the power of his Word. He is in Person identical with his Word, and his Word is itself his Act. However, when the (self-objectified) Word of God condescended to participate in created existence in order to become Word to man, personally addressing him in the medium of human speech and physical event in space and time, he entered into the divided and finite condition of word, person and act and into the duality of number and word, that characterized created reality.[53]

God's free self-objectification establishes the very relation demanded for the reciprocity, dialogue or responsiveness found in that revelation. Sin engendered difference is also overcome in the context of created and then re-created relatedness grounded in this free, gracious decision of God. God's objective self-disclosure requires intuitive and discursive thought on our part, while God yet remains free of controlling human scrutiny. As in all genuine knowledge, the proper object directs how it is known and the method of expression, and in the faith-relation the knowledge of God requires true repentant thinking, prayerfulness and worship. God has disclosed himself as Person and his self-objectification is personal Word inhering in God (*homoousion*) to which faith is in direct intuitive and dialogical relation. Thus, like Martin Buber, Torrance emphasizes that true objectivity requires personal communion or dialogical relation with God, while the human subject must reject the temptation to take to the self a dominant or creative role which would falsely replace the objective encounter with self-encounter. This Word of God's objective self-giving can never be bounded by those human words which arise in responsive expression, therefore theological conceptions resulting from the coming and encountering Word must remain "open up" or transparent for the objective Word which is itself the Truth of God. In the self-giving movement of God in Jesus Christ, God acts toward his *telos* in his creative-redemptive purposes.[54]

Upon these bases we will now follow Torrance's own theo-logical "movement" as he "thinks after" the way God has taken toward us from the concrete level of his self-disclosure in Jesus Christ.

Incarnation and Torrance's Realist Theology

> Clearly, for the eternal Word of God to become understandable and
> communicable in the mode and character of word to man he had to share to
> the full in the space-time distinctions of human existence in this world . . . .
> This is not to say, of course, that he ceased to be the (transcendent) Word of
> God he is in the Creator . . . he appropriated human form within the frame
> of earthly life and action and speech . . . . In Jesus Christ the Word has
> become physical event in space-time, meets us in the indissoluble connection
> of physical and spiritual existence, and is to be understood within the
> coordinate levels of created rationality.[55]

Introduction. In his unique objectivity, God is said to open himself to the world and humanity in the world by informing us of himself in a way that no created being can. Here Torrance recognizes and even emphasizes that God maintains the infinite mystery of his uncreated Being behind a "veil of ineffability," yet God also is said to objectively unveil himself to contingent beings in the world as "the transcendent Source and sustaining Ground of all created being and created intelligibility, and therefore of all our knowing of him as well as of the universe he has made."[56] As divine Object-being over against the world, he who is unveiled and made known as he who is yet ever Subject-being, God interacts personally, actively and intelligibly with the created order. God's relatedness to and for the world in his self-objectification in it for realist human knowledge of himself means that we are graciously allowed to share in God's own knowledge of himself. This "ellipse of knowing," as we have seen Torrance term it, is said to be established only within this sphere of created interactive relation.

> . . . God's uncreated Intelligibility and our creaturely intelligibility, God's
> self-witness and our human understanding, are correlated so that there arises
> among us within the conditions of our earthly and temporal existence
> authentic knowledge of God in which God's self-revealing is met by human

acknowledgment and reception, and in such a way that our knowing of him, however inadequate, is made to repose ultimately (level by level, or economically to the ontological) on the free creative ground of God's own Subject-being.[57]

Torrance is firm then that God has condescended to be known as he is in himself. This is knowledge of the eternal, transcendent God in the midst of the creaturely intelligibilities of the world. Nothing is known of God but that which comes by his active self-disclosure. No faithful inquiry can occur without a prior Word from God. Therefore he says that "it is not surprising, then, that in strict accordance with the nature of its object theological science replaces the category of discovery with that of revelation."[58]

It is this revelation, the active and sovereign self-objectification of God to be known redemptively as he is in the movement of his openness toward the world in Love, which is said to be found in the Incarnation of the Word. This is particular, historical and unique Word, the freedom of the eternal within temporal human existence, which is the center of Torrance's understanding of God's self-objectification known only from its historical facticity. He says that God has fulfilled his own objection to human sin and estrangement in the Incarnation, life, death and resurrection of the eternal Son of the Father.[59] It is of greatest importance for understanding Torrance to see how he emphasizes that in the incarnation "God accredits Himself to us" by coming in Grace to lift existing persons up out of their frailty and creating that "capacity" to know God.[60] Hence divinely founded reciprocal knowing and theo-logical activity arise from the "objectivity of the Object," wherein dialogue occurs in this "community" of conversation which is centered in and created by his incarnate Word. Because of incarnation, this dialogue can occur, as it must, on earth and within the context or sphere of human relations. In Jesus Christ above all, the world is the created place within which God reveals and shares himself with mankind, giving himself in human form there in order to be known as he is. This is finite knowledge, indeed, but yet true knowledge of God out of God. There, says Torrance, "God's Word assumes and makes use of and comes to us through creaturely objectivity . . . in and through that creaturely objectivity . . . we meet His divine objectivity."[61] In Jesus Christ theo-logical knowledge is specific creaturely objectivity covenantally bound with the divine objectivity. Torrance asserts then that one can never arrive at knowledge of God's ultimate objectivity from the contingent not-God. Rather, one is bound unconditionally to that creaturely objectivity which God has himself freely taken in the incarnation of his Word in Jesus Christ. Knowledge of God arises a posteriori in and from that historic person.

Torrance says that face to face with the incarnation the rationalist is scandalized by the fact that ultimate objectivity is then unconditionally bound to contingent and creaturely objectivity, bound to the weakness of the historical

Jesus. But this place is the only one given where, in the movement or way of God to mankind, God has given himself to be known directly, not as *Deus nudus* but as the One who is self-disclosed to be truly known as Redeemer as well as Creator. Torrance is emphatic that one cannot get behind the creatureliness of Jesus, that very contingent objectivity, wherein God has now and forever given himself as the Object of human knowledge. The attempt to reach God apart from Jesus is "not only scientifically false, but reflects the *hubris* of man who seeks to establish himself by getting a footing on ultimate reality."[62] The knowledge of God and scientific theology can only go the way of unconditional assent and obedience to the Object in the way he has given himself to be known within temporal, contingent existence. For Torrance finally epistemology, specifically the knowledge of God, and thus theological realism and scientific methodology, all flow in and from Jesus Christ the center who is the self-objectification of God for us by partaking of actual humanity. The Word in Jesus Christ is again said to prescribe how knowledge of God shall be ordered. The "order" of the human knowledge of God is in and from Christ the Word by the Spirit. Torrance's conclusion then is that in God's self-objectification in Christ he imposes himself upon the mind to the end that the mind coheres and conforms to that Truth of God in Christ.[63]

Incarnation as Covenantal Meeting of God and Humanity in the World. Like Buber, who said that "in the encounter itself . . . we are confronted with something compellingly anthropomorphic, something demanding reciprocity, a primary Thou,"[64] Torrance's centering on the incarnate Word means that one and no other is God's active coming to mankind for real, personal and cognitive meeting where human life is lived. Thus, the anthropomorphic element can never be wholly shed in the human knowledge of God. Incarnate Word is not sloughed off finally when knowledge of the "Absolute" is attained. In entering space-time creation and created rationality as transcendent Lord, the Word of God did not enter as a stranger, but rather in the incarnation the Word came to that which was his own, and yet into the contingent and temporal as the utterly different—in other words unitariness and yet duality, resulting ever from the divine *ratio* and Act in his Being, interactive relatedness and distinction. God's Being is said to be identical with his Word, and his Word is his Act. When God's Word "condescended" to partake of existence in a way utterly new, he became in a final way that Word to mankind in human speech and human being, physical event in space and time. Incarnation means the real "becoming" of God's "constant" Being.

> He came as genuine man, physically conditioned in space and time, in whom willing, speaking and doing are different, who thinks and forms judgments, whose acts follow upon his decisions, whose words are in addition to his person and whose works are in addition to his words, but who in none of

these things is self-sufficient, for as man he lives and thinks and speaks and acts only in inseparable relation to his fellow-men and in dependence upon the physical creation. Clearly, for the eternal Word of God to become understandable and communicable in the mode and character of word to man he had to share to the full in the space-time distinctions and connections of human existence in this world and operate within the finite conditions of created rationality. This is not to say, of course, that he ceased to be the Word of God he is in the Creator, but rather that he appropriated human form within the frame of earthly life and action and speech in such a way as to take up the frail finite conditions of the creature into himself . . . as his actual speaking of it to us.[65]

In covenantal relation, Creator and creation, the world and persons in the world have been made to correspond to God while being distinct from God. But the world itself has no revelatory meaning and power in detachment from the Word of God upon it and in it. The world and its contingent rationality leave only a rational question with regard to the ground of such orderliness and apprehensibility. Therefore in obvious and developed proximity to Barth, Torrance ever affirms that God's way into the world is by the incarnate Son of the Father. The Incarnation is God's fullest statement of his interaction with, in, and for the world, and this Act of his Being in history dictates the nature of all relations of God with his creatures. But this God-world-human relation founded in Christ cannot be reduced and generalized, he says, into something exemplary for all of God's relations with the world. The Incarnation then is absolutely singular, the place and active source in and from which his relations in the world are centered. Note carefully the terms and concepts used in the following statement by Torrance.

The Spirit and the Word cannot be interpreted in terms of immanent principles or norms within the creaturely processes, but as the power and presence of God the Creator supervening upon the creaturely world in the transcendent personal fashion, through the commanding Word of God, through the incarnate Person of the Son (cf. *homoousion*).[66]

Herein one finds Torrance referring to the economy of God and to the "new" relation which God has established and maintains by the incarnation. God's transcendence, a transcendence always understood not as crudely spatial but as ontological, means for Torrance that in all of God's relatedness with and in the world, preeminently in the incarnation, God will not be less or other than himself in his relation to the world. "Transcendence and immanence are not mutually exclusive predicates of God in Torrance's view . . . (God) may be both at once so long as he remains God."[67] In the incarnation of the Son of the Father, the transcendent God himself and no other is found to be freely present in and for the world as actually human, yet constantly himself.

It is also noteworthy to find in the quotation by Torrance above how he always speaks of God's presence as moving "upon" the world, or "upon" and "impressing" his truth on human thought. This is Torrance's expression for God's sovereign, dynamic, objectively self-disclosive coming which is conceptually characteristic of his particular emphases in all notions of divine relatedness to the world, but especially in the incarnation. God's active disposition to the world while indeed Lordly and free must never be perceived to be alien. What is "natural" for the world is the "supernatural" of God. God's acts in the world are not contradictory, but occur in the contingent world as grounded in its relation with God. Torrance's regular use of "upon" gives emphasis to his point that the Act of God flows directly from his Being, and not by supposed byways or paradoxically or tangentially as though God were cut off from the world. Even when God is said to use "media" Torrance's point is the same. As God is in himself, so too God is in his Acts *ad extra*, that is, in the sharing of God's free objective self-giving to creation in his Acts of creation and redemption.[68]

But the way of this "upon" of God is preeminently, uniquely and finally "though the incarnate Person of the Son." Torrance does broadly and vaguely speak of God's ongoing interrelation with creation as "vertical" or "from above," or of his "speaking" with the Old Testament prophets and of God's relation to Israel, as necessitated by his centering of all thought on the incarnation. Yet Torrance is at least clear that now, after the incarnation of the one and only Word which is God, and by means of Christ's continuing humanity, and by the effective presence of the Spirit, God has done something "new" and final in his movement and presencing to and within the world. As said earlier, Torrance reckons God's free union with the world and humanity, this "hypostatic" union in Jesus Christ, to be the basis and center for all of God's relations. Since the incarnation, God will not be without the world. God's being "among us" in the world can never be or be properly thought without the one who is incarnate God. He says then, "Now that the Incarnation has taken place . . . theology . . . is prevented from thinking of a relation of the Spirit to creation or to men except in and through the Person and Work of the incarnate Son."[69] God is not so much thought to be now coming "down" (vertically) upon creation, though that element remains in Torrance's thought, but more, the transcendent God is said to come to us in the world as one within and belonging to this order as God-man, while maintaining ontological difference as transcendent Creator and Redeemer. This refers to the divine "overlap" of the world in the humanity of the incarnate, crucified, resurrected and ascended Jesus Christ.

> This world of ours in space and time is actually intersected and overlapped, so to speak, by the divine world in the *parousia*, or advent and presence of Jesus Christ. He was acknowledged and adored, therefore, as one who is

God of God and yet man of man, who in his own being belongs both to the eternal world of divine reality and to the historical world of contingent realities.[70]

And by this bearing of the Word in Christ by the Spirit upon human nature, knowing and thinking, then representatively all of creation is in fact lifted to a higher redemptive orderedness, for all now participate, in a real sense, in reconciliation in Christ who is head of all creation. Torrance maintains that it is part of the Son's incarnational life and work that in him God's redemption would penetrate into and reunite human life and the contingent order of creation to God's creative purposes.[71] The grace of the Lord Jesus Christ is the ultimate answer to evil in the reconciling purposes of God, triumphing over disintegration and disorder and pain in the cosmos as the victorious *Logos* of God. Such is God's inextricable alliance with the world in his decisive Act in the incarnation.

Torrance further believes that the fact that God has thus allied himself with contingent existence and effected redemption of creation from within its own ontological bases strengthens the place of the human being in the creation (cf. below). Physical and spiritual reality are within the embrace of the divine purpose as assuredly grounded in God from the fact of the incarnation and embodiment of God's own personal mode of being and action as Word.[72]

But while this relation of the incarnate Word to creation is critical to Torrance's theo-logical understanding of the whole scope of divine redemption in Christ, and for grasping redemptive "content" of Torrance's primary concern for human restoration to God, the incarnation is then found to center upon the human knowledge of God in the gracious opening of God to be known as Lord in the faith relation. It is critical for Torrance's theological purposes to clarify and emphasize the fact that the two are one—the realist knowledge of God does not separate revelation from reconciliation. In the incarnation, humanity is said to be given an integral place in the knowledge of God as drawn into immediate relation to God in Jesus. Such a one is "opened up" or "adapted to" the knowledge of God in communion with God in the Holy Spirit. The role of the person in the knowledge of God is based in the fact that in his Word here God speaks personally in the incarnation. In the incarnation of the Word and by the Spirit alone the Object of knowledge encounters, confronts, and heals, addressing the "hearers" as subjects in the subject-Object relation wherein God ever reigns as lordly Subject.[73] In God's objective revelation of himself historically, God grounds human beings as personal subjects in personalizing communion with himself. Torrance is clear then that it is there and only there in Jesus Christ, and in that way, that one can know God in distinguishing him in his divine Being and Objectivity from ourselves and our subjective responses.

God in His utter difference and complete otherness nevertheless turns Himself toward man, and it is only as such that He gives Himself to us to be known, i.e., on the ground of his self-adaptation to our humanity which also lifts up our humanity into communion with God.   This is the epistemological significance of the Incarnation to which we have been forced back again and again . . . we are summoned to know God strictly in accordance with the way in which He has actually objectified Himself for us in our human existence in Jesus Christ.[74]

Torrance repeatedly refers to the newness of God's Act in Jesus Christ in a way which seems at times to portray something of a prior "absence," or at least a very different level of Word-world relation, and therefore a discontinuity in the divine continuity in relation to creation. Yet there is a tension here, for Torrance's clear emphases are upon the one and only Word who is God and the eternal Son of the Father, he who was once for all incarnated that humanity in the world may share in God's own knowledge of himself unto reconciliation. In what sense was the Word of God related to the world and to Israel before the incarnation other than as transcendent, divine Source of the world's coherence and orderliness (*Logos* of the *logos*)? But this type of relation as "External" Source of intelligibility would sound quite "Newtonian" and would seem to negate subsequent incarnational self-disclosure.   Torrance's answer here is simultaneously forceful and yet paradoxical as an outworking of his principle of theo-logically following after the inherent Rationality of Grace.

Formable Word and Preparation for the Incarnation. In several places in his works Torrance refers to the encounter and struggle between God and Israel. If the Word, as subsisting within the inner consubstantial relations of the Holy Trinity, is to enter the creaturely as speech to mankind by the medium of human words it must be directed to humanity in community, and therein it must create and be creating reciprocity between God and humanity and from person-to-person. Torrance believes that God's singular relation to Israel had a critical and preparatory role to play in the unfolding of God's covenant relatedness to mankind in the reconciling knowledge of God.

Considering "God's historical relations" with Israel in an "anthropomorphic" way, Torrance says that in God's desire to reveal himself and make himself actually knowable to humanity he chose one nation/people out to subject it to intensive interaction and dialogue with himself to the end that he might prepare this people in the service of his self-revelation. Considering "God's historical relations" with Israel in this way, Torrance says that in God's desire to reveal himself he established a special relation of covenanted kinship with Israel to increasingly imprint himself upon the being, thinking and acting of that nation so that it would thereby be molded to become the channel of the divine purpose of revelation.

> A two-way movement was involved: an adaptation of divine revelation to the
> human mind and an adaptation of articulate forms of human understanding
> and language to divine revelation . . . (God's long historical dialogue with
> Israel means) the penetration of the Word of God into the depths of Israel's
> being and soul in such a way that it took human shape and yet in such a way
> that the human response (faith and theology) it called forth was so locked into
> the Word in God that it was used as the vehicle of further address on the part
> of that Word to Israel. That ever-deepening, spiral movement of God's self-
> revelation to Israel was far from . . . painless . . . (in order that Israel
> would) become pliable and serviceable within the movement of God's
> intimate self-giving and self-communicating to it as a people set apart for that
> end.[75]

This sounds like some kind of pre-incarnation incarnation, except that it occurs
at the community or national level. Yet Torrance's development of thought here
seems to point more toward God's active, interactional, and dialogical
preparation for the place, the people, the mindset, the language, under God,
wherein the incarnation would then occur.

This covenant bond tightened, he says, as Israel's covenant goal was that
it   would   be   the   place   of   God's   space-time   revelation   and
reconciliation—"entrusted with the oracles of God (Rom. 3:2)"—creating new
patterns of thought, understanding and speech as appropriate means of
communication. The Word of God encounters the "carnal mind" in the world.
It is at odds with and calls into question the human subject and its patterns of
thought and existence. The particularization of the one covenant of Grace with
Israel meant that it became aware of itself as a people grasped by the Word.
This Word which created the world is said to have created in Israel the place of
corporate reciprocity, whether by assent or dissent, and also the way for deeper
penetration of the Word into Israel's life, culture, religion, history and language.
The Word, by means of the priestly and prophetic movements, "broke through"
the naturalistic, pagan thinking which obstructs the knowledge of the living God.
In all of Israel's history and struggles, says Torrance, "the Word of God kept
pressing for articulation within . . . covenant reciprocity,"[76] taking verbal and
written form in the matrix of Israel's life and thought.

Yet as the Word encountered Israel only in its "formable" state, as
Torrance puts it, it was not yet full but still taking shape in human thought and
speech, deposited in the Scriptures through which the Word of God could
continue to be heard in the living power and majesty of his Person.[77] In this
processive and durative encounter of the self-revelation of the living God with
the "carnal mind," the Word is said to have been preparing the way for that
final manifestation of revelation to mankind. Only then, at last, could the
personal Word be met by faithful reception on the side of mankind. "In the
fullness of time" and within Israel's faith and expectation, the Word became
flesh, God and man, and in him the covenanted relation between God and Israel,

and thereby also all humanity, was embraced in reconciling and restorative fulfillment once and for all. In Jesus Christ the Mediator, Torrance says that the revealing God and the understanding of humanity wholly coincided.[78] Within Israel the incarnate Word has been mediated in a way whereby a divinely prepared form of obedient response was part of Israel, as reflected in the figure of the Servant of Yahweh through whose passion the new covenant would be established. Israel was adapted to the purpose of God, becoming the "womb for the incarnation of the Word and a matrix . . . for the reception of the incarnational revelation"—Jesus born of Mary from out of the "organic correlation of Word and response in the existence of Israel, to be the Word of God made flesh in the life and language of humanity and . . . Word heard and expressed" as the perfect human response for all.[79] In Jesus Christ, the Word of God, "God from God and Light from Light," God is understood by Torrance to have communicated himself, becoming speech to and for humanity through the medium of human words, "man to man." From sheer Grace in Jesus Christ, God has assumed humanity into covenant union and participation in the Truth and Life of God, founding a wholly new situation. All that was before is relativized in Jesus of Nazareth, himself the final and fulfilling Word and Act of God, the revelation of God who brings unity, wholeness and completion.

"Light of Light," "True God of True God." In contexts where the modern physics of light becomes an analogy for the "theology of light," Torrance expresses the *sine qua non* nature and role of the historical incarnation of the Word of God from another perspective. Finding that the human need is to know God, the problem is that God is unapproachable, inaccessible because of the nature of his divine Light or Truth as beyond human, finite capacity. The knowledge of God demands that God-established and human elevating reciprocity and reconciliation between God and mankind. By incarnation only and conclusively, says Torrance, the invisible Light and Truth of God, he who is "Light of Light," is made visible, discernable, knowable, while yet remaining in indissoluble oneness with God as the very eternal *Logos* and Love of God himself.[80] By his coming and becoming for us in the incarnation, the Word/Son is accessible and knowable.

The incarnation then does not make Jesus, like the John the Baptist figure in the Grünewald altarpiece, a mere creaturely pointer to the presence of that "invisible light" beyond himself, which he is not. Rather Torrance's assertion is that Jesus is the invisible God made visible so that in Christ (to extend the metaphor) "God's own transcendent Light in personal and concentrated form has moved directly into the physical world of luminous phenomena created by him and become uniquely man within the contingent structures . . . of existence."[81] He is Uncreated *Logos* in created *logos*, the Uncreated Light and Truth of God within the created light and objectivities of the world created by him. The incarnation is then found to be so absolutely, epistemologically, methodologically and theo-logically central and formative of all appropriate thought, in assenting faith-ful response to the self-revelation of God, because Jesus of Nazareth is understood to be the actual embodiment of the Light of God within the world. To know him in faith is to know the Father whom to know is to know the eternal God in the only way he can be known, namely, out of God. Torrance finds Jesus to be then one and the same being with the Light to which he economically also bears witness, of God and to God.[82]

Therefore it becomes necessary to truly "hear" and learn from the Word, to faith-fully keep pace, faith-fully thinking after the movement of that Word to and in the world. Torrance asserts that one must develop that *a posteriori*, kinetic way of thinking in obedience to and in accordance with the dynamic and personal way of God's Truth. Only in this way is there that penetration into the intelligible Reality of God in Jesus wherein God's Word and Light coinhere, as does the Son with the Father (see below). Then in union and communion in and with Jesus, human beings as hearers of the Word are enabled to "see," "hear" or "know" the "Light" of God and thereby live by that grace founded participation in God's Life and Truth. Of this redemptive knowing in participative relation by faith in the incarnate Word, Torrance explains that there is no need to convert the divinely given data into "word," (as is the case with mute creation) for human apprehension.

> It comes to us . . . in the form of Word, not, to be sure, in the first instance at least in the form of creaturely human word, but in the form of the eternal Word who inheres in the Being of God and is the ultimate creative Source of all "word" . . . . In God himself Light and Word are one and indivisible . . . think of God as revealing himself to us through luminous Word or audible Light . . . how Jesus Christ is presented to us in the Fourth Gospel, in his identity as Word with the Light of God and his identity as Light with the Word of God . . . in God himself and in his work . . . the Word who was what God was, became flesh and dwelt among us . . . . No one has ever seen God, but the only begotten Son who belongs to the innermost Being of the Father has made him known . . . in Jesus Christ, the incarnate Son of God, the luminous Word or the audible Light of God himself, has beiome one with us in our human nature and condition . . . to be both the eternal Word of God and human word, both the uncreated Light of God and created light, in the indivisible unity of his life and person.[83]

Though being "God of God," the Word's coming and becoming as human was in order to communicate and interpret his own divine Person humanly, so that human beings as such would hear him, meet him in reconciling encounter. The incarnation is the self-objectifying disclosure of God to be known as Subject in the God-manness of Jesus Christ who comes to actually "dwell" in space-time as "the Mighty Creator Word and Light of God." His personal coming effects the "calling forth" from human subjects the ability to have faith in him and the power to receive him "as the very Word and Light of God into our human lives, and thereby to become children of God."[84]

But beyond this, the centrality of the incarnation of the Word means for Torrance that the Word, by or through the word of the Gospel, "encounters" or "comes to" the existing hearer now. While Torrance will vary in his description of this "Word-encounter" as experienced in the present of the person, the basis is quite clearly the Kierkegaardian notion of "contemporaneity" (this is indirectly confirmed by Torrance for whom the "realism" of the Kierkegaardian dynamic and Barth's early understanding of revelation, along with that of Emil Brunner, are crucial, see below). The coming of God in Christ by the Spirit which calls out faith and creates capacity in the human subject in the knowing relation is, from the time and point of actualization in the historical incarnation, the very way the Truth of God still "comes" to encounter the human being now through the kerygma.[85]

Incarnation and Realist Knowledge of God. With the Nicene Fathers and against the Arians, Torrance finds that all Truth of, and thus knowledge of, God is said to move from the essential and eternal bond, relation and coinherence of Jesus Christ, the Incarnation of *Logos* in history, with God—oneness in Being between incarnate Son and the Father. "As at Nicaea," the Father-Son relation has absolute primacy for Torrance as well. However important the works of Christ are for Torrance, this is not finally the way Torrance advocates for the knowledge of Christ and of God in Christ. This is because God in his objective self-givenness is said to dictate the way, and God as Father is approached only through the revelation of the Son in the world. Only Christocentricity fosters genuine knowledge of God. True and precise scientific knowledge of God means that one must allow God's own nature as revealed in the world to determine how he is to be known and how he is to be thought and spoken of. Torrance says that this happens when "we approach God as Father through Jesus Christ his Son, for the Son is of one and the same nature and being . . . as the Father . . . the one way of access to God the Father."[86] In terms of his emphasis on critical realist knowledge of God as theology's proper Object, Torrance must emphasize that humans *qua* human must be given "a point of access to him which is both in God himself and in our creaturely existence." This has occurred "in the incarnation" as the place where "God's self-revelation as Father takes place through his self-giving to us in Jesus Christ his Son."[87]

This then is understood to be God's freely given access to himself which, "for our sake," must occur within the creaturely conditions of space and time and within all of the boundaries of what contingent, alienated persons may apprehend. Yet this self-giving in the in-fleshed Son is then also a giving in and from a center in God's own Being. It is finally because of "both sides" that all understanding, conceiving and speaking of God can and must be regulated and

tested by appropriateness to God as known in Jesus Christ. For this reason
Torrance will refer to the "bi-polar" nature of God's self-revelation of himself
in the world to existing human beings. This "bi-polarity" in his thought is in
marked distinction from the bi-polarity which is said to be in God in process
thought. Torrance, rather, finds in the incarnation an unmistakable and essential
"bi-polarity" in God's revelation of himself to mankind in that first God is God
and not human, while in the historical incarnation of the Word God has become
human, indeed "the particular Man, Jesus Christ," without at all ceasing to be
God. In him God and human nature are actually and eternally united in one
Person, "eternal Word of God has assumed human nature and existence into
oneness with himself in order thus, as truly divine and truly human, to become
the final Word of God to man and the one Mediator between God and man."[88]
Thus the "bi-polarity" means that God reveals himself in interactive relation to
the world as transcendent God, Creator and Redeemer, in terms of humanity,
in terms of that which God is not. "Revelation is not only the uncovering of
God but the uncovering of the ear and eye of man for God . . . not only act
from the side of God but also from the side of man." Herein Torrance is
consistent in his emphasis upon the need to "think together" or to think
obediently after the "unitariness" of the full circle of God's redemptive Word.
The Humanity of Jesus is the actual substance of revelation and the place where
God is known. The incarnation is said to show revelation to be not only the Act
of God in humanity and from the side of humanity, but also act of humanity
through real human obedience to the Word of God.[89] This is a crucial, indeed
a primary, theme in Torrance's understanding of the movement or "logic" of
God in the Person of the incarnate Son. Jesus is our obedience, our faith, and
our worship.

> The Incarnation was wholly act of God but it was no less true human life
> truly lived in our actual humanity. Jesus Christ is not only Word of God to
> man, but Believer. In his obedient life he yielded the perfect response of
> man to the divine revelation which is that revelation in human form . . . .
> Revelation is entirely God's action but within it, it is the concrete action of
> Jesus Christ that mediates revelation and is revelation. Revelation is
> supremely God's act but that act is incarnated in our humanity, giving the
> human full place within the divine action issuing forth out of man's life. The
> human obedience of Jesus does not only play an instrumental but an integral
> and essential part in the divine revelation.[90]

Torrance's emphasis on the freedom of God for, to and in the world is
applied also to his understanding of God's freedom to actualize, from the side
of humanity, our understanding of the divine self-disclosure and obedience to it.
God in Christ is free to effect or realize in humanity real meeting with God and
to give "capacity" for the Word, which Torrance reckons out of Grace from zhe
side of God by the Holy Spirit and not from human subjectivity. In the

"encounter," the Spirit is said to effect within the person that which leads to real knowing and then understanding of the revelation in faith-fulness. From this side of the "triadic God-man-world" relatedness and the redemptive action of God in Christ, the revelation of God fulfilled in the incarnate Son displays that God provides mankind with a "truly human but divinely prepared response," which is also the "divinely given objective reality of our knowledge and response, and the divinely appointed norm and pattern of our knowledge and response."[91] In the whole "Humanity" of Jesus, and from there in the whole obedience of his incarnate life, being and knowing, Torrance sees this crucial bi-polarity of the revelatory relatedness of God who is transcendently free "for us" from within. He is the way of human knowing as our humanity is, in him, assumed into oneness with the Word. He is reckoned then to be also the basis and superstructure of all faithful theo-logical expression, because he is the content of the reconciling knowledge of God, the pattern, the way all knowledge of God must take to and for the service of the Word of God. Scientifically this is said to be necessary because this is the way God has historically taken "for our sake."[92] Epistemologically, then, if there is to be real knowledge of God in the world God must give that "point of access" which is both in God and in contingent human existence. God as Father is approached through the incarnate Son because our knowledge of the Father in the Son is "grounded in the very being of God and is determined by what he essentially is in his own nature . . . in Jesus Christ we are really enabled to know God in accordance with his own nature as Father and Son."[93] In this, Torrance believes that God is really known in the (Christological) way which is both "godly" and "scientifically precise" from the objective revelation (*homoousion*).

But here again it must be recalled how Torrance understands the redemptive, triadic God-world-human relation, and revelation in Christ as revelation and relation in ontological difference. The knowledge of the living God as Father as given in, and hence known through, the inner logic of the Christological pattern of revealing. This means human recognition of the fact that God infinitely exceeds all that persons can think or say of him. True knowledge of God is also said to be true knowledge of that difference. Yet Torrance is sure that this knowing, while indeed finite and creaturely, is real or true knowledge of the objective Reality of God as he is in himself. In the faith relation, true knowing of God is not a comprehending but an apprehending of God, not partial in the sense of "part of," but "in part the whole God, who exceeds what we can apprehend within the embrace of our human thought and speech . . . (as) justice is done to both the ineffable . . . reality of God, and to accurate positive knowledge of him" mediated in and through Jesus Christ.[94] As it is basic in Torrance's thinking from Christ that only God can know God, then only from or out of the God-man can God be known by finite, fallen persons. Only God's self-knowing is in strict accord with God. But then real knowledge of God must occur then by Grace, whereby one actually shares in the knowledge which God has of himself.

This forces out into the open another issue which is also at the heart of Torrance's "unitary theology," that is, the Holy Trinity. It is must be proleptically broached here as an important element of Torrance's theo-logical realism and expression of doctrine out of the knowledge of God in Christ. Torrance believes one can know God only if God brings one finally into communion with himself, in and through Christ and by the Spirit, into the inner relations of his own eternal being as Father, Son and Holy Spirit. Clearly this is understood as the sharing of the knowledge God has of himself, as made actual and therefore possible through the incarnation of the Son of God and the Son's mediation of the Spirit of the Father and the Son. In this "Nicene" way he sees the incarnation to be God actually communicating himself, his very Self. Ultimately the triune God is immediately present to us in his own being in the incarnate Word.

> . . . God has embodied in our human existence the mutual knowledge which
> the Father and the Son have of one another, and in the Holy Spirit he gives
> us communion in the mutual relation of the Father and the Son and thus
> makes us share in the knowledge which the Father and the Son have of one
> another . . . through Jesus Christ we are given access to the Father in one
> Spirit . . . for the incarnation of the Son opened the way to knowing God in
> himself, as nothing else could have done. In Jesus Christ the Son of God
> took our human nature . . . so completely that he came among us as man and
> by what he was as man, he revealed to us what he was and is as God.[95]

It is only in sharing the Son's knowledge of the Father that human thought and speech of God may really have God as object and thereby to really have positive content sourced in God. As will be found subsequently, this mutual knowledge of the Father and the Son as the ground of human knowledge of God is not meant to be a detraction or depreciation of the pneumatological element in Torrance's Christological-Trinitarian theology, for he maintains firmly that it is only in and through the communion of the Spirit that human beings partake of this sharing and knowledge.[96] But Torrance's Nicene understanding finds that the faith of the Church, whether it concerns creation, salvation, or eschatology, is wholly understood to flow from this Father-Son relation in God revealed in the incarnation.

Still, in all talk of difference and finite human capacities, Torrance is committed to the fact that human minds and capacities are actually opened and thinking extended under the direct impact of God's self-revelation in Jesus Christ by the creative operation of the Holy Spirit. In this way out of God and to God, human mind and thought are made, in some real measure, increasingly appropriate to their divine object, in this historical actualization of the self-giving of God. It is in this way, he says, that persons are thereby "initiated into accurate knowledge of him determined by what God really is in himself and as he manifests himself to us."[97]

But what Torrance means by "access to the Father through the Son and in one Spirit," as this is actualized in history by the Incarnation, means that his stress upon the "accuracy" or "precision" in the knowledge of God is not meant in some "narrow biblicist way of thinking and speaking about God . . . (but rather that we must allow) our thought to be informed and determined by the truth of God to which they (the Scriptures) direct us."[98] The nature of such thinking which Torrance calls "mystical knowing" as it relates to "encounter" with the Word will be examined below. The influence at this point not only of Kierkegaard, but especially the "early" (as well as "later") Barth and Brunner, becomes even clearer here. The Truth of God in Christ, the pattern and inner logic of God's Word conveyed through Scripture is that which encounters, lifts, adapts, creates and leads faith-ful human thought ever "higher" into the Truth and Life of God. Torrance consistently stresses the proper cognitive relation to, and thus the objectivity of, the Reality known.

> . . . we are given access to the closed circle of divine knowing between the Father and the Son (then) only through cognitive union with Christ, . . . stress on cognitive union with the incarnate Son of the Father (is) greatly reinforced by Pauline teaching about adoption and union with Christ and Johannine teaching about mutual indwelling between us and Christ . . . the mutual relation of knowing and being between the Father and the Lord Jesus Christ constitutes the ontological ground for our knowing of God, for in and through it our knowledge of God the Father is objectively rooted in the eternal being of God himself. Thus through union with Christ (and in the Spirit) we are given access to knowledge of God as he is in his own being.[99]

Like Barth, Torrance's Christocentrism is then finally Theo-centrism, without ever losing the former, as he follows after the Word to thereby really know God out of God in himself. By the incarnation, the "closed circle" of knowing and being in God has been injected into contingent existence, thereby "intersecting our human knowledge of one another and of the world in such a way that in Jesus Christ we may share in the very knowledge which God has of himself."[100] In this way, after God's own movement, Torrance calls theology back to its proper ground so that it will kinetically think the Being and Act, and Act and Being of God in balance and together in the incarnate Christ.[101]

Incarnation and Reconciliation-Redemption. But our discussion of the real knowledge of God in and by the incarnation has stressed what might be termed the "Nicene" side of Torrance's Christocentricity (what Torrance sees as the Nicene emphasis upon God's Being in his Act). Torrance is just as concerned with the redemptive aspect of the revelation of God in Christ, as reflected in the thinking of Calvin and the Reformers. Conceptual knowledge of God in Christ has as its goal or purpose "life eternal." The "coming" of God in Grace is then also understood to be the "order of redemption." This "side" in Torrance's scientific theology (in contrast to much previous discussion) has no analogical counterpart in the natural sciences. But theological science, as a *scientia specialis* concerned with disciplined form of rational activity, must remain in strict accordance with the self-given Reality of the living God who, in Jesus Christ, has given himself objectively in redemptive Love.

Torrance stresses then that the incarnation of the very *Logos* by which all things were created is the movement of the ultimate Love of God, thereby personally penetrating the structured objectivities of the world in a new way in order to creatively reorder the world and humanity from within (as *Logos* of the *logos*). But this underlines how the incarnation is also "the deep ontological intersection of the (disordered) patterns of our world" by the order of God's self-giving Love, "in order to inject into them a re-ordering at a different level."[102] Torrance speaks in terms of the world's evil, wrong and disturbance as "taken in command" by Jesus Christ, so as to be made, in spite of itself, to serve the ultimate triumph of God. Yet his accent falls on how this historical intersection of the world's and humanity's disorder, irrationality and evil by the Word of God's Love incarnate necessarily "involves the atoning passion of God in Christ, by which our disordered existence is restored to order even in its ontological foundations beyond anything that the creation is capable of in itself."[103] Torrance will sometimes put this in the form of a contrastive juxtapositioning, or in terms of the drama of God's opposition to the world's disintegration—his participation in the world that it would thereby undergo "healing" by its Grace grounded partaking of the ordering Word within itself. The "sheer presence and passion of God himself in the Cross" is spoken of as the "intersection" of the world's darkness by the light of God, evil by goodness, irrationality by the Rationality of God, disorder by the creative and regulative purpose and order of God's Love. The incarnation is then said to create a "field" of redemption. The God who confronts us in the entire life, death and resurrection of Christ is then "deep but not devious," in the sense that God is "Light and in him there is no darkness." He is faithful to the perfect Law of his own eternal Being and purpose, to the invincible order of his redemptive Love in the world.[104]

Torrance's expression of the redemptive "Act of God in his Being," which he wants to think together in a balanced way (following Barth) with the "Being of God in his Act," tells much about Torrance's understanding of the effectual bearing of the incarnation upon the creation. In following the way in which he relates the divine order in Jesus Christ to the irrationality and disorder of the world, one must first recall Torrance's use of terms from the physical sciences as he speaks analogically or illustratively of the intersection of symmetries and the breaking of the symmetry at a lower level by symmetry at a higher level. In this way disorder seems to continue, but it is "opened out through a cross-level integration" which brings about greater richness and depth of real order. Torrance asserts then that the symmetrical ordering of God's love in the incarnation "breaks into" (not as alien) the apparent symmetries of the world, with all of its actual disorder, breaking those discordant symmetries, "taking them up, redeeming and transforming them in a profound ontological reordering." Revelation and reconciliation must be thought together out of the unitariness of the incarnation of the Word.

> In this intersection of the divine symmetries with those of our existence in this world, we are made acutely aware that God is Light and there is no darkness in him, that God is Love and there is no dissonance in him, that the activity of God is always an ordering activity and there is no disordering element in it but we are also made acutely aware that the intimate linking of our world to such a God through the incarnation and resurrection of his Son inevitably thrusts our world forward into a future very different . . . . The breaking of the active and redemptive divine order of Light and Love into the spatio-temporal patterns of our existence is bound to be at once eschatological and teleological . . . restoring them to their true forms in the creative purpose of God . . . to a consummation in the ultimate victory of God's Love.[105]

Torrance takes the historically actualized, present and eschatological reconciliation and redemption in the world with full seriousness because the incarnation occurred within the empirical correlates of the world and humanity, so that faith-ful theological science is bound to think together its teleological redemption in Christ with the contingent rationality of the created world.[106] Again, Torrance understands that in Christ the good but disordered creation was taken up into God in order to bring reconciliation and transformation of creation in restored relation to God. Therefore the incarnation is God's penetration into human sin, alienation and guilt, and thus his coming for us in and under the judgment of God. As the Word of God incarnate, says Torrance, Jesus Christ has delivered humanity from bondage to negation, to recreate relation to God, to realize perfect humanity on earth, and to offer up to the Father that true human response to God from within the estrangement and injured existence of mankind.[107] The Word of God is thus said to have reached humanity and founded knowledge, reciprocity and reconciliation within its existence in the world. In his passion and resurrection, Jesus brought about rebirth of humanity in its whole physical and spiritual existence. In Jesus' entire Being and Act together as one, Torrance reckons God to be actively and actually there, directly affirming the goodness of what he has made and fulfilling his Word in the original creation of the world. This was "involved in every act of mercy and healing in which the commanding fiat of the Creator was found on the lips of Jesus."[108] In the person and action of Jesus he finds that there is a saving, a restoring, a healing of the creation within its physical and spiritual conditions by the Son's sharing in its existence with all of its limitations and afflictions.

Therefore Torrance states that ". . . only through the full participation of the Creator with us . . . can atonement for sin and redemption from evil power issue in the actual restoration of what God has made."[109] In Jesus God has redeemed the world and humanity from eventual nothingness, yet without the violation of its creaturely nature, in his redemptive "Yes!" Thus Christ is understood to be not only the ground of our being from beyond existence, but he also has now, by the incarnation, become the ground of our existence from within.[110] In the intended unitariness of the two sides of Torrance's theo-logical thinking out from the incarnation, one sees him coming again and again to God's Act, effecting self-communication out of his own Being, and his Being in his Act, for the real, redemptive knowledge of God. Such redemptive revelation accomplishes transformation of the world.[111]

Torrance's intention then is also to think together and clarify the God who is God and God who is God for the world and humanity in the incarnation whereby revelation and reconciliation are shown to be one. The self-revelation of God to be known out of himself as he is according to his own mode of rationality cannot achieve its *telos* in Torrance's theology unless it is a revelation which does effect human reconciliation in the faith-knowing relation within the community of the Church. It is from within the onto-relatedness and "overlapping of symmetries," or the "field" of divine-human encounter founded and given in Jesus Christ, that Torrance speaks of the incarnate "tension." He says that while Jesus was wholly the obedient Son throughout life, he still had to learn obedience; while "conceived by the Holy Spirit and born of the virgin Mary," he was yet "born within the womb of a sinner," and within the range of sinful human flesh; as "Son of Adam" he was born into the desolation and alienation of human "God-forsakenness," pushing his way forward, growing in wisdom and grace before God and man.[112] This growing and learning of the Word and Son of the Father is then esteemed to be the Son's own historical struggle with sin on behalf of and within our humanity. Jesus Christ is thus seen to be "bending human will" to submission and faithful response to the will and Truth of God. This too is the way taken or chosen in the movement of God, the way the incarnate Word takes in the midst of sinful humanity in vicarious suffering, judgment and atonement.

As Torrance has as his design to think together unitarily revelation and reconciliation in Jesus Christ, he is concerned then to make yet clearer the nature of God's self-revelation as engendering true faith-ful knowledge of God, which is reconciliation, transformation and eternal life. For this reason he states that revelation means a "communion through the reconciliation of the estranged parties . . . entails the entry of the Mind of God into our darkness and estrangement in order to redeem our understanding and to achieve its reconciliation to the Mind of God."[113] For Torrance's theo-logical movement of thought, revelation is unthinkable apart from that whole movement of divine humiliation from conception and birth to the Cross and resurrection. The Word of God made human poverty and distortion his own so that in himself he accomplishes and is that "atoning exchange (whereby) God's revelation achieves its end as revelation to and within a sinful world."[114]

Torrance on the Incarnation: A Summation. As a result, thought from the incarnate Word, in life, death, resurrection and, indeed ascension, back to God the Father and real knowledge of the Holy Trinity becomes also a movement of thought back from the Father to the incarnate Son in order, thereby, to grasp this aspect of the "logic of grace," the nature and significance of the incarnate activity of the Son. As a direct result of the Word becoming flesh and dwelling among us, Torrance claims that there can and must occur that axiomatic thinking forced upon one by the intrinsic structure of God's Reality, thinking which allows the Truth to impress itself on the mind and then penetrates into the inner intelligibility of the Truth of God in the inner coherence of God's Being. This would prove problematic to logical deduction and abstractionist forms of thought alien to the revealed mode of Rationality. This line and kind of thinking, which Torrance finds most fully in Athanasius, is one which affirms the incarnate Son's inseparability from the Father. Otherwise what Christ did *pro nobis* was not directly an Act of God himself. Then all that Jesus Christ was and accomplished would be of no ultimate significance for us and God would be seen as indifferent to the human condition (cf. below on the *homoousion* doctrine, versus dualist Arians).[115] By rejecting such "dichotomous" thinking, Torrance holds that the supreme Truth and Love of God, which is God himself, is revealed in and stands as the basis of the Gospel, making the incarnation absolutely decisive and redemptive.

In thus following and developing the Barthian "balance" of the Nicene "Being of God in his Act" (theology proper and Christology) and the Reformation emphasis upon the "Act of God in his Being" (soteriology) in the incarnation, we have found that Torrance intends to express the oneness of the direct Act of God the Father and the incarnate activity of the Son. Torrance approaches the "God with us" and the eternal and historical Father-Son relation in its varied doctrinal facets in order to emphasize both epistemological significance for the realist human knowledge of God in Jesus Christ and the soteriological or reconciling-transforming significance. All is said to rest "upon the downright act of God himself in Jesus Christ, that the act of God takes the concrete form of the actual historical man Jesus."[116] Torrance's "realist approach" to the incarnation leads him to emphasize the Pauline teaching about the way in which God in Jesus Christ has substituted himself for us, that is, in making human sin and death his own so that human beings may be able to participate in his own righteousness and life. Torrance calls upon Irenaeus and Eastern (Alexandrian) Church tradition in maintaining that the way of the eternal Word in uniting himself with humanity has effected redemption and thus the mode of rationality needed in the theo-logical calling. The "whole incarnational assumption of our human nature (with emphasis upon Christ's death and resurrection) was at the same time a reconciling, healing, sanctifying and recreating activity."[117] Torrance repeatedly confirms the Eastern Church's Christologico-Soteriological principle that that which was not taken (by the Word of God in becoming flesh) was not healed.

In bringing together Torrance's incarnational thinking regarding this "reconciling exchange" occurring in Jesus Christ, we must give further "economic" clarity to the fact that it is Torrance's contention that human alienation before God and distortion in mind and thought are one and integrated. The incarnation means the healing and reconciling of the human mind unto the Truth of God by the redeeming effect of God's self-revelation to humanity in Jesus Christ. This is because redemption in the Son is also redemption by the *Logos* whereby persons recover the true knowledge of God in Christ. Wanting to avoid Gnostic distortion, Torrance's stress is placed more heavily on how redemption in Christ and realist knowledge of God's gracious self-objectification in him means redemption and knowledge, regeneration and illumination.[118]

Therefore, against all "alien" modes of thought which would sever the realist, redemptive knowledge of God from human existence, Torrance points to Christ as the place where God is to be directly known by the Holy Spirit. The fact that this occurs in and through creaturely media is, again, not to negate this for these space-time media are made "transparent" or "transparencies" for that revelation (cf. above). The Word of God must be just that, and not the self-projected human word about God which has no grounding in God's self-objectification. It must be God's own Word as God is and as God speaks it as Word, the personal mode and activity of God's Being.

> . . . it has been addressed to us and has actually reached us, Word that has called forth and found response in our hearing and understanding and living—otherwise we could not speak of it. We do not begin, then, with God alone or man alone . . . but with God and man as they are posited together in a movement of creative self-communication by the Word of God. Word by which He creates and upholds . . . and gives them room for their relations with Him. It is the mode of His Being in which God goes forth to meet man, freely relating His divine life to him within the conditions of his creaturely nature . . . enabling him freely to relate his human life to the majesty of the divine Nature . . . . A profound reciprocity is created in which God addresses his Word to man by giving it human form without any diminishment of its divine reality as God Himself speaks it . . . . Thus the Word of God communicated to man includes within itself meeting between man and God as well as between God and man . . . . This is Jesus Christ, the Interpreter and Mediator between God and man, who as God of God in unqualified deity and Man of man in unqualified humanity, constitutes in the unity of His incarnate Person the divine-human Word.[119]

The incarnation is the Act of God's own Being, the movement and coming of God in Christ within the spatio-temporal domain, which is "open up" to the transcendent, asymmetrical, interactive relatedness of God, Creator and Redeemer, by the Word, says Torrance. In Jesus Christ Torrance finds the true and theo-logically needed balance of the knowledge of God's divine Being in his Act and God's redeeming Act as it is grounded directly in his Being. In the incarnate Word, Jesus, and by the Holy Spirit, God is known in his inherent Intelligibility and uncreated Rationality, the transcendent *Logos* of the immanent, created *logos* of the world. By the Spirit through the Son, God as Father is known because he has thus economically given himself to be known. This epistemological point is supremely significant to Torrance's theo-logical thinking out from what he believes to be the actual way God has taken in the world, as scientific theology then thinks after this its own proper object.

The Holy Spirit and the Realist Knowledge of God in Torrance's Theology

But one cannot read far in Torrance's theology, especially after *Theological Science*, without finding the important connection he makes between the realist knowledge of God in Jesus Christ and the critical role played "economically" and epistemologically by the Spirit of God. This has been briefly referred to above. Torrance maintains that the *kerygma* announces to alienated human beings that not only has the Love of God and Truth of God, God himself, come to dwell in distorted human existence in order to transform it and to be redemptively known within it, and that faithful human response to God has been made in the Person and self-offering of Jesus Christ "for our sake." But it also proffers this as the "divinely appointed and provided response in which we may share freely as through the Spirit we participate in the vicarious obedience of the Word made flesh."[120] For Torrance "Word and Spirit" are absolutely crucial for the reconciling knowledge of God and in the redemptively necessary, faithful human response in communion relation through Christ to God as Father, grounded in the Trinity.

Torrance's Christological-Trinitarian theology is properly understood only if one recognizes that his Christocentricity, the place where God is self-revealed and known, is necessarily Pneumatological as well. One must ever remember Torrance's scientific stress upon the *a posteriori* nature of the knowing relation, namely that authentic knowledge cannot begin with a theory of knowledge regarding what can and cannot be known or revealed (*a priori*) and then move from that theory, as independently argued, to supposedly develop actual knowledge. Nor can the abstract question, "How can one know God?" be posed and then from the human answers examine and explain what is known. As with any objective reality, an epistemology can be developed of the knowledge of

God only from actual knowledge of God. Form cannot be cut off from content
nor method from the actual subject matter of that knowledge. If "God is only
known out of God" then "it is God who makes possible our knowledge of Him
by giving Himself to us as the object of our knowing and by bringing us into a
relationship with Him in which we are made capable of knowing Him."[121]
Again, God's nature prescribes the way he is to be known. But what is the
understood role of the Holy Spirit whereby the knowledge of God actually forms
within human being, thinking, expression and activity? With regard to the
knowledge of God, Torrance's interest in the Person of the Holy Spirit is like
his concern for Christocentricity and the incarnation. Human beings are
bounded within the limited range of creaturely consciousness and perception.
Torrance notes that in epistemology the concern is with the formal aspects of
knowledge, the "how" and the "what" as these properly arise in human
understanding under the real impact of the revelation of the object. But with the
epistemological relevance of the Holy Spirit this is not so because God is said
to personally give himself to be known objectively and realistically. He reveals
himself to be the proper Object of theo-logical inquiry. But with the Spirit's
activity in the economy of God in the world the concern is rather with what
Torrance calls the "non-formal." By this he means that with this given Object
of knowledge there is uniquely that which "outruns all forms of our
understanding, and with the abrupt acts of God through which our understanding
of him arises but which cannot be reduced to forms of our understanding."[122]
Epistemological "forms" thus fall off as one is faced with the Act of God which
is not to be adequately explained from the side of the human knower alone. For
all of his emphasis on the self-objectification of God in Jesus, we see here again
that Torrance never negates God's constant otherness and ineffibility. Rather
it is under God's self-revelation in Jesus Christ and the creative operation of the
Holy Spirit where he says that there occurs an opening of the mind and the
expanding of our thought far beyond creaturely finite limits until, in some finite
measure, it is made appropriate to the divine object. Preliminarily, Torrance
says that it is the Spirit who personally "actualizes the self-giving of God in
Jesus Christ and so enables us to receive and apprehend what is beyond
ourselves altogether, the self-knowledge of God himself incarnate among us in
Jesus Christ."[123]

Torrance emphasizes, with his Christocentricity, that there is no knowledge
of God apart from the Spirit, given both the "economy" of God's self-disclosure
and the fact that God is Spirit. Therefore knowledge of God in truth is
actualized in the human being, in human knowing, as he is known in and by the
Spirit. There is no independent "epistemology of the Spirit" as some
epistemological basis apart from the Father and Son relation, as though
knowledge of God were explicable from the side of human understanding in
place of the Holy Spirit. Torrance's concern is with that activity of the Spirit
in the human knowledge of God where "epistemological forms" break off and

the human being is set over against the Act of God, which is ineffable, but yet from within alienated human nature. When the knowledge of God occurs, this carries with it the assurance that the human subject cannot attribute it to the self, but can only speak of how the knowledge comes into being by referring beyond the self to God's gracious acting upon and within the person by the Spirit.

Borrowing St. Athanasius's terminology, Torrance explains this more theologically and Christocentrically in ways which prove important, directing thought to another central issue in this chapter, that is, the nature and relation of the "economic" and "ontological" or "immanent" Trinity. He says that one must remember that the Son of God is the only *Logos* and *Eidos* of Godhead. The Trinity is not mere "subject, object and relation" which falsely reduces the Spirit to the mutual love relation between Father and Son. This fails to give full understanding and reality to the distinctive, incommunicable, personal Being of the Holy Spirit and the Spirit's epistemological role. Torrance maintains that in and through the incarnate Word of God, God reveals himself as Father, Son and Holy Spirit (subject-object-subject), and is truly believed, known and reverently acknowledged in accordance with his divine nature, glory and rationality. In and through the incarnate Form of God in Christ, God's "Face and Image are revealed" so that human knowledge of God is "shaped and formed through the conformity of our minds to Jesus Christ . . . by letting our thinking obediently follow the way God Himself has taken in Jesus Christ we allow the basic forms of theological truth to come to view."[124] But this can only take place when, by the Spirit, the being and nature of God is brought to bear upon the human being so that faith-ful thinking occurs under the compulsion of God's Reality. Thus the Holy Spirit is the Spirit of Truth. By the activity of the Spirit the Spirit is not made knowable in himself, but thereby Christ is known as God and Savior.

> . . . there is *aletheia*, for truth is the unveiling of what was hidden, the manifestation of the divine Reality—that is why He is called the Spirit of Truth: it is through His agency that Jesus Christ is revealed as the Son of the Father . . . . He does not show us Himself, but shows us the Face of the Father in the Face of the Son . . . yet because it is through Him that the Word of God was made flesh and through Him that the Word continues to be heard and believed, because it is in His Light that we see Light and by His creative operation that we know the unknowable and eternal God . . . . He is Himself God of God, the Holy Spirit of one substance with the Father and of one substance with the Son, who confronts us in His own person with the ultimate Godness of God . . . . He utters the Word but does not utter Himself, and therefore He directs us through Himself to the one *Logos* and *Eidos* of Godhead in Jesus Christ in accordance with whom all our knowledge of God is formed in our minds (Trinity).[125]

Torrance asserts that the Spirit casts his eternal "Light" upon the Father through the Son and on the Son in the Father, thereby bringing the Being and Reality of God from his "hiddenness" to bear directly upon the human being who is reciprocally brought from darkness, un-truth and alienation to communion with God in Christ. The Person of the Spirit is the very living Action and Presence of God effectively relating the divine Word to the human, creaturely forms, which the Word became in Jesus Christ.

But how is such a self-disclosure of God the Father in Christ by the Spirit related by Torrance to human knowing, thinking, and expressing, given the fact that the knowledge of God that Torrance is immediately concerned with is human knowledge of God?   On the one hand, while often speaking of "encounter" with God in largely Brunnerian terms, reminiscent too of the early Barth, Torrance is yet insistent that knowledge of God is not something heightened or spiritualized toward the ecstatic supra-rational. Still Torrance speaks ambiguously of this knowing as "mystical," and even as "unknowing." He desires to stress here that the miraculous nature of the Spirit's activity creates in the person the ability to know God according to God's own mode of rationality which is beyond human capacities. But this is not meant to be the negation of one's rational and critical powers. There seem to be two sides to Torrance's thinking here. It is enablement to apprehend God, which Torrance wants to portray without having to transcend human nature in its space-time setting, while at the same time one must be "lifted up" to a different level of knowing capacity and relations.   Torrance holds that scientifically this capacitating or lifting must be the case. Yet like all sciences, the knowledge of God, and then human response in theological science, demand activity and judgments which are sober and self-critical.[126]

But Torrance also speaks of this knowledge of God in Christ by the Spirit as a relationship which is "translogical." The direct, and personal action of the Being of God upon the human being by the Holy Spirit has no counterpart in natural sciences, and it "cannot be logicalized, corresponding to a relation between language and reality that cannot be resolved into language alone."[127] In the divinely and objectively dictated way of knowing God in communion by faith in Jesus Christ and through the Spirit, the human reason "is adapted and adjusted to knowledge of God" in accordance with God's own ontological nature as Father, Son and Holy Spirit, to the end that initiation takes place into accurate knowledge of God under the determination of what God actually is in himself. The Spirit of God is therefore found to be of central soteriological and "epistemological relevance" because Torrance is concerned with modes of knowledge tested for their real basis in actual knowledge of objective Reality. The Spirit enables persons to know beyond and above the self, distinguishing the God-ness of God in revelation. Knowledge of God in the power of the Spirit is then an ongoing process of informing, forming and re-forming as centered in Christ.

Persons then cannot have objective, knowing experience of God, or exercise faith in him, without conceptual forms of understanding, however preparatory or "tacit" such insight may be. This is the Spirit's role in theological knowledge. By the Spirit's enlightenment, one can and will begin to think and speak directly of God in and through the media of human forms of rational experience and expression. This is done in the Spirit under the guidance and control of the inner rationality of the divine Being, the Word and visible form of Godhead.

> It is only through the Spirit that such trans-formal experience is possible, for it is by His Power that we are enabled to know beyond ourselves and to distinguish (God) . . . so that our knowing falls under . . . what He makes known of Himself. This is knowledge with a transcendence in form and an indefinite range of enlightenment beyond anything else in our experience, in which our thinking becomes objectively rooted in the eternal Word in the Being of God and acquires out of that Word a basic conceptuality that does not vary with the many forms of man's self-centered and objectifying modes of thought.[128]

The Holy Spirit, as truly and personally free toward creation from beyond it, brings God's creative purposes to completion. Torrance's theo-logical bases are formed here by what he sees as the Spirit's personal relation toward persons out of the inner relations of the Trinity by the Son, the direct participation of the Spirit in the Godhead revealing God within the subject-object structures of human being, and the Spirit's effecting of both revelation from God and inward human response in reciprocity with God. Through Christ and by the Spirit, then, depth renewal occurs in the existing human being so that "con-science becomes a knowing together with Christ and with one another in Him, and always out of a centre in (Christ)."[129] By the Son, the Spirit works in that "saving exchange" of the eternal Son-Word's "riches" for human poverty, the Just for the unjust, effecting from the human side renunciation of self for Christ and realization of the "Godward side of our life" in order to direct all human knowing away from its own subjectivity to the "objective Reality of God's own Being and Word."[130] By the Spirit human relations with the objective Reality of the triune God are brought to their *telos*.

Only in the *monogenes* Son is the *eidos* of Godhead revealed. But thereby one is said to be able to know the Spirit, where Father and Son are also known, because it is in the Spirit "sent" to persons by the Father through the Son that true knowledge of God is mediated and actualized. Knowledge of the Spirit (not as independent) of God the Father is derived and controlled by knowledge of the Son. The Spirit comes as Spirit of the Father and of the Son to reveal the Father in the Son and the Son in the Father. God as Spirit is to be known in the "spiritual" way, not from without or from that which is external to God but from what he is within himself. Torrance is maintaining then, against "dualistic" or disjunctive "Arian" thinking which equates the limits of understanding with the limits of reality, that by the Lordship of the Holy Spirit in Christ that God can be known only through and out of himself as his revelation breaks through the *a priori* conditions of human subjectivism. Or, as Torrance says quoting Barth, "the Holy Spirit stands for the unconditionality and irreversibility of the Lordship of God in his revelation."[131] As understood by Torrance in the "Nicene way," the Person of the Holy Spirit, as internal to God and sent from the Father in the name of Christ, bears witness to Christ. The Spirit of Truth leads human beings into all truth, graciously giving direct access to the intelligibility of God while maintaining as inviolable the ultimate, transcendent mystery and ineffability of the Being of God. This yes and no is obviously critical to Torrance's understanding of the "God-man-world" or "God-world-man" relation and interaction. In the Spirit one is "lifted up" to have knowledge of God as he is in himself and is yet "restrained by the sheer holiness and majesty of God's Being as unapproachable Light from transgressing the bounds of reverent and lawful inquiry."[132] Having found that this is the Holy Spirit's epistemological relevance out of God's self-disclosive movement unto redemptive, participative knowledge, Torrance also gives extensive discussion to the propriety and activity of the Spirit in the epistemological basis of this knowledge of God. While the question of the relation of human cognitive and semantic acts to the divine Being was discussed in some measure earlier, this issue is important here for grasping Torrance's connections between God and human knowing and thinking of him. We have found Torrance to say that real knowing is first concerned with the relation of one's knowing and speaking to being, and that there must be real distinction in that relation (*diastasis*) between what one knows and one's knowing of it if there is to be real knowledge at all. Nevertheless Torrance is equally emphatic that in authentic knowledge being shows through to the knower, even though it is not known how this happens. As it is with natural scientific knowledge of contingent reality so too with theo-logical knowing. Torrance represents the scientific knowledge of God as a double action by which the Reality and Rationality of God gives himself along with the appropriate mode of knowing him, while the one knowing God actively and faith-fully responds by knowing God in his self-disclosure, allowing the impress of his Truth, his Word, himself to fashion that knowledge. This brings about that transparency in the created media of God's historical revelation and the correspondence-coherence in that human knowledge of God, and then in theo-logical thinking and expression (being and language). What he means by this is preliminarily explained when he says that "a relation takes place in which there is a disclosure of being from beyond our forms of thought and speech which we must distinguish from our thinking and speaking." In knowledge, thought and speech must arise from reality/Reality, and then transparently, actually and instrumentally point beyond themselves, and be open and incomplete in themselves.

But how does this relate to the epistemological role of the Spirit, the propriety of the Spirit for and in human knowledge of God? Torrance speaks of the Spirit as the presence (immanence) of the transcendent God and that apart from the Spirit persons would not know the divine Being or, to put it another way, God would not be effectually self-given here in his Reality and real distinction from our thinking and referring to him. In the knowledge of God one has to do with the Spirit of God in his sublime exaltedness whereby one is up against the ultimate Source and Ground of being beyond all finite being. For this reason Torrance says there is that epistemological diastasis between God's Reality and our knowing because the Being of God remains transcendent and his Truth retains his own Majesty even as Object of knowledge. Indeed, he says that one learns what objectivity really is under the Lordship of the Spirit. The Spirit's presencing and bearing of the very Being of God upon human experience and knowing creates the relation to God in Christ which the knowledge of God requires to be real knowledge. By the Spirit, empirical relation to God occurs in Christ and therein one is given direct or "intuitive" knowledge of God, an intuitive knowledge and relation which ever remains under the Spirit's control.[133]

But the realist knowledge of God also means that the Being of God acts upon the human subject by the Spirit who is that active, creative "presence" of God to persons. While human reference, thought and speech, cannot as such be related to God, that relation actually takes place by the action of God in the Spirit. The activity of the Spirit is the epistemological base of knowledge of God because by that action one meets "God's Being in his Act and his Act in his Being." By the Spirit "God's own Being is wholly present in His activity so that the given Object of our knowledge is actively at work in our knowing of it, creating from our side a corresponding action in which our being is committed."[134] For this reason theological activity in this sense is understood to be engagement in the movement of thought which corresponds to the movement of the Spirit by participation in it as a form of kinetic thinking which partakes in that which it seeks to know. To know the eternal *Logos* incarnate one must know him in a way "apposite to that divine becoming and happening in space and time, and therefore, *kata pneuma*."[135] This Torrance correlates to a Kierkegaardian "leap of faith," which he says is the opposite of the irrational. Rather it may be compared to Heidegger's leap of thought in opening the original source of being. Theology as a movement of thought from within the movement of God's self-revelation means that one is confronted and transformed with that which is wholly new to the knower by means of repentant rethinking. But this is something of which ultimately only God can be the Author and Ground, whereby the human subject is carried beyond the finite self to genuine knowledge of God by the Spirit, and thus into participation in the self-knowledge of God.

Torrance stresses herein as well that the Being of God who thus acts upon us is by nature eloquent, speaking Being, and God speaks in Person and he speaks himself. As God's Being-in-his-Act and his Act-in-his-Being are one, Torrance says further that God's Being and his Word are likewise related because God's Act is his Word and his Word his Act, for by his Word God communicates himself. The "propriety of the Spirit" to Father and Son is then found to manifest in that same unitary but double activity in which through the Spirit, God declares his Word and that, through the Spirit, the Word of God comes to existing persons as dynamic communication and creative Word-event. By the Holy Spirit one has union with Christ, which means that partaking of the communion between Father and Son and Son and Father results from that activity whereby the Spirit utters the Word.[136] Torrance's contention for the proper pneumatological emphases and the relevance and propriety in human knowledge of God leads him to say that the Spirit is also at work "shining" the Light of God or "sounding" the divine Word in and through human thought and speech. For this reason Torrance concludes that God does not disclose himself apart from such but always through them as those "transparent" media of disclosure. Here the Spirit is understood to be active and free not only as creating and present to contingent creation, but as the "personal presence and action of God to the human creature both to give rational life and sustained relation to Himself and to open the mind to receive and understand God's self-revelation" unto faith and love.[137] Therefore the Spirit uses those creaturely realities as the media of divine revelation in a way in which knowledge does not and must not terminate on them but upon the Being of God. God's presence and power in human existence is God actively directing us through contingent realities to immediate, intuitive knowledge of himself in his own ultimate Reality. This understanding of mediated, yet direct, knowledge is said to reflect the way of God in the whole history of his covenant relations with his people as preeminently and decisively fulfilled in the incarnation of the Word. Through the Spirit-inspired apostolic witness centered upon Christ the Word, God by the Spirit is said to "come to us" enwrapped in the historical, biblical forms which, as distinct from Word, yet direct all our ettention to that center, Jesus Christ. For all of his "divine ineffability and transparency," the Spirit's speaking the eternal Word and Light of God is done in order to relate the creaturely forms of revelation to God himself, to create that necessary transparency, so that they "become diacoustic and diaphonous media through which God discloses Himself to us in his own Word and Reality and makes us capable of knowing Him beyond ourselves."[138] As consequently faithful and open to the Truth by the Spirit, human statements about God, first in the Scriptures and then in theological statements, are true in being open to the Truth of God. Their truth is acquired at the highest "level" by pointing beyond themselves in witnessing to the infinite Truth of God which transcends all human thought and statement. By the Spirit, God is present and accessible to human knowing and hence knowledge is profoundly conceptual and rational.

Finally, Torrance makes the further epistemological-anthropological point that by the Holy Spirit in Christ the knowledge of God occurs not only within human rational structures but also within human social and personal structures. The Spirit's activity is characterized in Torrance's terminology as "personalizing Spirit." The Holy Spirit is said to confront persons with his personal Being by addressing them in his Word and opening them out toward himself. Thinking the individual and corporate together unitarily (cf. onto-relations), Torrance sees the address of the Spirit in the Word as healing and restoring the faith-ful human subject while upholding personal relations first with God and then with fellow human beings in the context of community, especially the Church.[139]

Act of God and Human Faith-Knowing in Torrance's View of Realist Knowledge of God

In one sense all of the "concrete" and "economic" elements and structures for the actual human knowledge of God in Torrance's theology are now in place. But there is at this point in Torrance's theo-logical expression and formulation a crucial connection from what God, from the Father through Christ the Son and in the Spirit, has done and is doing objectively and redemptively in the world and for existing humanity to what occurs in the point and "time" of "meeting" when revelation-Word and enlightenment are existentially met in human faith. If God does disclose himself objectively in Jesus Christ and by the Spirit, how is that God-human "encounter" to be understood? Torrance is certain that contingent, finite persons, as a result of the nature of the revelation of God, do receive realist, conceptual, cognitive knowledge of God as God is in himself. What is the "linchpin" that Torrance uses to integrate this question in his efforts for a Christocentric-Trinitarian theology which is truly unitary as it reflects God's active, triadic "God-man-world" relatedness as Creator and Redeemer?

As rooted in his Scottish realism, Torrance's insistence upon the cognitive, conceptual and intellective, as well as the transformative and reconciling, knowledge of God through Christ and in the Spirit is here basically consistent and understandable from what has been discussed previously. This involves a structured understanding in formal acts of cognition with the subsequent movement of theo-logical thinking. This is then Torrance's development of this conceptual structure by reference to the proper Object and thereby what he formulates regarding human advancement in the cognitive modes of rationality which arise as God communicates himself. We have seen that from the Wbrd which God is and by which he reveals himself in the world, the knowledge of God, and thus theology, are understood by Torrance to be fully rational processes. Yet it is also true that the Word as utterly unique Object has its own form of cognition proper to it, valid in its own right and its own nature (as is true in principle of all objects of scientific investigation). Torrance stresses that though God is apprehended without a discursive process yet this is not without the human act of conceptual cognition. Again, this is an interesting dual claim. This is not a partial knowing, but yet it is a knowing which does not at all exhaust God's transcendent Reality and mystery.[140]

Encounter/Word-Event. Torrance's theo-logical principle and the way of theo-logical science, in which he believes he is following the theological method of the Nicene Fathers, Calvin and Barth (and analogically Einstein, Polanyi), is that the nature of the truth, its mode of rationality, dictates the way it will be received or known, and that God has chosen to communicate himself to us here in the form of "personal Being in the specific form of active life and being in our historical existence . . . revealed in Jesus Christ." This demands a human knowing relationship to it within that temporal realm. In Jesus Christ and by the Spirit God has come here in Person and as Person to person. Because of what Torrance finds to be the unitariness of God's personal Word and Act, our human knowledge of God must be understood in terms of "encounter" (*Ereignis*) with the living God who is eloquent, speaking Word, by nature.[141] Revelation encounters the knowing subject not as does the divinely established intelligibility of the determinate world (or "number rationality") but as "Word rationality," the inherent rationality and intelligibility of God to be known personally, redemptively and cognitively, whereby real contact with divine Reality truly occurs. Here human knowledge is said to be brought to proper unity by which "the *Logos* of God Himself presses itself convincingly upon our minds."[142] God, who is known only out of himself, seizes the knowing subject from beyond the self so that actual knowledge of the ultimate Rationality of God is found to take place. In this encounter reason is "enlightened" or "lifted up" from beyond the limits of created rationality. An infinite extension of intelligibility beyond the person and the structures of existence is disclosed so that God's own ultimate Rationality establishes or impresses its own law within the depth of human rationality. God's Word opens and lifts the mind by the Spirit, thereby penetrating the sinful, self-enclosed structures of life. As Torrance sets up the God-human "encounter," referring to the divine compulsion, he speaks of how there in that meeting we find ourselves to be up against the "fundamental datum of God's self-revelation as the divine Word incarnate in our human existence." God is said then to "take our minds under (his) command in such a compelling and ultimate way that Jesus Christ gives decisive content and structure to our knowledge of God . . . the objective centre."[143] Through Christ and in the Spirit the God-human meeting still occurs for existing, historical persons now. While not alien, Torrance says that God has entered the creaturely as the transcendent and different. The Word continually enters the divided and finite as human, meets and recreates existing persons.

The gracious, dialogical and reconciling relation which God has historically founded within humanity in Christ must be understood both in its foundational, "substitutionary" aspect, wherein meeting, reconciling and faithful human response has already occurred in Jesus, and the dynamic, ongoing, face-to-face encounter of persons with God, as the Truth of God in Christ by the Spirit is met in the present, in the "moment" of the Word-encounter. Biblical anthropomorphism is said by Torrance to be far from mere projection of the human into the divine, but is obversely reflective of the stress placed upon the majestic objectivity and transcendence of God. God in his utter difference and otherness is yet the living God who "turns himself toward mankind" and only in that way does he give himself to be known. God the divine Subject-Object is said to be known in true objectivity only within and through personal, dialogical communion with God in the encounter rooted in Jesus Christ where God now confronts one with a compellingly anthropomorphic, reciprocal and primary "Thou" in his movement to adapt himself to our humanity and our human knowing by means of the historical incarnation. There one is lifted up to communion with God and there one is summoned to know God strictly in accordance with the way he has given himself to be known in the world. Thus, it is first Torrance's point that the present existing individual be brought face to face with Christ for only there in such meeting is our humanity disclosed as diseased and in-turned and self-willed. This human existence needs to be adapted back, bent back to God. In one sense, Jesus did this in the entirety of his incarnate life, death and resurrection. It is finished. But in Christ by the Spirit "the human subject is established before God by the out-going of the divine love to him, while he on his part is brought to respect the objectivity of God as he learns to love God for his own sake."[144]

Torrance makes a critical point for his argument in saying that Jesus Christ "embodied in himself the personal address of God's Word to man and the personal response of man to God's Word." As Mediator he *is* the communion, or, in a sense, the encounter.

> Thus, in Jesus the final response of man toward God was taken up, purified through his atoning self-consecration on our behalf, and incorporated into the Word of God as his complete self-communication to mankind, but also as the covenanted way of vicarious response to God which avails for all of us and in which we all may share through the Spirit of Jesus . . . the real text of the New Testament revelation is the humanity of Jesus . . . Jesus in whom we have both the Word of God become man and the perfect response of man to God offered on our behalf . . . . In him our humanity, our human understanding, our human word are taken up, purified and sanctified, and addressed to God the Father for us . . . that is the word of man with which God is well pleased.[145]

In the incarnation God penetrated the human constitution and in himself converted it back to love and obey God, "not my will but Thy will," and Jesus is himself the meeting, the vicarious human response in all of his life and activity to God. It is for this reason that Torrance emphasizes that "faith," which is that appropriate knowing relation with God objectively given in Christ by the Spirit, is not based on or from the existing self. Faith in the foundational God-human encounter in the world in Jesus Christ is said to be reciprocity and community between God and mankind in the polarity between the faithfulness of God and the answering faithfulness of humanity in Jesus Christ, that is, his faith not ours.[146]

But, again, how is this sharing linked to the human being living in the present? According to Torrance, the other side of the encounter occurs in order that in the hearing of the Gospel within the Church the objective, historical event of the incarnation encounters one in the present. In that Word-event one is engaged or in "personal encounter" with God in which his Word has penetrated into our existence creating relation and real reciprocity, thus inviting response and the knowing assent of faith to God's transcendent glory in his Word. In this faith-meeting with God, Torrance sees elements of freedom and compulsion which correspond to the interrelatedness of Word and Event in Jesus Christ. Objective historical Fact and personal Word encounter one through the *kerygma* with a determinate and articulate rationality grounded in God's Being and Word. Jesus Christ is only known in accordance with the innermost necessity of his Being. Encounter with God does not happen then by God's overwhelming the person with the immediacy of his transcendent glory but graciously in one's existence and worldly relations through the medium of humanity and human word.[147] By means of Kierkegaardian "contemporaneity," Torrance sees the God-human encounter founded in Christ as given in the subject's present existence where he is known freely in and through the Truth by the *kerygma*, or apostolic witness of Scripture, as the human mind falls under the compulsion of the coming of the Truth of God in the person's present existence and situation. This is the "second moment" in the objective movement or action of God in humanity for knowledge of God (the "first" being the incarnation, the "third" being fagth-ful theo-logical expression in the establishment of scientific "disclosure models") taking place in the human "moment." This "occurs" as the objectively grounded possibility of the person of Jesus Christ becomes subjective reality in actual human knowledge as connected to that Christ. In this "moment" the Holy Spirit meets and reveals God in Christ himself to the human subject here and now, in the world, while "lifting" the person, enabling, all in a face-to-faceness with the coming of God in Christ over against the individual. As such the Spirit of Christ opens the existing subject up subjectively toward the objectivity of God as Lordly Subject.[148] God's Act in Christ by the Spirit in the individual's present existence is esteemed to be the personal speaking of God in his Word as the Object encounters one as lordly Subject addressing subject(s) over against him to effect reconciliation and restoration of theo-logical knowledge. Again, this is direct, intuitive knowledge of God in his Word and Spirit within a divinely founded dialogical relation centered in the Truth of God Himself. In acting, addressing, demanding and creating relation, dialogue and reciprocity in humanity in the incarnate Christ, and thus upon the ground of the real knowledge of God, God in Christ by the Spirit founds in the "moment" of face-to-face encounter a "trans-subjective relation" of God and the human subject whereby the person is taken out of self in its incarcerated subjectivity and un-truth and made capable of objectivity, thereby becoming a true subject.[149] In the "moment," Word by the Spirit comes immediately to the subject via the God established media in the world for real healing relation in Jesus Christ.

Torrance has indirectly stated that his understanding of revelation is a mediate view between that of Barth and Emil Brunner, and that his work *Calvin's Doctrine of Man* was intended to heal the rift between the two on this matter.[150] His own theo-logical expression and use of Kierkegaard bear this out. While Torrance has been found to be firm regarding the relation between faith and rationality, faith as realist knowing in relation to God in Christ, there is also in his thinking of the God-human encounter in the moment provocative terminology and description of the Word-event traceable to the "mystical" traditions in Christian thought. The mystery of God's comprehensibility and intelligibility disclosed in the Word often brings out from Torrance this type of "mystical" or even "existential" representation, particularly when coupled to his emphases upon "unknowing" and borrowed elements from Kierkegaard on the revelation of God in Christ in *Philosophical Fragments* and *Concluding Unscientific Postscript*. Because of this issue, a brief excursus on Torrance's interpretation and use of the thought of Soren Kierkegaard will be undertaken here.

Regarding Torrance's concern for the contemporary question regarding the possibility of knowledge, he says variously that the question of the possibility of knowledge cannot be raised *in abstracto* or *a priori* but only *in concreto* and *a posteriori* (cf. above). Kierkegaard, he says, rightly attacked that abstract way of thinking which ignores the concrete and temporal, thereby abolishing the actual and real.

> It is false . . . to answer a question in a medium in which the question cannot arise, and therefore it is wrong to pose the question as to possibility in abstraction from the reality which alone can give rise to it. That is why it is a contradiction to infer existence from thought, for "thought takes existence away from the real and thinks it by abrogating its actuality, by translating it into the sphere of the impossible." This means that in any branch of knowledge we begin within the knowledge relation where we actually are,

and seek to move forward by clarifying and testing what we already know
and by seeking to deepen and enlarge its content.[151]

Torrance interprets Kierkegaard as saying that in each legitimate area of
knowledge/science there is the presupposition of the reality and accessibility of
the proper object and the possibility of knowing it further without ever stepping
outside of the object's own actuality and inner rationality.

In learning from Kierkegaard, Torrance concludes that while abstract
thought considers both possibility and reality it can sustain the relation of
possibility to reality only because it has falsified its notion of reality by
attempting to think it within the medium of possibility. Kierkegaard modified
traditional logical procedure in order to make room for thinking actual existence
without falsely transforming it into necessity.[152] Actual knowledge of the
proper Object of theology requires a mode of rational thought within the subject-
object relation which would be in genuine accord with and adequate to the
nature of the object. For Kierkegaard the object of theological knowledge is
Truth in the form of personal Being, namely, Truth as active Subject. But this
Truth must be known in a way that is appropriate to its nature as Subjectivity
because only in that way will the knowing subject be in the truth in relation to
it. The mode of apprehending the Truth belongs to the Truth. "Truth is
Subjectivity."[153]

Authentic human subjectivity is only possible when the existing person
encounters the objectivity of the divine Subject which is the experience of faith,
the "highest passion of subjectivity." In faith before the objective divine Subject
the existing individual so encounters the Truth that the person's whole existence
is involved and transformed into conformity to it. Apart from this encounter the
Truth is not known. But within the faith-knowing relation Truth is found not
only on the side of the object known but also in the knowing subject. This is
Kierkegaard's meaning in saying that "the mode of apprehension of the truth is
precisely the truth,"[154] says Torrance. This subjectivity is found to lie upon
the objective ground in the divine Reality of God given in Jesus Christ.
Kierkegaard's point was that when the issue of truth is raised in an objective
way then the knower is directed objectively to the truth as an object to which
he/she is related, though he/she does not focus attention on the relationship but
on the Truth itself. The question of truth raised "subjectively" means that the
knower is directed subjectively to the truth and it is only then that the focus is
on the subject's relation to the truth.[155] The object of faith is not confused
with one's faith nor is it upon the construction of subjectivity. Torrance affirms
that in Kierkegaard the very passion of faith is the opening of the knowing
subject out to the most objective of all realities, God himself as he actively
discloses and gives himself to be known by the knowing subject in Jesus Christ.
To know the Truth is to encounter the Truth, to be made contemporary with the
Truth and to be in right relation to he who is the Truth. In that way one is

understood to be in the truth with the Truth, "the god" who is "teacher" and
"savior," by whom the "moment" is decisive.[156]   As an example of
existentialist misinterpretation of Kierkegaard, Torrance interestingly mentions
Karl Barth in the transition from *Der Romerbrief* to *Die Christliche Dogmatik*,
and through Anselm to *Die Kirchliche Dogmatik*, where Barth sought to reject
all existential interpretation and the *analogia entis*. In this way he developed his
doctrine of God's Grace in Christ as learned from St. Anselm (*fides quaerens
intellectum*), Calvin (*omnis recta cognitio Dei ab obedientia nascitur*) and
Kierkegaard (the relation of the possibility to the reality of the incarnation) over
against all aprioristic forms of thought.   Though Barth's few and negative
references seem to offer a problem here for Torrance, he is firm that a corrected
understanding of Kierkegaard forced Barth's theology back ever more and more
upon its proper Object, God self-disclosed in Christ.[157]

Torrance's profound admiration of and dependence upon Kierkegaard at
this juncture on the question of the objective knowledge of God arises too from
Kierkegaard's profound and transformative way of "thinking movement."
Torrance says that Kierkegaard sought to go beyond mere logical connections,
which tended to lose existence, by developing a mode of thought appropriate to
real movement and transition, thought which is itself a free movement
inseparable from actual becoming. This necessitated that he give attention to
objective movement in the proper object of knowledge and to subjective
movement of the subject in relation to the object, says Torrance, while it also
means refusing to isolate pure thought from the entire activity of the empirical
subject, especially the human will—thinking within the historical medium which
involves decision. This "becoming" is said to have had no real place in
traditional logic. Real thinking is the movement of thought from known to
unknown involving transition and act in accord with objective movement. This
faithful following of the object is, according to Torrance, what Kierkegaard
termed the "leap" or, in theology, the "leap of faith," that is, "the activity of
the reason in obedient reaction to the action of Truth, an activity analogous to
the Truth in time, or to the Truth in action."[158] Like Einstein's relation with
Newton, Kierkegaard's concern with realist, objective Truth led him to reject
notions of time and space taken from the static point of absolute rest. Rather
he injected needed dynamism into modern thinking, especially the knowledge of
God in Christ given in and from the economic and historical movement of God
for us.

> . . . knowledge of Jesus Christ as Eternal Truth in the form of historical
> being involves a modification in our theory of knowledge, in fact a change
> in the logical structure of our consciousness. . . eternal Truth encounters us
> also as temporal fact . . . . This time-element or movement, cannot be
> eliminated from our knowledge without falsification. Theological statements
> require to be related to the Truth in time if they are to be truthful but they

require to be continuously upheld in that temporal relationship through living participation in the movement of the Truth, if they are to remain true . . . . Theological thinking is historical thinking . . . but (more) through participation in the eternal which has entered into the historical and gathered it into inalienable relation to the Truth in Jesus Christ.[159]

As he interprets and uses this aspect of Kierkegaard's thought, Torrance finds in it a scientific way of coming to the nature of theological understanding and communication which always involves and partakes of the divine movement of reconciliation. The problem of divine-human difference and opposition is magnified when brought up against the fact of one's own untruth, severance from the Truth, and the fact that one can know the Truth only by its being given to the end that one is reconciled with the Truth. Torrance sees here the epistemological relation to the Truth of God given in the "god in time" as grounded in atoning acts and completed in the reception of forgiveness.

If human reason is to act rationally in the face of this objective Act, God in Christ, it must allow the nature of this Truth to prescribe for it the mode of rationality or thinking and the mode of demonstration appropriate to it. That being so, says Torrance, Kierkegaard recognized that because the Truth is the Eternal moving into time human reason must move with it to know it and to break with other false or alien habits of thought and rationality which have been developed from determinate rationality. Like Einstein and Bohr in physics, Kierkegaard is said to have followed God's movement, the Truth becoming incarnate in Christ, in order to acquire the proper mode of rationality for the knowledge 'f that Truth acting here—"kinetic thinking."[160]

Such rationality has to move across a logical gap lying between knowledge acquired and knowledge yet to be acquired which cannot be logically inferred from the already known. It is, in Torrance's view, real *metanoia* or repentance of prior understanding that occurs in one's contemporaneous encounter with Jesus Christ the Word by the Spirit for the apprehension of the objective Word of God in the very way it has taken in its incarnate movement, its economic movement in the world.[161] Shunning *a priori* axioms, Kierkegaard is said to have been able to think into the dynamic of the self-revelation of God, penetrating the inner logic of the incarnation of the Word, the very place where the individual is met now in that same movement within the "field" of the triadic "God-world-man" and "God-man-world" relations.[162] One can only know that Truth by entering personally by faith into historical and knowing relation with that incarnate Reality in time. This is necessary in order to thereby be made contemporary with it in the "moment" of encounter. Only such theologic is found to be appropriate to the Incarnation.[163]

The Intuitive Knowledge of God and the Mystical Apprehension of Truth. The knowledge of God in Christ by the Spirit is "intuitive" knowledge.

It is direct, immediate (though given through created media), and cognitive. Faith, as the appropriate way of knowing in relation to God, has been found, in Torrance's thinking, to be itself rational, cognitive. Following his understanding of Kierkegaard on faith-rationality as the faith-ful "thinking after" of the objective movement of God in Christ, and Barth's understanding of faith in Christ as a real knowing, Torrance says that "faith is the very mode of rationality which the reason takes in its faithful adaptation to what it seeks to understand." The "epistemic process" properly advocated by the historic Christian faith is that we believe in order that we may understand and thereby be strengthened in the hold of authentic belief upon the mind. This faith or belief in God is correlated with the intrinsic rationality of the Object, and is the accordant response to the transcendent Ground of all created being and intelligibility as given in his Word.[164]

We have established that first the very center of Torrance's understanding of the knowledge of God is the fact of the incarnation of the Word of God. There is also the human participation in Christ by the Holy Spirit and the effective encounter with the Word of God as one is made contemporary with it as founded upon Christ who, as Mediator, is our participation and our dialogue in the Truth of God. In Jesus Christ the knowledge of God is already a human experience. Realization or actualization of knowledge in the existing human being occurs in terms of personal participation in the Son's own relation of knowing and loving with the Father. He breaks down in himself all impediments to reception, especially here the noetic. God is thus said to take one into the closed Father-Son polarity where such knowledge is realized and has already been "translated" for us in Jesus and made present to us by the Holy Spirit. There one may share the mind of Christ. In relation to the living Word, the sole given Object of theological knowledge and investigation, the way of knowing and thinking cannot then be a positivistic mastery but a rational Word-event.

If to know God is to know him according to his own intelligible Reality and to partake of his uncreated Rationality, then when describing this faith-knowing as "intuition" of the Truth of God (or the apprehension of the human being by the Truth), the capacity to know in this relation is not an autonomous power of the mind (*intellectus agens*) to partake of truth via mysterious insight. Yet the intuitive knowledge of God is not found to be in any sense the negation of human rational powers.[165] Indeed, the opposite is meant to be the case. Torrance emphasizes that the knowledge of the Word of God does not arise from logic, for there is no such logical road or bridge in theological knowledge (even as there is no logical road to the laws of causality), but rather "intuition" reflecting the surrender of the mind and thought to the "sheer weight or impress of external reality upon his apprehension."[166] Torrance is not asserting that "intuition" can be reduced merely to a situation of a knower unexpectedly taken by the clarity of the Truth, because in many ways, despite his terminology, his stress is not so much upon the intellective only but upon an ongoing intelligibility occurring in dialogical relation toward ever increasing profundity of knowledge and expression. Torrance, like Barth, asserts that theological Truth is self-evidencing which points again to the decisive, self-disclosing Act of God upon the mind whereby one "intuits" the knowledge of God in Christ and by the Spirit when the Word "seizes our minds and sets up within them the law of its own rationality . . . (true concepts) arise in us through direct and intuitive apprehension of reality in its own evidence and objective hermeneutical force."[167]   While Torrance never quite expresses his view in terms of complete coercion in the knowing-reconciling relation to God in Christ, he clearly regards the force of the Truth to be so "self-evidencing" that the person is brought "under the compulsion of (God's) divine Being . . . under the light of His Truth which is His divine Being coming into view and becoming in our understanding and knowledge of Him what He is consistently in Himself and in all His relations with us."[168]   But this is actualized only if we do not obtrude ourselves and our subjectivity in the way of God's light and truth, but rather repent of such and hear the Truth out of the Truth in a truthful way. It is this Word or Truth which is said to personally come to and encounter one rationally within one's historical existence while ever retaining his own Truth and Majesty. Therefore Torrance says that there is no way to demonstrate the Truth outside the Truth who unveils himself to us in real meeting.

> Through His Word God confronts us with the inner speech of His divine Being and through His Spirit He evidences Himself to us in the presence of His reality, in such a way that He creates in us the capacity to hear, recognize and apprehend Him, and evokes from us the consent and underspanding of faith in His self-revelation. Knowledge of God is thus conceptual in its essential root (*fides esse nequit sine conceptione*, as Anselm said), with a conceptuality that derives from God's self-revelation in Word, but which we have to bring to articulate expression in our understanding, with a conceptuality that finds shape in our human forms of thought and speech, yet under the control of God's own intelligible reality . . . . We know God only in that we are seized by His reality. It is in response to that divine grasping of us that our human grasping of Him takes place . . . an act of "under-standing."[169]

From this vantage point in Torrance's thinking, "intuition" or the "intuitive knowledge of God" refers to God's active self-evidencing of his own Reality which engenders real human apprehension of and intellectual assent to the Word of God which it "compels" in the mind under the Lordship of God over that very intuitive knowledge of him. The personal, self-revelatory nature of God's Truth calls for the corresponding personal response of faith, but faith never negates that primary issue for Torrance that the Truth must not be covered over and lost in the subjectivity of the knower—"the sheer objectivity of God." The knowing subject cannot enter into the actual content of the knowledge of God, though human participation is essential to that knowledge because the person cannot know God outside of the one in whom it is actively given in the world.[170] Yet, as has been stated previously, this knowing is also referred to in terms of "mystical knowing," and even "unknowing," and the theological outcome as "mystical theology." Given his emphases upon the priority of God's transcendence, his objective self-disclosure, the realist, cognitive, as well as dialogical, knowledge of the Triune God, there would seem to be discrepancy in the apparent need for the negation of the rational and the kind of apprehension in which, like the neo-Platonic mystics, there is the need to leave the human and to climb "up" to an absorptionist relation with the One/God.

To understand Torrance here one must recall again the centrality of incarnation as unitarily coupled to the active presence of God the Holy Spirit, and the sense Torrance makes of "encounter" and conceptions of "contemporaneity" in the intuitive and assenting knowledge of God. As actual knowledge of the Triune God occurs only in and by the economy of God's redemptive self-giving in history, the knowledge and understanding of God is not taken abstractively, not even from Holy Scripture, but by means of a movement of thought "up" from level to level initiated in the "field" of Christian experience and faith as one penetrates by the Spirit into that which is otherwise beyond human capacity. Like the Nicene Fathers, Torrance wants to follow the way that theological knowing and thinking has been commanded to go, given the *homoousion* relation.[171] As "truth" always denotes for Torrance the state of affairs ontologically prior to the truth of cognition or statement, this includes implicitly an oughtness. The Trinity in itself is the supreme Truth as all finite entities owe their truth by reference to the Being of God. The Truth of God is that he is what he is and reveals who he is as he is, confronting, encountering historical persons in that freedom and majesty of his own Reality and in the prerogative of his own Truth, Being and self-evidence. The God who relates himself to us is he who confronts as Lord who, in human intuitive knowing, is infinitely inexhaustible in his Truth and is the Source of all adequate human conceptualization of him. Therein one is allowed to participate in and to express the "ellipse of knowing" founded and maintained by God the Father in Christ and by the Spirit with human beings. The knowing subject is "locked into" a multi-leveled structure of intelligibility and truth of infinite range and grounded ultimately in God's own eternal Being.[172]

But that intuitive knowledge of God instantiated in dialogical relation in encounter with God as Father through Christ the Son and in the Spirit, that understanding of the Word of God beyond all human words or creaturely being and embodied in Jesus Christ, can be obstructed or eclipsed by *a priori* or inappropriate conceptual forms. Closed, dualistic modes of thought limit and distort apprehension of the Truth of God. For this reason the knowledge of God, says Torrance, requires that one go the way of "disciplined unknowing" of all prior thinking and conceiving that is not in accord with that revelation of God. Torrance believes this discipline or negation is necessary if the mind is to be open to the purity of divine Light and Truth. Borrowing from St. John of the Cross, and used in terms of his own program of realist knowing, Torrance says that this "leads to the pure imageless knowing of faith that comes from the hearing of God's Word," which is so needful because the concern is above all "to know God himself who is the source of all illumination."[173] Truly, the knowledge of God is inherently problematic for human beings because of the unapproachable nature of his divine Light. But against much of the mystical tradition Torrance states that the difficulty here is not that God is beyond all light and understanding, for God is wholly luminous or intelligible in himself. Following St. John of the Cross again, he contends that God is unapproachable because of the "sheer invisibility of his uncreated Light" resulting from the fact of the "transcendence of his Light over our finite capacities" which, in a sense, puts "God in the dark for us."[174] But additionally, God's "unapproachability" for our knowledge of him is said to result directly from the inability of impure human minds to bear the sheer purity of his divine Light."[175] We are also sinfully estranged from the glory and Truth of God.

In this context of the question of the knowledge of God and the utter difference of the holy God from the contingent and creaturely, Torrance holds that such knowledge can only occur by that establishment of reciprocity between God and humanity whereby the uncreated Light of God adapts itself carefully to the lowly human mental capacity while creatively reconciling and "elevating" the knowing subject to communion with God. By forgiveness and cleansing and healing occurring in Christ and by the Spirit, the mind transparently receives the transforming emition of God's Light. Of course, all knowledge of God in this two-fold relationship between God and the person is mediated through the incarnate one in whom the invisible Light of God is made visible, temporal and accessible.[176]

But one knows God only by cultivating the "extra-logical" relation to God in that faithful, dialogical bearing of the mind upon God himself in order to increasingly assume the epistemological unity of form and being in what one knows and in the knowing of it, as governed by the ordering principles founded by and in God's self-revelation.[177] The intuitive knowledge of God is then said to be in accord with the way God has given himself to be known by faith, worship, thankfulness and meditation in the Church. The "mystical" aspect of the knowing relation is meant to operate correctively at the very point of human conceptualization by sustaining the non-formal intuitive relation to God, while negating false directions in thought and speech used to refer to God. Torrance explains that this "mystical" knowing and "mystical" theology are necessarily apophatic factors in the real knowledge of God.

. . . rational structures of space and time through which God has made himself known to us, and relates them back to the ineffable Being and spiritual Reality of God in such a way that it not only reminds us of their finite limitations but keeps them ever open toward the inexhaustible Mystery of God's Love . . . we must learn to forget, which is the other side of the heuristic outreach to what is new and hitherto unknown.   The art of "unknowing" (*agnosia*) is far from being easy. To apprehend the new, old ways of apprehension must be left behind, for the new cannot be known through assimilating it to what we already know . . . there that mystical theology through its enlightening marginal control of theological reflection and dogmatic formulation can fulfill its true service in our knowledge of God . . . theologians must allow mystical theology to indwell dogmatic theology if dogmatic theology is to have the objective depth in its correlation with divine revelation which it needs if it is to fulfill its task in a godly way worthy of the Being and Nature of God.[178]

As the result of the redemptive and re-creative coming of God through the Son in the Spirit, the knowing relation which the existing human being participates in is direct and intuitive by the encounter in the Word-event. Therein, in Christ the Word in one's existence now, one may know, by way and in the way of the economy of God, the Being of God in that Act and the Act of the Being of God, to which thought must be ever more closely conformed and refined through repentant thinking or unknowing of the false notions and modes of thought which are contrary to the true objective Reality of God in Christ.

While the outcome of all knowledge of God occurs by means of his Christocentricity, Torrance's methodological focus upon and in the incarnation of the Word, is said to be ultimately knowledge of the eternal, ontological or immanent Trinity. This must be further unfolded and clarified if Torrance's full position is to be properly represented.

The Knowledge of God as Trinity:
The Ground, Grammar and Telos of
Thomas Forsyth Torrance's Theology

Introduction

For the first two decades of his theological writing Torrance's focus regarding the question of the knowledge of God was almost entirely given to emphasis upon the incarnational and Christocentric. References to and citations of Torrance, when this concern for knowledge of God was mentioned or discussed, would mention only Torrance's early incarnational conceptualizations.[179] The incarnational emphasis and its formative relation to theo-logical knowledge and structuring is still central and true in Torrance's theologizing; Christ is *the place* for all true theo-logical thinking after the movement of God in the world.   There God has objectified himself in order to redemptively be known as he is in the world by human beings.   But that which had been given comparatively much less explicit emphasis in his thought, the ontological Trinity, God's eternal Being and relations within himself, has become with fullness of clarity the finale or *telos* and ultimate ground of knowledge of God, of reconciliation, of the doing theology in the service of the Word of God, for Torrance.   It is for that reason that Torrance's mature theology is referred to here as Christocentric-Trinitarian.   If, as Torrance vigorously maintains, that the eternal, ontological Trinity has disclosed himself economically in space-time from the Father through the Son and by or in the Spirit, then God's own internal relations can and must be known after the actual economy into the world and for humanity which he has chosen.   Thus, much like Barth, Torrance asserts that scientific necessity requires that one think after (*Nachdenken*) the objective way of "God to us" by the Spirit, in and through Christ to the Father, and thereby to finally know God in God's Godness as ontologically triune and the *perichoresis* or coinherence of Persons "therein." This means that one is to actually participate in the knowledge God has of himself in a realist, objective way.   We have given much discussion to Torrance's real incarnational or Christocentric and pneumatological emphases, with his understanding of God's active coupling of his self-revelation with knowledge in encounter, the Word-event, intuitive knowledge and repentant, mystical knowing of God from the Truth of God in Christ.   But the question is then posited: what is the revelational, conceptual, ontological connection Torrance posits between what is revealed by the Spirit and in Christ, or between Christ the incarnate Son and the Father, and between the economic and ontological Trinity?   As so strongly influenced by the Nicene Fathers and St. Athanasius in the Eastern Church, Torrance points always to the *homoousion* doctrine of the Nicene-Constantinopolitan Creed.   As observed earlier, this means for Torrance that God is toward us in Christ (the economy) what he is in himself from all eternity (Trinity).   The "homoousial" relation, Father, Son and Spirit, is found to guarantee the realist, objective knowledge of God against all dualist thinking which splits God from world-humanity.   It is Torrance's "epistemological linchpin."

The Epistemological Centrality of the Homoousion and the Economic Trinity

Torrance repeatedly emphasizes that the Nicene Fathers thought "scientifically" from the Son to the Father (that is, "theo-logically"), from Jesus Christ to the Father who sent him, therefore understanding Jesus Christ to be "of one being with the Father" (*homoousios to Patri*) and "God of God, Light of Light," says Torrance. Torrance's point is that there is an absolutely critical "organic" connection to be found within the relation of the Father and the Son (and the Spirit). It is the link which ties the whole of Torrance's Christocentric-Trinitarian theology and the knowledge of God out of himself together. Torrance's position is that the knowledge of God is a rational event (Word-event) and is properly knowledge (*scientia*, conscious and actual relation to Object) and conceptual both in cognition and expression, and that theological knowledge begins from where God is actually known as given concretely in the world. All of this is grounded in God's own Being. For this reason Torrance emphasizes and gives central epistemological and theological place to the Nicene *homoousion* doctrine, or the "homoousial relation" between eternal Father and eternal Son incarnate in Jesus Christ.[180]

Christian theology is said to arise out of actual knowledge of God given in and with the concrete and temporal. Christian theology, according to Torrance, is therefore concerned with the concrete, space-time fact of God's self-disclosure, with God himself here. Hence there can be no anthropocentric beginning point except in the sense of that one place where the Word became flesh, truly human. Here human thinking is established within the area delimited by actual knowledge of God. Thinking and speaking must ever and only be by and from the divine fact itself, as given from beyond itself and creation, and which is in no way dependent upon human discovery. It is said to be known in its ultimacy and objective Reality in the participation of the faith relation.[181] Therefore the continuity of being and nature between the given, concrete fact of Jesus Christ and the God who comes to be known is understood to be all important—the consubstantial relation between the Father and the Son.

The "reciprocity" which God establishes with humanity in Christ means to Torrance that God communicates himself to humanity in a movement of love which penetrates into the human structures, thereby founding the law of love and that circle of knowing and loving which rests finally upon the free ground of God's own intra-trinitarian Being and Activity. The Communion of love in God has interpenetrated human existence in Christ in a way which forms a community of love and gives to human beings place of participation to share in God's own Communion of Love within the homoousial and interpenetrating/perichoretic relations of the Father, Son and Holy Spirit.[182] In the participatory reciprocity that God creates by his own triune Being, the person in Christ by faith realizes that God is and lives in a Communion of mutual Love as the one by whom personhood and mutual relations then come into being in mankind.

As Torrance thinks especially of the patristic paradigm, finding their struggle so related to his own corrective concern against the modern re-entrenchment of "dualism," he maintains that the central evangelical truth reaffirmed at Nicaea was that Jesus Christ is God's Son or God's Word and that

God's Son or Word is Jesus Christ. The Arian and Sabellian successors of the older ebionite and docetic heresies had to be confronted with Jesus Christ as God and man in one Person because if he was not really "God of God" then no divine reality was to be found in anything he said or did on the one hand and if he were not human then what God accomplished in him had no soteriological relevance for human beings in their contingent space-time situation. Herein the decisive issue for saving faith was, again, the nature of the relation between Jesus Christ the incarnate Son and God the Father.

In declaring the incarnate Son of the Father to be "of one being with the Father," among the other crucial affirmations, the Fathers at Nicaea meant that the incarnate Son is of identically the same being as the Father—"it is the self-same God who is revealed to us as the Son and the Father . . . the incarnate Son is the very same being as God the Father . . . (and it) expresses the distinction between them that obtains within the oneness."[183] Torrance concludes that the all-important *homoousion* doctrine resulted when the Nicene Fathers objectively, indeed, scientifically penetrated into the inner substance of the Gospel and the in-sight that "Jesus is Lord," the inner logic of the incarnation, and brought to expression by "disclosure model" the ontological substructure upon which the evangelical message in the New Testament about Jesus Christ rests. In a real sense, he sees the Fathers to be penetrating from "level to level" through the interrelated, open levels of God's truth grounded in God's own Being. To Torrance then the Nicene *homoousion* is both revolutionary and decisive for theo-logical thinking after the way of God for us because it clearly expresses the fact that in Jesus Christ what the eternal triune God is "toward us" and "in the midst of us" in and through the Word made flesh he actually and truly is in himself from all eternity. To put that another way, the penetrating insight of the Nicene *homoousion* doctrine is found to be that God is in the transcendent internal relations of his own eternal being (the *perichoresis* or coinherence of the triune Persons) the very same Father, Son and Holy Spirit that he is in his self-revealing and redeeming activity in space-time for mankind.[184]

Torrance then finds the significance of the "all-important" *homoousios to Patri* to be in its declaration that as Jesus Christ shares equally with the Father in the one Being of the Godhead he is the embodiment of the entire Being of God and is God's exclusive self-revelation. If he is not such, says Torrance, then Jesus is finally and only creature and external to God, different from God's Being and foreign to him. In a sense, it is all or nothing. If this is rejected then the necessary result is, whether for the "theological dualism" of Arius, Schleiermacher or Bultmann, that God is utterly unknowable because no merely creaturely being, however esteemed or exalted, can mediate any authentic knowledge of God. If final distinction or separation is made between the being of the incarnate Son and the being of the Father one cannot maintain that there is any oneness between what is presented in the Gospel as the revelation of God and God himself.

> If what God is in himself and what he is in the Lord Jesus Christ were not
> the same, there would be no identity between God and the content of
> revelation and no access for mankind to the Father through the Son and in the
> Spirit . . . . God would be for us no more than an absolute blank, of which
> we can neither think nor speak . . . . If it is not with God himself in his own
> being that we have to do in revelation, then it is not with theologia . . . but
> with mythologia, not with theology but with mythology that we are
> concerned. Moreover, if Christ is detached from God, then he himself is no
> longer central to the substance of the Gospel, but is only a transient variable
> representation of God, a detached symbolic image and no more.[185]

The *homoousion* means the self-communication of, and hence the realist
knowledge of, God in Christ as he inherently and eternally is in his own Being.

Positively Torrance so stresses the epistemological-soteriological
importance of the Nicene *homoousion* for his own theology, and correctively for
"dualistic" modern theology, because in that expressed understanding of the
relation of Son to Father he sees both effectual reference to the Truth and
opening of thought and understanding to the historical fact of God's
condescension to impart himself redemptively to us in Jesus Christ. There is
then epistemological and ontological connection between the love of Jesus here
and the love of God which has not stopped short of the actual dilemma of human
existence. God is thereby also known to be love in himself. Therefore all is
said to depend upon the unity in Being and Act and Word between Jesus Christ
the incarnate and only begotten Son and God the Father.[186]

The *homoousion* says then that God is no Unknown behind the back of the
historical Jesus, but is known as he is in Jesus Christ, thereby binding together
creation and redemption in the wholeness and reality of Christ, the personal
Being and Act of God in the world. Torrance says this means that the whole
life of Jesus is to be regarded as embraced within the coinherent relations of the
Holy Trinity. God's own Being is intrinsically "eloquent," and in his self-
revelation to humanity in his Word God speaks out of himself communicating
his very Self in the incarnation of the eternal Word. This is dynamically and
ongoingly true in the present of the Word-event as well, when, by the Spirit,
Christ encounters one across the centuries through the apostolic witness to the
Word.[187] The *homoousion* insight penetrates into that incarnation of the Son
within the contingent ontological structures of human existence whereby "he
actually establishes within it the laws of his own internal relations and our
rational understanding takes on the imprint of what it is given to know, the
triune Reality of God himself."[188]

On the basis of the hypostatic union in the one Person of Christ, there can
be, says Torrance, epistemic reference substantiated in reality, the reality of God
and mankind, because he finds that the incarnation falls within the spatio-
temporal structures of humanity in the world and it likewise falls within the Life

and Being of God. The *homoousion* is reckoned to be not only the "ontological and epistemological linchpin" of Torrance's own theology but, in his opinion, of all truly Christian theology.[189] In this doctrine, everything is said to hold together and the God-world interactive relatedness, which God has established in Creation, is grounded in its fullest and final expression and Act in Christ. The consubstantiality of Son and Father is the "linchpin" because it uncovers the one saving economy of God and the eternal Being of God without leaving Jesus Christ behind as a "vanishing point."

But here the useful scientific concept of multi-leveled, open interrelatedness is applied to the eternal Trinity. Torrance asserts that in Jesus Christ, who is of one being with the Father, one must think in cross-leveled reference from that basic level to what he calls the "theological level." In this way he finds that the *homoousion* insight takes the form in which Jesus Christ is toward mankind in history, in love and grace, redemption and sanctification, and pointedly in the mediation of the divine life, what he is inherently in himself in his own Being.[190] The Being and Act and Act and Being of God are known in their unitariness for humanity in and from Christ. But in this cross-level movement of faith-ful theo-logical movement of thought from the second level to the third, the *homoousion* insight takes the form in which God is in his economic, redemptive and self-disclosive movement toward us in Jesus Christ what he is inherently, essentially and eternally in himself, in his own triune Being. The Holy Trinity is not different or detached from what God personally discloses himself to be in Jesus Christ, the Word in history. The *homoousion* expresses that

> . . . our experience of God in Christ is not somehow truncated so that it finally falls short of God, but is grounded in the Being of God himself; it means that our knowing of God is not somehow refracted in its ultimate reference, but actually terminates on the reality of God . . . this movement of reference on our part is grounded in the movement of God himself condescending in the free outpouring of his love to be one with us in the incarnation of his Son, and in and through him to raise us up to share in his own divine life and love which he eternally is in himself.[191]

In this way, Torrance finds the scientific, the theo-logical, the objectively given and commanded (Word) way to be the theological counterpart to Einstein's critique and rejection of the disjunctive Kantian approach to knowledge as he too broke through it to ground scientific knowledge on the objective intelligibility of the universe. Theologically the *homoousion* insight is then found to be not a movement of human thought whereby what is known subjectivistically of Jesus is read back into God, a mythological projection of human subjectivity (e.g., Schleiermacher and Bultmann). Rather the critical edge comes in the "homoousial" reference, especially from the second to the third "level," where thought obediently moves from the economic coming or Act of God in space-time back "up" to what God is immanently in himself. But this thought remains grounded in the objective condescension of God himself in Jesus. Anthropomorphic images are controlled from "above" by the objective, intelligible relations within God himself.[192]

While Torrance does not stress the application of the *homoousion* to the Holy Spirit as often as he does to the foundational Son-Father relation, he is clear that this is just as true and as critical to the redemptive, revelatory economy of God. This is because of the Spirit's activity as the divine presencing and the critical role of the Spirit in the Word-event or encounter, creating contemporaneity to the Word in the "moment" by faith. In this way, and in a way appropriate to the Spirit's own personal mode of Being, Torrance says that it may be said that what the Holy Spirit is toward us in the divine acts of revelatory re-creation and sanctification in Christ he is inherently in himself in the coinherent relations of the Godhead. The Spirit then is also of the very Being of God and not some detached gift or emanation from God. The Holy Spirit is toward existing persons, the presencing of God for human communion with God. Therefore he is in his own Being God, God of God, of one and the same being (*homoousion*) with the Father.[193]

But Torrance also emphasizes the proper difference in the Nicene usage of the *homoousion* of the Spirit and of the Son in both the *oikonomia* and in his inner perichoretic relations from all eternity. As the *Logos*, the Son is said to be the mode of Being in and by which God utters himself, and thus it is in the economy of God and in the incarnation of that Word that God has expressed himself to us in an event in the world. In the mode of Word, according to Torrance, the economy of the Trinity acts in such a way that an epistemic bridge is established in Christ between existing human beings (humanity) and God, a "bridge" which is factually grounded both in the Being of God and in the being of humanity. Thus he stresses that in Christ the economy of the Trinity and the homoousial relation of Son with Father is inseparably bound to that God-man union whereby the incarnation of the Son/Word constitutes the epistemological-soteriological center in all human knowledge of God. Again, this is said to be so because it is rooted in the world and in the eternal God simultaneously. It is in and through that economy of the Word, who is one being with the Father, that existing persons do have real cognitive access to God as he is in himself.[194]

Likewise, Torrance finds in God's objective self-disclosure the crucial role of the Spirit's relation to and difference from the Son revealed, and thus the "homoousial" relation proper to the Spirit in the economy of the Trinity as well. By reference to the *homoousion* of the Son with the Father and the hypostatic union in Christ, constituting him the epistemological center for the knowledge of God in the world for existing human beings, Torrance finds that knowledge of the Spirit comes to clarity. The Spirit, he says, is not knowable in his own personal mode of Being, as is the Son, for he is not embodied or "enwrapped" in the concrete structured objectivities of the world or brought within the limits of human knowing at the creaturely level as has the Son. Because the Spirit is "God of God" but not "man of man" then knowledge of the Spirit in the economy of God rests directly upon the ultimate objectivity of God as God, that is, without mediation by secondary objectivities and only "indirectly on those objectivities through relation to the Son." In the economy of God's self-revelation in the world in the incarnate Son "the Spirit is the creative Agent in our reception and understanding of that revelation."[195]

In applying the *homoousion* in ways appropriate to the Spirit as to the Son, Torrance believes again that thinking is lifted up from level to level and from the level of the "Economic Trinity" to the level of the "Ontological Trinity." As a result of this process of cross-level reference one at last reaches the refined concepts, and particularly the inner relations in God, by which theology expresses the ultimate constitutive relations in the eternal God, i.e., the perichoretic and personal relations "in virtue of which (God) is who he is as the Triune God . . . of God's inner Being."[196]   Many would find this "penetration" to be a presumptuous intrusion into the inner Glory of God's Being, into the transcendent majesty of God's eternal, ineffable triune Being. But Torrance's point is that it is to this very penetration (and refinement), to this very knowing and participation, to which one (particularly the theologian in the Church and in service to the Word) is called and commanded through Christ and in the Spirit.   The God whom one comes to know by the gracious self-objectifying economy of his infinite condescension in Jesus Christ is the God who is self-given therein to be known and known to be infinitely greater than the human being can ever conceive.   For this reason, while he affirms that through Jesus Christ and in the Holy Spirit one does have realist knowledge of the eternal, ontological triune Godhead as he is, still Torrance is also equally emphatic that "it would be sheer theological sin to think of identifying the trinitarian structures of our thought (as faith-fully responsive) and speech about God with the constitutive relations in the Being of the Godhead."   By the very nature of the "levels" of thought and expression which follow and think "up" after the free economy of God's prior movement "down," all true theological concepts and statements inevitably fall far short of the glory of God to which they refer beyond themselves.   Their truth, again, lies not in themselves as statements but in their appropriate reference to, dependence upon, and service of clarification for the eternal Truth of God, which is ultimately that by which they were first brought into being in human understanding.   Thus Torrance contends that the very inadequacy of these concepts and statements to God (their "relativity") must be understood as necessary to their truth and precision.[197]

By faithful reflection upon or thinking after one's encounter with God's objective self-giving, one is drawn level by level into that "ellipse" of knowing and loving, which Torrance finds to include then both God and oneself in Christ and by the Spirit. The subject is embraced by a knowledge of the Reality of God which opens out finally into the eternal relations within the divine Being. Torrance emphasizes that in this way persons are brought to know God in such a way that he is known to be in his eternal Being the Love and Truth which God the Father is toward us here through the incarnate Son and in the Spirit. This means that one knows God's inner trinitarian Being to be an eternal movement of Love. The knowledge and love of God, which is inherent within this communion of God, then interpenetrates human relations in that "reciprocity" of love through Christ and in the Spirit. There is borne in the human subject the unalterable conviction that God is also in himself eternally a fullness of relations of Love in the Truth of his Being.

> The Love with which we are loved by God is the Love with which the Father, the Son and the Holy Spirit love one another in the Trinity, and the knowledge with which we know him is a sharing in the eternal knowing in which the Father, the Son and the Holy Spirit know one another coeternally. What God is toward us in the structure of love relations which he has set up between us and himself, he is in himself as God . . . (this is the outcome of proper scientific penetration into) the essence of the evangelical message that God so loved the world that he gave his only begotten Son for our salvation, namely, that God is antecedently and eternally in himself the Communion of Love which he has manifested to us in his revealing and saving acts.[198]

Jesus embodied the Love and Truth of God himself to "meet us directly and personally within our human being," and by the Spirit God lifts us up to actually share in the Reality, the Love, Truth, and Life of God. In Jesus Christ penetration is instantiated concretely in human terms to "interpret" God to humanity and humanity to God, bringing the two "near" and mediating the Spirit of God to mankind. In this way God has adapted human nature to receive that Holy Spirit. Therefore Torrance says it was necessarily Christology which "became the natural starting (point) for a doctrine of the Trinity."[199]

Thus the crucial *homoousion* doctrine means that in the concrete locus of Christ and in the Spirit thought penetrates into the non-observable, intelligible Reality of God to grasp Christ in his wholeness, his essential *Logos* constitutive of his incarnate actuality. It then conjoins Christ's human historicity and divine eternality, at once divine and human as indivisibly One, overthrowing the obsolete dualisms in the face of the unitariness of God's movement in the world. In this way, scientific theological thought is said to work with rational structures in the knowing of Christ which are correlative to the self-disclosure of God as ultimately impressed upon human thought by the inner relations of the one God who encounters and saves existing human beings in Jesus Christ as Father, Son and Holy Spirit. Torrance's emphasis then is that God's self-communication to and for us, and by means of the incarnational penetration into human existence in the medium of the space-time world, was enacted so that "it would set up within it the laws of its own internal relation," and that human rational understanding would take the "imprint" of that which it has come to know, namely the triune Reality of God himself.[200]　　Torrance's theo-logical "penetration" has been finally for the purpose of thinking after the self-revelation of God in Jesus Christ into the deep, objective structures and ground of the redemptive economy.　It arrives finally at the ontological Trinity which is the Ground and Grammar of all theological understanding, or the realist knowledge of God, with reference to which every aspect of God in his relation to the world is to be understood.　Torrance asserts that "in the Trinity we have the ultimate constitutive relations in God himself, the fundamental Constant upon which the intelligibility and objectivity of all our knowledge of God finally repose, invariant . . . through all of the relativity of human factors."[201]

Finale: Thomas Torrance's Understanding of Realist Human Knowledge of the Ontological Trinity

Theo-logical "arrival" at the final resting "place" of human thought upon God requires that gracious self-disclosive, self-giving "economy" of God to make himself objectively and really known in the world and in the reconciling relation occurring in human faith-knowing as appropriate to God's Being from the Father, through the Son and in the Holy Spirit.　Torrance believes that from the initial, intuitive knowledge of God in Christ the response of faithful, scientific and thus theo-logical thinking in conceptualization and expression must take the way given whereby, like Einstein's "structuring" in physics in *Physics and Reality*, the "knowledge of God's self-revelation to us . . . is the actual ground on which our knowledge arises."[202]

Torrance has described the first level of the knowing of God as the level of experience and worship as one first encounters God's revealing and reconciling action in the Gospel in the covenantal setting of the Church.　At this level we have found the focus to be the "contemporaneous" encounter with Christ in the "moment" within one's own existence.　This meeting with God in Jesus Christ by the Spirit through the Gospel is said to refer to "the evangelical and doxological level" of knowing.[203]

The level of encounter with Christ in space-time means a knowing which is open to and referential beyond itself to that economy or self-giving movement of God in Christ, to "the theological level," in which inquiries are directed to God in this "field" of evangelical and doxological experience where God is found to reveal himself to us as Father, Son and Holy Spirit in the three-fold movement of his love in self-revelation and redemption whereby the inquirer arrives at the basic concepts of "Father," "Son" and "Holy Spirit." These are three distinctively personal modes (not in the "modalist" sense) of divine action and ways of being.　This level of knowing and speaking of the "Economic

Trinity" Torrance understands to be that which is concerned especially with the "Act of God in his Being," as God communicates himself to mankind to be known in the world while remaining what he is in himself in his own Being. In this orderly action of revelation God speaks to us "really and truly and without reserve" in Jesus Christ and his Holy Spirit.[204]

But in the responsive and faithful movement of theo-logical thinking "up" from the Trinity *ad extra*, in dynamic coming and self-disclosure, to the Trinity *ad intra*, resting upon the epistemological "linchpin" of the *homoousion* relation of the three Persons, the God one knows via his infinite condescension in Jesus Christ is the God known to be infinitely greater than can be conceived. All true theo-logical concepts must fall short in themselves for their truth lies in God, the Object of their real referentiality. Again, this is no mere "way of negation." Torrance finds in Christ that the summons to respond not only in initial knowing but in rational thought and speech in ways worthy of God's self-disclosure remains intact as a commandment.[205] Therefore when he speaks of scientific theo-logical knowing in those very terms, it is a "higher theological and scientific level" in relation to the Truth of God's own Being in himself. Torrance is referring to a yet deeper penetration into the self-communication of God.

> At this level we are explicitly concerned with the epistemological and ontological structure of our knowledge of God, moving from the level of economic trinitarian relations in all that God is toward us in his self-revealing and self-giving activity to the level in which we discern the trinitarian relations immanent in God himself which lie behind, and are the ground of the relations of, the Economic Trinity—that is, we are lifted up in thought to the level of "the Ontological Trinity" or the "Immanent Trinity," as it is variously called. This is a movement of thought in which we are compelled . . . to acknowledge that what God is toward us in the three-fold economic activity of his revelation and redemption, as Father, Son and Holy Spirit, he is antecedently and eternally in his own Being in the Godhead.[206]

This closing expression, as often referred to previously, becomes Torrance's central theme here; it is his midpoint conceptually, methodologically and in theo-logical expression. It is the passage of thought from the Trinity *ad extra* to the Trinity *ad intra*. Epistemologically it is said to be movement of thought from the lower "theological" level to the highest level. Scientifically, the higher level, the level of the Ontological Trinity, controls the lower level of knowing, though the Economic Trinity and Ontological Trinity are obviously one. This is reflected conceptually and rooted methodologically in the *homoousion*, but it is also necessarily true if the knowledge of God is actually that, and not some existential human subjectivity falling back upon itself. There is but one divine Reality of God in himself (his Being in his Act) and in God's saving and self-disclosing activity toward mankind (the Act of his Being).[207]

This movement of thought, grounded in the incarnate Word, and from the economic to the ontological relations in God, has the preeminent role for Torrance's scientific theology because in Jesus the human knower is by faith in touch with "real, intelligible relations immanent in God . . . though by their ineffable nature they defy anything like complete formalization," while "they are the ultimate constitutive relations in God."[208] These real coinherent relations in the eternal Being of God are therefore held to be the ultimate, external ground upon which the intelligibility and objectivity of all human knowledge of God is finally based. The immanent trinitarian relations are said to give all theological doctrines unifying simplicity within the Godhead itself.

It has been found that for Torrance all genuine knowledge in any field is held to involve knowledge in accordance with the nature of the realities with which one has to do therein, i.e., in terms of their own internal relations or intrinsic structures. So too Torrance's theo-logical thinking from Jesus Christ, following what he finds in the thought of Athanasius and Cyril of Alexandria, understands the Trinity in this highest, ultimate and ontological sense to be the subject matter of theology par excellence. The Trinity is theologia or theology in its purest form, the pure science of theology, "the ultimate ground of theological knowledge of God, the basic grammar of theology, etc., for it is there that we find our knowledge of God" grounded and lying upon "the final Reality of God himself."[209] Theology is only grounded therein, that is, in the intrinsic relations of God and in God, and it is that Objective Reality which controls and governs all true, realist knowledge of God from the beginning to the end of the process. In this way too Torrance wants to think together unitarily in Jesus Christ *De Deo Uno* and *De Deo Trino* which are too often falsely bifurcated. He says that this results many times from a detachment of natural theology from revealed theology. The Truth of God means that God is eloquent and active by nature, Word and Act, *Logos* and *Energia*, and in him Word and Spirit are not separated from *ousia* and *physis* or, therefore, from *aletheia*.[210]

It was observed previously that Einstein understood the supreme task of physical science to be arrival at those universal, elementary laws (foundational truths) from which knowledge of the universe is built, the complete unitary penetration of natural events. In a similar way, Torrance believes that scientific theology must carry through a critical revision, unification and simplification of the whole of theological knowledge as theo-logical thought is carried through to that "basic grammar" of all Christian theology, the Holy Trinity of God.[211] But further, the *homoousion* doctrine refers to the coinherent relations within the one Being of God, to which the distinctions in the self-revelation of God in the redemptive economy pointed. This too is critical for Torrance and this "scientific" level of knowing God's own eternal Being in Christ. And like Athanasius he concludes that this coinherence (*perichoresis*) is not mere linking of the distinctive properties of the Persons in a way which finally is external to each, but a complete mutual indwelling in which each Person, while remaining what each is, is wholly in the others as the others are wholly in him.[212] But again it is ever important to Torrance's understanding of the Christological pattern in thinking "back" and "up" to the Holy Trinity that the starting point is never left or held as unimportant when the highest level is reached.[213] Jesus Christ and the inner logic of the incarnation ever remain in the heart of theological science as the disclosure place and the grace pattern in and by which God is known and thought in himself.

Therefore Torrance's shift of emphasis from Christocentricity (though Trinity was never lacking) to that of Christocentric-Trinitarian thinking in his later writing has also shifted his way of speaking of the Holy Trinity in relation to Christ, given that God is eloquent (Word) by nature and Act by nature, as a result of his further thinking on that theo-logical and epistemological "linchpin," the *homoousion* doctrine. This has meant some shift of emphasis for Torrance from looking at the Trinity in a more strictly Barthian way as Revealer, Revealedness and Revelation to those *perichoretic* internal relations of the eternal, ontological Trinity.[214] According to the "later" Torrance, the impact of God's historical self-revelation has led not only to understanding of the hypostatic union of Christ and the *homoousion* relation between Son and Father (and Spirit) but also to the *perichoresis*, indicating the mutual containing or mutual involution of realities, or coinherence of persons. While the term was originally used to grasp the way in which the divine and human natures in the one Qerson of Christ interpenetrate each other without the integrity of either being damaged by the other, Torrance uses the term at the next and highest level as the logic of grace, in the Christological and then Theological levels of understanding, was followed through the Economic and finally to the Ontological Trinity by means of the *homoousion* doctrine and the concept of *perichoresis* in God. As a result this *perichoresis* concept has now been "refined" by Torrance and made to give disclosive reference to the eternal, mutual interpenetration of the three Persons in the one God. But once *perichoresis* is thus refined to apply at the highest level to the Trinity it can no longer be applied to Christology at the lower level without great damage being done to the doctrine of Christ.[215] It is in relation to such theo-logical thinking that Torrance has come to reject not only the Hegelian Subject-Object-Relation expression of the Holy Trinity, but eventually also Barth's Revealer-Revelation-Revealedness formulation in favor of a Subject-Object-Subject expression of the Supreme Being of God in his eternal, interior, interpersonal relations. In order to properly reflect the Spirit's distinct and personal Mode in God's self-giving, Torrance emphasizes this subject-object-subject theological structure to reflect the actual structure of God's two-fold movement of self-giving or self-communication from the Father, i.e., through the Son and in the Spirit as governed by the "articulate" content of what God has revealed through the incarnate Son or Word.[216]

Doctrine of the Trinity as Scientific Disclosure Model. Einstein's "Theory of Relativity" is said to be a prominent example of a higher order theory characterized by logical simplicity and comprehensiveness, as it arrives at universal 'lementary laws from which knowledge of the universe is built. It is then a conceptual instrument through which one may discern inherent relatedness in the universe. This is said to be the nature of the effective unitary penetration of reality found in Einstein's theory. As scientific theology is said to have the same task in relation to its proper Object, the doctrine of the Trinity, as grounded upon and from the eternal relations of the three Persons in God, is held up by Torrance as just such a refined "disclosure model." As a "disclosure model," the doctrine of the Trinity is comprised of a "minimum of basic concepts immediately derived from divine revelation (Christ) and our intuitive apprehension of God in his saving activity in history." Other secondary elements are brought together in such a way that "through this doctrinal model we allow our understanding to come under the articulate revelation and power of God's own Reality and seek to grasp in our thought," by the Spirit, "what God communicates to us of his own unity and simplicity."[217] Torrance's concern is obviously with the knowledge of God out of God and not with some "system" *per se*. To that specific end though Torrance believes that advancement is made to develop a higher order "instrument," like Einstein's "Relativity Theory," which, as a doctrinal system of the greatest conceivable "unity" and "paucity" of fundamental notions, would be that "through which we can provide a revisable conceptual representation of the ultimate intelligible basis of our knowledge of God,"[218] the triune Being of God.

For this reason Torrance says that the use of anthropomorphic terms like "father" and "son" are valid for theo-logical expression only to the extent that such terms are effectively correlated with the fundamental human experience of God controlled by his self-revelation in Jesus Christ. He says that one can no more escape the anthropomorphic in theological speech than one can do without the self-disclosure of God from Father through the Son and in the Spirit. But the expressions used therefore arise from the revelation of God and are intended to be properly referential and ultimately transparent in order to direct attention away to the ineffable Reality of God himself. We recall that Torrance accords to human language an important role in the disclosure process if it arises from and is then appropriate to that reality to which it refers. In that properly scientific situation there is real relation between language and being whereby language serves and becomes "transparent" to that to which it points. Torrance maintains that true theo-logical concepts fulfill their function in the revelatory process when they enable us to actually grasp through them something of the inner "perichoretic" relations of God, which are themselves the fundamental relations in and behind all human experience of God in Christ. This inadequacy of our formulation of the Trinity of God is again said to be critical to its actual truth in relation to the Truth of God. As a "disclosure model" it is that whereby

"God's self-revelation impresses itself upon us, while discriminating itself from the creaturely representations necessarily employed."[219] This disclosure model allows the very Tri-unity of God to so bear upon the mind that the Truth of his own inner relations are set up therein as the laws of our faithful understanding of God himself.

Scripture is again found to play a critical role for Torrance as scientific theology penetrates through Scripture to attain to the inner *ratio*, the ultimate Truth of God, as such thinking scientifically follows the inner logic and movement of Grace in Christ and by the Spirit. All of this is said to lead to ever deeper and richer understanding of the oneness of God in light of the Trinity. Torrance says that one comes to epistemological terms with the Triunity of God as the mind yields to the Trinity of God's self-communication as Father, Son and Holy Spirit, which "is natural, for the knowledge of God requires for its actualization an appropriate rational structure in our cognizing of him." Thereby "the intelligible content of God's articulate self-revelation realizes itself in our faith and understanding."[220] Thus there is out of God's self-giving movement and Act in Christ and by the Spirit an epistemic coordination between what human beings know of God and the God who is known, the inherent intelligibility of the Object and the corresponding modifications in the understanding and thinking of the knower.

To Torrance this doctrine is no "disposable" model. It can be and is properly to be used as a "disclosure model" through which the hypostatic trinitarian relations of Father, Son and Holy Spirit may be allowed to directly bear upon human understanding and knowing of the eternal Trinity of God in a creative and deeply informative way. For that reason, of course, like all "disclosure models," this doctrine is subject to revision in the objective light of that which is continually disclosed and understood more fully by it, so that in the process the model more and more adequately reflects and serves its Object. In using the doctrine of the Trinity in this way, theology is prevented or corrected from dualistic thinking about the Trinity by way of a projection of some this-worldly "trinity," as formulated out of human epistemological structures, into God (e.g., Augustine). Rather this "disclosure model" arises from the Act of God and serves human knowledge of the triune God.[221] Torrance is convinced that through the work of scientific theology, as it thus serves the Word of God in clarifying the real inner correlation between the human knowing of God and God in his own Being, thinking can and must reach yet more deeply into that intimate circle of knowing and loving in God. It has been founded by God between himself and mankind in the world so that we would be able to gain firm conceptual grasp of God, however limited. In such knowing, Torrance finds no allowance for placing God at human disposal, but that in this very knowing relation one knows God to infinitely transcend all forms of human thought and speech and worship. Indeed one has truthful relation to God by virtue of that very disparity.

In this way theological science . . . may carry its inquiry reverently to the point where the intrinsic intelligibility of the created universe is discerned to derive from and ultimately to repose in the uncreated Rationality and eternal Love of the Creator . . . . Once we replace the trinitarian understanding of God by another with its simple mathematical unity our minds are no longer able to get a proper grip upon his Reality and we suffer from . . . "a conceptual letting go of God" . . . . It is in and through Jesus Christ alone that we have been able to reach an understanding of God in his inner divine relations which enables us to apprehend him in some measure as he is in himself and thus to be able to distinguish his transcendent Reality from the subjective states and conditions that arise in our knowing him. This is the knowledge of God the Father through the incarnate Son and in the Holy Spirit which has the creative effect in those who live in communion with him of personalizing and humanizing their being.[222]

Theological Realism. In this entire unfolding of the ultimate "ground and grammar" of Torrance's theological science, we have found to be largely at work with the general contrast between idealism and realism, emphasizing the human ability to distinguish between image or idea and reality, the self as subject from the objects of knowledge and our knowing from the content of our knowing. It is significant that in Torrance's most recent works he has come to acknowledge the proper role of idealism to proper thinking as a proper idealism enables one to avoid giving ultimacy to that which is not ultimate. Thus for Torrance it is an aspect of and must be thought with his critical realism.[223] This capacity to distinguish and to know objective reality he understands to be the very essence of rational behavior. In acts of perception and knowledge, meaning is displaced away from the self and its subjectivism so that even when something is adopted as a sign (as in mathematics) for something else, attention rests upon what the sign refers to. The sign here is a transparent medium of operation. The modern epistemological, cosmological and then, particularly and especially, theological dualism, which has "broken" the knowing relation in knowledge, has been Torrance's concern. It is that dualistic separation of God from the world and from all objectivity to be known truly therein which he has sought to overcome through both critique and his positive theology after the Way of God in his Word and by his Spirit for realist knowledge of God by existing persons. Torrance's positive-corrective theo-logical expression has been our primary concern here. Objective reality, which for theology is properly God in his self-givenness, has ontological priority over all of our human referencing. Theological thinking, as in all truly scientific activity must be properly, critically realist. It must be thinking on the basis of a non-dualist or unitary relation between empirical and theoretical ingredients in the structure of objective reality and in one's knowledge of it.

It is for this reason that Torrance regards the *homoousion* doctrine as a faith-ful expression and disclosure model of the oneness in being in the relation of the incarnate Son with the Father. The truth of this doctrine is absolutely critical to the realist knowledge of God and thus to theology as scientific and realist (cf. endnote 186). In the *homoousion* Torrance says that "we have an intensely compressed and far-reaching act of scientific theological activity within the community of the faithful empirically correlated to Christ and his Gospel," because by it the Church's understanding was grounded firmly on a "unitary basis both epistemological and ontological" entailing a unity in being and intelligibility in God's own self-disclosure in Jesus Christ. There is also in the human understanding and knowing of God in Christ a unity of being and intelligibility, and to the extent that human knowing submits to the priority of God's objective grace it falls "under the compelling power of that self-giving and revealing of God in Jesus Christ."[224] Therefore Torrance believes that as a scientific device or instrument enabling human thought to refer images in observation imagelessly back into the intelligible ground from which they arise in the eternal relations in the Trinity (thereby disallowing mythology), the *homoousion* concept must be allowed to be operative in theology.[225] Just as God discloses himself to us in concrete existence, so he enables us within our concrete existence, where he has given himself to us, to apprehend in theologically realist terms he who infinitely transcends the concrete creation without allowing deifying objectifications of our creaturely concepts. Scientific theological concepts arising under the impress of the revelation of God are then reckoned to be transparent media through which Christ encounters and confronts us with himself, "clothed in the power of his Spirit." Theological Realism is grounded in God.

> It is as our communion with God the Father through Christ and in the Spirit is grounded in and shares in the inner Trinitarian consubstantial or *homoousial* communion of the Father, Son and Holy Spirit, that the subjectively-given pole of conceptuality is constantly purified and refined under the searching light and quickening power of the objectively-given pole in divine revelation. Within that polarity Christian theology becomes what it essentially is and ought always to be, *logike latreia*, rational worship of God.[226]

Conclusion

For corrective antithesis and positive expression in relation to modern theological dualism after Descartes, Newton and Kant, among others, Thomas Torrance has found in the modern physical sciences after Maxwell, particularly in Einstein and Polanyi, a restoration of "classical" realism and rigorous objectivity of thought which he believes to be so needful again in theological thinking (theological science). Among modern theologians, he has found in Karl

Barth one who has pioneered the restoration and advancement of such scientific theological thinking from the proper Object, God's self-revelation in Jesus Christ, where God is objectively known in realist terms. By following and refining Barth's scientific theological thinking "after the way God has taken in the world," as God has objectified himself therein to be known redemptively, Torrance works to think yet more fully after the Act-Being and Being-Act of God in Christ by the Spirit in which God is truly known to be in himself what he is toward us in Jesus Christ and by the Holy Spirit. The "*homoousion* insight*,*" the recognition of the oneness of being in the relation between Son and Father (and Spirit) is found to be of critical importance if God is to be redemptively known. By thinking faith-fully and retrogressively "back" or "up" from the way God has taken, God is finally known by Grace in his own eternal, ontological Triune Being, even in the eternal perichoretic relations in God. Such is Thomas Torrance's positive and restorative theological expression of (and example of) scientific theological thinking from the Word of God in Jesus Christ. In this way human theological statements are said to actually derive from and refer to the real Word of God that has come to us from the side of God (contra Bultmann, et. al.). Such theo-logical statements do not "bend back" upon humanity, having only worldly, subjectivistic or existential "meaning." In this "scientific" way out of Christ, Torrance believes that the Church and the culture beyond can again know and understand God realistically and scientifically out of himself.

As Torrance endeavors to lead the way back to theo-logical intelligibility and objectivity in the Church's theological task under the impress of God's self-disclosure by the Holy Spirit, the outcome is meant to lead not only to a reformation of theology in its specific scientific task among the sciences, but also to an increasing ecumenism in the light and under the impress of God's redemptive, recreative movement toward humanity in his Word, and the healing of our "split, fragmented" culture that lies in the throes of a degenerative pluralism, which is perceived as a further outcome of its epistemological and cosmological dualism. But the role Torrance claims for himself, like Karl Barth before him, is that of servant of the Word in the Church of Christ. For Torrance then true scientific theology is meant to be an active engagement in that cognitive relation to God in obedience to the demands of God's interactive Reality and self-giving which has created the relational "field" in which such unitary (field, onto-relational) thinking can and must take place.

The question is now whether Torrance has accomplished his theo-logical purpose. Responses to this question have varied, but the question is an important one here and must be pursued in the next chapters.

NOTES

1. Torrance, *TS*, p. 180.

2. Torrance, *GG*, p. 112, 114.

3. Torrance, *TCFK*, p. 331.

4. Torrance, *TRst*, p. 113.

5. *cf.* Torrance, *CFM*, p. 142.

6. Torrance, *TS*, pp. 29-46.

7. Ibid., p. 138.

8. Ibid.

9. Ibid.

10. Ibid., p. 206.

11. Robert J. Stamps, "'The Sacrament of the Word Made Flesh': The Eucharistic Theology of Thomas F. Torrance," (unpublished doctoral dissertation, University of Nottingham, 1986), p. 35. Cf. Torrance, *TS*, pp. 49-50.

12. Torrance, *CTSC*, pp. 118-119. Cf. Torrance, *TS*, pp. 42-45.

13. Ibid., pp. 80-82. *cf.* p. 51 and Torrance, *TS*,. pp. 46-50.

14. Torrance, *GR*, pp. 63-64.

15. Kierkegaard, *Philosophical Fragments*, pp. 32f.

16. Herein Kierkegaard adds the Christological point that ". . . in the course of His human life He was the Being and Word of God's Truth incarnated in our creaturely being, the Truth enacted in the midst of our untruth, the Truth fulfilled from within man and from the side of man and issuing out of human life in faithful and obedient response to the Truth of the Father. As such He is the source and standard of truth, the one Truth of God for all men. In Him God turns in Grace toward us and makes Himself open to us, summoning us to be open toward Him and to keep faith and truth with Him in Jesus . . . . It is in this Man that we come up against God's own personal Being in which He bears directly upon us with the presence and impact of ultimate Truth. We know Him truly as we know under the compulsion of His divine Being, that is, of His being what He is and by His nature must be, and under the light of His Truth which is His divine

Being coming into view and becoming in our understanding and knowledge of Him what He is consistently in Himself and in all His relations with us. This is Truth which we can meet and know in our concrete existence through personal encounter and rational cognition, yet Truth who retains His own Majesty and Authority, Truth who so bears witness to Himself through His Spirit that we may testify to Him and reiterate His witness, Truth who makes Himself the object of our statements and the truth of their reference, and yet who transcends all our speaking of Him." Ibid.

17. Ibid., p. 144.

18. Ibid.

19. Ibid., p. 202. Cf. Karl Barth's break-through discussion on *fides* by means of his engagement with Anselm's thought in *Fides Quaerens Intellectum* and *CD*, I/1, 11-25.

20. Ibid., p. 211. It is important to understanding of Torrance's position on the self-revelation of God and encounter to follow how he says that theological thinking is both Christological and communal as a result of the Incarnation, i.e. the Truth as Personal Being coming into time, establishing a historical community whereby the Truth of his Person, the historical Jesus is to be known and expressed only in personal and historical relations (community). "Theological knowledge is found just there within the historical Church where both individual and corporate reception and communication of the Truth take place from generation to generation. This is not to deny that the Truth comes to each of us and to the community directly through the Word and Spirit of Christ. He does come to us directly but not apart from His coming personally and historically through the Word communicated by other historical persons. Christ communicates Himself to us personally in and through the historical Church where the Word is mediated to us in temporal acts by others, and where through that Word He comes immediately in direct address and personal meeting. Thus the Truth is received and communicated, and therefore known from generation to generation, within the Church as the Community of Christ revealing Himself through His Word, and of those who conjointly hear and receive it, in short, within the Church as the Body of Christ. . . . Because of the personal and historical nature of the Truth of God in Jesus Christ theological knowledge arises within a certain delimited sphere, where the Truth is personally and historically received and communicated. Theological thinking takes place within that sphere of actual knowledge--it is not free thinking that strays wherever it likes beyond the bounds laid down by the nature of the Object. Theological thinking is in no sense arbitrary, but is unconditionally bound to its proper Object, in orderly correspondence with his nature."

21. Ibid., p. 211-212.

22. Ibid., p. 140.

23. Stamps, "The Sacrament," p. 38.

24. Torrance, *TRn*, pp. 28 -29.

25. Torrance, *MC*, pp. 16-17.

26. Ibid., p. 17.

27. Ibid., pp. 18-19.

28. Ibid., pp. 26-29. Cf. also pp. 32-33.

29. Torrance, *TRn*, pp. 28-29.

30. Ibid., p. 249. Cf. also pp. 28, 126, 137; and Stamps, pp. 38-39; Torrance, *CFM*, chapter three; and *RST*, pp. 86-93.

31. Torrance, *TS*, pp. 18, 61, 68. Cf. also Torrance, *TRn*, pp. 123-126.

32. Torrance, *STI*, p. 71. Cf. Torrance, *GG*, pp. 5, 30-31; *TRst*, pp. 103ff., *GR*, p. 144, *TS*, p. 101.

33. Torrance, *TS* pp. 30, 66, 101. Cf. Torrance, *DCO*, pp. 85-86.

34. Stamps, "The Sacrament," pp. 47-48. Cf. Torrance, *The School of Faith: The Catechisms of the Reformed Church* (New York: Harper and Brothers Publishers, 1959), p. CI. Hereafter referred to as *SOF*. Cf. Torrance, *TS*, pp. 101-102.

35. Torrance, *CFM*, p. 23. Cf. Torrance, *TS*, p. 67.

36. Torrance, *SOF*, pp. xli-lii. On p. xliii Torrance says, ". . . the whole world of signs which God in His Covenant mercy has appointed to correspond to Him only has revealing significance, and therefore can be interpreted only, in relation to His Covenant will for communion with man and in the actualization of that Covenant in the course of His redemptive acts in history. Thus while the whole of creation is formed to serve as the sphere of divine self-revelation, it cannot be interpreted or understood out of itself, as if it had an inherent relation of likeness or being to the Truth, but only in the light of the history of the Covenant of Grace and its appointed signs and orders and events in the life of the Covenant people, that is to say, according to its economy prior to the Incarnation and according to its economy after the Incarnation. And this means, further, that the whole of creation in its relation of the history of the Covenant can be understood only in the light of the Incarnation which is the goal of the Covenant, for in it creation is lifted up into the light and glory of God." Cf. Torrance, *TS*, pp. 43, 68, 137, and *TRn*, p. 222.

37. Robert J. Palma, "Torrance's Reformed Theology," *Reformed Review*, vol. 38, no. 1 (1984), 13-23.

38. Ibid., p. 211-212.

39. C. Baxter Kruger, "The Doctrine of the Knowledge of God in the Theology of T.F. Torrance: Sharing in the Son's Communion with the Father in the Spirit," *Scottish Journal of Theology*, vol. 43, p. 387.

40. Quoted in Ibid., footnote, p. 381. Cf. Torrance, *GR*, p. 145, 158-159.

41. Torrance, *TRn*, p. 80, 210. Cf. also p. 226, and *STI*, p. 75.

42. Thomas F. Torrance, "The Doctrine of the Holy Trinity According to St. Athanasius," *Anglican Theological Review*, LXXI:4, pp. 396ff.

43. Torrance, *TS*, p. 216-217. Cf. pp. 215-222 and "logos of man," pp. 222ff. Cf. also Kruger, p. 370-371.

44. Ibid., pp. 46-47. Cf. pp. 49, 53, 157, 206.

45. Ibid., p. 234, 352.

46. Torrance, *CTSC*, p. 118. Cf. pp. 121-131.

47. Ibid., p. 132. Note here Torrance's discussion versus both Barth and Calvin on the mystery of election.

48. Ibid., p. 133. Noting that just before this Torrance elaborates at length on the real freedom of God (*voluntas*) in Creation, pp. 122-129.

49. Torrance, *TS*, pp. 157-158.

50. Ibid., p. 39.

51. Ibid.

52. Ibid., p. 25f. and 39. Cf. pp. 39-40, 205-222.

53. Torrance, *CTSC*, pp. 124-125.

54. Gray, "Theology as Science," pp. 224-228. Cf. Torrance, *TS*, pp. 40, 45-47.

55. Torrance, *CTSC*, p. 126.

56. Torrance, *RST*, p. 138.

57. Ibid., p. 139.

58. Torrance, *TCFK*, p. 91.

59. Torrance, *TRst*, pp. 238-239. Cf. below for more detailed discussion on this crucial part of Torrance's theology.

60. Torrance, *TS*, pp. 132-133.

61. Ibid., p. 136.

62. Ibid., p. 137.

63. Ibid., pp. 137-138. Notice how Torrance speaks of Christ, Person and Word/Message, saying on Ibid. pp. 147-148, ". . . because He is Person and Message in One, He is the Truth who both authenticates and interprets Himself. He is the Truth truthfully communicating Himself, and enabling us truthfully to receive Him. He is the Truth communicating Himself in and through truths, who does not communicate Himself apart from truths and who does not communicate truths apart from Himself. It is a communication of truths, but of truths that cohere in the one unique Person of the Incarnate Word of God, and it is a personal encounter in life and being with Christ, but not in abstraction from a Message. It is personal Truth that not only comes to us in the form of Word, and therefore in and through words, but has Word in its very content. In other language, this is Truth that is both personal and propositional, but uniquely personal and uniquely propositional in the unique nature of Christ. As Person and Message in one this Truth communicates and interprets Himself; He accredits Himself to us and draws us out of our autonomous efforts to penetrate into the Truth and establish it, by confronting us with Himself as the Truth and establishing us in relation to Himself as the Truth. Reception and understanding of this Truth, participation in and interpretation of it on our part, must be analogous to this two-fold nature of the Truth. The Message is not received except in personal relation to the Truth, and personal communion with the Truth does not take place apart from the reception of the Message. Therefore our theological statements have a truthful reference to this Truth when that reference is at once personal and propositional, that is dialogical." Cf. Torrance, *TCFK*, pp. 91-92.

64. Martin Buber, *I and Thou*, pp. 14-15, in Ibid.

65. Torrance, *CTSC*, pp. 125-126.

66. Torrance, *SOF*, p. xcvii. Cf. Stamps, "The Sacrament," p. 50.

67. Stamps, "The Sacrament," p. 51. Cf. Ray S. Anderson, *Historical Transcendence and the Reality of God: A Christological Critique* (Grand Rapids: Wm. B. Eerdmans Publishing Company, 1975), and that very notion he develops herein Christologically, i.e., "historical transcendence."

68. Torrance, *TRn*, pp. 117, 222. Cf. also where among many places this is developed in Torrance's writings, e.g., *STI*, p. 69, *SOF*, p. CII and XCV.

69. Torrance, *SOF*, p. XCVIII.

70. Torrance, *GG*, p. 39.

71. Torrance, *SOF*, pp. cxii-cxiii. Cf. cii-ciii and Torrance, *GR*, pp. 162-163. Torrance asserts on *GR*, p. 144 that ". . . the Fourth Gospel with all its immense stress upon the humanity and obedience of the Son opens with the Prologue in which we are told that the Creator Word has become flesh, Himself one of the creatures made through Him, in order to effect the enlightenment and regeneration of man by working within his creaturely existence and serving it from below and by sharing with him His own sanctified humanity. Without the incarnation of the Creator Word the fallen world would crumble away finally and irretrievably into nothingness, for then God would simply be letting go of what He had made and it would suffer from sheer privation of being. But the incarnation has take place. Once and for all, the Creator Word has entered into the existence of what He has made and bound it up with His own eternal Being and Life embodied in Jesus Christ, yet without violating its creaturely nature. In this union of the Creator with the creature the eternal Word of God who is the ground of man's existence from beyond his existence has now become also the ground of his existence within his existence, undergirding and sustaining it from within its natural processes in such a way as to establish his reality and meaning as human being and to realize his distinctive response toward God in the fullness of his creaturely freedom and integrity."

72. Torrance, *DCO*, pp. 138-139. Cf. an important added discussion on pp. 140-141 almost immediately following.

73. Torrance, *TS*, p. 307.

74. Ibid., p. 310.

75. Torrance, *MC*. pp. 17-18.

76. Torrance, *GR*, p. 148.

77. Ibid.

78. Torrance, *MC*, pp. 18-19.

79. Torrance, *GR*, p. 149.

80. Torrance, *CTSC*, p. 93-94. In *TRst*, pp. 129-130 he says, "We begin with faith in Jesus Christ as truly God and truly Man, and seek to unfold our understanding of the double fact that in Jesus Christ the Word of God has become man, has assumed a human

form, in order as such to be God's language to man, and that in Jesus Christ there is gathered up and embodied, in obedient response to God, man's true word to God and his true speech about God. Jesus Christ is at once the complete revelation of God to man and the correspondence on man's part to that revelation required by it for the fulfillment of its own revealing movement. As the obedient answer to God's revelation Jesus yields from the side of man the fulfilled reception and faithful embodiment which belong to the content of God's complete revelation of himself to man. In the Hebrew idiom revelation is not only the uncovering of God but the uncovering of the ear and eye of man for God. It is revelation which achieves its end in man and does not return void to God." Such discussion is common in Torrance's works.

81. Ibid., p. 95.

82. Ibid. Thus, Torrance's central theo-logical point that "The incarnation is the actual embodiment of God's Light within the objective empirical realities of our world in such a way that Jesus Christ is acknowledged and worshipped as God of God and Light of Light, of one and the same being with the Light to which he bears witness. Thus he constitutes in the reality of his divine human Person both the invisible radiation and the creaturely reflection of the eternal Light which God is. At the same time the Incarnation of God's uncreated Light within the realm of created light does not involve in any way the overwhelming or swallowing up of created Light, but the very reverse, the assuming, confirming and finalizing of the reality of created light in God himself so that it is given a stability and a reliability beyond anything it could have by itself in its contingent nature. Thus in Jesus Christ we have contact, as St. Paul argued, not only with the image of the invisible God, but with him in whom, through whom and unto whom all things were created, for he has priority over all and all things hold together in him . . . . Conversely expressed, Jesus was the life-giving Light of God translated into the form of a particular human life and at work among men precisely in its identity with that life. That is to say, Jesus was not just the most perfect man, the most human being that ever lived, shot through and through with divine Light, but God himself in his divine Light living among us as man. In, with and through Jesus the uncreated Light of God crossed the 'dark' barrier of his invisibility into our realm of crated light and creaturely visibility, and at the same time penetrated into the great darkness of our rebellious self-alienation from God in which even the light that is in us has become darkness, in order to redeem us from its power and bring us into the Light of the divine Life." *CTSC*, p. 95-97.

83. Ibid., p. 101-102.

84. Ibid., p. 102.

85. Ibid.

86. Torrance, *TF*, p. 52.

87. Ibid.

88. Torrance, *TRst*, p. 130. Note that Torrance also uses the term "bi-polarity" to refer to the divinely established interactive God-world relation.

89. Ibid., p. 131.

90. Ibid.

91. Ibid., p. 132.

92. Cf. Torrance, *STI*, p. 52-53ff, as a very strong elaboration of this viewpoint in expressing the way/movement of God in self-revelation and thereupon "The Christological pattern of Truth."

93. Torrance, *TF*, p. 53.

94. Ibid., p. 53-54.

95. Ibid., p. 55.

96. Ibid., p. 56.

97. Ibid., p. 56-57.

98. Ibid., p. 57.

99. Ibid., p. 59.

100. Ibid., p. 60.

101. Torrance, *TS*, p. 205.

102. Torrance, *GG*, p. 133.

103. Ibid.

104. Ibid., p. 134.

105. Ibid., p. 135.

106. Ibid., p. 136.

107. Torrance, *GR*, pp. 142-143.

108. Ibid.

109. Ibid., p. 144.

110. Ibid., pp. 144-145.

111. Ibid., p. 154.

112. Torrance, *TRst*, p. 132.

113. Ibid., p. 133.

114. Ibid.

115. Torrance, *TF*. p. 147. Cf. Torrance, *GR*, pp. 99ff.; 139-140, 147-149, and 157-158; *STI*, p. 73.

116. Ibid., p. 148. Cf. pp. 148-158.

117. Ibid., p. 163.

118. Ibid., p. 166.

119. Torrance, *GR*, pp. 137-138, 146.

120. Ibid., pp. 152-153.

121. Ibid., p. 165.

122. Ibid., p. 166.

123. Torrance, *TF*, p. 56.

124. Torrance, *GR*, pp. 166-167. Cf. Torrance, *RST*, pp. 190-191.

125. Ibid., p. 167. Cf. Torrance, *TF*, pp. 191-250 for extensive historico-theological analysis and exposition ("The Eternal Spirit"). Cf. also Torrance, *GG*, pp. 164-167, for a very important elaboration of this issue.

126. Ibid., p. 168.

127. Torrance, *TS*, p. 294. Cf. also pp. 273-277.

128. Torrance, *GR*, pp. 170-171. Cf. In *RET*, pp. 23-24, Torrance gives explanation that "Everything hinges on the reality of God's self-communication to us in Jesus Christ, in whom there has become incarnate, not some created intermediary between God and the world, but the very Word who eternally inheres in the Being of God and is God, so

that for us to know God in Jesus Christ is really to know him as he is in himself. It is with the same force that attention is directed upon the Holy Spirit, whom the Father sends through the Son to dwell with us, and who, like the Son, is no mere cosmic power intermediate between God and the world, but is the Spirit of God who eternally dwells in him and in whom God knows himself, so that for us to know God in his Spirit is to know him in the hidden depths of his divine Being. Father, Son and Holy Spirit are not just the operational modes which God's manifestations take in his saving contact with us in the transient conditions of our creaturely existence, and which could only have a metaphorical and not a real significance; they are distinct personal subsistences and relations of being which God is in his own eternal Reality as God, independent of his revelation to us or of our knowing of him. That is to say, the economic forms of God's self-communication to us in history derive from and repose upon a communion of Persons immanent in the Godhead. It is as our knowing of God passes from what is called the "economic Trinity" to the "ontological Trinity" that we have *theologia* in the supreme and proper sense knowledge of God on the free ground of his own Being, knowledge of him in which our knowing is controlled and shaped by relations eternally immanent in God. Without this advance from knowledge of God in his relation toward us (*quoad se*), knowledge of God toward us is not ontologically grounded in God, but is at the mercy of our knowledge of ourselves. If God is not inherently and eternally in himself what he is toward us in Jesus Christ, as Father, Son and Holy Spirit, then we do not really or finally know God at all as he is in his abiding Reality. From the perspective of its transcendental relation to God, Christian theology must be considered as unbounded precisely because it treats of God who in his unlimited and eternal Reality infinitely transcends our conceptions of him. However, since we may know God only insofar as he has condescended to accommodate his self-revelation to our creaturely reality and the finite measures of our minds, which are what they are through his design, Christian theology must be considered to be bounded by the actual way in which God has chosen to relate himself to us in this world. The only knowledge possible for us is that which he mediates to us in and through this world. We do not and cannot know God in disjunction from his relation to this world, as if the word were not his creation or the sphere of his activity toward us. This is not to say that we reach knowledge of God by way of logical inference from the world, but rather that we may know him only within the field of relations set up by God in his interaction with the world he has made, even though in that field we know him as the Creator of the universe who transcends it altogether. We know God, then, in such a way that our knowledge (*theologia nostra*) is correlated with the world as his creation and the appointed medium of his self-revelation and self-communication to mankind. Everything would go wrong if the creaturely reality of this world were confused with or mistaken for the uncreated Reality of God, or if knowledge of God were cut off from the fact that it is our knowledge, that is, knowledge of God by us in this world."

129. Ibid., pp. 171-174.

130. Ibid., p. 174.

131. Torrance, *TF*, pp. 203, 206-207. Cf. pp. 204, 208, 211-213, 256, especially regarding the knowledge of the Father, of the Son, of the Holy Spirit inseparably and only through the one movement of God in self-revelation from himself and through himself in a triadic way, and the relation of external relations to internal relations of God.

132. Ibid., p. 215. Cf. especially here relating to the resurrection, Torrance, *STI*, p. 85, and Torrance, *GR*, pp. 175-192.

133. Torrance, *GR*, pp. 175-176.

134. Ibid., p. 177.

135. Ibid.

136. Ibid., p. 180. Torrance's discussion herein of the relation of Word and Spirit in the Being and Act of God in their inseparability and distinction is most helpful in understanding Torrance's emphases and perspectival point.

137. Ibid., p. 183.

138. Ibid., p. 185.

139. Ibid., p. 192.

140. Ibid., pp. 21-22.

141. Torrance, *TS*, pp. 29, 138, 143, 154. Cf. Torrance, *KBET*, pp. 98-104.

142. Torrance, *GR*, p. 45.

143. Ibid., p. 99. Cf. pp. 137f.

144. Torrance, *TS*, pp. 309-310.

145. Torrance, *MC*, pp. 88-89.

146. Ibid., pp. 89-95.

147. Torrance, *GR*, pp. 155-156.

148. Torrance, *TS*, p. 52.

149. Ibid., pp. 307-308. Cf. pp. 56, 136-137, 150; and Torrance, *RET*. pp. 24-25, and *GR*, p. 161.

150. Bauman, *Tabletalks*, p. 3.

151. Torrance, *TS*, p. 2.

152. Ibid.

153. Ibid., p. 4. Cf. Soren Kierkegaard, *Concluding Unscientific Postscript*, pp. 169ff.

154. Ibid., p. 5; and Kierkegaard, *Postscript*, p. 287. Cf. Torrance's positive response to the interpretation of H. Diem, *Die Existenzdialektik von Soren Kierkegaard*; J. Brown, *Subject and Object in Modern Theology*, chapters I, II and VII; and J. Heywood Thomas, *Subjectivity and Paradox* in footnote five.

155. Ibid., and Kierkegaard, *Postscript*, p. 178.

156. Ibid., p. 6.

157. Ibid., p. 7.

158. Ibid., pp. 153-154.

159. Ibid., p. 154.

160. Torrance, *TRst*, p. 73.

161. Ibid., p. 74. Cf. Torrance, *RST*, pp. 89-91.

162. Torrance, *TCFK*, pp. 278-279. *cf.* pp. 288-289 and the relation of such thinking to Karl Barth.

163. Torrance, *RST*, p. 91.

164. Torrance, *CTSC*, pp. 69-70. Cf. Torrance, *TFCK*, pp. 195-198, 202-203 on faith as knowledge and faith as reason. Cf. also Torrance, *TS*, pp. 292. 11.

165. Torrance, *TRst*, p. 68. Cf. Torrance, *TS*, p. 11, 54.

166. Torrance, *TS*, p. 118.

167. Torrance, *GR*, p. 21. Cf. Torrance, *TS*, pp. 118f. and Robert Stamps, "The Sacrament," pp. 21-23.

168. Torrance, *TS*, p. 143. Cf. pp. 141-143, 11-14, 129-130, 165-168, 239-241, and p. 215 in particular.

169. Torrance, *GR*, pp. 21-23.

170. Torrance, *TS*, p. 87. Cf. p. 100, and Torrance, *TRn*, p. 239, *TS*, pp. 30, 85, in connection to God's self-presencing as Spirit. In *GR*, pp. 176, 184 Torrance asserts "On the one hand, then, the Holy Spirit through His presence brings the very Being of God to bear upon us in our experience, creating the relation to the divine Being which knowledge of God requires in order to be knowledge; but on the other hand, the Spirit through His ineffable and self-effacing nature reinforces the impossibility of our conceiving in thought and expressing in speech how our thought and speech are related to God, so that our thoughts and statements by referring infinitely beyond themselves break off before Him in wonder, adoration and silence, that God may be All in all. Through the Spirit empirical relation to the divine Being takes place and within it we are given intuitive knowledge of God, but the mode of our relation to Him and the mode of our knowledge of Him must be in accordance with His nature as Spirit, and therefore even though we have empirical relation to Him and intuitive knowledge of Him, they are not amenable to the kind of control which we exercise in relation to creaturely objects. It is rather we who fall under the overwhelming presence of the divine Being and come under the control of His Spirit in our experience and knowledge of Him. . . . He determines, within the created world, within man's life and history, and within the subject-object structures of his existence, certain facts and events as the signs or the mediate objectivities of His revelation, yet in the living presence and power of His Spirit God is Himself personally present in the midst directing man through these determinations to immediate intuitive knowledge of Himself in His own ultimate Objectivity and Reality. This sign-world which God has appointed and uses in our mediate knowledge of Him comprises the whole history of His covenant relations with His people as fulfilled in the incarnation of His Word in Jesus Christ, and it comprises the whole realm of the biblical revelation with its created forms of thought and speech and worship called forth from human life under the inspiration of the Holy Spirit and appointed as the medium which He continues to use in the revelation of God to man. Thus God still comes to us clothed in the historical and biblical forms of His revelation which (whether B.C. or A.D.) directs us to Jesus Christ in the centre, for it is in Him that God has objectified Himself for our human knowing, but through the power and presence of the Holy Spirit we are enabled to meet God and know Him directly and immediately in Jesus Christ, and under the compulsion of His Being and Truth upon us in Christ to formulate in our own statements our understanding of Him--yet all this only within our human existence and history and their rational, linguistic and social structures." Cf. also Torrance, *CTSC*, pp. 136-142, 148-154.

171. Ibid.

172. Ibid., pp. 140, 144.

173. Torrance, *CTSC*, p. 92.

174. Ibid., p. 93.

175. Ibid.

176. Ibid., p. 93-94.

177. Torrance, *RST*, pp. 123-124.

178. Ibid., pp. 125-126.

179. Cf. the works of Brian Gray and even the later work by Douglas Trook (on Trook, see below chapter six endnote eight). E.g., later works of Torrance such as *RST*, *GG*, *TF*.

180. Torrance, *GG*180., p. 161.

181. Torrance, *TS*, pp. 26-28.

182. Torrance, *RST*, p. 182. By the use of the term *perichoresis* the Church Fathers spoke of relation in the sense of coinherence.

183. Torrance, *TF*, pp. 124-125. Cf. Torrance, *TRn*, pp. 243f.

184. Ibid. p. 130.

185. Ibid., pp. 133-134. Cf. Torrance, *CTSC*, pp. 104-106.

186. Ibid., p. 135. Cf. p. 141 where Torrance further explains that "The evangelical significance of the *homoousion* is very apparent in its direct bearing upon the saving acts of Jesus Christ, in healing, forgiving, reconciling and redeeming lost humanity, for its asserted in the strongest way that they are all done out of a relation of unbroken oneness and communion between Jesus Christ and God the Father. The cognate significance of *theopoiesis*, however, lies in its stress upon the oneness in agency as well as in being between the Son and the Father, thereby identifying the saving acts of Jesus Christ in the Gospel as the downright acts of God himself for us and our salvation. It thus throws into sharp focus the divine finality and validity of those saving acts, by insisting in the most uncompromising way that they are the kind of acts which only God the Father Almighty, Creator of heaven and earth and of all things visible and invisible can do."

187. Torrance, *CTSC*, pp. 105-106. Cf. Torrance, *RST*, pp. 182-183.

188. Torrance, *GG*, p. 155.

189. Ibid., p. 160.

190. Ibid., p. 161.

191. Ibid.

192. Ibid., pp. 163-164. Cf. especially Torrance, *TS*, p. 160.

193. Ibid., pp. 164-165.

194. Ibid., p. 165.

195. Ibid., p. 166.

196. Ibid.

197. Ibid., p. 167. Cf. especially Torrance, *RST*, pp. 182-185 for extensive discussion of his understanding of the Christological pattern of all knowing--in him the movement of God out of himself. Cf. also Torrance, *MC*, pp. 57-82.

198. Torrance, *RST*, p. 183.

199. Ibid., p. 184.

200. Torrance, *TCFK*, p. 255. In his highly significant article, "Theological Realism," in *The Philosophical Frontiers of Christian Theology*, ed. by Brian Hebblethwaite and Stewart Sutherland (Cambridge: Cambridge University Press, 1982), pp. 185-186, Torrance says of the doctrine "Here, then, in the *homoousion* we have an intensely compressed and far-reaching act of scientific theological activity within the community of the faithful empirically correlated to Christ and his Gospel. In the *homoousion* the understanding of the Church is firmly set on a unitary basis which is both epistemological and ontological, for it entails a unity in being and a unity in intelligibility in God's self-giving and self-revealing in Jesus Christ, and correspondingly in our knowing of him in so far as it is allowed to fall under the compelling power of that self-giving and self-revealing in Jesus Christ. As such the *homoousion* both clarifies and expresses the fact that in the Nicene theology the worshipping and enquiring Church was enabled to grasp God, in some real measure, in the depth of his own reality in such a way as to affect the whole structure of the Church's understanding of him, and yet in such a way that there is no suggestion that the transcendent mystery of God can be captured and comprehended within the bounds of our creaturely conceptualities for God in the beauty and majesty and light of his being infinitely exceeds all the Church's theological or dogmatic formulations. As we move from Ecumenical Council to Ecumenical Council in the history of the Church we find that its developing theology can be traced back from all decisive points to this central affirmation and its essentially doxological character in the Nicene Creed."

201. Ibid., pp. 255-256. Cf. Torrance, *GG*, p. 155.

202. Torrance, 202 *GG*, p. 156.

203. Ibid. Cf. Torrance, *RST*, pp. 189-190 makes the following crucial statement: "It must be noted that the primacy and centrality of the Incarnation in all our relations with God implies that the anthropomorphic elements inevitably involved in the reciprocity established by God between us and himself, far from being eliminated are actually reinforced, but now it is Jesus Christ the one image-and-reality of the invisible God who constitutes the critical point of reference to which we must constantly appeal in putting to the test and thinking away all inappropriate and unworthy ingredients in our creaturely and anthropomorphic images, concepts and terms.   This applies also to the self-communication of God to us within the space-time structures of our world, where spatial and temporal ingredients are inevitably involved in our knowledge of God.   As themselves the hearers of our creaturely rationality the space-time structures of the world constitute the rational continuum in and through which we communicate with one another and in and through which God communicates with us. Hence we cannot opt out of them without opting out of the spatial and temporal ingredients in our knowledge of God, any more than we can opt out of the very rational structures in which we have our being, think, live, and speak. Thus we cannot but think of the Triunity of God from out of this triadic subject-object-subject structure in our worldly inter-personal existence, but it is one that serves God's trinitarian self-revelation to us only as it is taken in command and adapted by that revelation and thus made to point infinitely beyond itself. Here too, however, it is through critical reference to Jesus Christ, the incarnate Word and Truth of God, through whom God reveals himself to us as the Lord of our being and understanding, that we have to put all spatial and temporal ingredients to the test, thereby filtering away from our conceiving of God all that is inappropriate to or unworthy of the Holy Trinity. Hence, once again, we discern the crucial significance of the fact that in and through the Incarnation God's self-communication and self-revelation to us have penetrated into and taken commanding form within the subject-object as well as the subject-subject relations of our human existence."

204. Ibid.

205. Ibid., p. 167.

206. Ibid., p. 158.

207. Ibid.

208. Ibid., p. 167. Cf. p. 168 on the move from the second to third epistemological level, from the economic activity of God toward us as Father, Son and Holy Spirit to the ultimate set of fundamental concepts and relations resulting in the theological goal of one's reproducing in thought and speech the ultimate constitutive relation in God, the holding finally to the Ontological Trinity with the Economic Trinity.

209. Ibid., pp. 158-159.

210. Thomas F. Torrance, "Truth and Authority: Theses on Truth," *International Theological Quarterly*, 39 (1972), pp. 215-216.

211. Torrance, *RST*, pp. 160-161.

212. Torrance, *TF*, pp. 303, 305.

213. Ibid., pp. 306, 303.

214. Torrance, *KBET*, pp .113, 145.

215. Torrance, *GG*, pp. 172-173.

216. Torrance, *RST*, pp. 190-192.

217. Torrance, *RST*, p. 161. Cf. Torrance, *GG*, pp. 168-178.

218. Ibid.

219. Ibid., p. 162.

220. Ibid., p. 163. Cf. Torrance, *KBET*, pp. 184-193, and Torrance, *RST*, p. 173-183, especially the latter as Torrance analyzes historical developments in these theological concepts in the Eastern and Western Church, pointedly the property of the Greek patristic insight of the *perichoresis*. Cf. also *RST*, pp. 190-191.

221. Ibid., p. 192.

222. Ibid., pp. 198, 200.

223. Torrance, "Theological Realism," pp. 169-174.

224. Ibid, pp. 185-186. On pp. 188-189 Torrance asserts further that "Classical theology has always regarded the self-mediation of God to us in Word and in Spirit as inseparably one. That goes back to the teaching of St. Paul that through the Son and in the Spirit we are given access to God, for in the incarnation of his Son in Jesus Christ and the presence of his Spirit mediated through Jesus Christ, God has established such a relationship between himself and man that has made access to himself a reality for man. This is the twofold communion in Word and Spirit between God and man and man and God stressed by St. John. But his Word, as patristic theology reminds us, is not some 'word' detached from God, but *enousios logos*, Word who eternally inheres in the being of God even when incarnate and addressed to us on earth and in time; and this Spirit is not some 'spiritual activity' detached from God, but *enousios energeia*, Spirit who inheres eternally in the being of God even when he comes to us and acts upon us within our creaturely existence. That is to say, in the incarnation of his Word and in the coming of his Spirit God has actualized for us the openness of his own being and intelligibility within the conditions, realities and intelligibilities of our contingent being in such a way that neither his revealing of himself to us nor our apprehending of him

may be halted or negated by the conditions, realities and intelligibilities of our contingent being. In fact the real presence of God to us in the immediacy of his own divine Being as Holy Spirit is bound up with and mediated through his sheer unreserved self-humiliation and self-commitment to us in the incarnation of his Son, the Word made flesh. It is therefore in proportion to the realism with which we appreciate the *kenosis* that we can appreciate the realism of the *homoousion* of the Son, for they are the obverse of one another, and on that ground also appreciate the realism of the *homoousion* of the Spirit.   Thus the question whether there is ground for holding an evidential and conceptual relation to God in our knowing of him is an ontological question, or more precisely, a christological question.   It stands or falls with the question whether the incarnate Son or Word is of one and the same being with God, that is, with the very heart and substance, with the innermost sanctum of the Christian faith."

225. Ibid., p. 188.

226. Ibid., p. 193. Cf. Where the implications of this form of "theological realism" moves Torrance beyond Barth and clearly as a mediation point between Barth and Brunner on the one hand possibly a mediation point between Barth and Wolfhart Pannenberg on the other as he describes "the Transformation of Natural Theology"-- which he tries to tie into Barth's thought, at least in some implications, but which he concedes as going beyond Barth. In this "natural theology" is not to be understood in some *a priori* way or as a preface or preparatory discussion to theology in order philosophically to ground theology (e.g. the arguments for God's existence). Torrance finds the true and indeed necessary palace for "natural theology," the way in which the contingent order of the universe points beyond itself to God, to properly follow faith (*fides quaerens intellectum*) as reflected in the following sections of his later works, which are in fact the one's wherein this aspect of Torrance's thinking becomes finally explicit: *GG*, chapters one and four (especially pp. 75-109); *CTSC*, chapter four; *STI*, pp. 69-74; *RST*, chapter two; *TCFK*, pp. 290-296; *CFM*, chapters two and three; *DCO*, pp. 131-137. Cf. Palma, pp. 20-24.

Chapter 6

Representative Responses To Thomas Torrance's Restorative Programmed Expression Of Realist Knowledge Of God In The World

Introduction

We have observed the relationship between Thomas Torrance's corrective theological agenda, to overturn the general effects and thinking of modern dualism and its specific effects upon Christian theology, and his positive Christological-Trinitarian theological expression out of God's self-revelation in Jesus Christ, the Word made flesh. This is said to arise from Torrance's own personal "encounter" with God's Truth incarnate in Jesus Christ.[1]

Torrance is calling theology back to be again the "rational worship of God" (*logike latreia*). Theology ought to be, as truly scientific and as servant to the Word of God and the Church's task of thinking out the faith, in strict accordance with the movement and truth of the Word. To this end the methodological rigor of the physical sciences toward real objectivity and realist knowledge of the proper object in the disclosure of its own inherent intelligibility and rationality was found to be of great importance to Torrance analogically, epistemologically and methodologically. Positive theological science is then understood to involve the actual knowledge of God and therefore the assent and conformity of human thought to the authority and Truth of its proper Object, the Word of God. At the heart, Torrance intends his theology to be, in the context of the modern theological task, "Nicene" and doxological with its focus on the

Mediator Jesus Christ. This means then that it follows the inner logic of the incarnation by the enablement of the Spirit to thereby reach its ultimate end, the knowing of the Holy Trinity, which is the "ground and grammar of all theology." By his understanding of the interrelated levels of truth, authority and knowledge in realist science and the key connection (*homoousion*) between real human knowledge of God in the Word made flesh and God's own Being and knowledge of himself, Torrance maintains that he can assert that human beings, through Jesus Christ and in the Holy Spirit, can and do have realist theological knowledge within the faith-knowing relation.

It is for this reason that Torrance espouses a Christocentric-Trinitarian and, indeed, unitary theology as derived directly from its ultimate grounding in the Trinity, God in the eternal, perichoretic or coinherent relations, Father, Son and Holy Spirit. Thus we see the centrality of the *homoousion* doctrine of Son and Spirit, the Christocentricity, the focus upon the God-man (hypostatic) union in Jesus Christ, and the empirico-theoretical (form and being) methods shaped by the ultimate Acts of God's own Being for Torrance's theology. Such unitary, realist, and objective theology, arising in faithful submission to these realities, unified in Christ and the homoousial relation of Son to Father, is found by Torrance to undercut the modern dualisms (Cartesian, Newtonian, Kantian) which have such "destructive effect" upon the sciences, and particularly upon the real, redemptive, re-creative knowledge of God in the world (e.g., Schleiermacher, Bultmann). Torrance has attempted to formulate his theology upon what he believes to be the only ultimate unitary basis for such, the Trinity, and thus upon Jesus Christ who is at once human and divine. But the creation, as itself the place and medium of God's redemptive self-revelation, is also crucial as it is ultimately integrated from above by God's creative bearing upon it, that is, his bi-polar, asymmetrical, interactive relatedness with it (the creation-redemption nexus).

Torrance then understands his theology to be realist theology, not simply as affirming the reality of the Holy Trinity and the Acts of God as independent of all human knowing, but in seeking to follow after the emphases of "classical Christian theology" which maintain that God is open to knowledge in himself by his own self-revealing reality. He concludes that the Truth of God objectively encounters the knowing subject to the end that one knows God truly (however limited that may be because of human finitude) out of himself. While rejecting representative apprehension, Torrance's "Calvinistic" assertion of direct intuitive knowledge of God in his Word does not at all negate the role of created media in divine revelation. Indeed, he wants to emphasize this. In revelation in the world the creaturely becomes "transparent" to and for the Word of God. By these media, God in Jesus Christ and by the Spirit comes encountering one personally and contemporaneously through the Scriptures which both direct attention beyond themselves to the Word and are that medium through which the Word of God/Truth of God shines. Realist and rational theological thinking and expression seeks to serve and facilitate the communication of and encounter with this Word of God.

In this sixth chapter the focus will be upon representative responses, favorable, unfavorable and mixed, to Torrance's theological purposes, outcomes and positive, constructive expression. Having set forth indirectly and directly Torrance's own positive interpretation and expression of the theological task and theological science as realist, unitary and objective out of the Word made flesh, ending teleologically and ultimately (foundationally) in the ontological Trinity (in chapters two through five), here we will examine representative analyses of this aspect of Torrance's theology, and later examine each of these in order to establish the propriety or impropriety of each response to Torrance. In this way attention will be directed increasingly toward the question as to whether Torrance's theo-logical expression out of Christ can open the way toward the accomplishment of that which he intends to accomplish, given the totality of his principles or bases as grounded in the divine-human relation in Christ the Mediator. How do prominent interpreters of Torrance understand and assess the direction, method, and success of his theology as truly "scientific"? Is he even being understood? Does Torrance himself fall into a "dualistic disjunction" of his own? This, and related issues will become explicit through chapters six and seven.

Representative Responses to Torrance's Realist Theology
Representative Positive Responses:
Robert J. Palma and W. James Neidhardt

Robert J. Palma's Theological-Scientific
Affirmation of Torrance

Enlarging on the thought of E. L. Mascall, who said that Thomas Torrance is "one of the very few British theologians of recent years who have seriously enquired into the nature of the discipline to which they are committed,"[2] Robert J. Palma mentions four areas where Torrance is said to have made his most significant contributions to the tasks of Christian theology. Each of these has direct bearing upon our central concerns here regarding Torrance's understanding of realist theological knowledge of God in the world. These four contributions are, first, "theological discipline through obedient listening;" second, "theological integrity through real integration;" third, "theological advance through scientific understanding;" and fourth, "theological relevance through real relations."[3] In the first, "theological discipline through obedient listening," Palma finds that Torrance is one of only a few in the history of the

Church to have given sustained attention to the nature and method of scientific theology. Torrance, he says, has shown theology to be a disciplined mental activity arising from the Christian theologian's ordinary, intuitive knowledge of God self-given in Christ Jesus in which the theologian must strive to lay bare its inner logic. Torrance, he says, has shown that theology is not free to determine its own subject, methods or questions, but rather it is under the authority of its Object so that theology obeys the demands of God's self-revealed Reality, and only therein gains genuine theological freedom in knowledge of the Truth. Torrance is seen to have called theology back to inquiry that is obedient to its proper Object. As Palma says, "While Karl Barth spoke of this freedom, Torrance has incorporated it within an extended account of the disciplined questioning that is required if theology is to be genuinely scientific."[4]

Second, Palma maintains that Torrance has contributed to theology by emphasizing "theological integrity taken through real integration." In opposition to the fragmented, atomistic and mechanistic way of thinking in the modern era (cf. logical positivism), Torrance's theology has been an example of theological wholeness by his avoidance of abstract, artificial integrity derived from alien principles not actually found in the proper Object and which are thus derived from a false separation of form from being, empirical from theoretical, dynamic from ontological, phenomenal from the intelligible structures (noumenal). Unitary, relational thinking and "field" structures or patterns (*Gestalten*) are found to be the scientific way of thinking. This unitary way of thinking reflects the existing whole realities and dynamic relatedness within and among the realities of theology, the relatedness to and of the Holy Trinity, God's creation of and "asymmetrical" interactive relatedness to and with the universe, the incarnation of the eternal Son in the indivisible reality of Jesus Christ, the space-time interrelatedness of creation and incarnation, and the universe with its pervasive trustworthiness associated with the invariant properties of light. In his critical reception and thinking together of the Patristic (Nicene) focus on God's Being in his Acts and the Reformational focus upon God's Acts in his Being, Torrance is said to have not only thought together the Reformation thought with the Catholic teaching of the Fathers (as did Barth) but to have moved to a higher plane and a higher unitary theology by pursuing the objective demands for holistic, dynamic and field theoretical modes of theological inquiry.[5]

In clear relation to these, Palma asserts also that Torrance has done much for "theological advance through scientific understanding," referring of course to Torrance's ongoing participation and the cross fertilization occurring in the dialogue between theology and the natural sciences. Indeed, Torrance is referred to as a philosopher of science in his own right. Palma points out that Torrance has recognized and clarified the contribution of each to the other and the prospects for further, fruitful interaction. But Torrance has also strongly emphasized that both theological science and the other natural sciences must maintain their own peculiar integrity which for each is formed by the respective proper objects in their self-presentation and mode of rationality and therefore their own proper method of knowing as dictated by those objects. Yet each science remains open to the others in terms of complementarity, fortification and clarification. But Palma adds that Torrance properly and needfully recognizes that all of these sciences, theology as much as the others, are human endeavors, pursued within the same space-time continuum. This means that clarification of similarities and differences between theological science and the other sciences is required in the interest of theological purity. Torrance has thus put theology back upon its own proper ground, the only place where it can be true to the law of its own being, and therefore truly scientific. Torrance hds been able to find in such interaction confirmation of theology's own ultimate, regulative beliefs regarding the order and contingency of the universe, freeing theology from dualism, alien methods of knowing, false determinisms and the Newtonian "closed" universe. Field theory, Polanyi's recognition of the personal factor in knowledge, the open and contingent intelligibility of the universe, the relational concept of space and time, the concept the multi-leveled unitariness and rationality of reality, the multi-leveled structure of human knowledge of reality, and the physics of the invariability of light have all been used by Torrance epistemologically, analogically and methodologically for aid, insight and correction in relational, objective and scientific thought and expression of that which is apprehended. In this way, says Palma, Torrance has made highly significant use of (for example) the incarnation and resurrection not only to overcome the dualistic "receptacle" or "container" notions of space and their effects on theo-logical science but also to think appropriately from Christ and those empirical correlates of God's self-revelation in Christ. This results in a conception of space reflecting the ontological and dynamic relation between God and the physical universe and in terms of unitary fields of dynamic structure with important epistemological, cosmological and theological implications. Lessons from the new physics have helped Torrance to bring critical clarification and expression to the faith. The "new physics" of Einstein and Polanyi have helped him to secure and advance from theological gains of the past, while giving articulation to the Christian faith from within a scientific culture, says Palma.[6]

The fourth area of particular contribution by Torrance Palma calls "theological relevance through real relation." Modern culture wants immediate and therefore shallow and false relevance. Torrance does not share this desire, but in his pursuit of theology with its own meta-science, or method and mode of rationality, he expresses a dynamic and relevant witness to this culture which has been shaped by the scientific revolution. Torrance takes his position from the fact that where there are no helpful relations to be found in being, human logic and statement cannot create such. Human beings cannot found or create relevance. True relevance is grounded independently of the existing subject. Basic to Torrance's lack of anxiousness about relevance, then, is that in Jesus

Christ the Truth of God is already relevant to humanity and its need. Palma
believes that Torrance has contributed to true theological relevance by rejecting
the accommodation of the Christian faith and the gospel message to passing
trends of culture, to "abstract formal categories," reductionism, and all false
relevance which is part of the modern sickness of humanity. Those who partake
of a false, existential relevance wrongly, but inevitably, convert theological
statements into anthropological and even autobiographical statements (in-turned
subjectivism). In this way genuine theological relevance is lost. Against this
direction in modern thought, Torrance is then found to be dedicated to positive
theology with its own proper meta-science so that in this way he might make
faithful and penetrating inquiry into the objectively given subject matter of
theology, while listening to other sciences. He actively engages in such inquiry
in order to bring to view the dynamic and "triadic" God-world-human or God-
human-world relation in the self-revelatory, self-objectifying movement of God's
dynamic interaction with and for humanity within the empirical, space-time
world. Genuine theological relevance is the pursuit of scientific objectivity, of
a realist positive theology, out of the Grace of God's self-givenness, being
concerned with the "utter lordship of the Object, its absolute precedence, for
that is the one all-determinative presupposition of theology."[7]   God's
condescension in Jesus Christ means that theology is to be done in faithfulness
to this its Object. Such theology will be relevant to all existence, to all of
humanity, for it is grounded in real, reconciling (onto-) relations. This ought
to reconstruct and to unify the foundations of human culture.

W. James Neidhardt's Scientific-Theological Affirmation of Torrance

W. James Neidhardt, associate professor of physics at the New Jersey
Institute of Technology, has taken a positive position akin to that of physicist-
theologian Douglas Trook.[8]   In a lengthy introduction to Torrance's *The
Christian Frame of Mind*, Neidhardt speaks of Torrance's realization of the need
in theological science for a unitary understanding of inner simplicity and
intelligibility as the goal and content of every science (for example, the simple
but transforming implications of $E=MC^2$ and "Jesus is Lord"). He says that
like J. Clerk Maxwell, Torrance is aware of the vastness of God revealed in
Christ and the narrowness of the formal theological-systems—that all human
expression here is true only to a point and acceptable only as these expressions
are allowed to appropriately point inquiry beyond to that hidden realm where
thought weds fact, where the mental operation of the theologian and the Act of
God in Christ are seen in their true relation. Torrance's recognition means the
demand that all theological expression be put to the test of the actual way God
has chosen to take, God's factuality in the world. All such scientific theological

expression under the impress of the Word must then be seen as theory which is both provisional and revisable in the light of increasing penetration into the Truth of God.

But Neidhardt's central purpose is to underscore, clarify, and engender greater appreciation for Torrance's concern for theological knowledge by his consideration of themes in Torrance's theology as related to Einstein's relativity theory. Neidhardt, as a physicist, also speaks of "the unitary character of theological and scientific knowledge" in Torrance's thought.   Neidhardt commends Torrance's emphasis on unitariness, the scientific need to think together empirical and theoretical factors in real integration. When Torrance calls for theology to be faithful to its task as a creative science in the context of the unitary implications of physics, it is said to reflect the fact that Torrance agrees with Einstein that all theory and doctrine results from reflection upon ordinary experience in the light of one's intuition of reality and basic intellectual convictions (ultimate beliefs) about reality.   From such reflection the (theological) scientist makes a heuristic jump of imaginative insight, which Neidhardt describes as an "informed, speculative and bold leap to postulate a logically-not-obvious new theoretical structure"[9] which cannot be tested directly. If successfully tested via deductions from it, the theory or doctrine is found to reveal a hidden intelligibility which undergirds the realm of human experience. The discovery of such hidden intelligibility is the motivation and goal in all science. In theological science it is the search for understanding of God's ways in the world and with human beings. Neidhardt says then that Torrance has thus rightly concluded that the Nicene *homoousion* doctrine is just such a helpful scientific theological concept which does justice to the biblical evidence for the consubstantial unity of Father and Son in God. As a result of Torrance's work, there is said to have been clarification of the profound congruence existing between the unitary structures embodied in scientific and theological intelligibilities.[10]

In referring to the "relativity theory—the absolute underpinning of the relative" as it plays a crucial role cosmologically, epistemologically, analogically and thence theologically in Torrance, Neidhardt explains that Torrance has again correctly observed (and used) that when Einstein rejected the notion of space and time as absolute, defining them in terms of their relation to the human observer's physical frame of reference, that he did not abandon objectivity. The opposite is the case. Einstein, he says,

> . . . was convinced that the basic laws of nature are always and everywhere the same, regardless of their respective physical frame of reference. In his relativity theory, Einstein primarily stressed the invariant, that is the unchanging nature of physical law which, secondarily, results in the relativism of observational details with respect to different observational frames of reference. Torrance (rightly) points out that although Einstein

abandoned the absoluteness of space and time, he did not view the simplicity and order of nature as mere constructs of the human mind (an oft repeated misinterpretation).[11]

From a Christian perspective, Torrance is said to rightly assert that the invariant character of physical laws is rooted in the faithfulness, constancy and utter dependability of God's own inherent Rationality and intelligibility and love revealed by God in all of his Creation. But beyond that, says Neidhardt, given the striking and unusual appropriateness of mathematics in relation to the external world as used by the physical sciences, Torrance argues that science is possible only by the correlation actually existing between our mental patterns of intelligibility and the lawful structures of the contingent intelligibility embodied in reality.[12]

A third theme which Neidhardt brings out in his affirmation of Torrance's integration of theology and relativity theory is that "in creative science the invisible explains the visible" and not the other way around. Most people see natural science's progressive growth as the result of the fact that in science the "visible" or phenomenal guides interpretation of the "invisible." The contrary is the case, and Torrance has explained how physical theory develops "invisible" conceptual "objects" which explain the behavior of "visible" phenomena. In general relativity the space-time metric field is a key invisible conceptual "object" which determines the visible motion of all matter. Following Polanyi, Torrance holds that great scientists make their discoveries by imaginative postulation of "invisible" hidden patterns (*Gestalten*) which explain the phenomenal. In the same way, says Neidhardt, Torrance follows the traditional Judeo-Christian epistemological principle that the creature is truly known only in the Creator's light, the temporal understood only in the light of God's invisible Truth.[13]

Neidhardt is also most appreciative of Torrance's Einsteinian rejection of the dualist receptacle or container model of space and time, that is, "the physical universe—a relational rather than container model," is grounded in and thought from relation to God as Creator and Redeemer, especially in the Incarnation of the Son of God. All of this is made more comprehensible by the use of a relational and interactionist model rather than the container notion of the space-time continuum. The universe then is not a "bucket" into which all energy-mass structures of being are "poured" but more a "stage" forming the expanding outer boundary of the interactional relations of its objects and events. The relational character of the uncreated Reality and Rationality of God, who is the unitary, triune community of divine knowledge and love relations in himself, and created reality is found then to be a positive ongoing theme in Torrance.[14]

To these issues in Torrance's integration of the insights of physics with theology for the knowledge of God, Neidhardt adds the related theme of "field theories—an expression of the relational character of reality." He explains how

Torrance sees in field theories a number of relational-structural elements which are analogous to concepts in Judeo-Christian theology. Analogy for Torrance is understood disclosively rather than pictorially, a God-created correspondence existing between two knowledge structures representing distinct objects or relationships to be understood as having similarity within dissimilarity or commonality arising from certain aspects of realities at different logical levels of reality. For Torrance's theo-logical purposes, field theory, as developed by Maxwell and Einstein, has called the theological scientist, along with the physicist, toward the goal of a "grand unified field theory." Torrance is said by Neidhardt to rightly believe that this goal in physics is consistent with and, if rightly understood, is motivated by the first article of the Nicene Creed, the affirmation of faith in one God, Father Almighty, Maker of heaven and earth. This emphasis on creation by God is basic to Torrance's primary point that the profound biblical theme of God's guarantee of the trustworthiness and wholeness of Creation means that the entire cosmos, heaven and earth, is an intelligible, orderly continuum, a structural unity. The creation reveals the unique, unitary character of God as it is imprinted or traced upon the creation itself.[15]

Neidhardt also focuses on that characteristic epistemological, cosmological and methodological theme in Torrance, his understanding of the created, contingent "universe—a multi-leveled yet integrated whole." This integration of Christian theology and the Einsteinian view of the universe's interrelated levels of being is recognized to be of great conceptual importance for Torrance's theology. Theological science calls for thinking that moves "back up" through the divine economy level by level to rest finally in the eternal perichoretic relations of the persons in the Trinity of God. Neidhardt explains that from the creative expression in the Nicene Creed, Polanyi's heuristic understanding of science and Ilya Prigogine's irreversible thermodynamics seen in the light of relativity theory, Torrance recognizes the universe to be increasingly disclosed as scientific thinking follows the ascending gradient meaning of the universe in richer and higher forms of order, with the lower levels explained in terms of the higher, invisible, intangible realms of reality. This unitary perspective is said to heal perspectival splits and to create syntheses. Material and spiritual dimensions overlap and the knowledge of God and of his creation go hand in hand, bearing constructively upon one another. The "multi-leveled" universe points to and is open to the transcendent Reality and Rationality of God which is beyond it while sustaining and providing meaning to it. It is this same process of objective understanding which is applicable to the knowledge of God.[16]

Neidhardt also commends Torrance for showing that "theology and natural science (are) allies rather than foes." He rightly explains that much of Torrance's active integration of theology and natural science has been done as a transformational extrapolation of Einstein's well known remark, "Science without religion is lame; religion without science is blind." Judeo-Christian theology motivates and gives meaning to natural science which reciprocates in sharpening and clarifying theology's scientific methodology and need of proper objectivity. This reciprocity is said to be made possible by open dialogue and by the recognition that both are concerned with the discovery of a shared intelligibility which is a result of both the divine order revealed in God's interaction with humanity in the world and the contingent order revealed through humanity's exploration of the universe. Neidhardt believes that such a clarified interrelationship (distinctiveness and reciprocity) integrates theology and natural science into a greater whole whose unitary intelligibility is grounded in the relation between the divine and contingent order. But again, as Neidhardt points out, it is all grounded in the interactive relation of the divine and contingent order, uncreated and created rationality, and thus finally upon the Act and Being of God. Neidhardt says that Torrance is correct in his understanding of that relation to be

> . . . the loving intelligibility of the living God which is supremely revealed in the entering of the Creator into his own space-time Creation. The incarnation of Jesus Christ, his life, death, resurrection, and particularly his sharing in and redeeming human creaturehood on the Cross, is a central component of all Torrance's pioneering efforts to integrate into a larger whole scientific and theological intelligibilities.[17]

Such integration is intended to follow the example of the Nicene Fathers of the early Church (particularly Athanasius) as these sought not only to communicate the gospel but to transform the thinking of the prevailing culture, thereby allowing the objectively given knowledge of God to take root. These points were discussed in earlier chapters.

These two positive responses adequately reflect Thomas Torrance's great efforts to restore theology, as rooted in realist knowledge of God out of God's objective self-disclosure, to its proper scientific task, and to restore theological science and the physical sciences to their proper relation of complementarity as each pursues its calling within the contingent intelligibilities of the world. But there are other voices of response to Torrance and these, however effective or short of the mark, can be helpful too in unfolding the real nature of Torrance's Christocentric-Trinitarian theology out of the Word made flesh.

Representative Negative Responses: Carl Henry, Donald Klinefelter, Ray Anderson, Richard Muller, Thomas Langford, Ronald Thiemann

Introduction

These representative critics of Thomas Torrance's theological position do not always set themselves wholly against Torrance but find in his thinking problems bearing directly upon his theology and the knowledge of God. Discussion will center variously around those issues connected to that question of the realist knowledge of God in Jesus Christ. These responses will be subsequently analyzed and assessed with regard to their actual viability, and to that extent used preliminarily in our larger process of critique and correction here.

Carl F. H. Henry's Critical Analysis of Torrance's Realist Theology

Henry's criticisms of Torrance and his line of theological thinking have come in varied contexts over several decades. Focus here will be upon Henry's criticisms directed at issues of logic and what he sees to be Torrance's irrationality, despite Torrance's expressed desire for the opposite in and for theology. He says that Torrance insists that theological knowledge be free of imprisonment in logical connections, that the Truth cannot be known in terms of fixed categories. Rather the truth requires a Kierkegaardian movement of thought to go beyond logical connections. Such thought requires *decision* beyond logic in a "leap of faith." This "leap" Torrance calls true rationality. But, says Henry, if the *logos* structure of the universe and logic are tentative then what basis is left for asserting the permanent validity of Torrance's own comments about theological knowledge? Henry says that this means we must take Torrance at his word regarding the unsatisfactoriness of his own theological ideas and conceptions and words about God. The human mind must be altered to be able to recognize divine revelation as concerned for the fullness of meaning while the Truth of God resists all formulation. But how then can one be sure that this fullness of which Torrance speaks is a fullness of meaning? In the question regarding the realist and objective knowledge of God, there is said to be a problem of the ontologic and the theologic as well. In other words, "how are we to relate the *logos* of man (thought and reason or rationality in the world) to the *Logos* of God?"[18]

While agreeing with Torrance with regard to the crucial nature of the Johannine *Logos* doctrine and that God has made himself known in a final and decisive way in Jesus Christ, Henry believes that Torrance unjustifiably transforms the fact that God objectifies himself for and meets us in Jesus Christ into an eclipse of general revelation, a devaluation of prophetic revelation and a cognitive deflation of all *Logos*-revelation. He is said to do less than full justice to the Old Testament when he declares that in the fact of Jesus Christ God has now at last broken into that closed circle of human and world alienation. This means, according to Henry, a conceptual reductionism of general revelation, of scriptural disclosure and in fact that very revelation in

Jesus Christ which is so central to all of Torrance's theology. In emphasizing
that in Jesus Christ God's Truth is personal, Torrance is also said to forget that
all truth as truth is personal in the sense that objective truth "exists only in and
for a living mind."[19]

Henry agrees with Torrance that humanity lives in untruth and in
opposition to the Truth. As a result human ideas and the world are twisted and
resistent to the Truth, from which comes God's demand for repentance. But
when Torrance relates this to human, epistemic deficiency rather than volitional
rebellion he is found to have contravened the biblical understanding. Torrance
requires, then, a radical alteration of the human cognitive capacity because real
knowledge of God's revelation in Christ necessitates real change in the logical
structure of human consciousness, which endangers the incarnation itself.[20]
Torrance's answer lies in his distinction between human word and the Word of
God, which is inseparable from God's Person and partakes of the hypostatic
relation between humanity and deity and is communicated in the form of
mystery. As Henry describes Torrance's position, the Truth of God is said to
be communicated to humanity in the form of mystery in the concrete fact or
event to which "the Truth is nevertheless infinitely transcendent." In affirming
the dialogical nature of the Truth of revelation Torrance does set himself against
the dialectical and existential views that revelation cannot be cognitively known.
Yet, says Henry, "the dialogical objectivity of revelational truth espoused by
Torrance nevertheless erodes the universal validity of theological truth. 'The
Message is not received except in personal relation to the Truth.'"[21]

Henry agrees that theological truth is bound to God's sovereign revelation
and will, but then Henry elucidates what he sees to be Torrance's problem in
connection to the thought of Kierkegaard. This is the heart of Henry's criticism.
Regarding the role of "decision" and truth, Henry asserts that it is one thing to
say that decision is necessary for efficacious appropriation of the truth, another
to say that private decision establishes the truth-character of the truth for the
individual. He finds Torrance to be standing on the edge of this distinction
when he says that theological statements involve a spiritual relationship to the
extent that they are truthfully related to Christ instead of insofar as they are
truthful. In defending his position against charges of irrationalism, while
claiming it to be in fact the way of obedient reason to the Truth, Torrance can
say that "knowledge of Jesus Christ as Eternal Truth in the form of historical
being involves a modification of our theory of knowledge," indeed, "a change
in the logical structure of consciousness."[22] But Henry responds by asserting
that if one cannot know the truth of revelation apart from existential inner
decision, then one cannot be held accountable for personal rejection. One would
be immune to revelation given the utter difference of the Logic of this "divine
lightning" from that of the human *logos*. Torrance's way is found to allow for
no objective revelational knowledge.[23]

The chasm in human theological statements is said by Torrance to only be

overcome in Jesus Christ. But this exception in respect to Jesus, he says, cannot
be brought together with what Torrance claims for the inadequacy of all human
words and concepts. Given that the discrepancy is overcome in the God-man,
then, thinking anthropologically, Henry questions Torrance saying,

> . . . if human nature only under these conditions can incarnate the Logos of
> God to possess the truth of revelation in epistemological form, and if
> coherent knowledge of God requires a structural change in the mind of man
> made possible only by personal union with the Godhead, then the price paid
> for preserving the truth of revelation simply cannot be reconciled with the
> teaching of Scripture. Theological truth available only on this questionable
> basis of incarnation leaves us not only with the problem of how we can ever
> inherit this truth that requires such "divine humanity" for its knowledge, but
> also how even so discerning a theologian as Torrance came into its
> possession.[24]

Torrance does not explicitly claim that knowledge of God negates or alters our
humanity per se, but the encounter means there is "lifting it up above to
participation." Yet Torrance asserts many things about the "moment" of
encounter or the "event" of revelation that the principles of his positive theological expression may negate.   Vigorous assertion does not overcome
incoherence.

But Henry develops this point by stating against Torrance that Jesus did not
come as the founder of a new logic or new religious language. Torrance admits
that the revelation of God in Jesus Christ is divine Truth actualizing itself in our
humanity and communicating itself through human speech, but he warns against
looking to human speech (*lalia*) without actually hearing beneath and beyond it
the actual Truth of the divine *Logos* to which it points. Henry claims that
Torrance has denied that God's revelation is externally and objectively given in
valid form. Word becomes real only as internal response and subjective decision
(*Entscheidung*). Torrance clearly considers human words and concepts to be
unuseable for actually bearing or being divine revelation, being at last but
pointers to and the open occasion of disclosure from beyond at a higher level.
Words are bound up with the Word behind and through them and this Word
does reach us through words. But Henry adds that Torrance has also said that
theological statements (like the mind) require a "structural shift" in order to be
made then, in some sense, adequate to the nature of God's Truth which they are
made to convey.

In all, Henry is questioning whether the God spoken of in Scripture reveals
himself to humanity in a "dialogical revelation" or whether the Truth of God
which meets us in the *Logos* meshes with humanity and human knowing in an
activity of rationality which comprehends both the Infinite and the finite in one
and the same logical level (to put the matter in "Torrancian" terms). The *imago*

Dei is an important part of Henry's epistemology. It is not surprising that Henry's understanding of the "image of God" stresses the rationality of humanity. If the image of God includes categories of thought and forms of logic ample to the service of God, and if this has not been destroyed by sin, it need not be the case that in the rational divine Word that one is face to face with a transcendent Reality which cannot be reduced to, or better, be made manifest in and as part of the creaturely dimensions.[25]

More narrowly, the singular nature of the living God, who is ever affirmed by Torrance to be the proper Object of human knowledge, means that Torrance's theology of revelation may involve the unique use of language or conceptual forms, says Henry. What'it absolutely cannot do if theology is an objective, realist and rational science, is to assert the necessity of some unique logic. If the knowledge of God is conceptual, in Torrance's sense, and the *Logos* is revealed both ontologically in Jesus of Nazareth and epistemologically in these conceptual forms, then Torrance is found to limit God's power and freedom in his self-revelation. God is then unable to speak intelligibly in the space-time world. Torrance is said to be taking away from revelation the status of universally valid information, that is, that nothing that God discloses, not even, for example, that God is one or justification by faith, can be understood as simply true.

> The revelation of the God of the Bible surely includes much that is permanently and universally valid. The truth of divine revelation is not time bound . . . in the sense of requiring sporadic updating simply because divine action in time is essential to historical revelation. Torrance's activistic view of divine revelation would, if consistently applied, seem to permit only a situational theology.[26]

While strongly asserting the rationality of revelation as cognitive, conceptual and intelligible, Torrance wants to avoid the "purely intellectual" view of truth. Henry finds that truth of statement for Torrance is concerned primarily with the reference of statements to the reality of things beyond. Torrance's is then a "representational" epistemology whereby truth of statement is said to refer to reality or Truth beyond so that the mind in fact cannot grasp the real.

Henry also finds in Torrance's insistence upon "open" (toward God) rather than "closed" concepts appropriate to the knowledge of God the toppling of the objectivity and knowledge of God that he is so concerned to maintain. He perceives that Torrance's reasons for such stem from his desire to show God's sovereignty and incomprehensibility, the utter dependence of human knowledge of God on God's own initiative, that the finite cannot "hold" the infinite, etc., but that this requires "open" concepts rather than "closed" (knowledge capable of propositional expression) does not follow. Torrance's reasons are said to be "rationalizations" from a speculatively imposed theory of religious knowledge

by which Torrance himself seems to have been given some objective
propositional knowledge of God which his own methodology disallows to all
others (e.g., how does Torrance know that there is an ultimate objectivity which
cannot be enclosed within creaturely objectivities by means of which we
encounter it?). Torrance insists that we have "genuine apprehension" of God
and that knowledge arises by the conformity of rational cognition to that
objective Word of God. But except by a colossal "leap of faith," Henry asks
how anyone can be assured of objectivity of knowledge when no statements are
accorded universal validity, but as "open" they can carry only inexpressible
"information"? Are we, as existing persons, not actually robbed of all
universally valid knowledge of God in this view? While Torrance talks of
"levels" of objective reality, whereby seemingly paradoxical statements at one
level are not to be read "in the flat" (phenomenologically) but in their openness
to and interrelation with levels "above," Henry questions Torrance's whole
attempt to both disjoin and correlate human concepts and knowledge of God.
Torrance is said to have been overcome by what Henry sees to be the struggle
inherent in the subrational consequences of his Barthian position, to which
Henry has much antipathy.[27]

Before leaving Carl Henry's criticisms, it is of interest here to refer briefly
to Torrance's response when this writer engaged Professor Torrance with regard
to Henry's views.

> . . . the farrago of nonsense you send me from Carl Henry! His whole
> position rests on the divine inspiration of logic, and the nominalist identity
> of truth with the terms that refer to the truth. Moreover it rests on an
> immense error in which he thinks that logic refers to the relation between
> terms and reality, when it has to do with the relation of statements to one
> another or the relations of ideas consistently with each other. I do not know
> what one can do with one like Carl Henry whose reason has clearly not been
> humbled by the Cross of Christ . . . . Jesus, the Incarnate and crucified and
> risen Word who IS Jesus Christ comes to us through space and time and
> through the Holy Scriptures as through closed doors. He does not come in
> the kind of way you can specify with linguistic or logical tools, as Carl
> Henry thinks, but in the power of the resurrection—really comes.[28]

Ray S. Anderson's Critical Analysis of
Torrance's Realist Theology

Ray Anderson takes a position largely in accord with Torrance and within
the larger "Barthian" school of thought, though not uncritically. He is also
much influenced at important points by Dietrich Bonhoeffer and the late
Glasgow theologian Ronald Gregor Smith. In a published work which began as
Anderson's doctoral dissertation done under Torrance's supervision, *Historical*

Transcendence and the Reality of God: A Christological Critique, Anderson discusses a number of criticisms, as well as affirmations, of Torrance's thought. But there is one criticism of Torrance's position which is more pertinent to the concerns here than the others, the nature of revelation in Torrance's thought. Anderson explains that what is at stake for Torrance "in giving up that which a concept of propositional revelation seeks to preserve" has to do with the pole of transcendence which lies in history and thus can serve to inform one's act of faith "in the Spirit" of its transcendent grounds in the person of Jesus Christ. "Historical transcendence," that is, transcendence as an actual historical experience in the world, is crucial for Torrance and it is that which is at stake because "if the cognitive link with the content of God's transcendence as historical act is broken, the act of faith must supply its own content to the divine Word."[29] This historical "pole" of God's manifested transcendence in Christ can be truly revelatory only as it informs faith of its own transcendent grounding. Therefore Scripture is said to have the quality of transcendence only with regard to its cognitive link with the ontic reality of God's own "historical transcendence," (i.e., incarnation). The ontic and noetic can then relate to each other without some human anthropology being forced in between the two. Anderson develops this point in relation to Torrance.

> However one redefines propositional revelation to avoid the distorting element of "rationalism" (which is itself the insertion of an anthropology), this is the concept which must be preserved. T.F. Torrance, while carefully avoiding tho implications of propositional revelation, attempts to state the case for the place of Scripture in a double sense, both above the Church, and thus transcendent of the words of man, but also in history, and thus subject to all human finitude . . . . One can appreciate the efforts of Professor Torrance to maintain both the authority and the humanity of Scripture; but I am not so sure that it can be done by giving the Scripture both a transcendent and an immanent relation to man, and thus separating its transcendence from its historicity. For the problem of how one determines when it is "above the Church" and when it is merely "under the judgment of the cross" introduces a (problematic) position . . . that is, it can only be determined by how one "hears it in his situation."[30]

The rationale (or "inner logic" of the incarnation) of "historical transcendence" has made it clear to Anderson that the transcendence of God was most completely revealed when the Son of the Father was under the judgment of the Cross, so that in Jesus the word of man was the Word of God. He says then that "if this rationale is allowed to expose the rationale of Scripture, we would find that Scripture has this same 'kenotic' function within the rationale of historical transcendence."[31] This means that Holy Scripture would not have a "double place" as existential (beyond) and historical but as the pole of transcendence which confronts one completely as a revelation in history with all of the limitations and conditions which history imposed upon the Person of the Word made flesh.. But then the "transcendence" of Scripture, if such be recognized at all, is not found in either the existential pole of the hearer nor even as the hearer is "enlightened" by the Spirit. The "transcendence" of Scripture would lie in the very human and historical word of Scripture itself. Anderson's point is not "rationalistic" but that the "historical transcendence" of Scripture as "revelation" needs to be recognized as forming a critical pole of transcendence within which God places one responding in faith to the revelation of God in Jesus.[32]

Richard Muller's Critical Analysis of Torrance's Realist Theology

In a context whose focus is Karl Barth and the ongoing place of Barth's theological thinking in the twentieth century, Muller makes a significant, critical reference to Torrance's "Barthian" position in theology. He explains that the basic issues and themes in nineteenth century theology have remained for much of theology today, and no matter how much Barth signaled a revolt against such "culture Christianity," he barely disturbed the basic theological program of the older "liberalism." In fact Barth's thought itself arose, he says, from the nineteenth century's basic directions and he carried forward many of its basic notions. Many elements in Barth's thought are grounded in the "liberalism" of Kähler, Herrmann and even Troeltsch's views on the "absoluteness of Christianity" among the religions via his Christ-centered appeal to revelation.[33] Barth's radical severing of Christian revelation from religion and his Christocentrism is said to reflect his debt to Schleiermacher, Dorner, Ritschl and Herrmann, while the "history of religions" approach is set aside and nineteenth century "theological rebels" and "outcasts," Overbeck and Kierkegaard, are brought in. Barth's "rebellion" was of limited significance and created no new epoch in theology, nor did it end nineteenth century theological liberalism.[34]

These points are used to shed light upon Torrance's proclaimed theological task in overcoming theological dualism and in grounding theo-logical knowledge in the actual, objective Word as the continuation and development of Barth's own theological program (cf. chapter one). As Barth's theology is seen to be rebellion against the Schleiermacherian and Ritschlian theologies, the development of his thought makes it clear, says Muller, that such Barthian thought participates in and remains indebted to that very "dualist" post-Kantian context so that even in issues where Barthian thought is said to differ from "liberalism," such as the historical study of religion and the relation of theology to natural scientific investigation, these same issues have remained crucial to theology throughout this century. (Torrance's emphases on the necessary relation of theology and the natural sciences may possibly be seen as the pushing of Barthian theology back into the stream of thought and the public arena, cf. Wolfhart Pannenberg). Of "Barthian" Torrance, Muller says

> With the exception of a few students who chose to become "Barthians" and
> follow the thought of their master almost slavishly, repeating with awe
> certain Barthian phrases like "God's Being in his Act and his Act in his
> Being" or "the identity of God with his self-revelation," Barth's theology
> reposes in splendid isolation both from its own ("liberal") past and from the
> theological present. There is, in other words, a continuing Barthian
> movement of a rather limited scope and impact which, together with other
> movements typical of this pluralistic age . . . has stood alongside rather than
> in the center of the post-Reformation orthodox and the post-Enlightenment
> liberal trajectories.[35]

Thomas A. Langford's Critical Analysis of Torrance's Realist Theology

Like Anderson, Thomas Langford comes critically to Torrance's position not as one wholly at odds with Torrance but as one who takes seriously and who in some ways shares Torrance's basic theological commitment and hope. Wanting to understand more fully Torrance's position, it is Langford's purpose to criticize his theo-logical expression to the end that Torrance develop his thought on themes upon which both are agreed for theological science.[36]

Focusing here on those points of criticism connected to our concern for Torrance's realist knowledge of God, Langford says that while Torrance is largely correct about the nature of science, his view of theology as science has only formal points of similarity with physics. Yet the basis of Torrance's argument is that science as science has learned to be open to its object. In this Torrance is more profound than most who falsely perceive that to be "scientific" means to be "antidogmatic," thereby actually missing the issue. He finds that Torrance's stress on faith is much too "rationalistic" and thus loses necessary elements of trust and obedience (though Langford, like Torrance, sets himself against notions of faith as non-cognitive). This sets the stage for Langford's analysis of the theme of the "objectivity of knowledge" wherein it is said that the proper object of knowledge for each particular science must be allowed its integrity and formative power to shape and direct all interpretation of itself. Therefore Torrance maintains that human knowledge of God as humble acknowledgement of the objectively given Word of God, which controls all thinking about it, means that scientific theology is done in a relation of cognitive obedience to God only and objectively in Jesus Christ. And there in Christ this occurs dynamically through the Holy Scriptures which are the "garments" of God's personal coming to encounter us now in Jesus. Theological statements, like Scripture itself in principle, are said by Torrance to have no truth in themselves but only as they are related to the Truth as it is in Jesus. In this dynamic way God is continually re-speaking himself so that in the Word-encounter Jesus is made present to the hearer. Langford points out that in this way a duality is formed so that human words (Scripture, then subsequently theological statements and doctrines) may be incontrovertibly true as derived from God, yet they are also simply culturally conditioned symbols. This would seem to reflect or potentially point toward a kind of "hypostatic union," one which Torrance does not acknowledge in his felt need to emphasize the divine difference to all creaturely words.

Here Langford says of Torrance's theo-logical formulation of the self-communicating movement of God in the Word-event of Jesus, occurring as it does from beyond through the Scriptures, whereby theological statements are then verified "through conformity to the biblical revelation," that Torrance does not deal adequately with what he means about the nature of this "biblical revelation" as he calls it. Torrance appears, he says, to be open to the problems that Hermann Diem uncovered in Barth's thought. Diem found that Barth did not provide for adequate interaction between dogmatic work and scriptural exegesis.[37] That is even more applicable to Torrance. It is Langford's concern here to understand the relation of human theological statements to the Truth of God. Therefore this is central, absolutely critical to the larger question. Does Torrance take all of Scripture as equal? While formally all Scripture is seen as open to God's power, the question Langford raises is a historical one. How are differences in interpretation to be judged and then theological priorities set? He says that while it is true that we can never claim that God must be himself the content of human statements about him, still "where does this leave the deposit of written theology? Where does it leave the Scriptures? The creeds . . . . Can one claim that some forms . . . are more susceptible to God's influxion than others? If so on what grounds?"[38] Langford is correct in saying that Torrance's answer is to refer to the validity of the way and forms of self-revelation which God has actually chosen to take in the world, that is, historical assessment. Yet while Langford finds that this is a significant point, this is not fully useable or successful. Theology then becomes a science without a technology.

From this basis, Langford develops his criticism on this question of theological statement, with regard to Torrance's development of the analogical understanding of statements about reality which must correspond to their "transcendent reference." Note carefully how Langford perceptively describes Torrance's position on the relation of knowledge, statement and Reality.

> The verification of these analogue complexes is by repetition of the original intuitive experiences that gave rise to them . . . . What Torrance has said is that there seems to be an impassable gulf between Reality and any statement about Reality. Nevertheless, certain sets of analogic existence-statements

arise out of engagement between this reality and cognitive man; these statements provide one with a paradigm through which it is possible to enter again the originating relationship—if in attempting to utilize the paradigm one remains open as the original self-giving of Reality re-presents itself.[39]

But for all of that, Langford still wants to know how Torrance is able to adjudicate among rival claimants in the Christian community. Torrance believes real objectivity, more faithful thinking after the Word and scientific theology will itself decide the issue by the one Object which will judge all and will itself found the Truth. This is at the heart of Torrance's own personal ecumenical rationale. The uniqueness of Jesus, as the object of Christian rationality and as "concrete universal," is meant by Torrance to be self-evidencing truth, and this is fine, but Langford is not convinced that Torrance has actually worked this out. Torrance's desire to make the center of theological knowing, thinking and worship Christological is clear and logical, but the hermeneutical question remains.

> What remains in doubt is whether this event gives rise to one or many legitimate interpretations . . . we fall back once again upon the biblical medium of the event of Jesus Christ. For Torrance theological statements are to be compared to scriptural statements which are judged by the living Christ who reveals God. The question which remains paramount is how the theological statement is to be compared to the biblical statement. What is the hermeneutic? . . . how (is) any given set of theological statements proffered by theologians to be judged by the constellation of statements found in the New Testament.[40]

Through the subject-object relations at the ascending "levels" of interpreter to biblical text, then biblical witness to Jesus, Jesus to God and God's self-revealing in Jesus, Torrance asserts that one must advance and synthesize their interconnections by being drawn into and thinking out from that faith-ful participation by the Grace of God. Clearly, says Langford, Torrance's assumption underlying his answer to the relation of Jesus to the New Testament witness is that the Holy Spirit can in fact draw the interpreter into and through the text to its nucleus, Jesus Christ, and through Christ to God.[41]

Donald S. Klinefelter's Critical Analysis of Torrance's Realist Theology

Donald Klinefelter analyzes Torrance's theology from the viewpoint of an analytic philosophy of religion. Over and over one finds in Klinefelter responses which reflect his empiricist insistence. As a result, he has great difficulty with Torrance's senses or definitions of objectivity and scientific rationality which begin with the actuality of the proper object of a science and the commanding role of the inherent intelligibility of that object in the realist knowing of it, while also viewing autonomous reason as a diseased form of rationality and as in fact subjectivism with no real relation to external reality. Torrance's further emphases upon the Object, God, of theological science and his antipathy to positivistic scientism and dogmatic empiricism all surely put the two at odds. Thus Klinefelter speaks of Torrance's constructive efforts to "rehabilitate" theology as science and his confidence in the ultimate rationality of the Object of theology as at best roughly analogous to the faith of the natural scientist, and as a presumptuous endeavor traceable to his scientific realism.

Klinefelter sees many problems with Torrance's connection between theology and the physical sciences. Thus there is the question of theology's truly "scientific" nature. He says Torrance stresses "that both natural science and scientific theology operate through a methodological exclusion of one another . . . they move in opposite directions . . . two mutually exclusive ways of knowledge," therefore in what sense can there exist complementarity and analogy to the natural sciences? Indeed, in Torrance there are found to be ambiguities or potential dilemmas, or at least lack of clarity, regarding his method, and finally an epistemological or ontological dualism ". . . (to which he has) not yet found a satisfactory solution."[42] Are theological and physical science two ways of knowing? Torrance's problem is then understood to be the traditional problem for dialectical theologians in that logical clarification of the relation between the theological and natural sciences and their respective objects is regarded as not appropriate in the light of modern developments. Beyond that the natural sciences are held by Torrance to be unable in themselves to grasp the wholeness and uniqueness of the Truth of God as expressed in the incarnation. The "concrete universal" of Jesus Christ cannot be grasped by the analytical methods of formal logic. How can the "natural" be used to test or verify the "supernatural"? As Torrance follows Kierkegaard's thought, his view of theology's peculiarity is said to leave Torrance with real methodological problems. There is then only an indirect, formal comparison with the other sciences by the analogy of proportionality with no direct transfer of method or language. This prompts Klinefelter, throughout his analysis of Torrance's theology, to question his "implicit dualism" and to ask that if his work is philosophical theology then

> . . . why the apparently arbitrary reliance on Christian revelation to control all epistemological questions? Why the apparently unwarranted appeal to a "special" type of analogy, to a "unique" knowledge of ultimate Reality in addition to proximate realities? Why the abrupt dismissal of logical argument or proof in any ordinary sense? Why the insistence on the actuality of an extraordinary "concrete universal"? . . . formulated in such a way as to defy refutation, that is, they are so logically odd . . . . Nearly all of these cluster

around the appropriateness of the crucial analogy on which Torrance appears to rest his case, namely his appeal to the "scientific" character of theology.[43]

Klinefelter's point is that the very differences between theological and natural science would seem to be so great that all real comparison and relation is doubtful, especially given that fact of the differences in their "objects," and thus in their "rationalities" and their "objectivities." Torrance seems to push the use of the terms to real distortion. This theological position is said to posit such a radical distinction between knowing and being and between different kinds of knowing that Klinefelter cannot see how this can be coordinated in the same universe. While natural science cannot presuppose the content of actual knowledge, will Torrance allow the same kind of interrogation and ignorance in theological science? Apparently not, says Klinefelter. Torrance insists that actual knowledge within theology is knowledge of the Absolute, Christological and trinitarian, coming "full-blown in the historical Christian revelation in a way quite incommensurate with normal scientific discovery."[44]

On the relation of theology and philosophy in Torrance, Klinefelter focuses on how Torrance understands Truth and formal logic, and struggles with Torrance's Kierkegaardian emphasis on the dynamic thinking appropriate to the dynamic, personal God in his desire to think together correspondent and coherent truth. Torrance, he says, must insist then that genuine theo-logical thinking involves a "leap" in keeping with the rationality of the Word of God which is "absurd" from the perspective of formal logic. Theological statements are "provable" only by assuming what is to be proved, that is, by "intuiting" the reality in its objectivity and unity. Torrance is said then to cut off theological statements from all other types of statement. He is not dependent upon philosophical analysis for verifying their validity, but only upon the content or internal structure, the being, of the objective reference. Klinefelter asks how can human statement refer to what is infinitely beyond the limits of human experience? And how can non-linguistic relations be represented in language? What objective standard could measure the strengths and weaknesses of Torrance's analogies? Thus he says that Torrance leaves us only with Einsteinian awe before the mystery, the fact of human knowledge of God. All verification is a combination of intuitionist, analogical and existentialist elements. Yet as "knowledge" *a posteriori* out of encounter with the objective Reality, theological statements are "empirical" statements which, if genuine, are said by Torrance to conform to the Word of God. Therefore all verification of scientific theology is finally by the Grace of God. Klinefelter says that "rather than supporting an advance to new theological frontiers they (Torrance's use of science and philosophy) serve instead as bulwarks protecting a sophisticated Barthian fideism."[45] Torrance's rationality and objectivity are found to be so peculiar it should be called something else. Theological rationality and ordinary rationality seem barely connected as one is led through the analogues to a "shock of recognition," a repetition of original intuitive experiences, and a direct cognition of the denoted realities. Whatever room Torrance gives to "natural reason," Klinefelter finds that Torrance falls short for not developing the empirical nature of *a posteriori* theological statements sufficiently to indicate whether they are "falsifiable" or are peculiar in this respect as well. Klinefelter emphasizes that Torrance has not moved far enough from his Neo-Reformation roots so that, all he has given are reasons why theoretical justification of any kind of knowledge is impossible, and therefore why what seems to be irrationality is really rationality when one is thinking about God.[46]

What of theology and history? The fact of Jesus Christ, and particularly the incarnation and resurrection, make the relation of theological science to historical science necessarily vital to Torrance, especially as he desires to avoid the dualistic problems of an idealistic history, a materialistic science, and the dualist error underlying the *Historie-Geschichte* disjunction. The historian too must go beyond description and narration to explanation, that is, to "Word rationality." Klinefelter finds that Torrance believes that one must treat the question of Christ as any other event, but must also learn to ask questions in two directions simultaneously in accord with the nature and acts of God and the nature and acts of human beings. This involves an interactionist rather than a dualistic understanding of the relation of God and history. This interactionist understanding means thinking out of Creation and Incarnation. But Klinefelter wonders about the relation of particular events to the Word's space-time movement and asks how one determines which events are decisive in interpreting God's intention. Why ask questions in two directions? How do source materials "interpret themselves," as Torrance claims? Now while Torrance asserts that faith is necessary to see the divine action in history in Christ, that is, to see the intrinsic process of hermeneutics in the incarnate *Logos*, Klinefelter is hardly convinced. He says that Torrance has tried to "maneuver out of the *Historie-Geschichte* dilemma . . . in his appeal to the complexity of the historical fact: we are confronted with a complex fact that includes its own interpretation as part of its facticity."[47] In other words, Torrance's view of this unique historical process, as characterized by an inherent duality arising from the interaction of God with historical agents, means that it is a process distinct from the kind of becoming found in common facts, and it tells of a dualistic tendency in his thinking. This leads Klinefelter to conclude that Torrance has not overcome the problem of modern dualism in order to found a proper scientific realism more firmly. Torrance is said to be caught within the very problem he wants to overcome. Klinefelter asserts that

> . . . the notions of complementarity and objectivity in science, bipolarity and duality in philosophy, and logical levels and complex facts in history, although quite suggestive in themselves, have not been appropriated by

Torrance's theology in such a way as to overcome his latent dualism.[48]

Torrance is found then to have been arguing for the interaction of God and world without ably defending this divine activity, often referring to it as mystery beyond explanation. But this is self-defeating because, while the "new theology" severs God from God-language, Torrance has severed God and God-language from any other realm of discourse. If that is so then theology is forced to silence before the questions directed to it by the world. While Torrance is said to rightly want to unite the ontological and dynamic elements in theology, Klinefelter concludes that he has not provided such a union.

Ronald F. Thiemann's Critical Analysis of Torrance's Realist Theology

In the lengthy second chapter of Ronald Thiemann's important recent work, *Revelation and Theology: The Gospel as Narrated Promise*, he describes the modern desire in theology to justify Christian claims to revelation by the dual strategy of asserting first that claims to revelation must be reasonable (or not contrary to reason) and second, that revelation refers to a special category of truths undergirded by a unique mode of knowing—similarity and dissimilarity (not knowable by ordinary uses of reason) in a dialectical relation. Such views in affirming revelation are found by Thiemann to require "unusual intellectual dexterity" to avoid irrationalism on one side or ordinary knowing on the other, either of which would negate any claim to revelation as actually warranted or needed after all. Thiemann gives considerable space to Torrance as an example of such thinking which falls prey to inevitable inconsistencies.[49]

Thiemann's criticisms of Torrance's understanding of revelation and theology as real knowing and as a special science focus on his understanding of "intuitive" knowing and what he sees to be Torrance's non-reciprocal understanding of one's relation to God in the non-inferential knowing encounter with the Word. Torrance is found to have followed the way of Kierkegaard rather than that of Schleiermacher as a model of revelation in his giving to revelation its exalted status in his theology. From this basis, to then say that God's revelation must conform to some *a priori* standard of rationality falls far short. Such a position, as Thiemann finds in Torrance, asserts the need to recognize and maintain the absolute prevenience of grace, and revelation is understood as that "impossible possibility" given in the "moment of crisis" shattering autonomous subjectivistic structures of existence in the supra-rational communication of that which lies beyond the grasp of human reason. This theological tradition on revelation stemming from Kierkegaard finds God to be creating in the subject the capacity to receive revelation through faith while simultaneously asserting absolute contrast between faith and reason, almost reveling in revelation's non-(or supra-) rationality. Thiemann believes that in Torrance one finds the most fully developed and interesting form of this position as Torrance claims both the absolute uniqueness and the full rationality of revelation, reversing Schleiermacher's method. At the center of Torrance's dilemma, he says,, is his attempt to ground both the uniqueness and the rationality of revelation in the intuitive, self-evident nature of the revelatory experience, i.e., "the same incoherent notion of intuition which undermined his predecessor's (Barth's) defense of revelation as the basis for prevenience and rationality of grace."[50]

Torrance holds that theology which accepts the absolute primacy of its proper object of inquiry can be considered both rational and scientific. By attending to its own unique object theology exhibits the key characteristics of scientific objectivity. Because of the peculiar, personal and lordly characteristics of its object theology must submit more radically than other sciences in keeping with its status as special science. But according to Thiemann this perspective ingeniously makes theology's flaw, its heteronomous obedience to God, into the very virtue which grants to theology its scientific, rational status. Theology's objective content cannot be discovered by the "mind's ordinary processes" but it must be given by the initiative of God. At the same time divine revelation is true in itself apart from human recognition of its truth. This is seen by Thiemann as "odd." If revelation is true independent of the process by which one comes to know it, that is found to be none other than a claim for irrationality, or at least non-rationality. Such is said to be faith's grasp of revelation in Thiemann's description of Torrance's position. Torrance argues that the theologian must understand and interpret revelation in accord with its own intrinsic rationality and the requirements or mode of rationality given by such. Revelation's *"Wahrheit-an-sich,"* as Torrance propounds it, sounds "strange," says Thiemann, because it goes against the modern epistemological turn to the subject since Descartes and Kant. One can no longer refer to objects independent of the mind's schematizing function. Thiemann is obviously correct when he says that Torrance is not a pre-critical thinker who ignores Kant's "revolution," rather he is aware and very critical of the modern focus upon subjectivity as the key to "knowledge." Thiemann also correctly interprets Torrance as asserting that knowledge arises from the mind's interaction with that which is given, and points to the importance of his rejection of the absolute priority Kant grants to the structure of reason in the formation of "knowledge."[51]

Further, Torrance reflects many contemporary complaints against Kant, but in contrast to most of these Torrance does not then seek for a historical and cultural relativization of the "categories." He looks rather to the renewed realization of the centrality of the object's role in knowledge formation, i.e., realism in epistemology. Rationality is adherence to the proper internal criteria of a discipline as these are specified by the object. Revision of understanding occurs as the nature of the object demands it. But Thiemann finds such "easy talk" about object and objectivity inappropriate before a transcendent object. The object of theology differs from that of physics. Torrance emphasizes this, for God is more emphatically self-revealing. We are said to think according to the inner compulsion of the gracious revelation of God whereby all statements about God are finally statements of God as one who places the individual's subjectivity in subordination to God's objectivity, and thereby is allowed God to interpret himself. Having so understood Torrance, Thiemann sees a contradiction between Torrance's assertion of revelation's uniqueness and rationality. "Reciprocal relation" between subject and object is said to be characteristic of all rational inquiry, but in defending the uniqueness of theology's object Torrance "denies that such reciprocity characterizes the relation between theologian and God." How can a claim to rationality be made for theology if it fails to exemplify that characteristic of objective, scientific discipline? Torrance, he says, is equivocating in his use of the terms "knowledge" and "rationality."[52]

> . . . Torrance's own account of theology's unique object appears to undermine the argument for formal rationality, thus providing the falsifying argument his critics seek. The argument for reciprocity . . . cannot be discarded when attention shifts to the peculiar nature of the theological object. Torrance cannot deny subject-object reciprocity and continue to claim that rationality and truth reside solely in the object without also denying theology's rationality. Torrance is faced with the following inconsistent triad.
>
> 1. Theology is a rational discipline exemplifying the characteristics of a true science.
> 2. The reciprocal relation between the investigating subject and the object of inquiry is a general characteristic of rational scientific activity.
> 3. Theology's unique object is the truth which imposes itself on the subject independent of the subject's reciprocal influence.
>
> The assertion of any two of these propositions demands the denial of the third. Since Torrance's argument requires all three assertions, his position appears doomed to inconsistency.[53]

To overcome this Torrance is said to appeal to "intuition." The human subject does not play a constitutive role in the revelatory relation. The human subject is reformed (or made true) in order to bring about correspondence to divine revelation's essential structure. Human categories are remade until they are united with God's self-interpretation. Thiemann believes that for Torrance revelation is intuition and vice versa and that intuition as revelation ("incorrigible causally imposed knowledge") moves Torrance to maintain that the theologian can apprehend God's essential reality. Revelation unifies our interpretation and God's self-interpretation thereby establishing correspondence between our assertions and God's Being. All of Torrance's position and argument is said to rest upon this concept of "intuition." This "intuition" is a "direct experience" or "encounter" by which one re-lives the original encounter with God. In this way the validity of pre-cognitive experiences is denied. In that case there is no distinction between personal and propositional revelation, for God reveals himself in his Word as mediated through scripture. Torrance is said to claim here that God directly imposes true propositions upon the mind and such divine imposition is unique to theology. Though he is a Kierkegaardian, says Thiemann, Torrance's defense of revelation finally forces him to a form of theological foundationalism.[54]

But Thiemann finalizes his criticism when he claims that for Torrance, as a foundationalist, his insistence that revelation is always linguistic "seals" his position's inconsistency. In his distinction between inferential and non-inferential beliefs, Torrance understands the non-inferential belief to be established independently of a framework of connected concepts but rather by direct relation to the object they represent. The Object establishes the framework of thought. But, says Thiemann, this means that the "proposition which grounds the conceptual framework must be true independent of the concepts for which it serves as the foundation." In point of fact, then, Torrance has "not provided a sufficient argument to justify his claim that the non-inferential propositions of revelation deserve the title knowledge."[55] Since "knowledge" is ordinarily applied to justified true beliefs, how can it be applied to an independent apprehension? Torrance's problem is said to be the same one which Barth had in his *Epistle to the Romans* he stresses both God's sovereign transcendence and his knowability. Torrance tries to solve this by granting to the Spirit mediating power to bring together Object and human being. But Thiemann asserts that the problem is that the Spirit of God is not the human subject but the "not-I" dwelling within. The subject only knows God to the extent subjectivity is conformed to the power of the Spirit, that is, only as the God within knows the God without. If that is so Torrance must hold that true knowledge and interpretation arise "at the expense of the goodness of the creaturely being . . . the human self remains hopelessly bifurcated in the act of knowing God . . . (this must be so if Torrance) hopes to maintain the self-evident incorrigibility of revelation."[56] But all of Torrance's defense of revelation is said to collapse by his appeal to "intuition" or "non-inferential knowing of God."

> How can we have knowledge of God? If we bring God into a context
> dominated by our categories and concepts, we treat him as if he were simply
> another object among the many objects we know through rational
> schematization. If we set God outside that framework and allow him to

create his own conditions and content of knowledge, then we cannot say how it is that we know him. The former option denies God his divinity; the latter denies us our humanity.[57]

Summary

These several viewpoints or responses to the theology of Thomas Torrance, positive, negative and somewhat mixed, are indeed helpful as they can be used to open up that "dialogical" process which Torrance advocates for all of the sciences. But more, these varied responses to Torrance's thought, variations reflecting not only something basic to the thought of the critic but issues central to Torrance's own "theo-logical" concern, enable one to take criticism of Torrance even further. At this point we will analyze and criticize these responses to Torrance, and thereby move on toward further constructive criticism of Thomas Torrance's formulation of Christocentric-Trinitarian theology as firmly rooted in the knowledge of God in the world in Christ.

Critical Analysis of and Response to Torrance's Critics

Critical Response to Carl F. H. Henry

In large part Carl Henry and Thomas Torrance talk past each other and tend inevitably to "compare apples and oranges." Several issues need to be mentioned before Henry's substantive points can be clarified. Henry and Torrance are more in agreement on significant issues than either ever admits. Yet there are also critical differences. Much of the difference lies in their views of logic and the role of human reason and rationality in relation to the self-disclosure of God. Henry is more explicitly Aristotelian, not as a Thomist per se, but he does believe that Aristotle's logic was not an invention but rather a discovery. This is also methodologically observable in his understanding of this logic in relation to the *Logos*-structure of being and to his consistent emphasis on the "law of contradiction" if there is to be rationality at all. While Torrance implicitly works with similar logic in his theological expression, Torrance is adamant against all imposition of *a priori* forms regarding what the real rationality of God must be in relation to the way/pattern he has taken in Christ. Rather the "theo-logic" of God is known only *a posteriori* out of his objective self-revelation in Christ and by the Spirit. Methodological differences between the two obviously ensue. They differ not on the fact of revelation but more on the how and where and content/nature, as well as the knowing of it. For Henry,

Scripture, by means of the process of revelation and inspiration, is the written Word of God, though he too says that Jesus Christ is *the* Word, Scripture being the Word in which the Word by the Spirit is known. To Torrance, this is judged as "nominalism," that is, the separation of Word from God. For Torrance, Scripture is rather understood to be the apostolic and human witness or pointer (though truly referential) to the Word or Truth of God, which is God himself who is ever dynamically and newly revealed in the "moment" of human existence through Scripture. For Henry, objectivity is only possible from within a logic in which humans participate—only then, or under such conditions, can the rationality of God be neither irrational, a-rational or non-rational. For Torrance, though, scientific objectivity is related to the nature of the object in its own internal structure and intelligibility. True rationality must then follow the proper object's mode of rationality. One cannot say *a priori* what can and cannot be disclosed or must be the way taken by God, but rather one can only hear in the knowing that occurs in the faith-relation.

But there are a number of points on which Henry has also clearly and simply misunderstood Torrance. Two significant problems are connected to Henry's perception of Torrance's use of "levels," which is so crucial to Torrance's understanding of unitary theological knowledge of God and theological science. There is also his criticism of Torrance's use of Kierkegaard's "irrationalism." Regarding his use of "levels" of truth, Torrance is not saying that theological concepts at the lower level are false but that their truth does not lie or repose in the concepts or statements themselves. For Henry the statements "the ball is red" or "the leaf is green" are true in addition to and in relation to the red ball and the green leaf. For Torrance the truth here is finally to be found only in the ball and leaf, and in the statements only as derived from, in relation to and in appropriate reference to the proper object. Torrance's point is that in the physical sciences, as well as in theological science, one cannot read the truth of something right off the surface of external reality phenomenologically. The "levels" theo-logical of knowing, and therefore of God's economy grounded in the perichoretic relations of the Trinity, are meant by Torrance to found statements in the Truth. The Truth of God is God in the uncreated Rationality of his own eternal being. Second, given Henry's Aristotelianism, Torrance's use and defense of Kierkegaard was bound to bring reaction from him. The objection is grounded also in the way Kierkegaard is interpreted by Henry. Torrance has understood Kierkegaard's "Truth as Subjectivity" as in fact theo-logical objectivity and realism, the subject's proper relation to the Object. What Torrance takes from Kierkegaard should not be regarded as irrationalism. While Torrance's use of Kierkegaard does apparently form a problem, it is not precisely in the way Henry describes it.

Yet Carl Henry has touched some issues which must be taken as possible difficulties for Torrance's emphases upon theological objectivity and realism. All objections must be understood in light of Torrance's own central theo-logical concern(s) regarding the interactive relation of God with the cosmos and redemptive, objective knowledge of God in the world in Jesus Christ. First, despite vigorous protestations, Torrance does much less than justice to the relation and "revelation" of God in the world before the incarnation event, and then what he does say in broad, vague, essentially unfounded terms about it seems contrary to his own position on the absoluteness and singularity of God's self-revelation in Christ, the one Word of God. Further, Torrance does seem to call for a conceptual reduction of revelation, not as Henry espouses, but rather that in the end Torrance holds to a kind of dialectical view of revelation and a Christ-Word mysticism. In fact, he seems to open himself to the very charge of "dualism" that he levels against others. If God is utterly different, if the *Logos* of God is radically different from created *logos* and historicity then what of unitariness and interrelation and real knowledge of God arising out of creation and redemption. Has he not either left Jesus Christ behind (in his true, real humanity) or made Christ/Word beyond history and human apprehension, given the fact that he speaks of the Truth as utterly transcendent and beyond all creatureliness, yet somehow apprehensible. A real "leap" of the "quantum" variety must occur given the fact that for Torrance Truth is not to be found in linguistic truthfulness itself. By "encounter" with the Word and Kierkegaardian "contemporaneity" all discrepancy, whether vertical or horizontal, is said to be overcome or over-leaped. But has he not created an historical problem and the negation of human creatureliness in relation to God by "lifting up" the knowing person into the divine as knowledge is actualized a-historically and "adoptionistically." While Henry's emphasis on the "constant" truth of God may well be inadequate, Torrance's "lightning" revelation akin to the early Barth's "tangential" revelation seems open to difficulties, given the central place in Torrance's thought for the ultimate Reality of God's eternal constancy as triune, the Lord who is ever faithfully relating and revealing himself interactively in and for the world and humanity.

Critical Response to Ray Anderson

While Torrance does in principle seek confirmation of his theological assertions in Scripture, still Torrance has not really dealt with or explained what he calls "biblical revelation." Torrance wants to engage in realist, scientific and unitary Christian theology in ways paradigmatically reflected in Athanasius, Calvin and Barth. After Anderson's comments Torrance seems to have sought to consistently unfold his thinking about and from Scripture and hermeneutics, but the basis has not altered and Anderson still touches rightly upon a gap in the "field" of relations grounded in Torrance's attempt at the formulation of unitary theology.

This is critical to the whole of Torrance's theological purpose and therefore to the realist knowledge of God in the world. In Anderson's terms, Torrance appears to lack a concrete, historical pole for God's transcendent, redemptive relatedness with the existing human being now. And the means Torrance does use do not overcome the dilemma, but rather make the problem clearer. As Bonhoeffer could not fully accept Barth's view of revelation as contingent to the human subject, suspecting traces of transcendentalism, so too Torrance's view seems again to at last fully remove God and God's self-disclosure from truly historical existence and thus into non-objectivity in the world. It may indeed be that Barth's "Being and Act" and "Act and Being" in balance is not quite adequate (see below). Perhaps if Torrance is to complete his unitary theology in terms of the realist, objective knowledge of God in the world through Jesus Christ and in the Holy Spirit, as he intends, then John Calvin's view of the historical Scriptures in relation to the Church may be a key to bring theo-logical completion in accord with Torrance's own Reformed theo-logical goal.

Critical Response to Richard Muller

Richard Muller's analysis, in its broad sweep in clarifying linkages in Barth's and "Barthian" thought to the liberal tradition, while obviously correct at many points, does not do justice to the real theological impact and energy of Barth, to the early dialectical theologians and to the thinking of the "mature" Barth. While Karl Barth began to be eclipsed in the 1940's by Bultmann and "existential" theology, and then the "shattered spectrum" of theologies, such as we are now experiencing, he (like Tillich) is being shown to be anything but fully exhausted in the first wave of prominence (cf. not only Torrance but Eberhard Jüngel, Robert Jenson and others). In both direct and indirect ways, through various aspects of his thought, he continues to exert an impact (cf. modern emphases on the Trinity in Rahner, Moltmann and Pannenberg). Even Muller's reference to the "Barthian" slavishness is much too flippant, casting aside current work which is developing in new ways important themes found in Barth. Barth's theology is no mere twentieth century footnote in the complexes and maelstrom of modern theology, and Torrance's often bombastic development of elements of Barth's thought, including natural theology and dialogue with the natural sciences, can in no way be reckoned as slavish.

Yet Muller does direct attention to issues which must be emphasized for developing consideration here. One is the relation of Barthian thought to and its ongoing participation in the dominant strains of nineteenth century theology, even in Barth's partial rebellion against such. Muller brings out that through Barth these themes, including his continued participation in post-Kantian (dualist) thought, are those of which Torrance too partakes, though also from a position of contention, correction and reformulation. It is epistemologically and methodologically noteworthy that Torrance, in contrast to the later Barth, makes much use of what he calls Kierkegaard's real objectivity and realism in the knowing relation. Muller's negative reference to Barth's balancing of the Nicene and Reformation insights in focusing on "the Being of God in his Act and the Act of God in his Being" and "the identity of God with his self-revelation" belies the crucial methodological and epistemological role these expressions play theologically and particularly in Torrance's thinking with regard to the bi-polar, interactive God-world relatedness, which receives so much of his stress in connection to the redemptive knowledge of God as he is in himself. These can be and should be helpful theological expressions serving the development of theological thinking from Christ and by the Spirit. But they may in fact be incomplete and too narrow in scope to do full justice to Torrance's realist, unitary theological intention to show forth God's real transcendence and relation in the field of human knowing in history, which he has found to be centered in Jesus Christ.

Critical Response to Thomas Langford

Langford has sought to engage Torrance's theology on a range of his own concerns and to get to the center of Torrance's own theological task, and thus to show Torrance's themes for both their promise and their lack. In a sense, Langford wants to help Torrance to accomplish his goal. This is certainly proper. But in focusing on the question of the truth of theological statement Langford has too often left implicit in the discussion that which must be made explicit in order to enhance his own contribution. It must be said too that while Torrance has probably overemphasized the cognitive aspect of faith as the proper mode of knowing God, yet Torrance does not forgo the crucial aspects of trust and obedience.

The critical points of difficulty, which Langford for the most part only alludes to, must be made explicit and be developed. Langford brings out Torrance's understanding of the self-objectification of God in Christ in terms of encounter and Word-event. In this way, Jesus is said to come and present himself immediately to the existing individual, while the individual is "lifted up" and drawn back to the original experience of revelation. This understanding is clearly linked, through Barth's view of history, back to Kierkegaard's concept of "contemporaneity," though Langford does not make such connection. As one is encountered by Jesus in the "moment" in one's present existence, and thereby drawn back or made contemporary to the original revelation through Scripture, one is drawn through the apostolic witness to the Christ-event and the Christ-center or level, and from there "level by level" to the highest level in God. But Langford alludes to the fact that Torrance still seems to assert the necessity of Scripture and to describe it in terms conspicuously parallel to his discussion of the hypostatic union and its relation and role to and for the creaturely, and yet as creaturely. Despite this, Torrance then cuts Scripture, as creaturely, away from the self-disclosive movement of God in the world, severs it as in principle the disposable medium through which the transcendent God reveals himself. The Word of God thus seems to be disjoined from the creaturely and historical as *God's* Word. This is clearly the case despite Scripture's supposed necessity for Torrance's own understanding of divine disclosure which is found to transcendently participate in and as the creaturely in Christ. But what then (to borrow from Langford) not only regarding the question of Scripture, but beyond Langford, what of the historical Incarnation of the Word? Has Torrance finally let go of the needed historicity of the divine Word? This would seem to be even more at the heart of the matter given Torrance's desire to serve theologically the interactive God-world relatedness and the objectivity of God's self-giving to be known in Christ and by the Spirit in every generation.

Critical Response to Donald Klinefelter

Even more than with Carl Henry and Torrance, we have here the meeting of two largely irreconcilable approaches. Basically Klinefelter is chiding Torrance for not being Klinefelter. He is critical of the "unitary" and "interactionist" elements in Torrance's theology because they do not show explicitly how divine activity is related to the world. This is an empiricist insistence or requirement for demonstrations of transcendent reality of the positivistic, scientist type which seems to fall under the criticisms of Einstein and Polanyi, as well as Torrance. While Klinefelter attempts to bring weighty criticism upon Torrance by broad interpretive strokes, in fact Torrance has not been understood adequately. It is the purpose here first to show a few of the prominent ways in which Klinefelter has not understood Torrance, and then to point out how he has also correctly raised a difficulty for Torrance, though it is somewhat different from the way he himself seems to conceive of it.

Klinefelter's own analytic and empiricist philosophy of religion puts him in opposition to Torrance from the beginning. To Torrance, one like Klinefelter looks at everything "in the flat" or at "one level," that is, phenomenologically. One of Klinefelter's difficulties in understanding Torrance's thought is Torrance's "theological," or "scientific," realism. He has numerous problems in seeing what realism is and is not in Torrance's own discussion and understanding of it. "Realism" is then transformed, reduced or shifted in Klinefelter's attempts to re-express it. When Torrance speaks of the proper methodology and mode of rationality of the post-Einsteinian sciences as that of faithful obedience to the proper object of each science, that is, to the object's inherent intelligibility and rationality, he is referring to that objective impress of reality upon the mind and the way of truth (mode of rationality) to which the scientist is called in order to know it out of itself. It is the same for aspects of creation or for God. Klinefelter falls back then into what Torrance would term dualist or disjunctive thinking. Torrance would emphasize that God, a human being or a stone are not to be approached methodologically in exactly the same way, given the differences in their natures, indeed in their being. Beyond this, when one inquires after the way God has actually taken, God is said to reverse or "invert" this process as he "questions us down to the root of our being." In this way too God is Object, but unique as well. This does not cut off theology from dialogue with other sciences but, according to Torrance, it actually establishes true objectivity, and therefore founds the basis for dialogue among all sciences (a dialogue in which Torrance has himself been a leader for decades).

Klinefelter also misunderstands the nature and significance of Torrance's epistemological and analogical use of Einstein's interactive "levels," which are crucial to Torrance's understanding of the economy and prescribed way of knowing of the truth of the Truth of God in the world. Over and over Klinefelter finds here in Torrance a "radical disjunction" or "dualistic tendency," seemingly because it is thinking endeavoring to rise above mere visible space-time connections. This interactive openness "up" and the issue of the apparently paradoxical as true at a higher level is as problematic for Klinefelter as for Carl Henry. Klinefelter repeatedly criticizes Torrance for not following empiricistic verification procedures in his entire theological program. It is maintained that only in this way can Torrance ground his theological program in any way that can be considered scientifically true. When Torrance points to his verification in Christ as the place objectively given, Klinefelter pays no heed but implicitly finds this to be arbitrary. Torrance's emphasis upon the givenness of the proper object for scientific thought and his refusal to use what would be, upon Torrance's own principles, a false *a priori* method severed from the actual Truth of God in Christ causes Klinefelter to write him off for his "Barthian fideism."

Torrance and Klinefelter are therefore fundamentally at odds as to the nature of scientific rationality, and not simply with regard to the nature of science after Einstein. But this is particularly true of the nature of God as transcendent beyond the world, and as interactively related to and self-revealed in the world. Thus Klinefelter finds Torrance's lack of scientism, his interactive levels of rationality and truth, his epistemology and method out of the appropriate object, that is, God's Lordly interactive relatedness with, to, in and for the world and objective self-revelation as irreducible to only space-time connections, to be too irrational, arbitrary and dualistic. Again, Torrance would find Klinefelter to be far too Newtonian and positivistic, obsolete and dualistic in his thinking, lacking in capacity to think kinetically. Torrance has no intention of being a mere "fideist," but wants to respond in knowledge to knowledge—*fides quaerens intellectum*. Klinefelter, for all of his interesting dialogue with Torrance, has finally missed much of Torrance's actual movement of thought.

Yet it is also the contention here that Klinefelter has found a real difficulty in Torrance's thinking. It is a difficulty though which is not to be understood exactly as Klinefelter has expressed it. There is an apparent problem of dualism. While asserted because of some of his misunderstandings and his empiricistic reasoning, Klinefelter has rightly mentioned a difficulty in Torrance's thought connected with his use of Kierkegaard. While I would agree with Torrance that Kierkegaard has been horribly misunderstood as a mere subjectivist and irrationalist (cf. the whole point of *Philosophical Fragments* on external Truth outside the human being who is in untruth, in contrast to the Socratic understanding), there is a problem with regard to Torrance's understanding of the nature of "encounter," and thereby in his understanding of the nature of history in relation to the encountering Word and the existing individual, which reflects a breach or gap that dualistically belies Torrance's strong desire for theological duality, interaction and unitariness in the knowledge of God in Jesus Christ. There is a lack in his understanding of space-time that necessitates Torrance's falling back upon something akin to the dialectical concept of revelation of the early Barth and Emil Brunner and the notion of the "Word-event" or "encounter" in the apparently timeless "moment."

Critical Response to Ronald Thiemann

Ronald Thiemann's anti-foundationalist wrestling with Torrance's thought regarding revelation mishandles Torrance's argument at the very critical points and junctures necessary to really ground his criticisms. While being selective here, we must begin our response by focusing attention on Thiemann's misrepresentation of Torrance's understanding of theology's difference as a science from other disciplines, especially regarding its proper mode of rationality or way of knowing its proper object. He finds in Torrance an absolute contrast between faith and reason and a Kierkegaardian reveling in revelation's non-rationality, thereby separating theology's way of knowing *a priori*, as utterly unique, from all other ways of knowing in the world. But for Torrance true faith in relation to the givenness of God in Christ is a real knowing in relation, and that far from being irrational or non-rational, this faith-knowing is a mode of knowing dictated by the inherent intelligibility of the object itself. God is indeed not understood to be some mere determined object, but the One who gives himself to be known in a relation which God has founded and does found by his own redemptive movement in and for the world he has created and providentially, personally sustains. Torrance does not argue that objective knowledge of God is in principle different, but that like all sciences theological science has a method grounded *a posteriori* in the command of the proper Object. This is true of all sciences, but *a fortiori* this is said to be most certainly true with God who is Lord, Creator and who speaks to us, and at the same time questions the "examiner" (epistemological inversion) "down to the roots of his being."

Indeed, the Truth of God, which is God himself, is interpreted as being independent of the process of knowing, for Torrance. But Torrance does maintain the necessity of subject-object reciprocity in theology as well. Torrance's actual understanding of scientific reciprocity is actually different from both Thiemann's own and from Thiemann's understanding of Torrance's viewpoint. For Torrance the subject-object relation never allows the subject to project into the object. The knowing subject never "adds" to the object, but only receives and assents and faith-fully responds to it in revisable expression. Therefore in reciprocity the human knower and human knowledge must be brought into ever greater conformity to the object which imposes its rationality upon the knower. Contrary to Thiemann, there is no difference among the sciences to be found in Torrance's thinking on the question in that sense. Before God as well there is to be true reciprocity whereby knowledge of God and theological expression arising from such knowing do not modify the "Truth" of God. Rather Torrance asserts that in reciprocity the consequent human theological expression of the Truth/Word of God must point appropriately to, serve and be transparent to the Truth of God as he is in himself ("disclosure model").

Though his statements lack clarity, Thiemann seems to claim that Torrance believes that revelation takes the form of "propositions" (theological expression) which are incorrigible. But this is most strange, for Torrance understands God's revelation to be God himself in his own objective self-giving and not propositions about God which are held to be detached from God. The revelation is said to be conceptual, yes, but not linguistic or in the form of propositions. Faithful theological statements engendered in human thought are said to result from the impress of revelation, but these statements are not revelation themselves. And theological expressions are hardly held to be incorrigible for Torrance. Rather they are seen to be highly revisable as theologians penetrate ever more deeply into the "Christological pattern of Truth" and its implications in submission to the Word. Further, theological statements can be in a real sense true, but not in themselves. They are said to be true only by openness "up," whereby they referentially point to (as signitive) the "level above." Thus as grounded in the Truth itself as it is within the ontological Trinity.

At the heart of much of Thiemann's criticism of Torrance is his understanding of Torrance's appeal to "intuition" as the basis for the rest of his theo-logical thinking. In calling intuition revelation and revelation intuition, with the implications he then seeks to charge Torrance with, Thiemann badly misses Torrance's entire discussion where he explains that the "intuition" (in "direct," "immediate" knowing) is simply the term he uses to refer to the collocation of faculties which together lead one into direct apprehension of the

Reality of God as graciously given through the Scriptures by the Spirit. Intuition is not revelation for Torrance. Intuition rather is immanent in the knower, and as such is egocentric, or specifically God-directed by the Spirit in Christ. In fact "intuition" to Torrance (following Einstein and Polanyi) is simply the epistemological process in scientific cognition enabling one to "explain," in a sense, how their knowledge is determined by their proper objects.

Therefore regarding Torrance's "inconsistent triad," Thiemann's first point is correct. Theology is understood to be a "rational, scientific discipline," according to Torrance. The second point is correct if one takes Torrance's and not Thiemann's own understanding of reciprocity in the context of scientific objectivity. Therefore, as it hinges on the nature Torrance's understanding of reciprocity, it is actually Thiemann who "equivocates" in misunderstanding or simply not accepting Torrance's meaning of reciprocity as related to that self-revealing Object. This problem is evident throughout Thiemann's discussion. Like Klinefelter, Thiemann also wants to understand Torrance from out of his own definitions and then to point up Torrance's inconsistencies.

Much of the difficulty Thiemann has with Torrance stems from his inability to grasp Torrance's understanding and expression of God's interactive, interrelational engagement with the world as Creator-Redeemer. As a result, he can only see revelation in essentially "all-or-nothing" categories. This problem is coupled with Thiemann's formulation of the "reasonable" and/or "unique" tension which arises from his own inability to see what Torrance finds to be central to the movement of God reflected in the *homoousion* doctrine regarding the oneness of the Persons and the relations in the divine economy. Therefore Thiemann sees the individual as "bifurcated" in the knowing of God by missing the nature of the relation God is said to have founded. Though transcendent, God, by the movement of grace in Christ, is not meant to be outside the conceptual, nor by the Spirit does Torrance intend to negate the humanity of the knower, but wants to restore our humanness which is what it is meant to be only in proper relation to God. As a Reformed theologian, Torrance would also find Thiemann too concerned to defend humanity's goodness and the importance of its subjectivity when it is in fact humanity that is in "untruth." Above all, he would find Thiemann too "Kantian," wanting to "dualistically" split noumenal from phenomenal.

Yet there is to be found in Thiemann a number of commendable insights, especially where he points out Torrance's view of direct encounter or experience of the Word which calls for the person to be "lifted up." The nature of that Word-encounter draws much from Kierkegaard, the early Barth and apparently Emil Brunner, and seems to negate the historicity of the Word while necessitating that the person be "removed" in some sense from the historical in the "moment." What occurs through Scripture "immediately" seems to become disconnected from any real space-time incarnation. Thiemann sees that

Torrance's Word is transcendentalized. It is also of importance that Thiemann argues that the category of "narrated promise" offers a way to reconceptualize the Christian doctrine of revelation in order to display the intelligibility and truth of Christian claims concerning God's actual relation to and priority to the human theological framework. The doctrine of revelation is said to be properly conceived not as an epistemological theory but rather as an account justifying a set of Christian convictions concerning God's gracious identity and reality, "a reasoned theological account of Christian faith and hope."[58] This is an affirmation, though, not of knowledge but that the God identified in and through the biblical narrative is a God Christians can be said to "know" in justifiable affirmations. But would such a "recall" by Thiemann to the text of Scripture and to textuality in fact deepen or complete Torrance's chosen theological task?

Recapitulation of Critical Responses to Torrance's Theology

In analyzing several prominent critics of Torrance's theology we have found much misunderstanding. Yet while differences, problems and misunderstandings were found to be plentiful, there was also found within each one (sometimes almost inadvertently) a criticism which seemed to "hit the mark" and which will prove crucial in light of Torrance's own purposes, his own perceived scientific theological task, his own understanding of a unitary theology, his own striving against theological dualism, and his own efforts to properly reestablish the objective, realist, redemptive knowledge of God in the space-time world out of Jesus Christ as grounded in and from the ontological Trinity. With and beyond Carl Henry it has been asserted that Torrance's form of Christocentricity does less than justice to the Old Covenant God-world relation, and yet he continues to speak vaguely and in sweeping terms of God's confrontation with Old Testament Israel in contrast to and in preparation for his Christological pattern of Truth. Also we have claimed that Torrance brings about a conceptual reduction of revelation by finally maintaining a more dialectical than dialogical view of revelation in a way which ultimately necessitates a Christ or Word mysticism. The use he makes of certain crucial aspects of Kierkegaard's and Barth's thought seems to lay him open, or at least make him vulnerable, finally, to the charge of the very "dualism" he works so diligently to overcome. Torrance's maintenance of God's utter difference, the *Logos'* radical difference from the historical human *logos*, despite a strongly espoused creation-redemption interrelation, means that either Jesus, as truly human, has been lost in an Arian way or set docetically beyond the reach of human existence. This forces the postulation of a non-historical vector in the form of Kierkegaard's notion of "contemporaneity." Torrance has seemingly created not only a problem connected to the Word's historicity and its relation to real human history, but a negation of the creatureliness of humanity wherein the "lifting up" of the human being by the Spirit to the divine in knowledge actualizes a noetic adoptionism.   In that "moment," the non-historical "lightning" of the Christ/Word encounter moves through the temporal without actual "coordinates" in the space-time of human existence.

Ray S. Anderson's responses to Torrance were found to be very near the mark.   Anderson has made concise reference to what could be thought of as a "gap" in the Torrancian "field" of "God-man-world" relations, despite his desire for a unitary theology.   In light of Torrance's theological purpose to reform thinking in relation to God's objectivity in Jesus Christ and realist knowledge of God by historical, existing persons, he seems to lack a concrete, historical pole for God's transcendent and redemptive relatedness whereby such knowledge and thinking could take place.   Torrance seems to suffer from what has been termed a Barthian "transcendentalism," finally removing God's Truth from the present, historical situation into non-objectivity (cf. below).   God's "Being in his Act and Act in his Being," while helpful, may well be less than fully adequate as a model of what Torrance wants to reflect.   Torrance's theological purposes may require a "third" element in clearer fulfillment of Torrance's own Reformed and Trinitarian theological bases.

Richard Muller correctly draws attention to the often forgotten or covered roots of Torrance's Barthian thought in nineteenth century theology.   Torrance is a participator, though often, like Barth, from a position of contention.   There may also be more neo-Kantian thinking in Torrance than he has recognized or admitted.   Torrance also makes much more conscious use of Kierkegaard than did the "later" (post-Anselm) Barth and gives much energy to defending Kierkegaard's theological objectivity and realism for his own purposes.   This reflects the fact then that Torrance's objectivity and realism and understanding of divine revelation are largely Kierkegaardian as well as Barthian.   Also, Muller's questioning of the adequacy of the Barthian balancing of the "Being of God in his Act and the Act of God in his Being" and "the identity of God with his self-revelation," each having much conceptual effect on Torrance theologically, epistemologically and methodologically, may preliminarily help point toward a greater adequacy whereby Torrance might more consistently do theologically that which he intends.

Despite his empathetic attempt to grasp Torrance out of Torrance, it was observed how Thomas Langford fell short at some crucial points.   Yet we also found that he did, along secondary lines of argument, make several significant and proper, if indirect, criticisms of Torrance.   In setting forth Torrance's view of objective self-revelation in the encounter or Word-event, whereby Jesus or the Word is said to come and present himself in the power of the Spirit in the "moment," Langford points out that in this way the person is "lifted up" into and to the "original" historical experience of revelation in the Word.   From this he also rightly alludes to connection through Barth to Kierkegaard, though not noticing the full linkage, and particularly to "contemporaneity" in *Philosophical Fragments*. One is said to be encountered in this way by Jesus in the present and simultaneously brought back through Scripture to the original place of revelation, the Christ center (or level), and from there finally to the highest level in the triune God. Here the prophetic-apostolic witness of Scripture to the Christ-event Torrance describes as apparently necessary for this process and also in terms reminiscent of the hypostatic union. But then Torrance actually detaches the creaturely realm and historical Scripture from the disclosive movement of God, and finally disposes of it as the human mind rises, via encounter in an almost neo-Platonic way, "up" level by level to the immanent relations in God above the creaturely. What of Scripture? Or more, what of the real, historical incarnation of the Word? These issues must be thought out in light of Torrance's expressed claims and purposes.

Donald Klinefelter seemed to be at cross purposes with Torrance more than any other critic examined here. Indeed, his misunderstandings were many. But Klinefelter's criticisms had some merit (though often for the wrong reasons) when seen and applied from within Torrance's own theo-logical purposes, that is, Torrance's own dualism connected with his strategic and formative use of the thought of Kierkegaard. Kierkegaard is no irrationalist or subjectivist. Yet his objectivity in relation to Jesus Christ, to the nature of history, to the human being in history, and the relation of history or the space-time continuum to the Word, all uncover an apparent "gulf" contrary to Torrance's own concerned drive for duality, unitariness, God-world interactive relatedness and realist human knowledge of God. Torrance's understanding of God's relation to the contingent world is lacking any real and historically present "field" of connection or relation, and this forces him to fall back upon a more dialectical view of revelation in the Word-event and a Christ-mysticism rooted in the timeless Kierkegaardian "moment."

Finally Ronald Thiemann is also much at odds with Torrance's "foundationalism," as it is vitally connected to "revelation," and to Torrance's own view of revelation as Thiemann seeks to lay a non-foundationalist basis for revelation. Thiemann properly describes and pinpoints Torrance's understanding of God's revelation in relation to the individual in the Christ/Word event. He recognizes Torrance's understanding of the revelatory "process" as one which seems to require the negation of creatureliness and removal from the historical. Further, Thiemann's emphasis upon the centrality of the text of Scripture, or particularly the biblical narrative may have merit for correcting Torrance and for establishing more firmly that historical pole of God's transcendence. This is so needed in light of Torrance's own theological purposes in relation to human existence, wherein one is now called as an existing human being in untruth to hear the Word of God and thereby to "know the one true God and Jesus Christ whom he has sent which is life eternal."

NOTES

1. Torrance, *RET*, p. 138. Cf. *TS*, ix.

2. E. L. Mascall, *Theology and the Gospel of Christ: An Essay in Reorientation* (London: SPCK), p. 46.

3. Robert J. Palma, "Thomas Torrance's Reformed Theology," *Reformed Review*, vol. 38, no. 1 (1984), 23-29.

4. Ibid., p. 24.

5. Ibid., pp. 24-25.

6. Ibid., pp. 26-29.

7. Ibid., p. 30. Cf. pp. 29-31.

8. Douglas A. Trook, "The Unified Christocentric Field: Toward a Time-Eternity Relativity Model for Theology in the An-/Enhypostatic Theology of Thomas F. Torrance" (Ph.D. Thesis, Drew University, 1985).

9. W. James Neidhardt, "Key Themes in Thomas F. Torrance's Integration of Judeo-Christian Theology and Natural Science," Introduction to Thomas F. Torrance, *The Christian Frame of Mind*, 2nd Ed. (Colorado Springs: Helmers and Howard, 1989), p. xvi.

10. Ibid., pp. xv-xx.

11. Ibid., p. xx.

12. Ibid., pp. xx-xxii. Here he finds that Torrance has been able to extend E. L. Mascall's seminal insight: ". . . There is a very close connection *de jure* between the Christian belief in a God who is both rational and free and the empirical method of modern science. A world which is created by the Christian God will be both contingent and orderly. It will embody regularities and patterns, since its Maker is rational, but the particular regularities and patterns which it will embody cannot be predicted *a priori*, since He is free; they can only be discovered by examination. The world, as Christian theism conceives it, is thus an ideal field for the application of the scientific method, with its twin techniques of observation and experiment." *Christianity and Natural Science*, (New York: The Ronald Press, 1956), p. 94.

13. Ibid., pp. xxii-xxv.

14. Ibid., pp. xxv-xxvi.

15. Ibid., pp. xxvi-xxxi.

16. Ibid., pp. xxxi-xxxiii.

17. Ibid., pp. xxxiii-xxxviii. cf. Torrance, *DCO*, pp. 32-34.

18. Carl F. H. Henry, *God, Revelation, and Authority*, vol. III, (Waco, Texas: Word Publishing Company, 1980), pp. 214-215, hereafter cited as *GRA*. Cf. Torrance, *TS*, pp. 153, 154, 205.

19. Ibid., p. 218.

20. Ibid.

21. Ibid., p. 219.

22. Torrance, *TS*, p. 154.

23. Henry, *GRA*, p. 221.

24. Ibid.

25. Ibid., p. 222.

26. Ibid.

27. Ibid., p. 224.

28. Thomas F. Torrance, Personal Correspondence, February 22, 1990.

29. Ray S. Anderson, *Historical Transcendence and the Reality of God: A Christological Critique* (Grand Rapids: Wm. B. Eerdmans Publishing Company, 1975), p. 213. Note on p. 212-213 on definition of propositional revelation: "In its highest sense, propositional revelation simply means that the Scripture constitutes the Word of God in its power to communicate as well as command the truth of God to man." The concern is that Torrance has lost the real historical presence God's transcendence (historical pole).

30. Ibid., pp. 213-214. Note Torrance, *TRst*, p. 138, where Torrance states that "As such the Holy Scripture, like the Apostolate, stands with sinners and among sinners, and belongs to the sphere where salvation is bestowed. That gives us the peculiar problem of Holy Scripture and its peculiar place. Holy Scripture is assumed by Christ to be his instrument in conveying revelation and reconciliation, and yet Holy Scripture belongs to the sphere where redemption is necessary. The Bible stands above the Church, speaking to the Church the very Word of God, but the Bible also belongs to history which comes

under the judgement and the redemption of the Cross. That double place of Holy Scripture must always be fully acknowledged, else we confound the word of man with the Word of God, and substitute the Apostles in the place of Christ."

31. Ibid., p. 214.

32. Ibid. Cf. Ibid., pp. 218-221.

33. Richard A. Muller, "Karl Barth and the Path of Theology into the Twentieth Century: Historical Observation," *Westminster Theological Journal*, 88 (1989), pp. 38-39.

34. Ibid., pp. 40-41.

35. Ibid., p. 47.

36. Thomas A. Langford, "T.F. Torrance's Theological Science: A Reaction," *Scottish Journal of Theology*, 25 (1973), pp. 155-156, 170.

37. Ibid., p. 162.

38. Ibid., p. 163.

39. Ibid., p. 165. Cf. Langford's illustration of the monk.

40. Ibid., p. 165-166.

41. Ibid., p. 167.

42. Donald S. Klinefelter, "God and Rationality: A Critique of the Theology of Thomas F. Torrance," *The Journal of Religion*, 53 (1973), 119-121.

43. Ibid., pp. 123-124.

44. Ibid., p. 125.

45. Ibid., pp. 127-128.

46. Ibid., pp. 129-130.

47. Ibid., p. 131.

48. Ibid., p. 134.

49. Ronald F. Thiemann, *Revelation and Theology: The Gospel as Narrated Promise* (Notre Dame: Notre Dame University Press, 1985), pp. 16-17. Cf. Thiemann's doctoral dissertation related to this issue, "A Conflict of Perspectives: The Debate Between Karl Barth and Werner Elert" (doctoral dissertation, Yale University, 1976).

50. Ibid., pp. 32-33.

51. Ibid., p. 34.

52. Ibid., p. 38.

53. Ibid.

54. Ibid., p. 40. In a crucial explanatory footnote on p. 165 Thiemann says, "The key aspects of a foundational epistemology are as follows: 1) a set of non-inferential self-evident beliefs which serve as the given or foundation of all knowledge, 2) a distinction between foundational beliefs and other inferential propositions, 3) a claim that foundational beliefs are justified immediately by a form of direct experience, 4) an appeal to the mental act of intuition, and 5) an assertion of correspondence between the self-evident beliefs and the language independent world."

55. Ibid., p. 41.

56. Ibid., p. 42.

57. Ibid., pp. 42-43.

58. Ibid., p. 7. Cf. pp. 154ff. I have had my thinking perfected on the shortcomings of both Donald Klinefelter and Ronald Thiemann in their criticisms of Torrance's understanding of revelation and the knowledge of God by Kurt A. Richardson, "Trinitarian Reality: The Interrelation of the Uncreated and Created Being in the Thought of Thomas Forsyth Torrance" (unpublished doctoral dissertation: University of Basel, 1991).

Chapter 7

Critical Analysis Of Thomas Torrance's Theo-logical Understanding Of The Realist Knowledge Of God In The World

> If I understand what I am trying to do in the *Church Dogmatics*, it is to listen to what Scripture is saying and tell you what I hear.
>
> —Karl Barth

Introduction

By way of preliminary critique and correction of the Christocentric-Trinitarian theo-logical realism of Thomas Forsyth Torrance, we pointed out in chapter six a number of concerns which, if true, pose real problems for his scientific theological purposes. We have found that Torrance's position does not do justice to the covenantal God-world-human relation. His formulation of the Christological pattern of Truth also appears to then produce a conceptual reduction of revelation which ends in the very existential, dialectical understanding of revelation, which is opposed to the dialogical view of revelation which he surely intends. In fact, it has been said that Torrance finally falls prey to a form of the very dualism, disjunction of real, historical God-human relation in Jesus Christ, which he is endeavoring to overcome and to theo-logically correct. This remnant of dualism has been linked to inherited aspects of the thought of Soren Kierkegaard and Karl Barth, and hence the apparent historical inadequacy of Kierkegaard's "contemporaneity" and Barth's

"Being of God in his Act and Act of God in his Being." This remnant dualism was said to potentially negate the humanity of the existing person in the knowing relation to God on the one hand and to endanger the real, historical incarnation of the Word on the other. The dualistic "gulf" which appears to remain and hence to undermine Torrance's purpose of correction and positive and unitary theo-logical expression ("disclosure model") was found to need a concrete, historical pole for God's transcendent and redemptive relatedness whereby realist knowledge and faith-ful, responsive thinking can take place in the service of the Church. Torrance's Barthian "transcendentalism" seems to remove God's Truth from the present historical situation toward non-objectivity. A firmly grounded historical pole for God's transcendent self-disclosure as truly reflective of God's economy and triune being is necessary to reflect Torrance's own intention more adequately. To bring this to more complete expression, step by step, will be the goal of this chapter.

This chapter will move from more specific, concrete criticisms to theo-logical correction. In order to develop the positive, corrective intention of this essay, we will first examine the apparent problems to be found in Torrance's "depth" hermeneutics and what seems to be his similarities to Neo-platonism. This will be followed by two important sections analyzing the thought of Soren Kierkegaard and Karl Barth at points which are vitally and, in fact, problematically influential upon Torrance's scientific theo-logical realism. Critique having thus been accomplished, the last sections of this chapter will focus on possible correction within the bounds of Torrance's own theo-logical intention in Jesus Christ and by the Holy Spirit. To this end we will examine the example of John Calvin, whose more textual and Christocentric way of approaching the theological task could be model of correction for the very points where Torrance appears to be lacking. We will subsequently set forth, in contrast to the Barthian two-fold "Being of God in his Act and Act of God in his Being," a three-fold "Hebraic" model which will reflect both Torrance's emphasis on theo-logical objectivity in history and his concern for real "God-man-world" interactive relatedness in a more complete way. This will lead finally to closing suggestions related in part to the thought of Hans Frei.

The Problem of Torrance's Realist, Theo-logical "Depth" Hermeneutic

This issue is indicative of central problems which Torrance faces if he is to adequately and consistently complete his realist theological purposes by theo-logical thinking out of Jesus Christ, the Word of God. Here we point out problems in Torrance's "theological" interpretation from the "Christological pattern" which has fostered distortion of the thought of various sources to the end that that horizon in interpretation is partially lost or obscured in the re-shaping dominance of Torrance's own purposive theo-logical horizon.

Torrance's "Depth" Interpretation of Scripture

Despite Torrance's occasional reference or claim to the place of the "apostolic" or "prophetic" witness to Christ as the creaturely place or the "inspired" human words through which Christ encounters the individual, one finds, contrary to Calvin and even Barth, almost no actual engagement with the text of Scripture. Rather he inevitably speaks through and beyond it (or "above" it) and beyond all such phenomenological references and processes to the Word as it is to be found transcendently in the depths of such human, historical witness. In contrast to other sciences, theology is said to have in the Holy Scriptures a normative human response to the revelation of God. The Holy Spirit works through these scriptures dynamically and continuously as God ever reveals himself anew through that witness of scripture. Torrance says that in this way God objectively impresses his Truth upon the theologian in the Church, particularly in a normative and causal instance engendering intuition.

Torrance's understanding of scripture and its role in the economic process of God's redemptive self-objectification reflects the crucial points of discussion and direct influence of Kierkegaard, the early Barth, Scottish realism, the epistemology of Polanyi and, to a lesser extent, the thought of Einstein. Scripture is seen as something of a conduit, creaturely medium, to convey the unique, conceptual self-revelation of God in Christ for the meeting of God with the existing person in the "moment." Scripture is the historical, contingent, human means whereby real knowledge of God the Word can and does move across the difference between God, or the Truth of Supreme Being and creature. And in the Word-event in the moment the Spirit effects intuitive, cognitive reception of the Word. For this particular end careful exegesis of the scriptures is of no real use. The theologian, Torrance says, must begin with the incarnation-resurrection framework in coming to scripture, and from that framework move back through the scriptural witness to the deeper, transcendent self-revelation of God which is not to be founded upon the "phenomenal surface" of the text. Reflecting Barth's "Forward" in the second edition of the *Epistle to the Romans* and Polanyi's "levels," he asserts that one must consider the "depth" of the apostolic tradition. One must allow the text of scripture to bear referential witness to the transcendent Word and so to allow the impress of the appropriate frame of understanding of the Word upon thinking in the integration of levels in bearing upon God's self-disclosure in Christ. Through the apostolic witness the Truth of God in Christ and by the Spirit is understood to be a dynamic movement of the Word which ever comes to meet persons. It is there, in that moment of encounter, that God is "heard" in "audits" or "auditory concepts," or simply with non-linguistic cognitive content.

But as has been mentioned, Torrance's "reading" of the deeper self-revelation of God in Jesus through or past the phenomenal surface of the text of the human witness seems to perpetually distort the phenomenal surface like the depth breaking through in van Gogh's "Starry Night." The surface is finally broken and almost lost in the theologian's rise beyond the historical text out of the encounter. Hence, the real text is the Jesus/Word met in the "moment," and then the concepts are "expressed" under the creative impact or impressment of the Object upon thinking. This of itself is not necessarily a problem were it not for the fact that it reflects the kind of problematic "disjunction" or "dualism" which Torrance has defined and which must be overleaped in the Word-encounter and contemporaneity with the original revelation in Jesus. Where is the unitariness of the God-world relation, historicity and of the revelation of God in Jesus Christ by the Spirit? Here Torrance has shortchanged the crucial pneumatological aspect of revelation in this "Being-Act and Act-Being" formulation. This seems to leave the Word "above" human existence and necessitates alteration of the human in order to effect the conceptual grasping of the Word.[1]

Torrance's "Depth" Interpretation of Athanasius

As Torrance analyzes and exposes the "faithful" thought of St. Athanasius out of Christ, St. Athanasius is regarded as the one (thus he is Torrance's supreme patristic "paradigm") who above all others submitted to the Word and restored theology and epistemology to proper scientific realism. Yet questions persist. Why is Athanasius made to sound so Barthian? How is it that Torrance sees transparently below the phenomena of the texts of Athanasius' writings a realism and unitariness when others have pointed out that Athanasius was much influenced by Platonic "dualism" resulting in what R. P. C. Hanson has called Athanasius's "space-suit Christology"? As with Torrance's theo-logical use of scripture, both in principle and far more so in actual practice, Torrance's depth understanding of the movement of truth below the surface here in Athanasius seems to be a process of imposition.[2]

Torrance's "Depth" Interpretation of Augustine

If Athanasius is perceived by Torrance as the early Church's pre-eminent champion of scientific, theological realism (with the Nicene Fathers), St. Augustine is oftentimes (though not without some appreciation by Torrance) interpreted to be the most influential and problematic theological "dualist" of the early Church and the theologian through whom (with St. Thomas) dualism became re-entrenched a second time in the Church's thinking and theologizing (thereby necessitating the restorative realism and objectivity of the Reformers). There can be little question of neo-Platonism in Augustine's thought. Yet as Augustine's thought matured as a result of the doctrinal factors and implications of *creatio ex nihilo* and incarnation-redemption and much more, there was a marked lessening of Platonism in his later writings. In fact, Augustine is considered by some to be often the more "unitary" thinker and Athanasius the more dualistic. The real difference seems to be that Athanasius' process or mode of thought out of Christ is more conducive to Torrance's understanding of what theo-logical thinking out of the Word must be as scientific. Though he is a fine patristic scholar in his own right, Torrance's "misrepresentations" of historico-theological and content is thought by some to be quite prevalent. According to Richard Muller such misrepresentation arises from the false connections Torrance makes.

> . . . (Torrance links) Augustinianism and Aristotelianism and then identifies this conjoint "Augustinian and Aristotelian metaphysics" (!) with a problematic dualism in the Christian tradition . . . an "Augustinian-Thomist tradition" which, because of its "idealism," somehow lessened the impact of the Christian doctrine of creation *ex nihilo* . . . . (yet) What is clear from the history of medieval theology and philosophy is that these traditions are distinct and merge only with difficulty. Moreover, it is the Augustinian view, not the Aristotelian, that is idealist or realist, and it is the Aristotelian view, as adopted by Thomas Aquinas, that elaborated at great length on the contingent or non-necessary character of the created order and that argued against any dualistic separation of form and matter.[3]

But here too Torrance has a formative "Christological pattern" to follow and theological paradigms to set against one another in a developing historical dialectic which culminates in the resolution found in Karl Barth (which he is seeking to bring to greater development and completion). From upon these bases interpretation follows. Methodological similarities to Reinhold Niebuhr could be raised at this point.

Torrance's "Depth" Interpretation of John Calvin

With Athanasius and Karl Barth, John Calvin is a first-order theological mentor for Torrance and as such he is used as Torrance's second paradigmatic historico-theological figure who endeavors to restore the Church back to the objective, realist knowledge of God out of the Truth of God in the Gospel of Jesus Christ. While Calvin's "Act of God in his Being" is also said to fall somewhat short of the needed, final, unitary Barthian balance, Calvin is said to have done much to restore the Church again to its realism and objectivity in Jesus Christ. Torrance sees (as he does in Athanasius and the Nicene Fathers) much non-dualist thought in Calvin as the Reformer is found to be *the* historical and theological precedent to modern non-dualistic, Einsteinian thought. This is said to be so simply because he did not hold to views later superseded by Einstein. But this does not establish the larger developmental point which Torrance is trying to make. Calvin also made much constructive use of neo-Platonism via Augustine (however strategic it may have been) and held to such proper scientific concepts as contingency and non-necessary existence and the unity of form and being as a part of what was for him the current Aristotelian world-view (despite his antipathy to excessive Aristotelianism in theology) which he did hold to.

> . . . Torrance consistently chooses the platonizing side of the tradition—Athanasius and Anselm, for example—as his allies. Yet it is precisely this side of the tradition which most frequently embodies the dualistic separation of form and being which Torrance sees as problematic.[4]

Calvin too is rendered or squeezed by Torrance into a "Barthian-Torrancian" mold. Indeed Calvin's theological method seems to show him to be one who usually thought out from what Torrance would term the Christological pattern of God's objective self-disclosure and the realist knowledge of God in Jesus Christ. But too often Calvin becomes merely a Reformation mouthpiece of Torrance's own restorative theological program.

Torrance's "Depth" Interpretation of Soren Kierkegaard

Soren Kierkegaard is often referred to and used by Torrance directly and indirectly. Clearly his work has a powerful, conceptual authority and effect on the thought of Torrance. This being so, and given Torrance's emphases on objectivity and realism, it is most important that Torrance defend Kierkegaard against charges of subjectivism, irrationalism and dualism. It is again the contention here that Torrance is largely correct about the prevalent misunderstanding of Kierkegaard as a mere subjectivist and irrational existentialist. The *Philosophical Fragments* in particular seem to direct one against such a conclusion, especially as coupled with Kierkegaard's use of irony, literary device, and passionate commitment. Yet beyond this there seems to be in Kierkegaard's influential understanding of God's self-disclosure, the event of Christ or Word, a difficulty reflected in his notion of contemporaneity (cf. below) which is carried over into Torrance's thought.

Torrance's "Depth" Interpretation of Karl Barth

In consciously moving beyond and bringing development to Karl Barth's thought, Torrance remains deeply indebted to the thought of this his theological father. While somewhat critical in places of Barth's conclusions, Torrance almost always seeks to soften any differences and to point finally to incipient forms of his own developments as though already to be found in Barth. Beyond all that has been referred to previously about Torrance's theological rootage in Barth's thought, it seems clear that Torrance's development of a proper "natural theology" out of Barth's theology is indeed a remarkable feat. It is as though Barth's *Nein!* to Emil Brunner and his antagonism to natural theology and to the *analogia entis* were actually only antagonism to a "form" or "type" of natural theology which was thought to form some theological *a priori* or *praeambula fidei*, and thereby establish philosophically the knowledge of God apart from the actual, self-giving of God in Jesus Christ. Therefore Barth's "Nein" was not a "No!" to a "natural theology" properly derived from theological reflection upon the actual "God-man-world and/or God-world-man" relations. Barth is said to have realized that the world as creation of God and the place of the incarnation of the Word must inevitably enter into the coefficients of theological statements and concepts—*a posteriori*. Barth's negation was then a negation only of a false natural theology arising conceptually from dualistic bases, which then problematically channeled naturalistic thinking into the Church and theology. Now it is true that Barth's wrestling with natural theology in the *Church Dogmatics* is not wholly negative. While he defines it as the theology which comes to us by nature expressing our "self-preservation and self-affirmation" against God and his grace, yet in his doctrines of creation and reconciliation the earlier rigid negativity is gone. Indeed he claims that the "lights" of creation are significant. Barth never doubted that God reveals himself in nature, though he did deny that this revelation is "natural."[5] Thus there may well be something in this claim in the potential sense in Barth, but one is hard pressed to find this as directly or as emphatically as it is given in Torrance's interpretation and formulation. This is a conclusion which Torrance almost concedes on rare occasions. But there is also coupled with this Torrance's further contention that in Barth's theology (as in St. Athanasius) one finds epistemological and methodological insights (that is, out of Barth's theological objectivity) which preceded the parallel forms in physics by several years. Barth's faithful "thinking after" the way of the Word in the world is said to have preceded that methodological breakthrough in objective thinking in modern physical sciences with their own proper objects. While others have noted such parallels between Barth and, say, modern physics, Torrance's exuberance seems to push the thought in the texts of Barth's writings (as with scripture, Athanasius, Augustine, Calvin, Kierkegaard) into the understood "Christological pattern" in a distorting way. Also, it is clear that the Barthian motif of greatest interest to Torrance, and the one to which all other emphases give way, is theological objectivity out of God's own objective self-revelation in Jesus Christ. But while this is central in Barth's theology, Torrance's

"Barth" seems often too businesslike and lacks much of the dynamism and sense of confrontation characteristic of Barth's transitional and even mature theological thinking. Torrance's hermeneutics seem to require all of this in order to unify all aspects of theology in relation to the pre-framework of Incarnation-Resurrection and the in-breaking of the Word of the transcendent Trinity.

Torrance's Use of Albert Einstein and Michael Polanyi

For Torrance's theo-logical purposes the thought of these two natural scientists (physicist and chemist), which for each developed into philosophical, epistemological and cosmological reflection later in life, is "baptized" for Torrance's own theological purposes. Einstein's and Polanyi's scientific realism and developed "unitary" thinking is much used, and with great effect, by Torrance, but in ways that are somewhat distorting (especially Polanyi) and somewhat forgetful, picking and choosing those elements most useful. But Torrance has a tendency to not only pick and choose, and then interpret in accord with his own purposes, but to avoid all mention of consequential aspects of the thought of these two scientist-philosophers (and all who have been mentioned above) which deviates from his own direction. An interesting exception is Einstein's favorable reference to the "God of Spinoza," which by means of some interesting and nearly plausible discussion, Torrance explains away.[6]

The point here has been that Torrance's own strong sense and mission of theological objectivity and realism according to the given "Christological pattern," as he understands such, and his own underlying Kierkegaardian "dualism" seem to force distortion in the outworking of his hermeneutical processes. The thought of all of these is thereby forced into what inevitably ends in very "Torrancian" sounding conclusions.

Torrance and the Question of (Neo-) Platonism

There are issues and aspects in Torrance's scientific theo-logical methodology and his positive theo-logical expression which strongly suggest at least parallels to Platonism and Neo-Platonism. Specifically there is possibly a significant parallel to be found in Torrance's use of "levels" of truth and scientific thinking "up" from "level to level" from Jesus, the incarnation of the Word, then re-tracing the way of the redemptive-disclosive economy of God through Christ and in the Spirit to the Father, and thereby to final "participation" within the eternal perichoretic relations and the eternal communion of knowing and loving within the triune God ontologically. At least in expression the similarities to Plato and to Plotinus are suggestive.

At the end of Book V and at the end of Book VI in *The Republic*, Plato unfolds his definition of the philosopher, the "two worlds," and the four stages of cognition. The passion of the genuine philosopher is to "see the truth" or to know the Forms (e.g., Beauty) as it is in itself. Plato's own realist emphasis is on "knowledge" of the unchanging, of essence.[7] From the contrast of sensible appearances with the eternal and unchanging Forms, and the genuine philosopher as the one whose concern is for knowledge of that real world (V. 474-480), the latter discussion of Book VI then describes the process of taking thought across the division of the "two worlds" and ultimately beyond to the vision of the Good. For Plato, the Good and knowledge of it is expressed in objective terms. Like Torrance's movement of objective knowing or thinking "level to level" up to the next level where thought at the lower level is made complete, Plato's stages or modes of cognition become ever clearer, ever more complete and certain than what was known at the lower stages. From the lower stage of knowing, *dianoia*, then *noesis* or *episteme* is understood as immediate knowing, or, in Torrance's terms, direct apprehension of the Truth.[8] This is all too similar to Torrance's advocation of the movement of scientific thought he has learned variously from Einstein, Polanyi and Barth.

Plotinus speaks in the *Enneads* of progressing, or the need to retrogress, from the multiple to restoration back "up" through intuition (*theoria*) and contemplation, to the divine source of all being. Thus one ought to reach the One by thought (cf. the superiority of *nous* to *psyche*). Thus in contemplating the absolute, thought moves beyond being (cf. Plato, VI, 509) and beyond even the Idea of Plato by diligent intellectual labor and by means of those intermediate stages (*doxa, gnosis*). In thus becoming as "alone" as the One in "knowledge," as reascended to the original source, there is experience of "ecstasy" or "flight of the alone with the alone."[9] And here too the emphasis on the movement of thought "up" is interestingly parallel to Torrance's call to vigorous knowing as "thinking after" and "up" from "level to level" to the "ground and grammar" of all theology in the living God, whom to know is to know not as beyond Oneness but in God's own triune relations. But again the divine "movement" sounds all too similar to Platonic emanations.

It is also important to note that Torrance's Barthian emphasis on the concept of revelation as that which has God not only as subject but as exclusive content has nineteenth century roots related to this question of neo-Platonism and Idealism. This concept of revelation as only God's self-revelation has a long history going back beyond Plotinus, but is not employed in the history of Christian theology until close relations to German Idealism arose. In Hegel and Schelling one finds the thought of the self-revelation of God in the sense of the strict identity of subject and content. Hereby God is revealed to human consciousness as it shares in the unique revelation of God as himself to himself. Again, this sounds all too familiar.

The crucial issue for Torrance though is not in thinking which reflects some platonic undergirding, but whether that dualist undergirding, if there, is overcome. Is Torrance fully able to think out the real historicity of the incarnation, the *ho logos sarx egeneto*, in a way in which divine Word truly partakes of the human nature, history, existence, life, speech, etc.? Or is Torrance's concern for the divine difference from the human, from the creaturely, finally to endanger his own theo-logical intentions and purposes? As we will show below the answer is yes, i.e., Torrance does have a problem at the heart of his theology and it stems largely from aspects of his theological thinking rooted in the thought of Soren Kierkegaard and Karl Barth.

The Roots of Torrance's Problem:
Analyses of Soren Kierkegaard and Karl Barth
on Divine Revelation and History

While other issues could be pinpointed regarding the bases of the apparent disjunction in that necessary jump across the gulf lying between the divine and the human (e.g., Scotian emphases on the divine *voluntas*,[10] or aspects and relations of his Scottish realism and foundationalism), Torrance's firm and conscious rootage in the thought of Soren Kierkegaard and Karl Barth, especially at the point of encounter, objectivity, realist knowledge, the relation of God to human existence in history, and the seriousness of such, call for examination.

Christ, Revelation and History in Soren Kierkegaard:
On Christ the Absolute Paradox

In seeking to understand Soren Kierkegaard's understanding about the person, work and implications of Jesus Christ, one must try to keep in mind both his method of expression and theologico-philosophical purpose. With purposeful irony, Kierkegaard presents the *Philosophical Fragments* as a "thought project of Johannes Climacus." Thulstrup calls it a "classical drama in five acts" regarding "what the highest truth is and how it can be apprehended by the individual."[11] Kierkegaard is not willing to follow the preoccupation with understanding, spreading and extending the Hegelian System, but sets forth a little "experiment." Kierkegaard asks how it can be that a human being is related to the highest truth. Does one possess it in himself or not? Can the truth be learned? In other words, much like Torrance, he is asking what is the relationship between philosophical Idealism and Christianity? Thus the formulation of the *Fragments* must be understood as first experimental, yet not without a responsible understanding of the doctrinal. Evans explains that:

> In the book, Climacus attempts to clarify what is distinctive about
> Christianity by pretending to "invent" it . . . . In attempting to isolate what
> is distinctive about Christianity, Climacus first characterizes pagan thought
> under the Platonic-Socratic principle of immanence: Essentially, the truth is
> within man already.[12]

Kierkegaard's "experiment," set against this "immanence," is undertaken to see
if there is an alternative way for conceiving Christianity. If there is an
alternative to the Socratic, then the result would be the importance of "the
moment." The alternative to idealism requires the re-creation of the person by
the "teacher" whose role is absolutely crucial. The teacher, as "outside" the
individual, brings both the truth and the condition for knowing which is not
already possessed.

    As the Church has proclaimed that Christianity was true by divine
authority, it has affirmed that "Jesus is Lord." Climacus is not claiming that
these were right in their assertion of Christological supremacy, but he is
attempting to clarify what Christianity is by exploring the meaning of its central
concepts. These mark out Christianity's difference from pagan thought.
Kierkegaard's Christology and his presentation of Christ for dialogical and
dialectical purposes as set before the existing individual are crucial. It was in
Christ and in the biblical account of the incarnation that he found the means to
express the difference, the difficulty and the historical decisiveness of the gospel
message. It is simply that in Jesus Christ God became human and that this is
the Absolute Paradox. It is an event of impossible proportions, the Eternal in
history. The unthinkable has happened. The uniqueness of Christianity is
balanced upon that most singular event which was neither anticipated nor
grasped by human understanding after its occurrence. It is the *mysterion* that
shatters. It is the Absolute Paradox. Kierkegaard's Christology is profoundly
and dogmatically set, then, in existential contrast to the Hegelian-Idealist
"System" in order to set forth a philosophical reflection on the nature of truth
in relation to God and history by means of Jesus Christ, the Historical
instantiation of the Eternal.

    Kierkegaard argues that, "The god, however, cannot be envisioned, and
that was the very reason he was in the form of a servant. Yet the servant form
was no deception, for if it were, then the moment would not be the moment but
an accidentality . . . (it) infinitely vanishes as an occasion."[13] For the learner
to form any conception of the god then it must be received from the god
himself. This is what Kierkegaard calls the divine "incognito" which the
individual cannot penetrate "without receiving the condition from the
teacher."[14] So while having concern for the tangible, the outward physical
reality of Jesus, he says that "to see this external form was something appalling:
to associate with him as one of us and at every moment when faith was not
present to see only the servant form,"[15] is said to be central to the problem of

the paradox. Christ, though, is no longer present physically. Yet the so-called immediate contemporary who saw Christ in only his physicality had no advantage. Indeed, the opposite may be true. True "contemporaneity," not in the immediate sense but in the non-immediate sense of faith, is that which discerns, affirms and responds to the teacher.[16]

Thus, empirical perception or historical evidence is not enough for belief. The empirical and historical cannot be that which mediates the transcendent. In ways very similar to Torrance, Kierkegaard evidently believed (in a problematic way as we will show) in the relation or "presence" of the transcendent in and to history. Yet history is simply the real occasion for the encountering of the transcendent. Contrary to his Hegelian contemporaries and their form of historical concern, Kierkegaard maintained that the transcendent can never become or be made merely an issue of objective historical facts.

While Kierkegaard seems to argue at times for a radical historical skepticism on par with David Strauss, and later Bultmann, he is actually reflecting a presupposition that he simply brings to history as history. He wants to clarify the actual place of history in relation to Christian faith and experience. His project, intending to deal with problems of thinking about God and God's relation to history, was done as a committed Christian, one who must "believe" in relation to historical events. If a specific "moment" in history is of vital significance for the acquisition of truth and the change of the existing individual to truth, then "the moment" or "Absolute Fact" at the heart of Christology and faith is necessarily distinct from relative facts of history. The "Absolute Fact" is absolute because it is historical yet equally contemporaneous to every point in time (simply because it is the eternal). Yet not all are equally near the "Absolute Fact" in faith. For Kierkegaard, faith and the historical are correlative concepts in relation to the Eternal. The fact is the "moment," the "revelation." It is the Eternal coming into time. It is Kierkegaard's formulation of this real incarnational coming and becomingness of God into time that is so critical to the adequacy of his Christology.

Kierkegaard's radical dialectic of history produces a dialectical confession about Jesus which is in basic continuity with the historic faith, while being interestingly "unorthodox" in expression. He asserts the historical existence of Jesus of Nazareth. On this level there were historical details about his physical frame and life that others could point out.[17] Beyond these there are the unique gospel assertions about Jesus which Kierkegaard acknowledges as historical but which have significance for his larger conception of who Jesus Christ is. In the *Postscript*, he refers affirmatively to the Lukan account of the virgin birth and early life of Jesus. But the incarnation, the god being born in time, is a fact barred from objective historical certainty. For human understanding it is a contradiction.

Alastair Mackinnon has made a good case regarding Kierkegaard's meaning here. He says that by asserting that the incarnation is a paradox Kierkegaard does not mean that it is a logical contradiction. Kierkegaard clearly denies this conclusion.[18] Rather the point concerns the relation between God and Man, God in time, and the incarnate God as a paradox, whereby the rationality of relation to God is something given by God to the historical relation. Kierkegaard's expression of faith in Jesus of Nazareth (the purely historical) as the God in time (the Absolutely Paradoxical/the moment) is not the outcome of an abstract logical process. It cannot be dealt with objectively as merely a time and space, world-historical thing.[19] Kierkegaard finds the illusion of ordinary objectivity in the Christian faith inappropriate, vain and fruitless in relation to "who" Jesus Christ is as the foundation for the faith response that lies in dynamic continuity with it, that is, the "therefore." Kierkegaard asks two important questions in *Training in Christianity* which relate to this issue: "Can one learn from history (profane history in distinction from sacred history) anything about Christ?" and "Can one prove from history that Christ was God?"[20] What is so offensive to Kierkegaard is that attempts to make the offense inoffensive actually effect a negation of the truth for faith.

Kierkegaard concludes that both the Hegelian speculative unity of God and humanity in Christ and the Enlightenment valuation of the moral teachings of Jesus are pagan, and the docetic tendencies of the theologically orthodox to dissolve and lose the reality of Christ's historical in-fleshing are both perilous. The divine essence of Christ is not to be nor can it be identified and objectified into some article for human scrutiny.

Kierkegaard's acceptance of the Chalcedonian tto nature doctrine of Christ is markedly non-Chalcedonian in expression and reflects the existential dynamic of Luther's Christology, despite Kierkegaard's well known critique of Luther.[21] The central issue of Christ, though, is not to be found in a theological confession or statement but for faith. The truth of the deity and humanity of Christ is pre-eminently a question and a reality for the living, personal realism of an existing person as a subject before God who is Subject. Contrary to the Hegelian speculative Christ and the Schleiermacherian Christ of profound God-consciousness, Kierkegaard's Christ as the divine incognito is reminiscent not only of Luther but of Pascal's belief that God is more hidden in the Incarnation than in creation.[22] "Look, there he stands—the god. Where? There. Can you not see him . . . he is the god . . . . Thus does the god stand upon the earth, like unto the lowliest through his omnipotent love."[23] By the will of God, the outcome is a double expression of the divinity of the divine. Deity is hidden in the truly human, thereby manifesting the nature of the god, the kind of God he is. God comes for sinful human beings.[24]

Such otherness in relation between God and existing persons negates direct expression within the human and the historical. Rather, as the god infleshed, Christ's tangential relation to the historical human continuum is real. He is no mere cosmic phantasm. But his real-ness was a veiling of the divine so that the only approach to the Christ, the only appropriate way of knowing, is by the affirmation of faith. Kierkegaard's Christ, then, is no mere protest against theological immanentism; it is also "confession" of the historic Christian faith which sets forth the requirements of the New Testament upon one who would be a disciple. Kierkegaard understands Christ as the paradoxical place where one is summoned to obedience to follow the god in time. Faithfulness is the consequent of Kierkegaard's all-encompassing, Christocentric response to the objective, soteriological work of the Saviour.[25] The "Who?" and "What?" of Christ, was, inevitably a "therefore!", that is, the faith response to the person of Christ. While maintaining something of a Kantian epistemology, Kierkegaard yet affirmed the Christological content of the historical Christian faith. The link with Kantian limitations to knowledge led him to portray Christ as an occurrence of the Eternal in history in such a way that real historicity becomes problematic. In the terms of later "Dialectical Theology," the Incarnation becomes "supra-historical." Yet in this lies Kierkegaard's point. It is the Paradox. Kierkegaard's Christological "content" is consciously non-contentful, a non-systematic expression of the living foundation with which, to which, from which and by which he calls "Christendom" back to the god in time.

Kierkegaard's Christology then cannot be understood apart from its radical consequence, faith. In the "moment," in the transhistorical-historical encounter between individual and Absolute Paradox via the incarnation event, Kierkegaard believes that one can find eternal happiness. Contingent human existence is altered in, before and by the Incarnate One. But again Kierkegaard's and thereby Barth's and Torrance's historical problem emerges. Can the non-immediate Incarnation, so crucial to the historical faith and faith consequence, be truly historical? And has the historical Jesus been lost to the "moment"?

The Christ Consequence. On the Christ-consequence one must say introductorily that Kierkegaard's theological and devotional writings do present a marked divine-human polarity, the otherness of Eternal God over against the temporality of humanity and its thought. Yet Kierkegaard's opposition to the immanental synthesis of the divine and the human that led him to the "diastic" portrayal of the God-man relation[26] is not without some real synthesis, interrelation or interaction of its own. The question of its effectiveness though is important. Kierkegaard concludes, "To believe is to believe in the divine and the human together in Christ, but in such a way as to markedly distinguish such from the Hegelian synthesis."[27] Sponheim asserts that for Kierkegaard

> There is a fundamental incommensurability between this God and this man. So it is that Kierkegaard speaks of the intrinsic incognito of the God-man, for a human being revealing God can never become an instance of direct communication. Indeed one may well wonder if one deals here with communication . . . . (for) The co-presence of this divine and this human does constitute a paradox of the most fundamental order . . . the God and

man who meet (in the Christ) are so understood that it is hard to see how one can speak intelligibly of the meeting.[28]

Sponheim's point about Kierkegaard's Christology and its unresolved tensions is accurate, yet Kierkegaard may well agree with this and point it out as central to his prophetic purpose of drawing attention to the true nature of the Christian faith. Yet by so doing the crucial historicity of the incarnation and the faith itself may be jeopardized in the process. "He, who was the truth, and the way and the life, he, who needed to learn nothing, he yet learned one thing: he learned obedience. In so close a relation does obedience stand to the eternal truth, that he, who is truth, learns obedience."[29] For Kierkegaard the historicity of the Absolute Paradox seems to be Yes and No. Can this be meaningfully maintained by Kierkegaard, and for Barth and especially Torrance who follow him?

Indirectly the *Fragments* and more directly *Training* take up the Christological consequence at the heart of Kierkegaard's thought. Indeed, this is the thesis of *Training*, focusing on the historical humility of Christ, his willing lowliness, the divine participation in human creatureliness. By focusing on the humanity of Christ as also exemplar of the Ideal, Kierkegaard seems to occasionally fall into seemingly Nestorian exclamations. But such is not his concern. Christ's lowly humanity sets before the disciple the suffering involved in witnessing to the truth. The imitation of Christ is a primary outcome to both Kierkegaard's Christology and his call to that consequential, decisive faith in the Absolute Paradox. Lowrie finds that for Kierkegaard the narrowing of the disciple's focus to the humanity of Christ comes by the individual's acknowledgement of the incarnational distinction in the person of the Christ.[30] "In Christianity, at all events, truth is not the goal but the way."[31]

In moving on to analyze Kierkegaard's understanding of the incarnate Christ and then his significant accounts and distinctions between Religiousness A and B, we must here distinguish between Kierkegaard's designations on the nature of "religiousness." Religiousness A is difficult to ascertain precisely, being almost amorphous in its nature. Kierkegaard saw that "Religiousness A can exist in paganism, and in Christianity it can be the religiousness of everyone who is not decisively Christian, whether he be baptized or not."[32] Such a one has fallen short of true Christianity. Further, Kierkegaard maintains that, "In Religiousness A an eternal happiness is something simple, and the pathetic becomes the dialectic factor in the dialectic of inward-appropriation."[33] "A" relates the eternal to time synthetically. "A" does not go far enough. History is finally lost or dissolved with the Eternal. This is religiousness as heartfelt expression of a generic sense of God, the numinous, or some expectation of eternal blessedness. All such lack historical decisiveness. This reflects the religiousness of most persons in the world. As Lowrie finds, "This is not to be taken as a disparagement of religion A, which in its loftiest exemplifications may well be regarded as man's tip-toe reach, the most exalted attainment of humanity."[34] Kierkegaard recognized that "A" must be present before there can be any question of one being brought face-to- face with the demands of religiousness B.

While Kierkegaard's stages or sphere's of existence overlap and interpenetrate (or better, reflect circles within circles), still there is a disparity that marks off the highest expression of the religious life, religiousness B, from other spheres of human existence. It denotes the misunderstood nature of faith-as-faith and its relation to history. For modern persons who perceive "faith" as easy, Kierkegaard felt compelled to reveal the difficulty to his contemporaries, as Bonhoeffer would do for the twentieth century. Kierkegaard's route proved to be, as is "faith" itself, an offense to many.

Again, the biblical account of the incarnation is central to Kierkegaard's understanding of faith (religiousness B). Kierkegaard interpreted the historical incarnation as the "Absolute Paradox," thereby establishing three critical points regarding faith and the faith: (1) the uniqueness of Christianity in the world, (2) the necessity of a "leap" of faith, and (3) the lack of either historical or rational advantage for faith.[35] Kierkegaard's Christology is ever at the heart of his understanding and critique of religiousness.[36]

The Absolute Paradox happened. The truly Christian reckoning of faith then hinges upon that shattering mystery of the Incarnation as "the paradox of paradoxes,"[37] making true faith inherently unique. Before the seemingly "absurd," authentic faith is manifested as the passionate self (subject-as-subject) decisively and existentially believes in the face of that Absolute Paradox. It is the "happy understanding of difference" before Jesus of Nazareth.[38]

The Absolute paradoxicality of the Incarnation whereby one bases eternal happiness on an historical event, an event not more than approximately certain, and an historical event that is contrary to its nature as historical, leads the subject to the epistemological boundary situation of human understanding. Kierkegaard, while not regarding the paradox as a logical contradiction, saw the paradox as a qualitative (not a logical) contradiction whereby two dissimilar realities are brought together to form a human perspective. The "leap" is not irrational nor is it subjectivism, but it is recognition or acceptance of the human rational end-line, the boundary of human finitude before the wholly other God who has come and become the servant in time. The incarnation is "precisely this limit to thought, the place where a man must recognize the complete inability of his thought to carry him further; it establishes then the point of decision."[39] Reason is not cast away in the faith relation to the paradox, but rather comes to fulfillment in the process of its own conclusive assent or self-submission to the objective reality of the god in time. Faith, then, is the happy passion whereby reason sets itself aside in relation to the objectively given paradox. One may then understand that the highest end is not understanding per se.[40] Understanding in itself cannot make one what one ought to be. It is the historical response to the Absolute Paradox which reveals the individual. Self is shown in the "moment" of Choice. Faith is the passion in which one's reason and the paradox come together happily in "the Moment."[41]

> How, then, does the learner come to an understanding with this paradox, for we do not say that he is supposed to understand the paradox but is only to understand that this is the paradox . . . . It occurs when the understanding and the paradox happily encounter each other in the moment when the understanding steps aside and the paradox gives itself . . . that happy passion to which we shall now give a name . . . . We shall call it faith. The passion, then, must be that above mentioned condition that the paradox provides.[42]

In this process, though, Kierkegaard seems to dissolve the real historicity of the Paradox into the "moment" of decision. The question as to whether the incarnation is actually the faith "moment" manifests itself here.

But is the existential decision, which arises from an unusual yet inherent "logic," itself the critical point? It seems that the choice to believe in relation to the Absolute Paradox is considered to be appropriate to the object, indeed necessary, as a subjectively rational and passionate commitment to the supra-rational reality of the self-given Incarnate One. It would appear true, then, that Kierkegaard's "faith" is neither irrationalism nor rationalism. Rather, by masterful irony, Kierkegaard wants to show the true way of real faith as grasping of the whole of living.[43] Jerry Gill, in commenting on de Silentio's discussion of faith in *Fear and Trembling*, says that

> . . . two equally absurd views of faith are contrasted, the rationalist being presented negatively and the irrationalist positively. The latter is a corrective, not in the sense of replacement, nor in the sense of striking a "happy medium," a compromise between reason and will. Rather it is a corrective in the sense that one sided views will dawn an awareness of the true character of faith as something to be lived, not defined or argued about.[44]

Still, Kierkegaard appears at times to make the incarnation into the very Socratic "vanishing point" he wishes to alleviate. Or has Kierkegaard in fact altered history to make "room" for the wholly other Eternal and its relation to time and the temporal call to discipleship?

Faith is a willing and obedient faithfulness arising dynamically from the "happy" encounter. But again, has the historical-transhistorical "moment" now become the central issue in Kierkegaard's prophetic Christianity where revelatory content forces the Choice and the Life before the existing individual? The literary form Kierkegaard uses embodies his message in example. His Christology is enunciated with such brevity, such indirectness, and with such enigmatic impact that his expressions about Christ are themselves in keeping with a marked avoidance of "content" as an end in itself. But if the historical content is but a place from which to leap, a means only, what can the historical Jesus mean subsequently?

Kierkegaard's understanding of the incommunicability of faith is also linked to his formulation of the incarnation. Such "happy under-standing" of difference before the Paradox will not manifest itself in Hegelian speculation. At the same time faith may not be able to manifest itself from the historical content (intellectual) of the faith alone.[45] Has Kierkegaard hereby met the Hegelian-immanentalist challenge with historical adequacy? Communication of "faith unto faith" here is at best a stammering approximation that can only point to and from the Absolute Paradox, the Incarnate One. One must ask about Kierkegaard's emphasis on the subjective "how" of faith. Has the historical incarnation become lost, superfluous or actually lifted from history because of the form or nature of his presentation of the Christ alternative for faith?

Paradox and Faith in History. Kierkegaard asks "Can the truth be learned?" In this way he initiates his discussion of the Socratic-Idealist perspective whereby the teacher is reduced to being only the "mid-wife" of knowledge in the process of eternal "recollection," or more broadly the immanental divine-human integration of being whereby the mind of man is the mind of God and the mind of God is the mind of man. Here the teacher gives nothing that the learner does not already have. The teacher becomes the historical vanishing point, the dissolving conduit of self-affirmation in and with the eternal. Therefore, the "Socratic" teacher is not critical in the final out-working of things. To this Kierkegaard wants to "dispassionately" bring that possible alternative.

> If the situation is to be different, then the moment in time must have such eecisive significance that for no moment will I be able to forget it . . . because the eternal, previously nonexistent, came into existence in that moment . . . if the moment is to acquire decisive significance, then the seeker up until that moment must not have possessed the truth . . . must not even be a seeker . . . . If the learner is to obtain the truth, the teacher must bring it to him, but not only that. Along with it, he must provide him with the condition for understanding it . . . (otherwise) he merely needs to recollect . . . the one who not only gives the truth but provides the condition is not a teacher . . . it must be done by the god himself . . . . The teacher, then, is the god himself, who, acting as the occasion, prompts the learner to be reminded that he is untruth and is that through his own fault.[46]

The teacher must also be understood yet more fully as "savior," a "deliverer," a "reconciler" and a "judge."[47] As the alternative to Idealism, the teacher who is the god and thus the "moment" (or "fullness of time") must then be decisive. "It must decide"[48] the person. The historical individual in untruth is brought into truth by the faith ("leap") response to the Eternal god in time, the paradox.[49]

Yet this relation between the historical Incarnation and the "proposition" of the Absolute Paradox as necessary to the subsequently existing individual has become a point of critical contention in studies on Kierkegaard. Michael Levine puts this question severally.

> Assuming that God is no longer in time how could one enter into a relationship with God at the present time? If God's presence was "required" at some time in the past why should that presence not be required now? . . . why would God have had to exist in time at all in order for man to enter into such a relationship with God? . . . whether God must be present and in what sense "present" if one is to receive the "condition" (i.e., the awareness of one's own state of sin) needed to appropriate the paradox.[50]

Is incarnation a necessity for Kierkegaard's consideration of the truth of subjectivity, or is the "proposition" itself all that is necessary? If the "condition" comes to a later individual in the same way that it came to the disciples who were "immediately contemporaneous" with the god in time, then, says Levine, "it follows that the actual presence of the God-Man would not be required for the dispensation of the 'condition,' but only to 'bring' it."[51] Must the incarnation be actualized or historical within Kierkegaard's scheme of subjectivity? If the "how" (response), the subjective passion for the Paradox, is itself the truth then in what way can the incarnation be critical to Kierkegaard's position?   Thus, Levine's question is whether or not Kierkegaard's concern for subjective appropriation has actually severed it from what he esteems to be the necessary historical basis, the incarnation.

> . . . Kierkegaard thinks that some connection exists between the objective truth of Christianity (i.e., the reality of the Incarnation as an historical event) and subjectivity in full measure. The latter, it seems, cannot be had without an awareness and acceptance of the former. One does not develop an infinite passion unless one has had the opportunity to become subjective through the "occasion for decision" (to use Bultmannian terminology), presented by an awareness of the paradox. But despite Kierkegaard's insistence on the necessity of the paradox and its importance it remains dispensable. His claim for the centrality of the paradox does not seem to me to be adequately reconcilable with his concept of faith or "truth" as subjectivity, or with his remarks about the subjective pagan.[52]

Levine's criticism regarding the relation between the historical paradox, the god in time, and the paradoxical proposition which confronts the existing individual in untruth touches upon the problem of history in Kierkegaard's, and hence Torrance's, presentation of faith. Levine concludes that unless Kierkegaard could in some way show why the actual, historical condition is necessary, only after which a person may be capable of entering into a God-relationship, then one may rightly question whether the historical incarnation is not a superfluous detail for Kierkegaard's argument after all.[53] Apart from some "ontological detail," which he believes would lack real logical weight, Levine finds that only "the proposition itself and not the truth of the proposition" is all that is required for Kierkegaard's formulation and subjectivity.[54]

In this, Levine is correct in finding fault with Kierkegaard's presentation of the historical incarnation. Kierkegaard has a problem potentially devastating to the whole notion of historicity, contemporaneity and the nature of history. Yet it may not be as Levine sees it in his critique. Levine's contention that Kierkegaard's claim of the "truth as subjectivity" has done away with any need for the "god in time" misses the nature of what Kierkegaard means by subjectivity and its relation to objective truth and by "faith" itself. Here Torrance's emphasis on and corrective of misinterpretations of Kierkegaard is relevant. The very "proposition" to which the individual responds is difficult to understand as actually "paradoxical" in Kierkegaard's sense unless the occurrence is not mere talk but has been "objectively" enacted in space and time. Paradoxicality and historicity are inextricably intertwined in Kierkegaard. How could the "unthinkable" be thought and expressed apart from the real coming and historical becoming of the Eternal whereby the instantiation of the god has enacted the Absolutely Paradoxical and given the condition? Could that which is historically untruth, strictly speaking, lead one from untruth to the truth in God—that is, is a God whose very "proposition" is apparently true, but which is at last factually untrue, be the God of truth who can lead the existing individual into the truth? But further, Levine gives more weight to Kierkegaard's assertion of the "truth as subjectivity" than does Kierkegaard. For Kierkegaard, subjectivity by its passion must and finally will be led into affirmation of that which is the objective truth strictly speaking.[55] The truth of subjectivity is grounded in the Object. Thus, Levine appears to misunderstand Kierkegaard's various usages of the term "truth" in *Postscript* on "Truth as Subjectivity." Kierkegaard is concerned with the historical actuality of the Incarnation. The "leap," the faith response or subjectivity is an infinite movement from the god in time to the God who has "comingly" manifested himself where we are. Apart from the historical incarnation, the existing individual is found then to be restoring itself by means of its own passionate subjectivity and the entire issue is thereby reduced again to "Socratic midwifery." Finally, Levine too casually dismisses the relation between the ontological and the historical in Kierkegaard's thought. For Kierkegaard, the historical incarnation founds the double reality of the change possible in the existing individual before the Absolute Paradox and the real change in history and its reckoning. True human change ("new creation") and true historical change ("contemporaneity") are found to be impossible apart from the real tangential relation and entrance of the Eternal in time. More subjectivity is simply not enough. Kierkegaard requires that change within the existing individual which the person of itself cannot bring to the self. As Tillich would later emphasize, there is something in being the Messiah, in being the one by whom human alienation is overcome, that requires an historical manifestation.[56]

Oscar Cullmann sees a different problem with regard to Kierkegaard's understanding of the relatedness of the individual to the incarnation. Cullmann finds in Kierkegaard's conception of "contemporaneity" what amounts to the abolition of the real time character of the New Testament salvation-redemption process. The biblical portrayal of one who has responded in faith to the *euangelion* is one who has responded to the historical Incarnate One. But the believer must live in the present with its particular relation to the whole of redemptive history. The believer does not live in the past with the apostles nor in the future.[57] Cullmann's point is most relevant to our larger discussion.

> To be sure, faith allows him to share at the present time in the saving gifts of the entire time line, even those in the future . . . . Thus the thing in question is not a sharing by the believer in the Lordship of God over time; it is not as though he were competent to leap over the periods of time. Even the believer remains in the present; this is shown by the fact that his participation in specific future gifts of grace is always provisional . . . but the Holy Spirit does permit the man to share in the gifts of the entire redemptive line.[58]

Christ, then, is not to be understood soteriologically as one apart from or in addition to but yet somehow related to real history by means of "contemporaneousness," but as the decisive "midpoint" of redemptive history. It is the biblical tension, not of this world and the Beyond or of "time versus eternity" as in Kierkegaard, but of present and future based on the victory of Christ in the real past. Compared to this

> . . . Kierkegaard, with his conception of "contemporaneity," mistakes the significance of the present for redemptive history. According to him faith transfers us back into the time of the Incarnation; it makes us contemporaries of the apostles. In this view it is correct that faith permits us to survey the entire redemptive line and to share in its fruits . . . but the concept of contemporaneity presupposes that basically time as redemptive time has already come to a standstill with Jesus Christ; hence we can only go back to him in order to enter the realm of salvation . . . when the first disciples uttered their original confession: "Christ reigns as Lord," this means rather that Christ the Crucified and Risen One comes to us. The redemption history continues; Christ sits at the right hand of God, now, today.[59]

Kierkegaard, says Cullmann, has rightly seen the Christ event as central to redemption, but Cullmann is correct in finding Kierkegaard to be misled with regard to the relation of God and history in Christ. Kierkegaard fails to recognize fully that the post-Easter present signifies a continuance in time of the redemptive process. Kierkegaard is grouped with those who speak of eternity invading time to communicate or reflect a kind of "oil and water" relationship. This way of conceptualizing God and time, which is so important to Kierkegaard in the *Fragments*, and those like Torrance and Barth (cf. below) who follow him, "implicitly destroys the redemption line, inasmuch as he really abstracts the present from it."[60]   Reality is portrayed to overlook "the fact that, according to the New Testament faith, Christ now rules invisibly over heaven and earth" so that while rightly centering on the incarnation, Kierkegaard is said vo wrongly see the need to overleap the centuries to the Christ event as "mid-point." Kierkegaard undervalues history and especially the present of the individual.[61]

In so criticizing Kierkegaard and those who follow from the standpoint of an inadequate viewpoint on the relationship of God to time, or *Heilsgeschichte*, Cullmann has exposed something significant in Kierkegaard's Christological position. The problem is historical and thus redemptive-historical, lying in the Kierkegaardian understanding of the nature of God and relation of God to history. The Eternal in time, the inexpressibility of faith, and the nature of true "contemporaneity" are the outcomes of such presuppositions. But has Cullmann accurately expressed the incarnation as it is developed in the *Fragments* and elsewhere? One may agree with Cullmann that Kierkegaard's salvation-history finally casts "mundane" history away. Central to this problem is Kierkegaard's emphatic and reactive declaration of the otherness of God and the utter qualitative distinction of God from time. But is the problem simply that by faith the believer is transferred back to the time of the apostles by faith as Cullmann says? Kierkegaard does lose sight of the place of all history, of the history of existing persons, which is so crucial to biblical understanding. But it is not so much by overleaping the centuries backward, for all that this would account for is a kind of historical or rather a trans-historical immediacy which is ruled out by Kierkegaard's negation of immediacy for anyone as a contemporary. The Kierkegaardian loss of real history arises not from some trans-historical retroactivity to a mid-point but from his paradoxical view of the incarnation whereby the action of the wholly other God is one of "comingness" from the redemptive-historical mid-point by which the centuries may be "overleaped" to encounter the believing person who then participates in redemptive time, God's time.

Kierkegaard sought to answer the question of the non-contradictory unity or unitariness of God's being and existence, a unity that impacts the lives of existing persons. That question requires the subsequent question "where?" What is the place of God's ontological being and historical existence in unity? Such a place would be the place of reconciliation. Kierkegaard deals with this by reference to one's "assenting to the god's having come into existence, whereby the god's eternal essence is inflected to the dialectical qualifications of "coming" and "existence."[62] Human thought, historical knowing, meets with its own boundary and collides with the incarnation. Thought meets the unthinkable, the Miracle, God's self-revelation in Jesus Christ, where thought's striving proves futile because of the factuality of God's self-giving there. The historical event which thought meets, the divine in existence, cannot be substantiated as an historical event. Not even its difference can be proven. Incarnation transcends reason because of the "absolute difference."[63] Only in the "diminutive moment" does the nature of such existence emerge by means of the "leap." Before the paradox, historical understanding as such is insufficient. What then can present one with eternal consciousness?

Kierkegaard's notion of "contemporaneity" reveals the nature of time for his understanding of history, God's relation to history and the way he reckons Christ and the religious life. The god in time cannot be revealed as such in time for this would require historical immediacy. Historical immediacy is negated by the nature of the Eternal and its difference to time and human sin. The Paradox repels such direct reasoning by transcending it. The moment "is actually the decision of eternity" arising from the "condition" the god provides. For Kierkegaard, this moment is simultaneously truly temporal and a point filled with the eternal. Actually there are two "levels" of reality co-existing side by side here. As merely historical the moment "in the more concrete sense is inconsequential." The moment then is the "point of departure for the eternal."[64] Yet the "moment" as historical is thereby lost in the Eternal because historical reasoning is transcended by means of the leap. The leap from the frontiers of historical thought in the face of the Paradox is a leap toward the god who *comes* to encounter the existing individual.

The god comes to and gives the condition in the moment. Apparent contradictoriness or paradox is not synthesized but transcended by and in the Eternal, much as quantum theory or incarnation is understood to be "resolved" at the next higher level in Torrance. The free "coming-ness" of the Eternal into existence as the Eternal makes possible the coming-ness of the Eternal to the believer in "genuine contemporaneity." This comingness of the god into existence occurs "in freedom," revealing himself as he wills, to which belief, as also free, corresponds.[65] The fact of the Eternal in time has freedom as its cause, but the result is change in history. The comingness of the god in time to the believer whereby contemporaneity is established is made possible because history is understood to have been changed or invaded by difference, and supra-history or faith-history, God's own time, has been superimposed in some relation to but "above" mere history. As the Eternal in time, the god can de-temporalize actual historical distinctions. As the Incarnation is then not directly or purely historical, neither is "the moment" nor the "faith" of the individual in relation to the Paradox in that mediating realm of encounter called "contemporaneity." History has been altered by the "addition" of a second "historical" (or trans-historical) continuum whereby paradoxical immediacy for faith is engendered by the indirect historicity of the Incarnation. By his view of incarnation, Kierkegaard has made history-qua-history of no final accounting and faith as that by which the individual encounters the god outside the direct historical realm. As a result, both the incarnation as paradox and faith as paradoxical are said to become incommunicable in history. This historical incommunicability is expressed conceptually in both the *Fragments* and the *Postscript*, but with dramatic effect in Abraham's faith in *Fear and Trembling*.[66]

It seems that Kierkegaard's use of Lessing's historical concerns and, to an extent, Immanual Kant's epistemological formulations in relation to historical questions has molded his answer to the issue of eternal consciousness for the existing individual. Kierkegaard's eagerness to overthrow Hegelian immanentism, with its equation of the mind of God with the mind of man and the mind of man with the mind of God in relation to Christianity and history, caused him to alter and bifurcate history by an emphatic divine transcendence. Further, his essentially "orthodox" Christology, the basis for his whole discussion of the life of faith, has been reactively formed and has altered the nature of the knowledge of God and of historical redemption in Christ. The knowledge of God as truly historical in the context of true historical, covenantal relatedness, "historical transcendence," would do much to shore up the line of thought from Kierkegaard to and through Karl Barth to Thomas Torrance.

Christ, Revelation and History in Karl Barth

Karl Barth's Conception of Revelation and Time. For Karl Barth as for Thomas Torrance, Jesus Christ is the objective reality and possibility of God's revelation to us, the Word of God. The fact or reality of the divine self-disclosure is necessarily first, for the concrete revelation of God in Jesus Christ whereby God is free for us must precede any question of the possibility as such. For Barth too, actuality establishes the possibility. This is linked to the order in the relation between revelation and history. The God who "has time for man" is the necessary *a priori* and therefore time and history must be assessed in the light of the *Deus praesens* in Jesus and not the other way around. This is in contrast to the understanding of the "liberal" tradition from which he came and in contrast to which he sought to form his theology. The outcome of this priority of the divine acting is that finite, fallen time is understood by its relation to the nature of the incarnational event. Jesus Christ is the present manifestation of the time of revelation, fulfilled time. This reckoning of world times to the Time, God's time, is to be seen redemptively as reflective of the love of God.

God's revelation in the event of the presence of Jesus Christ is God's time for us. It is fulfilled time in this event itself. But as the Old Testament time of expectation and as the New Testament time of recollection it is also the time of witness to this event.[67]

Later, Barth enlarges on his christocentric perspective on time and its meaning.

> Men live in the allotted span of his present, past and future life. He who was before him and will be after him, and who therefore fixes the boundaries of his being, in the eternal God, his Creator, and Covenant-partner. He is the hope in which man may live in his time.[68]

The revelation of God's self-giving is indeed an event. Yet there is the "assertion about a time proper to revelation," or the fact that "God has time for us." Like Kierkegaard, Barth reckons that this time is a distinct time which is real in God's revelation. This time as God's time is the only time God has for us. History and time, our fallen time, are not fully real and they are not revelation. Mankind has no other time, no other "real" time than the time of God's revelation.

This other time, reference to which is to be found even as early as *Römerbrief* and through the 1950's, reflects Barth's interaction with Overbeck,[69] and most importantly with Kierkegaard's thought. This real time (terms often used being *Urgeschichte* and *Ubergeschichte*) of God as fulfilled time is the "different" time, it is "new" and indeed a "third" time which has "its place because God reveals Himself, because He is free for us, because He is with us and amongst us, because in short, without ceasing to be what He is, He also becomes what we are."[70] Barth is insistent that this time, to be God's revelation, had to take place "in 'our' time."[71] But of itself this is not adequate and Barth is emphatic that God's revelation of himself cannot be esteemed as God's revelation unless we say "that this event has its own time."[72] It is "His own time for us" and as God's time it is real time. God's time for us is neither apart from His time nor is it our time or history. It is "eternal time." In an almost definitional statement, Barth says

> The time God has for us is constituted by His becoming present to us in Jesus Christ. If we say Jesus Christ, we also assert a human and therefore temporal presence. (It) is an eternal but not therefore a timeless reality. . . not a sort of ideal, yet in itself timeless content of all or some time. It does not remain transcendent over time, it does not merely meet it at a point, but it enters time; nay, it assumes time; nay, it creates time for itself.[73]

In this process of conceptual grappling, Barth has formulated an altered configuration of the time-eternity question since his earlier radical statements in *Römerbrief*. His Anselmic transition can be seen here. Yet problems seem to still be lingering in this new structuring of time and history. Revelation as revelation still has its own time which must remain distinct lest it be something else, merely historical. Barth's concern that his theology may partake of some anthropological grounding may well be at work in this.

His development of the "God's Time"/"our time" relationship only exacerbates the dilemma. While trying to set forth and clarify for understanding the revelation of God in Jesus Christ as factual and objective before humanity, which is said to live in fallen time, Barth continually falls back to his earlier emphases on the "otherness" or difference as such of God's revelation. The incarnation of the Word is that "real time" which "breaks in as the new time," as the "now and today of the Savior."[74]

> Here there is a genuine present . . . . The Word of God is. It is never not yet and no longer . . . . The Word spoken from eternity raises the time into which it is uttered . . . up into His own eternity as now His own time . . . . It (Word) is spoken by God, a perfect without peer (not in our time but in God's time, created by the Word in the flesh there is a genuine, proper, indissoluble, primal future).[75]

By attempting to cut through the gulf between God and man created by his earlier theology, Barth has constructed a situation between God and mankind that maintains the otherness of the divine, but which asserts the real coming-ness of God's presence in the sphere of human fallenness while yet remaining separate. Here Kierkegaard's notion of "contemporaneousness" again becomes significant for Barthian theo-logical formulation. God's self-revelation must

> . . . become our time, since He directs His Word to us; we are to become contemporary with this time of His. His genuine time takes the place of the problematic, improper time we know and have. It replaces it in that, amid the years and ages of this time of ours, the time of Jesus Christ takes the place of our time, coming to us . . . and to be seized and lived by us.[76]

In the event of Jesus Christ which is both the veiledness of God's revelation in Him and the "breaking through of this veil" by his self-unveiling, the veil that is torn is "our" time, general time. It is the triumph of God over our time by "his new time."[77] Human time and history is the barrier of the old age which shall pass away. Fallen time is "vanquished" and simultaneously indwelt "incarnationally," but not partaken of by God. The relationship between fallen time and revelatory time then is one of adversarial contradiction.[78] In Christ revelation becomes fulfilled history, and thereby that history becomes what it is and was not by the acting and present God. God comes to it as Lord, in third time.

Revelation, Time and Jesus. In speaking of God's coming in triumphant fulfilled time, we have usually spoken in general terms. Again, the place of divine manifestness, self-giving, in relation to "our" time is Jesus of Nazareth. It is a Christological-soteriological point for Barth, and central to his whole theological concern. Barth represents the presence of Jesus Christ as the presence of the "fulfilled time" and as the fulfillment of time in order to reflect something of the intentions of the Chalcedonian formula, while also responding to and expressing the faith-content in the face of current theological needs. If one esteems Christ's time as God's time and "the light of new time in the midst of old time" can one "see through and regard any part of this old time as new, fulfilled time"?[79] In light of Barth's "Word made flesh" emphasis as basic to his own reformulation of the whole theological task, his understanding of this relation between Jesus the Christ and the history of fallen humanity as such must be clarified.

Barth here takes up the notion of "offense." Along clearly Kierkegaardian lines of thought and expression Barth says that Jesus Christ as the revelation of the "God in time," the Other coming to us in "our" fallen time as being yet the Other, is "offensive." He is in a sense there before us in our time but again he is not. He is historical but of another "history." He is the incoming "over-history" in our history, set inimically against our fallen history and there he is the "unapparent and unknown" by whom the years 1-30 are simultaneously our fallen time and also the genuine time of God's Word. Of Jesus' offensive otherness Barth says,

> It is not a natural hiddenness but a hiddenness contrary to nature . . . . Amid this contradiction and resistance (of fallen man) arises the "form of a servant," i.e., the amazing existence of revelation before our eyes as though it were not revelation at all. This existence Israel prepared by crucifying their manifested Messiah. It was a drastic attempt to get clear of the offense of revelation, to make God's time the same as our time, to abolish and to level up that order of rank between these times which was becoming visible.[80]

The possibility of the actual manifestness of the divine Word in our time, by incoming, dominant distinction, is designated "miracle" by Barth. The two times cannot be assimilated one to the other or leveled off, but the "offense" of the revelatory presence of God in Jesus can and must be known in its very difference by "miracle." Fallen man desires to set aside the offense of revelation, desiring rather a Word that takes place in general, fallen time, to set the unknown Word made flesh before himself as though it was not hidden, unknown and different.[81] Fallen time is not itself the time and place of the redemptive acts of God. This is most emphatically true of the incarnate Christ's manifestation here, whose hiddenness or contrariness is a "necessary determination of revelation, and not a chance difficulty in understanding that might perhaps be got over."[82]   As a result, fallen persons in fallen time must think themselves away inasmuch as such a one is set over against God and is confronted by God in Jesus.   Apart from this self-negation the time reckoning of God's Word in Jesus is not possible for us.   In absence and loving difference he is present to "our" time in Jesus, in the miraculous event of the breaking in of new time into the heart of the old time by the one "special new direct act of God."[83]

How then can this miracle be actualized or completed in the redemptive coming of God's self-giving in Jesus if this difference is real difference?   For Barth, the difference as such is considered necessary, but it is the difference of God who is for us and wills us for himself.   Therefore the "miracle" of revelation is the "in spite of" or the "nevertheless."   Despite the difference, God's time is time for us whereby he must become "manifest in His redeeming action" in Jesus Christ as the object of faith.[84]

> . . . if revelation nevertheless takes place it can only take place in the form of a miracle. And if it is nevertheless to be an event, which a man confesses by saying "God reveals Himself," it can only be the confession of a miracle that has happened, but not the expression of an (historical) insight into the content, which he can also explain otherwise than by the special direct new act of God. Otherwise he again abolishes and levels up the order of rank, created by the divine act of lordship between God's time and our time.[85]

The impossible is possible for God.   Even the offense of the hiddenness and otherness of His revelation to man, "which impenetrably surrounds His revelation" in Jesus is no hindrance to the divine coming.   Fallen time and fallen man are not the criteria limiting the self-giving of God in Jesus.   Revelation actually occurs "in the freedom of God to be free for us and to free us from ourselves . . . to let His light shine in our darkness."[86]   By the coming of his Kingdom, the realm of fallenness must give way.

> Our time lies, so to speak, in the neighborhood, it stands under the sign and shadow of this quite different time. This time is God's time . . . our time is . . . overtopped and completely dominated by this, the fulfilled time. It is so overtopped . . . by it that in practice the remotest past and the remotest future times are in its neighborhood (contemporaneousness).[87]

The two times are found to meet in Jesus Christ, says Barth, in terms reminiscent of the *Römerbrief*, and ". . . in fulfilled time the earth is (made) one with the heavens which are arched over the whole earth."[88]   It is for this reason that "our" time must be taken from us.   Fallen time must be transposed, and fallen man must be transposed "away into that time . . . into the time of

Jesus Christ (contemporaneity)."[89]   Only in that time can Christ be
mediated.[90]

Again, if the mediation of God's coming and God's time for us in Jesus is
another and different time, how can this "miracle" of transportation be enacted
from the one domain of fallen time to fulfilled time? Barth does not assert this
miracle simply fideistically. Rather, this "crossing over" or trans-temporality
is said to occur in the "subjective reality of revelation." It is the work of the
Holy Spirit. By a "leap of thought," Barth points to the crucial pneumatological
enactment of "sign-giving by whose mediation revelation, or Jesus Christ,
reaches man . . . the way in which revelation comes to man (our trans-historical
encounter with Jesus)."[91]   By the Spirit revelation can take on an objective
revealedness, concealment and difference, and yet also become actual for the
person's subjective appropriation.[92] This too is revelation. God's revelation
in Jesus Christ as the fulfilled but other time reaches fallen time signitively
whereby ". . . objective revelation is repeated in such a way that it can come
to man in genuinely human form . . . (but) still remains a mystery."[93] By the
Holy Spirit the gift of faith is given whereby one may be presented with the
objective revelation of God in Jesus.

Critical Analysis of Barth's Understanding of Jesus Christ and History.
In responding to Barth's conceptualization of history in relation to the question
of God's objective self-disclosure to humanity by real instantiation of the divine
redemption and human knowledge of God, the influences on Barth's thought
must be clarified. Reference has been made to Overbeck. Attention here will
focus on what has been found to be Soren Kierkegaard's understanding of
history in relation to "the god in time," Jesus Christ, as we saw earlier in the
Philosophical Fragments. At this juncture in Barth's theology Kierkegaard's
influence is pre-eminent.

To move from the Idealist or Hegelian position epistemologically and
methodologically, Kierkegaard was found above to move from the crux question,
"Can the truth be learned?" to his Christological experiment that ensues if, in
fact, the truth can be learned.[94] If "the moment" is decisive, if the "teacher"
is no mere mid-wife in coming to the truth, then, in Kierkegaard's experiment,
"the one who not only gives the truth but provides the condition is not a teacher
. . . it must be done by the god himself."[95] For one to experience eternal
happiness one must be related to God. But as a person existing in time, this one
cannot enter relationship to God unless God has acted and entered time at some
point. Real relatedness of an existing individual to God comes, then, as one
affirms the statement of God's existence in time by a "leap of faith" and thereby
experiences "contemporaneousness" in an "encounter" with the trans-historical
truth of the Absolute Paradox in the Spirit. In this way, Kierkegaard is able to
assert that there was no historical and rational advantage (cf. Lessing's "ditch")
for one of Jesus Christ's own time regarding the question or need of faith.

Thus, for Kierkegaard, as for Barth, it is crucial that the revelation of God in Jesus was truly historical but also that this particular "historical" relation be unique. For both Kierkegaard and Barth the truly Christian reckoning of faith hinges upon that which was neither anticipated nor understood as such. Yet, faith in that one is the "happy understanding of difference." The absolute paradoxicality of the incarnation lies in its being an historical event which is contrary to the very nature of the historical. Thereby the individual is led to the epistemological boundary of human understanding.   As so rooted in Kierkegaard, there remains in Barth and then Torrance the distinction of two realities, inherently dissimilar, which must be overleaped by the final acceptance of the boundary, finitude before the real otherness of God who is still other even in "the god in time." In something of what Torrance himself would call a "Kantian" bifurcation, Kierkegaard has made the noumenal, historical "moment," "the god in time," non-historical.   As a result, Kierkegaard's "contemporaneity" and contentless "indirectness" in the "moment" bespeak a revelation that remains beyond human falleness.[96]   This problem largely remains in Barth and Torrance and in many of the variations in "Barthian" thought.

Though differing in his conceptual use of Kierkegaard at most points from his earlier, pre-Anselmian, work, Barth yet maintains something of a Kierkegaardian holdover at this point which threatens to undo some advances made by his study of Anselm. One finds in Barth's discussion of the incarnation and the self-revelation of God in Jesus Christ repeated references to "contemporaneity" and "indirectness" that are not mere linguistic links but real, substantial, conceptual links to Kierkegaard, and therefore with the "transcendentalizing" tendency in Kierkegaard's Christology. In one brief example, which also interestingly reflects something of Bultmann's existentialist thought, he says

> In revelation God stands in for us entirely. And so also the time He creates for Himself in revelation, the genuine present, past and future is presented to us entirely. It should, it can, it will become our time, since He directs His Word to us; we are to become contemporary with this time of His. His genuine time takes the place of the problematic, improper time we know and have. It replaces it in that, amid the years and ages of this time of ours, the time of Jesus Christ takes the place of our time coming to us as a glad message presented to us as a promise, and to be seized and lived in by us.[97]

The otherness of God, which must be set forth as present to us in Jesus Christ, remains outside "our" fallen times. This appears often to be an intrusion of an almost Platonic or neo-Platonic sense of difference regarding the relation of eternity to history. It finally excludes the necessary factuality of the *Deus praesens* and thereby distorts the existence of the existing believer in history.[98]

In a sense, Barth does within Christology, time and history (and therefore redemption) what he berates Calvin for doing in his formulation of election. Barth has not consistently followed the movement of the Word in forming his notion of history and the relation of God to space-time. As a result his conceptualization of distinction or two-ness (or realms of reality), which, though a problem in and of itself, is a clearer problem for Barth in the light of his own foundational understanding of revelation and Christology and for his entire redempto-theological purpose.

The outcome for Barth's Christology is a redemptive-historical problem lying in his understanding of the nature of God and the relation of God to humanity and the historical process. Like Kierkegaard, Barth sees God's relation and coming to time as one of Lordly difference. While in one sense wanting to express the non-contradictory unity of God's being and existence whereby we are actually confronted and grasped in existence here, Barth finally lets human, fallen history go as that which cannot be partaken of by the coming and self-giving of God. God's time for us is, like God's otherness, that of which the human as human cannot partake of. If God cannot, even as the Creator who comes in freedom to redeem, partake in human fallen time for our sake, how can one even by grace participate in God's time? Thus, in Barth's thought, Christ is understood to be the redeeming God for us, which means that he is claiming that the self-revelation of God for us has maintained a difference in this fulfilled time of Christ. The Word has remained aloof or is unable to partake so that then, by definition, even the Holy Spirit as the subjective possibility of revelation cannot overcome the diastasis. The Spirit as God must also be other and therefore unable to mediate the one who is himself meant to be the Mediator, Immanuel. Barth has re-formulated the situation of the liberal tradition by perceiving the historical setting as a separate domain from which and through which to ascertain the truth of God indirectly. There is then, as it turns out, a Jesus of (our) history and a Christ of faith (fulfilled time) discernable herein simply because of Barth's imposition of a bifurcated, transcendentalist notion of history in relation to God taken from Kierkegaard. Barth's understanding of the freedom of God cements that very distinction.[99] Barth's Christology, then, partakes to an extent of a "transcendentalism"[100] by which God in his freedom seems at last to move away from all real objectivity. Regarding Barth's own distinction of *Geschichte* and *Historie*, Richard R. Niebuhr has pointed out that for Barth revelation is meant to participate in those two kinds of history.

> In Barth's mind . . . these two orders of history require two modes of cognition. For profane history, ordinary experiential cognition suffices, but for God's immediate action, there is no human response that is adequate. Pure revelation demands a wholly passive attitude of man, for what happens

then and there . . . happens wholly and entirely externally to him, outside and apart from him. How then can revelation be known?[101]

Against his own theological desires, Barth has reduced the historical Jesus Christ to a theological form of Cartesian interactionism, and particularly in relation to Kierkegaard's "moment," a mathematical point, which as revelatory finally vanishes from our history. The Barthian desire to adequately reflect the factual instantiation of God's time for us in Jesus of Nazareth is finally beclouded in transcendental otherness and a "history" of its own that cannot be ours but only God's. The Christ, as the Word of God's self-giving for us, remains "transcendentalized."

It is this rootage in Soren Kierkegaard, and in Kierkegaard through Karl Barth's formulation and expression of this kind of God-world relatedness, which then creates in Thomas Torrance's own Barthian theo-logical formulation disjunctions or a "dualism" which threatens the onto-relational "field" of his own unitary theological purpose in Jesus Christ, the incarnate Word of God.

Resulting Inadequacy of Torrance's Barthian "Being-Act and Act-Being" Formulation of the Nature of Divine Revelation in History

Introduction

As observed in both Kierkegaard and Barth there occurs, at the critical point of actual historical relation by the self-disclosure of God in Christ in human existence, an implicit need in the "moment" to negate the human, historical actuality. There is a de-temporalization in the transcendentalized coming of the Word and in the encounter of the human in the Word-event in a Christ-mysticism. Barth clearly deepened and strengthened Kierkegaard's thought by clarifying true theo-logical/Trinitarian relations regarding the movement of God, and above all in the relation of the ontological Trinity to the economic Trinity, as well as in the relation of God to the world in his attempt to balance "God's Being in God's Act and his Act in his Being" in the real knowledge of God. Torrance has fully taken over this line of theological thinking as central to his own development of the Kierkegaardian-Barthian understanding of the objective reality of revelation to the end that in Christ and by the Spirit one may have realist knowledge of God. But Torrance has fallen into the same difficulty whereby in the "moment" the person is brought to mystical and non-discursive cognitive or conceptual "encounter" with the Word who "jumps" the gulf or difference, thereby negating all historical distinction in the "contemporaneity" achieved in the coming of the Word and "lifting" of the Spirit. Thereby the knowing subject's historical existence and very humanity is finally lost or reduced as one is lifted up to the Word transcendentally beyond the historical domain of the existing self. Torrance's theological purpose to establish "theo-logically" that Barthian synthesis of "God's Being in his Act and Act in his Being," while most helpful in affirming the oneness of God's redemptive self-revelation with his eternal Being (cf. the crucial *homoousion* doctrine), is not fully and economically adequate. It does not finally reflect the intended asymmetrical God-world relatedness he wants to portray, the openness of contingent creation to the Creator in real grace-established interactivity, or the real trinitarian nature of God's self-revelation to be known and his real, disclosive, economic presencing in the world as Father, Son and Holy Spirit.

The Question of Torrance's "Christ-mysticism" and "Mystical Theology"

What Thomas Torrance wants to accomplish in the service of the Church and above all in service to the revelation (Word) of God in Jesus Christ is an adequate "disclosure model" which reflects and serves that objective revelation of God. He wants to set forth with increasing scientific clarity the unitariness, the "field," of God's actual relations to and in the world, this being understood as an interrelational, asymmetrical "duality" which rejects all dualistic disjunctions between God, humanity and the world, as well as all monistic identity. He intends to overthrow the dualism and disjunctive thinking which he finds has again become entrenched as the modern mindset and which has forced modern theology into the isolationism of its existential, subjectivist experiences with a "Jesus" who timelessly meets one through the kerygma unto *Entscheidung* for personal authenticity. Thus, Torrance is endeavoring to negate, to correct, and then to express positive theo-logy in accordance with the objectively self-given Word of God whereby God is truly and redemptively known as he is in himself. In this way, proper theo-logical expression can again be that faith-ful and obedient "scientific" model by which God can impress ever more fully his redemptive Truth upon human thought, life and culture. Torrance does much to advance and develop the Kierkegaardian-Barthian line of theological thinking, yet he too stumbles again at basically the same point where Kierkegaard and Barth fell down, where all either holds together or falls apart according to Torrance's own principles. The link is to be found in the way, the place, the mode, and the nature of the Word of God in our history, in and as partaker of real human existence, in cognitive or conceptual and real historical relation to the existing individual there in community. There turn out to be two unreconciled sides to Torrance's thinking here. Torrance wants to serve the Word and to set forth the openness of God to the created world and the world to God, and the human subject in the world to the cognitive knowledge of God given objectively in space-time human existence. He wants to do this by faith-fully "thinking after" the economic "levels" of God's own condescending self-disclosure to humanity unto realist knowledge of God in himself as he is in the eternal, immanent relations within the ontological Trinity. Therein is the ground of all realist knowledge and rationality, and thus the "ground and grammar" of all theology. But in actual expression, formation and delineation of the historical disclosive situation in Jesus Christ and by the Spirit, Torrance's understanding of the Word as encountered also continues to maintain strong bases in Kierkegaardian-Barthian transcendentalism. At Torrance's critical theo-logical point where human knowing of God is meant to be actualized or instantiated in real historical relation, God seems to recede from the historical into non-objectivity for space-time human existence. Torrance's formulations and descriptions of that "moment" of encounter become descriptions of a Christ-mysticism very similar to descriptions of the existential Word-event as found in such prominent post-Bultmannian theologians as Gerhard Ebeling and Ernst Fuchs. The problem is that this kind of existential Word-event is a form of the very "dualistic" theology Torrance is trying to criticize, overthrow and correct. While desiring to follow the way actually taken by the Word in the unitary God-world-human, God-human-world relation in creation and above all and emphatically in incarnation, Torrance is left with a Word which, in the divine Act now ("moment"), remains beyond human reach. He needs and uses both Kierkegaard's and then Barth's non-historical notion of "contemporaneity" to bridge the chasm remaining between the divine and the human, God and history, and in order to provide the way of "mystical knowing" or "unknowing" in that moment for his "mystical theology." Anthony Thiselton has given much effective criticism of the modern theological-existential emphases on the "Word-Event" which are appropriate to this discussion. Thiselton has rightly pointed out that this approach comes too near to "word-magic," especially when the Word-event is spoken of as an event in which God himself is communicated. This "Word-magic" also inevitably devalues the "place of assertions" and the "complexity and variety of functions performed by statements" in the disclosure process.[102]

Torrance admits much difficulty on the issue of the actual knowing of God or the human, historical relation to God's self-disclosure. God is unapproachable and inaccessible in his divine, intelligible Light, in the sheer invisibility of his uncreated Light and Rationality as transcendent beyond creaturely, finite capacities. For this reason God is "in the dark for us" as the "thickness of that darkness is in proportion to the infinite excess of his Light over ours . . . by covering himself with Light as with a garment, God shrouds himself in a 'dark cloud' through which our minds cannot penetrate."[103] God is said to be unapproachable for human beings because of the inability of impure minds to bear the purity of divine Light. We would be overwhelmed by the utter holiness and absolute difference of God. While this is well and good and is meant to lead to the "gospel" assertion that God has adapted himself to humanity at the incarnation and reconciliation in establishing real historical relation, Torrance then simultaneously forces a divine retreat from the space-time domain of the dialogical and historical to the transcendental and dialectical in speaking of the tangential in-breaking of the Word-Act as timeless encounter-event in the present of the existing person which is somehow continuous with the original event of revelation, Jesus of Nazareth.   In that encounter ("contemporaneousness") there is said to occur union and communion with Jesus as one is "lifted up" by the Holy Spirit and enabled to see the invisible God and live.   Torrance does not hold this to be wordless, contentless or non-conceptual as is the case in much of the overtly neo-Platonic tradition, but, "with St. Anselm," he maintains that behind all of our understanding of created existence and divine revelation coming dynamically through the apostolic witness, that there is the ultimate, non-linguistic, non-discursive Speech or Word deep in the being of God known in the "conceptual" relation to the Christ in the "moment" by faith.   Torrance's Christ-mysticism in the "moment" of revelation is meant to be understood as, in some sense, "conceptual."[104]

Therefore, while on the one hand Torrance truly wants to follow faith-fully and think after the real interactive relation of God to, in and for the world as Lord, whereby God's revelation is said to become truly and actually historical, his Kierkegaardian-Barthian transcendentalism has forced a schism within his theological thinking so that a gulf is found finally to exist between divine and human at the point of space-time relation in the world.   This demands that existential Word-event (or "Christ-event") for theological "knowledge" and faith-ful response in the task of doing what he calls "mystical theology."   Thus we have seen Torrance speak of knowledge of God and scientific theology not only as "repentant" thinking, but as "unknowing" or "unlearning," as one is divested of all alien presuppositions under the objective impress of God upon thought, all of this occurring in the non-historical "moment" of encounter.   Only by such "mystical" theology, he says, can the "field" be cleared for appropriate modes of thought and relevant cognitive instruments, as grounded in the Word, can be formed to match the intrinsic intelligibilities of God's self-disclosure which are brought to increasing clarity.   In this way, the "science of God" is said to occur through a "reasoned movement of thought within the field of Christian experience and faith to penetrate into (the Object's own) intrinsic order and intelligibility."[105]   In this way, like St. Athanasius, Torrance wants to uncover and determine the ordering force and pattern of grace revealed in the Word made flesh, learning directly from the *Logos* of the inner Rationality of God's redeeming acts.   He says that like St. Anselm he is seeking to rise above all earthly authorities, biblical or ecclesiastical, and to know "intuitively" and "immediately" (or "directly") beyond the existing self the objective Truth itself, as given through the earthly forms and under the objective compulsion of the Truth and Rationality of God by the Spirit.   This is to faithfully and obediently know and declare the supreme Truth of God. Such intentions can, in the main, be commended.

In Kierkegaard, Torrance finds the needed objectivity and dynamic mode of thinking necessary to follow the object of theological knowledge out of the way actually taken. Like quantum logic, Torrance claims that Kierkegaard saw the need for a new "theologic" which would not fall prey to the static forms of formal deduction which are impotent in relation to real movement and transition. Torrance emphasizes that traditional logic cannot cope with the fact that the Truth has moved into time as a historical event. This is again to be truly appreciated and acknowledged as vitally important. But we have seen what Kierkegaard left unfinished and, finally, disjoined. This has not been overcome by either Barth or Torrance.[106] Yet it is clear that there is a sense in which this is Torrance's desire and goal. This final disjunction between the divine, history and the human requires a "leap" and thereby a negation of historical difference, a negation of the historicity of the Truth of God in Jesus Christ, and of humanity as such. This occurs because of "transcendentalist" assumptions which thwart a final completion of real interrelatedness as is necessary in Torrance's asymmetrical, unitary theo-logical whole as a disclosure model of God's lordly creative-recreative relation to the world as centered and founded in the real historicity and Mediation of the Word made flesh. Putting the point in patristic terms, Torrance is "Alexandrian" in his theo-logical desires and goals in and from the incarnate Word, but he is finally "Antiochene" (or even Nestorian?) at the crucial point of real historicity and historical relation or manifestness of the Word. On the one hand, Torrance wants the knowledge of God to be understood in terms of real historicity and real conceptuality, but he formulates the given "way" and "place" of the knowledge of God in terms commensurate with those who assert nonhistorical and nonconceptual knowledge of God.

Toward Possible Correction and Terminus of Thomas Torrance's Theology in Light of His Theo-logical Purpose

It would seem that Torrance has two basic choices (in different but effective ways) for overcoming the difficulty of a disclosive Word which remains yet beyond any partaking of the historical and beyond historical human knowledge contrary to his own theological purposes. Like Barth's "transcendentalism," rooted, we would assert, in Kierkegaard's understanding of time and the God-world relation, Torrance's own view causes God to recede from the truly historical into the non-historical or the non-objectivity of some other "time."[107]

Either Torrance must theologically go in the way of Paul Tillich or in the way of John Calvin. It is especially Tillich's understanding of the revelatory role of historical religious symbols which could be most helpful to Torrance for they do not merely mediate the wholly separate divine but actually and rightly participate in Being Itself, while not being confused with it.[108] Tillich would provide not only a way of real divine-human-world differentiation but importantly divine-human-world unitary interrelation. But while Torrance does rarely admit to having more affinity to Idealism than he usually acknowledges (in his later writings he admits the necessity of "Idealism" for truth), it is also clear that Torrance would find Tillich's thought too Hegelian and too necessitarian, as he would understand such. Torrance also would find herein the "Son" and "Spirit" relegated to mere moments in the self-realization of the "Father" in contrast to his "Nicene" trinitarianism. Torrance has said that while he finds much that is of worth and interest in Tillich (contra Bultmann) he believes Tillich to be, interestingly, both a monist and a dualist simultaneously. Therefore it is in Calvin's theological and historical "textuality" (and in a real sense one may refer to Barth's Reformed sense of "textuality") where one may find a more historical-human anchorage for the divine-human relations in historic and theological connection. This may give to Torrance's Barthian understanding of "the Being of God in his Act and the Act of God in his Being" and the simultaneous authority and humanity of the scriptures, which Torrance seems to indirectly acknowledge, another needed and completionary dimension. Following Ray Anderson, it may be said that scripture can become the one pole of transcendence ("historical transcendence") which, in and from God through Christ and by the Spirit, confronts the existing person as part of and participating in the revelation of God in history, with all of the limitations and conditions which history imposed upon the Word itself in becoming flesh. The "transcendence" of scripture is not then its fleeting existential role in the "moment" of the hearer wherein it then becomes disposable as creaturely and historical. It rather is to be found in the human and historical world of scripture itself as an indispensable pole of "historical transcendence" within which the objective Reality of God places the believer in Jesus Christ.[109] This would also more faithfully reflect Torrance's own strong trinitarian position by giving a more economically critical place to the pneumatological in the self-disclosive movement of God in the world.

But more, the revelation of God must not be understood merely as a contingency of pure Act united tenuously with humanity, but as the eternal Word of God which has truly and factually entered as Lord into real human history and into a specific human time and culture, taking shape in a context of interaction, real presence, real participation or partaking and real response. The point is, with Anderson, that "the Word acquired a history in which the verbal and written response became part of the transcendent act itself."[110] In principle, Torrance would seem to want to do this, seeing the need for interpretation as, in some sense, necessary for real, conceptual revelation, but this becomes disjoined in his theology from the real, objective revelatory movement of God in the world, and therefore the Word remains finally beyond the human as human and creaturely, and outside of contingent, human history, whereby that Word is said to reveal in the "moment" a "time" of its own. A more appropriate terminus is needed given the nature of Torrance's theo-logical, epistemological and soteriological goals. An analysis of John Calvin's view of the role of scripture, historical Word in relation to the Word of God and to the Church in the world, and its potential usefulness for Torrance will be examined in the following discussion. John Calvin has been chosen because of Torrance's Reformed heritage and his acknowledged debt to Calvin's thought.

John Calvin's Word Centered Response: An Approach for Torrance

In setting himself against much of the recognized ecclesiastical authority of the time, John Calvin felt impelled to point out that the true divine authority immanent in and for the Church was to be found in God's inscripturated Word. By means of this historical Word, the Holy Spirit of the exalted Christ could lead the Church effectively in truth and in life. All human authority was derived from or related to the Word by the Spirit of God. It will be necessary to take note of this side of Calvin's positive argumentation as he interacts with each realm of claimed authority in his *Institutes*.

Scriptural Word and Doctrinal Authority

Prior to his explicit response to the Roman Catholic Church's claims of "immanent" divine authority for the establishment of dogma (whether by council, pronouncement, etc.), Calvin looked to Scriptural examples of ecclesiological authority. In the Old Testament, Calvin saw the manifestation and exercise of authority as given by the Spirit as most clearly reflected in Moses, the Levitical priesthood, and the prophets. The central principle is that divine authority "is wholly given not to the men personally, but to the ministry to which they have been appointed; or (to speak more briefly) to the Word, whose ministry is entrusted to them."[111] No one has authority to teach "except in the name and Word of the Lord."[112] Crucial to Calvin's basic postulation of this Word-authority is the "witness of the Spirit" to the Scripture as the Word of God. This comes immediately from God. Since only God is a "suitable witness for his own word . . . . It is necessary that the same Spirit who spoke . . . should penetrate our hearts in order to convince us . . ." that the message of the writers of Scripture is of God and therefore faithful.[113]

Such a work of the Spirit applies not only in the context of the prophetic dynamic, but with special importance to the process of setting down divine truth in Scripture.

> But where it pleased God to raise up a more visible form of the church, he willed to have his word set down and sealed in writing that his priests might seek from it what to teach the people and that every doctrine to be taught should conform to that rule . . . (thus teaching) "from the mouth of the Lord" . . . then followed the prophets, through whom God published new oracles which were added to the law — but not so new that they did not flow from the law and hark back to it. As for doctrine, they were only interpreters of the law and added nothing to it but predictions . . . that whole body was the Lord's Word . . . and to this standard . . . (all) had to conform their teaching.[114]

To this Calvin adds that the apostolic expression-interpretation of Christ and his finished work set forth in the New Testament is not only part of the Word but, as the book of fulfillment, it is the critical locus of truth for the Church. In any case, none of the writers of Scripture were free to pronounce beyond the Word.

In thus stating his case, Calvin is laying a groundwork for continuity and discontinuity in the nature and character of Church authority and leadership. He distinguishes between the apostles and their successors, ". . . the former were sure and genuine scribes of the Holy Spirit, and their writings are therefore to be considered oracles of God."[115] Of those who follow, their "sole office . . . is to teach what is provided and sealed in the Holy Scriptures."[116] To be faithful to God now is therefore, by definition, to avoid the formulation of new dogmas. Calvin is consciously cutting off all notions of ecclesiastical infallibility in the realm of doctrine if it is claimed apart from whole submission to the rule of scripture and thereby to the rule of Christ. Any such claim, whether for tradition, council or pronouncement, is "contemptuous of God's Word."[117] The very nature of the Church as Christ's body submitted to him and unwavering against evil in the world requires that the Church and Christians find

> . . . firmness solely in God's Word. Then here is a universal rule that we ought to heed: God deprives men of the capacity to put forth the new doctrine in order that he alone may be our schoolmaster in spiritual doctrine as he alone is true (Rom. 3:4) who can neither lie nor deceive. This truth pertains as much to the whole church as to individual believers.[118]

Thus, while Christ is acknowledged and acclaimed to be Lord of the Church and present in it by the Spirit in governance and guidance, this immanent reality is said to be but the foretaste of his salvation, not the guarantor of new truth. Awareness of such in the Church ought to lead to careful self-limitation "within the limits of God's Word."[119]

Scriptural Word and Legislative Authority

For Calvin, the authority of scripture is not only prior and supreme in matters of doctrine, but it also rules in the life of the Church. Through the Word, taught and proclaimed, Christ as head rules his body. Calvin emphasized that the Word is truly over his Church, both in the exercise of present authority and as divine truth, and must be allowed to freely rule therein. Thus, "this is the perpetual mark by which our Lord has characterized his people: Everyone that is of the truth hears my voice."[120] This is held to be proper because the Church is Christ's Kingdom and, "he reigns by his Word alone."[121] Therefore, the acceptance of the authority of scripture means that the Church is "allowing Christ to rule within its life and to be the sole inspiration of its life."[122] Calvin emphasized over and over the principle that

> Whenever, then, God bids those pastors to be heard whom He sets over His church, His will is . . . that He Himself should be heard through their mouth. In short, whatever authority is exercised in the church ought to be subjected to this rule—that God's law is to retain its own pre-eminence and that men blend nothing of their own, but only define what is right according to the Word of the Lord.[123]

Spirit and Word (or Spirit through the Word of Scripture) govern in the Church so that all authority remains with the Lord himself. Calvin wanted all concerned to become clear on the fact, then, that God claims for himself the rule of his own people by the authority of his own Word.

Scriptural Word and Ecclesiastical Jurisdiction

Calvin's own volatile situation at Geneva clarified for him the crucial nature of Church jurisdiction. Though often accused of excessive "exercise" of what he perceived to be proper discipline, he held his point with relative consistency that "the whole jurisdiction of the Church pertains to the discipline of morals . . . [to] spiritual polity."[124] The Church's power of jurisdiction will, as an "order framed for the preservation of the spiritual polity,"[125] scripturally establish "courts of judgment . . . to deal with the censure of morals, to investigate vices, and to be charged with the exercise of the office of the keys."[126] Like many fellow Reformers, Calvin associated the power of the keys with the authority of the inscripturated Word.[127]

Calvin's strong sense of order and disorder in an age of uncommon flux left him often in a strait between two equally felt needs: the coherent peace and order of human life if it is to be truly human, and freedom in Christ. Clear for him, though, was the recognition that the overthrow of order was in fact contempt for "the sacred name of God."[128]   While probably somewhat overstated, Bouwsma's psychological perspective sheds light on this issue:

> . . . Calvin tended to equate righteousness with control, sin with unrestraint. "The Lord," he asserted, "cannot endure excess, and it is absolutely necessary that it be severely punished. It is characteristic of the godless always to run to extremes."[129]

Yet it is noteworthy that in actual pastoral practice Calvin was often exceedingly patient and went out of his way to make things right and allow for human frailties.[130]

In the realm of Church jurisdiction nothing is binding on consciences except for that which is specified in Scripture. Therefore the "command concerning forgiving and retaining sins and that promise made to Peter concerning binding and loosing ought to be referred solely to the ministry of the Word."[131] Regarding the doctrine of the keys which Christ has given and confirmed, it is not a merely human word, not of the apostles or their successors, but a word of God himself. Consequently, "the forgiveness of sins, the promise of eternal life, the good news of salvation" from God cannot be understood as mingled with the human and located in the hands of men by some reckoning of inherent divine authority. "Christ has not given this power actually to men, but to his Word, of which he has made men ministers."[132] As the holy bishops of the early church, who resisted the exercise of power in what could be esteemed as "civil" or secular ways, using the Lord's word alone, as was fitting (cf. excommunication), the ministers of the Church

> . . . have the Word of God with which to condemn the perverse; they have the Word with which to receive the repentant into grace. They cannot err or disagree with God's judgments for they judge solely according to God's law, which is no uncertain or earthly opinion but God's holy will and heavenly oracle.[133]

The power of Christ's minister is not, then, worldly power but is directly under Christ and thus is directly subjected to scriptural authority, direction and principles, by the Spirit.[134] The Church, as truly and faithfully Christ's, manifests his Kingdom only to the extent that it is obedient to his Word.[135] In rejecting the "Romanist" legal system as being humanly devised, Calvin proposed instead that the Church's authority rested only on scripture. For Calvin, the authority of scripture is not primarily to be found in its acknowledged inspiration ("the very Word of God"), but rather

> (Calvin's) argument is Christological. Christ is the wisdom and revelation of God, who alone has entered into the secrets of the Father. He is the source from whom the Old Testament writers drew their knowledge of God and when he became man he was the final witness to the Father. Hence his

> is the perfection of teaching. It would be impossible to surpass it, criminal
> to invent new. Let Christ speak and all be silent![136]

Thus, the Spirit of the church, which is the Spirit of Christ, is the Spirit of
Christ's inscripturated Word, who leads the Church into the knowledge of the
will of Christ by directing such into the knowledge of the Word of Christ.[137]

Christ and the Church's Focus on Christ: The Basis of Calvin's Emphasis on Scriptural Authority

Calvin's strong response to what he believed to be the problematic
medieval mixture of the divine and the human, the holy will of God with sinful
human inventions, came in the light of what he saw to be the eradication of the
Gospel of Christ, "like pouring sour wine into good." The very services and
ministries which the medieval Church proposed to promote Christ's redemption
in the people in its watchcare only multiplied Calvin's concern to challenge its
claim to authority.[138]

Throughout the *Institutes* Calvin attempts to set forth Christ as the central
focus and witness of the scriptures. The whole of this Word, one way or
another, presents God's active, redemptive self-disclosure concentrated preeminently in the one who has come to be Savior of men, Jesus Christ, God
come in the flesh.[139]

While there are several prominent sub-themes in Calvin's active and often
vociferous response to what he understood to be the late medieval teachings on
the blending of an immanent divine authority within the official hierarchy of the
Church, Calvin's emphatic point in asserting scriptural authority is again, as
throughout, Christological. To put the point differently, redemptive authority
in the Church is to be found simply and singularly in and from the Person of the
ascended, transcendent and ruling Christ as ever mediated in and within the
temporal dimensions of the Church by the Holy Spirit through the Word of
scripture as set historically over, within and before the Church.

In questions of authority in the Church in relation to doctrine, Calvin's
limitation of the Church's teaching to that which is disclosed by the Spirit in
Holy Scripture is so that, in their calling "to build up the Church," the ministers
must seek only "to preserve Christ's authority for himself; this can only be
secured if what he has received from his Father be left to him, namely that he
alone is the schoolmaster of the Church. For it is written . . . 'Hear him'
. . ."[140] Speaking of this in relation to apostolic authority in matters of
teaching, Calvin emphasizes

> . . . they are indeed commended with many notable titles. They are "the
> light of the world" and "the salt of the earth" . . . they are to be heard for
> Christ's sake . . . they show by their name how much is permitted to them

> . . . if they are "apostles" they are not to prate whatever they please, but are
> faithfully to report the commands of Him by whom they have been sent
> . . . . He (Christ) was the sole and eternal counselor of the Father, and was
> appointed Lord and Master of all by the Father.[141]

As Old Testament promise has turned to fulfillment and "the wisdom of God
was at length revealed in the flesh" declaring to all the present fullness of what
"can be comprehended and ought be pondered concerning the heavenly Father
by the human mind (ultimately "trinitarian" thinking),"[142] human beings must
esteem Christ as the basis and eternal capstone of God's self-revelation for
human liberation from sin and death.

> For it is as if, leading us away from ill doctrines of men, he (the Father)
> should conduct us to his Son alone; bid us seek all teaching of salvation from
> him alone; depend upon him, cleave to him; in short . . . hearken to his
> voice alone.[143]

Christ, the Lord and Teacher of the Church, reigns transcendently above all and
in this Church, His bride and pupil, in and through his written Word. To the
extent this is altered, distorted or lessened by human initiative in the Church, he
maintains that Christ is displaced and salvation imperiled.

In legislative matters, Calvin's assertion is that the souls of people are
called to deliverance and submission to scripture for ultimately the same
Christocentric reason. To compound things divine and human and thereby to
govern by any law except the Law of Christian freedom in the holy Word of the
gospel is not just an example of great impiety, he says, but is to disdain the
grace of Christ and to inflict consciences with human enslavement, consciences
Christ came to set free.[144] Essentially the question is one of Lordship for
Calvin.[145]

> In his law . . . has (already) included everything applicable to the perfect rule
> of the good life, so that nothing is left to men to add to that summary . . . .
> We hear that God claims this one prerogative as his very own—to rule us by
> the authority and laws of his Word.[146]

True polity in the Church is governance in responsive *a posteriori* submission
to that *a priori* disclosure of God whereby Christ the Word, truly and
transcendently reigns over the Church. By Christ and from Christ only, as
Head and Lord, the Church is built up by the Spirit of Christ in real relation in
and through the written Word.[147]

Calvin's opponents would claim that the Church is governed by the Holy
Spirit in matters of ecclesiastical legislation (Church constitutions) so that "its
authority resides in them."[148] Calvin responds that such points are simply
pious modes of self-glorification.[149] Rather, in hearing the voice of Christ

"the Church is first confronted with the transcendent Christ through his true Word so as to be delivered out of bondage" into the freedom that he has purchased for us by his sacred blood."[150]   Through the written Word of scripture people receive the revelation of God's glorious holiness and grace in the person and work of Christ. Through the scriptures, by the Spirit, Christ forms, directs and sanctifies his body, the Church. Through the scriptures and by the Spirit the Church is directed straight to its Source, Lord, Head and Savior, the Word made flesh. Thereby Calvin believes that the Church remains free from bondage, superstition, self-glorying and selfishness, to be true to its risen and ascended Lord in whom it knows God revealed.[151]

Finally, in matters of ecclesiastical jurisdiction, Calvin's view that the power of the keys is the authority of the Word is again pre-eminently Christological. The authority inherent in the capacity for binding and loosing is immediately the redemptive authority of the gospel of Christ, for "Christ has not given this power actually to man, but to his Word."[152]   This spiritual power, says Calvin, has been given

> . . . to destroy strongholds, to level every pinnacle that vaunts itself against the knowledge of God, to subjugate and take captive every thought to the obedience of Christ . . . . As this is done by the preaching of the doctrine of Christ.[153]

As "Christ cannot be properly known in any other way than from the Scriptures"[154] it necessarily follows for Calvin that in Christ's proper, abiding and transcendent Lordship over and in the Church "Christ is rejected when we do not embrace the pure doctrine of the Gospel."[155]

The point at issue in this section has been the relationship of Christ the Word, Christ's written Word (scripture) and Christ's Church. Or to put Calvin's contention with more clarity, it is the question of the place or relationship of the Word, the text of scripture, of Christ in relation to Christ's own ministry to the Church by the Holy Spirit. As Wallace has put Calvin's own perspective,

> . . . the Bible is not only the sole source of Church proclamation but also the sole authority that must rule the life of the Church. It has been pointed out that through the preaching of the Word of God Christ rules within His Church. The preacher of the Word is bound to turn to no other source for his testimony than to Scripture. This means that the Scripture is set over the Church by God as the authority that must be allowed full freedom to rule the life of the Church . . . . By accepting the authority of Scripture the Church is allowing Christ to rule within its life and to be the sole inspiration of its life.[156]

Given his great stress on God's transcendence and difference from the world and from human sinfulness, the scriptures, as God's "accommodation" to our frailty in his address to us, are a critical historical and authoritative aspect of God's redemptive disclosure in Calvin's theology. Indeed, for Calvin the scriptures are God's Word derivatively, functionally and mediately, but, under Christ and by the Spirit, they are Word of God. In this way, by allowing for and asserting an inscripturated Word as historical part of and within God's enactment of redemptive self-disclosure in the eternal Word make flesh and but by the Spirit, Calvin can effectively maintain the interactive relatedness of God, the space-time world and existing persons in the world — i.e. "historical transcendence." The authority and Truth are ultimately, transcendently, Christ's alone, so that in the Church "the doctrine of the Gospel is preached in purity, (so that) there we are certain that Christ reigns; and where it is rejected, His government is set aside."[157]

Calvin's understanding of the disclosive role of scripture in the divine economy by the Spirit was set and expressed in the face of much controversy. It is his textuality or his scripture-principle, as central to Torrance's own Reformed theology, that is being emphasized here. This Reformed tradition of theological "textuality" is appropriate to Torrance's own theo-logical purposes in order to bring a more complete unitariness to his Christocentric-Trinitarian theology, to his understanding of the real historical divine-human relation in Christ and by the Spirit wherein God is known redemptively as he is in himself.

It is at Calvin's very Christocentric-theological point in the economy of God's trinitarian self-disclosure that Torrance, if he would similarly maintain God's revelatory openness in the world in ongoing, truly historical interactive relatedness, could maintain a more fully "Reformed" position and would bring about the interactive connection needed. It is this Christocentric-Trinitarian emphasis which we will seek to preliminarily unfold below, "updating" Calvin and seeking to complete Torrance in relation to the Word emphasis, incarnation, Trinity and the text of Scripture in relation to ongoing historical disclosure of God in Christ by the Spirit.

Hebraic Three-fold "Being-Act-Interpretation and Interpretation-Act-Being": A Possible Way to Bring About Revelatory Relation Historicity and Humanity

While Calvin's own handling of Christocentric-Pneumatological Word-Scripture authority in objective relation to and in the Church and world as historical Word of God reflects its own neo-Platonic characteristics, still it recognizes the necessity of a historical and human part or pole in the movement of the self-revelation of God in the world. For Calvin, scripture is understood as participating, as part of the movement of divine disclosure as "inspired" interaction, response, witness and interpretation. This effects a fuller or larger unitariness of the triadic God-world-existing human relation than Torrance has produced while yet working under the influence of that problematic aspect of the thought of Soren Kierkegaard. To accomplish what he truly wants to accomplish Torrance needs to give the historical "prophetic and apostolic witness" of scripture to Christ a place of actual participation in and part of the historical disclosure of God in Christ in the world and in human existence, and not as a disposable conduit which, in fact, because it is historical and human, has therefore no real (ontological) part in the disclosure process of the Word made flesh by the Spirit. The scriptures of the Church are human, historical works which the theologian (contra the historian) judges, says Torrance, "from the *Urgeschichte* to which they bear witness" (that is the incarnate Word).[158] Despite the helpfulness he has found in Bultmann, Ebeling and Fuchs, Paul Ricoeur has spoken against the onesidedness of any "idealism of the word event" while wanting to "reaffirm the realism of the event of (real) history." Along lines whereby Ricoeur would criticize Bultmann and these post-Bultmannians, Torrance too seems to jump to and from human existence much too quickly.[159] Rather than Torrance being forced into what is, in his own terms, a disjunction in the subject-Object relation, thus necessitating a "lightning" Word-event akin to that of Ebeling or Fuchs, an Hebraic three-fold disclosive movement rather than the Barthian two-fold movement (Being-Act and Act-Being) could help Torrance's understanding of the revelatory process and relation in order to overcome the remaining remoteness of pure Act from our space-time existence. Understanding is not a non-linguistic, mystical event but is, as Ricoeur says, the result of interpretative work.

G. Ernest Wright, William Foxwell Albright and others have shown that the Hebraic perspective, reflected throughout scripture, stresses the revelation of God in real human history as interpreted theologically. Knowledge of God is therefore "historical knowledge" which is best expressed in the dialogue of events and in the revealed understanding of the meaning of the human struggle in the otherwise meaningless chaos of the triumph and defeat of human experience. This notion of "revelation in history" led Israel to preserve and write its historical traditions. Israelite historical knowledge of God, which led to its interest in history, is understood to have arisen out of Yahweh's having chosen the contingent forms of history as the way and place in which he has revealed himself in that covenantal relation. The basic thing which can be said about the God of the covenant, the God of the scriptures, concerns his historical actions. Through these actions and the theological interpretation of the meaning these acts, a new people is created.[160]

As Jewish philosopher Abraham Heschel has described, the scriptures deal with universals through narration and recitation of everyday particulars of history.[161] The God of scripture is, as Torrance himself says, not static but dynamic, and to be contrasted from the Greek view of God. Therefore one is reckoned to be able to actually and in realist terms know the living God in history. This same view Torrance is in a very real sense concerned to express, but apparently he cannot because of a remaining "gulf" between the divine and human reflected in his inability or unwillingness to recognize the real relation of God and to God as occurring not only in a transcendentalized "historical" Act, but then also in narrative and the cultural/linguistic/theological interpretation of the meaning of God's Acts in real relation to human history. Human existence is durational and narrative fits well with the nature of action in history.

George Lindbeck has expressed the matter by saying that a religion such as Christianity must be viewed as a cultural and/or linguistic framework that shapes all life and thought. Biblical religion is a communal reality that forms persons and which is made up of both linguistic and non-linguistic symbols along with a distinctive grammar for meaningful utilization. Scripture then functions interpretively to reveal the character and give description or identity to God as agent.   Scripture then needfully recounts and interprets God's deeds and purposes with and for existing human beings in their ever changing circumstances. These written accounts, these interpretations, reach their climax in what the four evangelists say of the incarnate, dead, risen, ascended and ever-present Jesus Christ whose identity as divine-human agent is enacted interpretively in the gospel stories of Jesus of Nazareth.   But this climax as God's Act cannot be severed from the events and interpretive accounts which precede it whereby it is concluded that the Jesus of the gospel accounts is the Son of the God of Abraham, Isaac and Jacob. A real sense of textuality and of interpretation as integral to and as part of the economy of the real historical, human revelation of God means, then, that at this historical "pole" of the redemptive process or movement of God as connected to interpretation, that the focus is allowed to be and is shown to be cultural, as this is expressed narratively and linguistically in the stories of Israel, of Jesus and of the early Church. Scripture's various historical genres, notably narrative, are crucial in their portrayal of life lived in the realities of this world in the light of God's character interpreted therein in relation to his historical acts.[162] This necessary historical God-human interrelatedness in the real relation of divine act and interpretation is what, given his goal, Torrance should include but finally lacks. In fact it may be said that Barth's attention to the linguistic or textual aspect of disclosure, in practice if not always in principle, puts him much closer to the mark of what is needed. Dietrich Bonhoeffer is another example of one who sought to ground transcendence more effectively (than has the Barthian tradition reflected in Torrance) in an historical reality extrinsic to one's own existence. This is a good corrective for Torrance. Torrance says that

> As such the Holy Scripture, like the Apostolate, stands with sinners and
> among sinners, and belongs to the sphere where salvation is bestowed. That

gives us the peculiar problem of Holy Scripture and its peculiar place. Holy Scripture is assumed by Christ to be his instrument in conveying revelation and reconciliation, and yet Holy Scripture belongs to the sphere where redemption is necessary. The Bible stands above the Church, speaking to the Church the very Word of God, but the Bible also belongs to history which comes under the judgment and the redemption of the Cross. That double place of Holy Scripture must always be fully acknowledged, else we confound the word of man with the Word of God, and substitute the Apostles in the place of Christ.[163]

While one must avoid a "docetic" scripture and affirm all aspects of the historicity of the prophetic-apostolic scripture, Torrance is clearly disjoining and dichotomizing the historical word of the witness of Scripture to Christ from the Word of God and is consistent with his principle of never confusing the objective Word of God, Christ, which meets or encounters us now in our existence, with creaturely things. But this finally disjoins the Christ of that "third" Barthian time of revelation from space-time existence and cuts Torrance short of the redempto-disclosive relation in Christ and by the Spirit which he desires. Why the necessary severance of transcendence for historicity? How does one determine when Scripture is "above" the Church and when it is under judgment? Somehow, in Torrance's formulation, the scriptures must, in the movement of God in real salvation history by the Spirit, constitute real Word of God in real relation to and under the living Christ in a way akin to that found in Calvin. This simply means that in this way scripture constitutes the present, historical Word of God in its power to "communicate as well as commend the truth of God to man." This could potentially be the needed pole of transcendence lying in history, and so it would work to "inform the act of faith in the Spirit" of faith's transcendent basis in Jesus Christ.[164] Only as it thus informs faith of its transcendent ground in the person of Christ is it revelatory. Without this cognitive link faith must, in Torrance's own terms, "fall back upon the self" and provide its own content. Torrance's "double place" for scripture, transcendent (in a creaturely sense) and under judgment, is unsuccessful, for one side is finally disjoined from the other and there is the danger of either the loss of historicity or a merely "situational" hearing.

The transcendence of God was most fully revealed when the Son was under the judgment of the Cross. In Jesus the word of man was the Word of God. If this be analogically applied, in and for Torrance's theo-logical purpose to scripture, then scripture as "servant" needs to be reckoned by Torrance as having this same "kenotic" function in the "logic" of God's gracious movement in historical transcendence. This would mean not a "double place," existential and historical, but that scripture would be the one pole of transcendence which confronts as a revelation in history with all the limits that history imposed on the eternal Word himself in the incarnation. Historical transcendence is at stake here for Torrance because Kierkegaard's influence has meant that his cognitive link with the real content of God's Being as historical action is (almost neo-Platonically) cut off. Without the further step to include the historical interpretive process then the human act of faith must provide its own almost "gnostic" content for the transcendent divine Word.[165] In our corrective for the completion of Torrance's own theo-logical model out of Christ and by the Spirit, scripture, as interpretation of God's historical acts, has the quality of "historical" transcendence (immanent relation) only with regard to its cognitive connection with the ontic reality of God's economic, historical transcendence through the Holy Spirit as ever epistemologically "relevant." In this way, Torrance's Nicene reflection of the divine economy "from the Father by the Son and in the Spirit" can be brought theo-logically from the pneumatological-interpretive response to the Act of God in the Son. In this way the Spirit can finally be given real economic function as it ought to have for Torrance's theology, given his own larger and narrower purposes and intentions.

Torrance and Scriptural Interpretation of Christ: A Brief Suggestion Connected to the Thought of Hans Frei on the Text of Scripture

In moving yet further toward a suggested corrective for Torrance's theology, as it relates directly to the key of the objective, realist knowledge of God by existing persons, there must be developed a more adequate interrelated three-fold understanding of the self-revelation of "God's Being in his Act and Interpretation" whereby one follows or thinks after "Interpretation made of his Act as it reveals God's Being" as more adequate to Torrance's own principles and purposes than the two-fold "Being-Act and Act-Being," which (against all of his intent) has left the Word of God beyond history and existing human beings. This needed addition would seem to be open to the literary-biblical insights of Hans Frei. Hans Frei, with Torrance, shares many of the spiritual and academic traditions of Calvinism and its Word theology.

It may be though that if the purpose here is to be truly corrective within Torrance's actual framework, intentions and goals that the thought of Hans Frei, as more consciously "Barthian," may be preferable for bringing out a greater or more complete realization of the role of the biblical text or of textuality and the biblical narrative in real historical participation in or as part of the self-disclosive movement of God in Christ and by the Spirit in the world. Unlike Torrance, Barth saw his *Church Dogmatics* to be not so much a system as the narrative of the event of Jesus Christ, with the resurrection reality as central. He sought to listen to Christ as attested in Scripture, to adopt the biblical writer's outlook, approach and method, and then to teach the result. Barth sought centrally to report the event of reconciliation, and so he placed himself as hearer or as theological exegete of the narrative of reconciliation believing that he should find Jesus Christ to be the unifying content of Scripture. Thus he intended to engage the text of Scripture through observation, reflection (*Nachdenken*) and appropriation of the literature, especially the central Gospel events. Here is found Barth's "scandal of particularity" as he emphasizes the dominance of one story, of one event over all others; it is the story, the witness, which points to Jesus Christ. Therein lies its authority for Barth. By his reflection or thinking after (*Nachdenken*) the text or narratives of Scripture, Barth is able to uncover the logic of the Gospel of the risen Christ and the role of the Holy Spirit therein.[166] Frei claims then that Barth effectively preserves the literal sense of the Gospel narratives, for example, while Bultmann and Ricoeur (as yet too Bultmannian to Frei's way of thinking) construe the narratives as expressions of faith's self-understanding couched in myth (though Ricoeur is surely clear that Word is prior to both faith and understanding). In his influential work *The Eclipse of Biblical Narrative*, Frei argues that in the nineteenth century the literal sense of the biblical narrative began to be distinguished from questions of historical reference or religious truth. This led to the situation where the biblical narrative was finally eclipsed altogether by the historical or ideal subject matter. The meaning of the biblical narrative was thought of either in terms of historical reference or ideal reference. In discussion similar to Torrance's own unitary (anti-dualist) concerns, Frei explains that in England and Germany there occurred the breakup of the harmony between historical fact, literal meaning and religious truth that modern theology has yet to recover from. The central issue for Frei, like Torrance, is whether or not a theologian affirms that salvation depends not only on what Jesus said and did, but rather that he actually existed as God come in the flesh. This affirmation of the incarnation, that God in Jesus Christ has directly intervened in the realm of finitude, is the "positivity" of the Christian faith.[167]

Frei's protest is against the whole of philosophical hermeneutics where one model of intelligibility is accepted *a priori*, and all texts, without regard to specific features, are placed under those categories of meaningfulness. Frei is also "Anselmian" in his thinking. He, like Torrance (following Barth), understands theology to be that endeavor which seeks to describe the Christian faith on its own terms. As Anselm sought to explain the logic of biblical language rather than transposing it into a philosophical conceptuality, even so he says that theology need not argue its own case before a philosophical court of appeal but must pursue its task to achieve understanding and clarity of its own beliefs (i.e., *credo ut intelligam, Fides quaerens intellectum*). Frei then is a theologian who wants to approach the Gospel narratives in particular to let them make sense in their own way. The reference to "literal sense" refers then to this Anselmian way. For this reason Frei points to Barth as the model for a narrative reading of scripture which preserves this "literal" sense without making history the test of the meaning of the realistic forms of the stories. Barth made no *a priori* demands concerning the kind of meaning the Gospel narratives may have. The text determines the rules for reading (*ad hoc*).[168] God's action must be the prior action, the self-revelation of God who is wholly free and not "generally" or "in general" available. Following Anselm and Barth then, Frei views theology as conceptual re-description. Therefore the task of theology is not to mold scripture into some other conceptuality, but to render the world of the scriptures intelligible on their own terms. Unlike myths, the meaning of the Gospel narratives is what the stories actually say and not what they supposedly symbolize. The Gospel narratives are said to be "history-like" in Frei's proposal ("realistic"). Here meaning is in great measure a function of the interaction of character and circumstances. Very importantly he says then that there is no meaning separated from the story, and therefore meaning is not to be found apart from the written narration itself. Like Torrance's emphasis upon the need for the unity of form and being, one sees here in Frei the assertion of the close identification of form and meaning in the realistic story. We see here too then a favorite and crucial scientific principle or issue for Torrance (as for Barth), that is, the necessity of letting the object of knowledge dictate the manner in which it is known. But Frei applies this much more consistentlypto the text of scripture than does Torrance. Lindbeck calls this Anselmian approach to scripture "intratextual" or making sense of the text of scripture from the inside, respecting the "literal" sense or what the text says, the story itself, whereby the literal reference of the story is the story's own world. The theologian must focus on and describe the world of the text and not leap to the world above the text or beyond it or in front of it. The text must be taken seriously on its own terms and its own relations.

But even more at issue, especially when Frei is seen in relation to Paul Ricoeur, is that Frei's reading of the Gospels focuses on the particularity and specificity of the identity of Jesus Christ. Jesus is the referent of the Gospels. This Torrance would also affirm. Ricoeur in contrast sees in the Gospels the manifestation of a secondary world, a way of being-in-the-world or in the divine presence. But like Torrance, Ricoeur holds to a disclosure model of truth which moves him to prefer the metaphorical over the realistic, literary descriptive character of the passion and resurrection narratives.[169] Torrance would probably prefer and would certainly need to combine disclosure and narrative.

While this is but a brief reference to Frei's hermeneutics and the crucial role he gives to the text of Scripture (with emphasis upon the Gospel narratives), one can find, in principle at least, Frei's textuality as a possible, healthy and needful corrective to Torrance's tendency to "transcendentalize," a tendency likely rooted in part in what Thiemann points to as Torrance's problematic "foundationalism" or theory about the religious dimension of human experience. Indeed, Thiemann (who is also much influenced by Hans Frei) sympathizes with Torrance's "Barthian" concern about the neo-Protestant tendency to correlate

Word with some innate human capacity. But Thiemann also rejects the "radical disjunction between human speech and divine reality." This solves the problem of cutting all actual and historical relations between the two while taking refuge in the "miracle of grace" to somehow bring them together. He says by contrast, "once God has claimed a piece of creaturely reality as his own and bound himself to it then we are warranted in accepting the God-forged link . . . if God has annexed some form of human language . . . that form contributes to our understanding of that communication."[170] Frei is then better able to hold together sense, reference and meaning, and thereby to avoid moving immediately to a world beyond the text, losing its world, the space-time world, the existing person, and thus the place where God has objectively come to be known in the mundane there-ness and then-ness of the incarnation of the Word of God.

But it should be noted that as Frei reads the Gospels as "history-like" narratives, insisting that the "literal" sense of the text is not to be equated with historical reference, that he seems to have cut off the question of historical reference. This aspect of his thought seems to be counterproductive for his own theological agenda and for Torrance's own principle in his consideration of the centrality of Jesus Christ as historical reference. Might this not be destructive to Frei's enterprise by in fact eclipsing not the biblical narrative but biblical claims to truth.[171] It would not here meet Torrance's understanding of correspondence-coherence truth. This also falls far short of Torrance's own perceived and determined theo-logical task. Frei himself says that the reader must somewhere decide whether to move from a literary to a faith judgment. Perhaps the fact-fiction dichotomy must be examined more closely. But real correction and completion for Torrance requires that the historical prophetic and apostolic texts not be severed from the economic movement of the self-disclosure of God as Act in history whereby the text of scripture as historical would again become only a vanishing Cartesian "point" of mediation. Scripture must unitarily be part of the very self-disclosive movement of God in the world centered in Jesus Christ. Torrance, like Barth and Calvin, wants to make it clear that humanity cannot find its own way to God. God must find and make the way to and for us here. It is the objective way God has taken in Jesus Christ. God's revelation, in the Barthian-Torrancian sense, must wholly relate God's Word, God's self-disclosure, to ongoing concrete human existence whereby these human words and human texts have participated and do participate as captive to his Word in the immanent, economic, operative power of God's Holy Spirit, the Spirit of Christ, the presencing or subjective Reality of God. Torrance's understanding of revelation only as Act or event without interpretation is but another "wax nose" which one can turn wherever one wants. The Exodus was but one of many tribal migrations and the crucifixion of Jesus of Nazareth was but one of thousands of such Roman executions. Meaning-ful Act or event cannot be unto itself without interpretation. The hermeneutical issue is central and Torrance has not properly addressed it. Event-qua-event is not self-interpreting as Torrance would seem at some level to have it and if he would then have interpretation sourced wholly in human perception, however "inspired" (as Torrance speaks of scripture in some vague sense), then one finds this to be sourced finally in human subjective perception as dualistically cut off from participation in the actual economy of God's self-disclosure. This lands one back into the very "dualistic subjectivism" and "relativism" which Torrance so wants to overcome. It seems finally that Torrance wants it both ways. He seems to rely implicitly on this interpretive principle but then denies it in formal principle. Scripture does witness to and point away from itself to Christ, but, reflecting Torrance's own economic emphases, this is not to say that it is not also truly (if at a more immanent or "lower" level) Word of God anymore than when Jesus "economically" spoke of and pointed to the Father in the Gospel accounts. Again, following Torrance, all must relate unitarily in the one economy of the living, triune God. When this writer questioned Torrance whether knowledge "about" God as coming from God in Christ was possible, he had finally to admit (as the contents of each of his books seems to necessitate, lest he allow that they speak merely human conjecture or even nonsense) that this was the case, but only in relation to the knowledge of God himself in Christ Jesus. This is precisely the point being made here.[172]   He arbitrarily limits the historical Word to the incarnation. Torrance identifies Word, self revelation, only with Christ as though to speak of interpretation as somehow, if at a lower yet unitary level, as Word, is to deny or denigrate Christ as the Word. But this is absurd. For his own purposes the Word must indeed first ontologically and absolutely be Christ. And yet the witness/interpretation can be unitarily an aspect of God's dynamic movement in Christ in the world without the Word being separated from God in Christ and by the Spirit. Indeed, for Torrance's own goal this seems "economically" necessary.

Interpretation or written witness as historical aspect of the unfolding economy of God's purpose to be known as he is ought to be seen in Torrance's own trinitarian scheme as also crucial to the role or manifestation of the Spirit in relation to Christ the Lord. In this way the Spirit need not and will not negate the historical, existing human (as does one side of Torrance's thought), but can fulfill the human at the very level of the historical, human word as truly human in a way which links unitarily to and fulfills the "incarnation," as Torrance himself would have it. Without this Torrance is forced to set forth the revelatory event or "moment" as "contemporaneously" above this human history thereby reflecting the "existentialist" and "dualist" gulf at the very point of necessary historical connection to this human present and sphere of being. Contrary to his own wholly trinitarian desire, Torrance's view of revelation, without this corrective, seems to actually make the role of the Spirit not simply one of economic "submission" but finally subordinationist.

In all of this Torrance has been found to at least partially negate, in his own positive theological expression, what he believes Immanuel Kant and all operating theologically out from Kant's epistemological basis (e.g., Schleiermacher, Bultmann, John Robinson) are said to have negated, that is, personal communicative, dialogical, realist and covenantal knowledge of God. If Thomas Torrance is to maintain his desired outcomes regarding the realist knowledge of the triune God as he is in himself in Jesus Christ within the basic Reformed outline he has set forth, then he must take something akin to this way of correction in the recognition of the crucial role of textuality and interpretative witness (scripture) as also part of the Word economy in Christ by the Spirit, as it was in Calvin. This will help to complete an incomplete and thus "broken" revelatory process in relation to the existing human being as human. Otherwise, Torrance must, by his own conception and definition of dualism, give up his notion of the realist knowledge of God which has a real content for the existing human being in space-time. He wants to bring to open, unitary and yet differentiated (asymmetrical) relation the phenomenal and noumenal realms to do away with the division as "gulf" without doing away with the triadic God-world-human distinction in relation (especially the transcendence of God as Creator-Redeemer). He seems to end with the (unwanted) negation, or better, the minimalization, of the phenomenal. Emil Brunner has himself admitted that in some real sense the historical scripture must be understood in a secondary way as being itself Word of God in the immanent economy of God's self-revelation.[173] For completion Torrance must see this too. Along these lines of correction it seems that Torrance can truly accomplish theo-logically what he wants to do, and thereby to set forth the realist knowledge of the triune God in the world as he thinks this out in a more fully and truly unitary, interactive way from the way God has historically taken in the world by his Word and Spirit. In this way he can overcome a kind of "arianizing" of the self-revelation of God in the world at the critical point of our historical, human existence and interpretation. Torrance can thereby fulfill in positive expression the entirety of the factuality of God's not remaining "aloof" but that he has concretely and fully brought about his own self-giving participation here in our space-time and in the humanness of our humanity to the end that we may know God and Jesus Christ whom he has sent which is eternal life.

NOTES

1. Note carefully the detailed criticism of Torrance's distorting theo-logical hermeneutics in relation to Scripture by James Barr in *The Semantics of Biblical Language* (London: Oxford University Press, 1961), pp. 45, 106, 125, 133-136, 152-156, 161-165, 171-175, 184, 194, 199, 201, 202-203, 204-205, 235, 259, 264, 277-279; and C. F. D. Moule, "The Biblical Conception of Faith," *Expository Times*, LXVIII, 175, cf. p. 222 for details.

2. John D. Morrison, "Review: The Trinitarian Faith: The Evangelical Theology of the Ancient Catholic Church," by Thomas F. Torrance, *Calvin Theological Journal*, 25, no. 1 (April 1990), 119-122.

3. Richard A. Muller, "Review of Transformation and Convergence in the Frame of Knowledge: Explorations in the Interrelations of Scientific and Theological Enterprise" by Thomas F. Torrance, *Westminster Theological Journal*, 47, no. 1 (Spring 1985), 137.

4. Ibid.

5. Karl Barth, *CD* II/1, pp. 121, 136; *CD* IV/3, pp. 1, 97, 110, 140ff. Cf. George Hunsinger's critical analysis of Torrance's reflections of and use of Barth in his recent work *How to Read Karl Barth* (Oxford: Oxford University Press, 1992), pp. 6, 9-12, 15, 20-21.

6. Cf. where Klinefelter takes Torrance to task for this.

7. Plato, *The Republic*, translated by Francis M. Cornford (Oxford: Oxford University Press, 1945), pp. 183-185 (V., 474-480).

8. Ibid., pp. 224-226 (VI., 509-511).

9. Plotinus, *Enneads*, translated by A. H. Armstrong (Cambridge: Harvard University Press, 1977), VI, 9, 9.

10. Cf. Stephen Strehle, *Calvinism, Federalism, and Scholasticism: A Study of the Reformed Doctrine of Covenant* (Bern: Peter Lang, 1988) especially pp. 24-43, 149-156, 386-392.

11. Niels Thulstrup, "Introduction," in *Fragments*, p. xvii.

12. C. Stephen Evans, *Kierkegaard's Fragments and Postscript: The Religious Philosophy of Johannes Climacus* (Atlantic Highlands, N.J.: Humanities Press, 1983), p. 24.

13. Kierkegaard, *Philosophical Fragments*, translated by Howard V. Hong and Edna H. Hong (Princeton: Princeton University Press, 1985), p. 63.

14. Ibid., p. 64.

15. Ibid., p. 65.

16. Ibid., p. 67-68.

17. Ibid., pp. 67f. Cf. Kierkegaard's perspective on this issue in both the *Fragments* (p. 101) and in *Training* (p. 125).

18. Alastair Mackinnon, "Believing the *Paradox*: A Contradiction in Kierkegaard?" *Harvard Theological Review*, 1968, pp. 633-636.

19. Kierkegaard asserts that "The existing individual who chooses to pursue the objective way enters upon the entire approximation-process by which it is proposed to bringing God to light objectively. But his is in all eternity impossible, because God is a subject, and therefore exists only for subjectivity in inwardness." *Postscript*, p. 178. Cf. *Training*, pp. 28-29.

20. Soren Kierkegaard, *Training in Christianity and the Edifying Discourse*, translated by Walter Lowrie, (Princeton: Princeton University Press, 1947), pp. 127, 134-135.

21. See Paul Althaus, *The Theology of Martin Luther* (Philadelphia: Fortress Press, 1970), p. 178-198.

22. Soren Kierkegaard, *Journals and Papers*, no. 3110, III, translated by Howard and Edna Hong (Bloomington and London: Indiana University Press, 1967-78), p. 421.

23. Kierkegaard, *Fragments*, p. 32.

24. Kierkegaard concludes, "Christ does not will to be God. In an omnipotent decision he has forced himself into being a single human being and must now very concretely suffer the total impotence of wretchedness with the cause of humanity upon his heart, must suffer being a poor individual man--and at every moment it is his voluntary decision that constrains him; he does, after all, have the power to break through and be God." *Journals and Papers*, no. 4651, IV, p. 395. In *Training*, pp. 128-31, Kierkegaard develops this when he says, "It was Christ's free will and determination from all eternity to be incognito." So when people think to do Him honor by saying or thinking, 'If I had been contemporary with Him,' and since it is Christ they insult, this means they are blasphemous . . . . Oh, loftiest height of self-abnegation when the incognito succeeds so well that even if He were inclined to speak directly on one would believe Him. . and now in the case of the God-Man! He is God, but chooses to become the impenetrable unrecognizableness that is possible; for the contradiction between being God and being

an individual man is the greatest possible, the infinitely qualitative contradiction."

25. In *Training*, Kierkegaard states, "There is a comfort which did not exist so long as Christ lived and which He therefore could not offer to anyone: the comfort of His death as the atonement, as the pledge that sins are forgiven. In His lifetime Christ is more especially the Pattern for his contemporaries, notwithstanding that He is the Savior, and notwithstanding that His life is suffering . . . yet the out-standing fact is that He is the Pattern , . . . But then He dies. And his death alters everything infinitely. Not that His death becomes the infinite guarantee with which the striver starts out, the assurance that infinite satisfaction has been made. . . that Christ died to save him, that Christ's death is the atonement and satisfaction." p. 270.

26. Paul Sponheim, *Kierkegaard on Christ and Christian Conscience* (New York: Harper and Row, Publishers, 1968), pp. 99ff.

27. Kierkegaard, cited in Sponheim, p. 173.

28. Ibid., pp. 176-177.

29. Ibid., p. 177.

30. Walter Lowrie, *Kierkegaard*, (London: Oxford University Press, 1938), p. 426.

31. Ibid.

32. Kierkegaard, *Postscript*, p. 495. cf. Ibid., p. 494. "The distinction between the pathetic and the dialectical must, however, be more closely defined; for religiousness A is by no means undialectic, but is more paradoxically dialectic. Religiousness A is the dialectic of inward transformation; it is the relation to an eternal happiness which is not conditioned by anything but is the dialectic inward appropriation of the relationship, and so is conditioned only by the inwardness of the appropriation and its dialectic."

33. Ibid., p. 497. Cf. *Ibid.*; p. 509. "Religiousness A makes the thing of existing as tenuous as possible (outside the paradox-religious sphere), but it does not base the relation to an eternal happiness upon one's existence but lets the relation to an eternal happiness serve as basis for the transformation of existence. From the individual's relation to the eternal, there results the how of his existence, not the converse, and thereby infinitely more comes out of it than was put into it."

34. Lowrie, p. 323.

35. Edward J. Carnell, *The Burden of Soren Kierkegaard* (Grand Rapids: Wm. B. Eerdmans Publishing Company, 1960), p. 83.

36. James Collins, *The Mind of Kierkegaard* (London: Secker and Warburg, 1954), pp. 161-62. Note the point Collins makes here, "(He) places emphasis upon the dialectical factors in religiousness to such an extent, that it cannot be deemed a mere continuation of the natural religious life. This dialectical tension is achieved by asking men to have faith in the mysteries of Original Sin and the Incarnation. The effect of this faith is to introduce paradox into the reality of man and God taken in themselves and not merely in their mutual relation . . . The Incarnation means that the eternal has subjected itself to the law of becoming, that the All Holy has taken upon itself the conditions of sinful existence, that God has become Man."

37. Carnell, p. 83. cf. Kierkegaard, *Postscript*, p. 528. "The paradox consists principally in the fact that God, the Eternal, came into existence in time as a particular man. Whether this particular man is a servant or an emperor is neither here nor there . . . it is not a greater humiliation for God to become beggar than to become an emperor . . . . If one would talk about God, let him say, God. That is the quality."

38. Kierkegaard, Fragments, pp. 44-49.

39. Evans, p. 116.

40. Kierkegaard, *Fragments*, pp. 38-39. Cf. Ibid., p. 44-45.

41. Note that in Kierkegaard's discussions, the "moment" is used much like Descartes' "point," i.e., the moment for Kierkegaard both participates in time and is not actually measurable--it is paradoxical. As we will note later, the concept of the "moment," along with "contemporaneity," becomes significant in the question of history and the nature of true religious belief in relation to the historical Incarnation.

42. Kierkegaard, *Fragments*, p. 59.

43. Jerry H. Gill, "Faith Is as Faith Does," in *Kierkegaard's Fear and Trembling: Critical Appraisals*, ed. Robert L. Perkins (University, Alabama: The University of Alabama Press, 1981), p. 204.

44. Ibid., p. 208.

45. Mark C. Taylor, "Sounds of Silence," in Perkins, pp. 182-188.

46. Kierkegaard, *Fragments*, pp. 13-15.

47. Ibid., pp. 17-18. Note Kierkegaard's significant discussion of the "moment" in conjunction with this issue in the *Fragments*, p. 18.

48. Ibid., pp. 20-21.

49. Richard Schacht, "Kierkegaard in 'Truth is Subjectivity' and the Leap of Faith," *Canadian Journal of Philosophy*, II (1973), p. 308.

50. Michael P. Levine, "Why the Incarnation is a Superfluous Detail for Kierkegaard," *Religious Studies*, XVIII, 2 (1982), pp. 171-172.

51. Ibid., pp. 172.

52. Ibid., p. 174.

53. Ibid., p. 172.

54. Ibid.

55. Kierkegaard, *Postscripts*, pp. 181ff.

56. See Paul Tillich's discussion on Christology and the critical role of "Jesus the Christ" in relation to the bearing of "New Being" in history whereby man is to be restored to his Ground of Being. *Systematic Theology*, II (Chicago: University of Chicago Press, 1957). Between the two thinkers there is much difference. On this point though the comparison is helpful.

57. Oscar Cullmann, *Christ and Time: The Primitive Christian Conception of Time and History* (Philadelphia: The Westminster Press, 1964), p. 76.

58. Ibid.

59. Ibid., p. 146.

60. Ibid., p. 168.

61. Ibid., p. 169.

62. Kierkegaard, *Fragments*, pp. 86ff.

63. Ibid., p. 87.

64. Ibid., p. 39-42.

65. Ibid., pp. 58-59.

66. Ibid., p. 87. Cf. Soren Kierkegaard . . . Soren Kierkegaard, *Fear and Trembling*, translated by Howard V. and Edna H. Hong (Princeton: Princeton University Press, 1983), pp. 92-93, 98-99, 112-120.

67. Karl Barth, *Church Dogmatics* I/2, translated by G. T. Thomson and Harold Knight (Edinburgh: T&T Clark, 1956), p.45. Hereafter cited as *CD*.

68. *CD* III/2, p. 437.

69. Peter Halman Monsma, *Karl Barth's Idea of Revelation* (Sommerville, N.J.: Somerset Press, Inc., 1937), p.147.

70. *CD* I/2, p. 49.

71. Ibid.

72. Ibid.

73. Ibid., p. 50.

74. Ibid., p. 53.

75. Ibid., p. 52.

76. Ibid., p. 55.

77. Ibid., p. 56.

78. Ibid., p. 58.

79. Ibid.

80. Ibid., p. 62.

81. Ibid., p. 63.

82. Ibid.

83. Ibid.

84. Ibid., pp. 64-65.

85. Ibid., p. 64.

86. Ibid., p. 65.

87. Ibid., p. 66.

88. Ibid.

89. Ibid., p.67. Here Barth says significantly that "The fulfillment of time by revelation means . . . that our time, the thing we suppose we know and possess as time, is taken from us . . . . Revelation destroys this appearance (of our possession of time), it unveils it as an untruth, and to that extent it takes our time away from us. Precisely as the time of grace that breaks upon us, it is the crisis that breaks into general time. This is where the offense of revelation arises. We are quite right to be shocked to death when revelation confronts us; for it is actually the end of our time . . . and it announces itself as immediately imminent . . . The fulfillment of time does not so far mean, of course, the completion, but it means only the announcement. The immediate imminence of the taking away of our time."

90. "So far as revelation is not yet redemption, not yet the breaking in, but (Mk. I) 15 only the "at-handness" of the Kingdom of God itself, our time is actually conserved. The fact that Christ has not yet come "in the glory of his Father" (Mt. 16), 27 the fact that God's new time is not yet the only time, that this very revelation involves in its self-restraint a delay, or holding up of the end of all things, means that a parallelism is maintained between fulfilled time and general time. Accordingly God's time is really the time God has for us, in the sense that by it our improper, fallen time--which is indeed our present time--is conserved, and continually make possible in all its exposed impossibility. To that extent we may say that the whole history of the world has happened in the way in which it actually did happen, not, that is, as the completed end of time and all things, but as the announcement of the end of all things in time itself. The grace and mercy of God, which become effective in that He has time for us, i.e., His, own time for us, answer to the long-suffering of God whereby He leaves us time, and our time at that, to adopt an attitude to this condescension, time, that is, to believe and repent. It is necessary to say that in this very relation between revelation and other history, between God's time and our time, rests the whole immense tension which revelation of necessity imports into every consciousness of history?" Ibid., I/2, p.68

91. Ibid., p. 232.

92. Ibid., p. 236.

93. Ibid., p. 233.

94. Soren Kierkegaard, *Philosophical Fragments*, translated by Howard V. Hong and Edna H. Hong (Princeton, N.J.: Princeton University Press, 1985), pp. 9-22.

95. Ibid., pp. 14-15.

96. Cf. John D. Morrison, "Christ, Faith, and the Problem of History in the Thought of Soren Kierkegaard," unpublished paper. For similar but for their own differently directed purpose, note the work of R.H. Roberts "Karl Barth's Doctrine of Time: It's Nature and Implications" in *Karl Barth: Studies of His Theological Methods* (Oxford: Clarendon Press, 1979), esp., 122-130 and John Thomson, *Christian Perspective: Christological Perspectives in the Theology of Karl Barth* (Grand Rapids: Wm. B.

Eerdmans Publishing Company, 1978), pp. 74-86, 98-99.

97. *CD*, I/2, pp.55 cf. I/2, pp.59, 61-62, 64-66, 111, 125, 166-168, 172-173,177, 204, 219, 223, 234, 269, 383, 359, 364, 375, 397-398, 408, 424, 463, 483, noting especially 499-501. On p. 499, Barth declares that the "knowledge of the priority of God as achieved in the Bible is the knowledge of the divine benefit, again--and here the circle closes--permitting and commanding us in the thought of Creator and creature to achieve calmly and clearly the unthinkable thought of the co-existence of absolute and relative, no, of the gracious God and of the men saved by His grace . . . . Again it is quite impossible that there should be a direct identity between the human word . . . and the Word of God, and therefore between the creaturely reality in itself and as such and the reality of God the Creator. It is impossible that there should have been a transmutation of the one into the other or an admixture of the one with the other. This is not the case even in the person of Christ where the identity between God and man, in all the originality and indissolubility in which it confront us, is an assumed identity, one specially willed, created and effected by God, and to that extent indirect, i.e., resting neither in the essence of God nor in that of man, but in a decision and act of God to man."

98. Richard R. Neibuhr, *Resurrection and Historical Reason: A Study of Theological Method* (New York: Charles Scribner's Sons, 1957), pp.84-85ff.

99. Dietrich Bonhöffer makes a reference to this problem or tendency in Barth's thought when he says of Barth, "Inevitably, exception must be taken from the first to the fact that the God--man relationship should be resolved in terms of pure act-subjects in the very content where revelation's transcendence of consciousness is unequivocally asserted. And the suspicion there from arising, that transcendentalism is lurking here somewhere, receives confirmation. God reveals Himself only in acts freely initiated by Himself." *Act and Being*, translated by Bernard Noble (New York: Harper & Row, Publishers, 1961), pp. 81-82.

100. Ibid., p. 82.

101. Niebuhr, p.84. Pointing to Barth's discussion of the resurrection within the larger question of revelation and history, Niebuhr states, "Karl Barth has said that in the resurrection event there is nothing our human faculties can touch. It is an essentially non-human event, yet in history, one cannot contest Barth's assertion that here grace more fully manifests itself than anywhere else, and the resurrection renders the final judgment on human boasting. But Barth has overlooked perhaps dimly seen but wrongly understood . . . the resurrection of Christ is an open historical event, one into which the disciples themselves were able to enter, and indeed one in which they were compelled to participate." Ibid., p.178-179.

102. Anthony C. Thiselton, *The Two Horizons: New Testament Hermeneutics and Philosophical Description with Special Reference to Heidegger, Bultmann, Gadamer and Wittgenstein* (Wm. B. Eerdmans Publishing Company: Grand Rapids, 1980), pp. 337,

354, 385, 443. Thiselton has much pertinent and related discussion to the question of Torrance's notion of Word and Word-Event in relation to history and the language of the prophetic-apostolic witness or Holy Scripture.

103. Torrance, *CTSC*, pp. 92-93.

104. Ibid., p. 104.

105. Torrance, *RST*, pp. 82-83, 87.

106. Ibid., pp. 87-91. *cf.* pp. 92-93, 95n., 123-127. A noteworthy similarity to Torrance's own theo-logical and epistemological emphases is to be found in Ian Ramsay. Ramsay too says that God is revealed via "disclosure models" which do not attempt to describe anything but are currency for a moment of insight. He parallels this to the disclosure models by which the universe reveals itself to humanity. In theology such models enable one to be reliably articulate when they arise in a moment of insight/disclosure and they are judged by their ability to incorporate the most diverse phenomena. But for all of the similarity with Torrance, Ramsay seems to understand that that which is "disclosed" is a nonconceptual, nondescriptive pointer to mystery. *cf.* *Models and Mystery*, p. 7, 12-17, 19-20, 60-71.

107. Dietrich Bonhöffer, *Act and Being* (London: Collins, 1962), pp. 81-82.

108. Paul Tillich, *Systematic Theology*, vol. I (Chicago: University of Chicago Press, 1951), pp. 239-240. Cf. Robert P. Scharlemann, *Reflection and Doubt in the Thought of Paul Tillich* (New Haven: Yale University Press, 1969), pp. 87, 97-99, 147-148, 155, 176-177. It is significant to note how effectively Tillich distinguishes between "originating revelation" and "dependent revelation." The first refers to a revelation occurring within a "constellation" which did not previously exist, i.e., "miracle" and "ecstacy." This revelatory event is consequently proclaimed, recorded and made the center of cult and sacrament, etc., i.e., "dependent revelation" as related and resulting expression whereby the revelatory event continues "horizontally" through time repetitively and in real participation in the originating disclosure. See *Systematic Theology*, I, pp. 126-128. Additionally, Tillich refers to the scriptures and particularly to the "New Testament picture of Jesus Christ" as mediating the original event in a way which seems to reflect participation in the whole of the disclosive process. See *Systematic Theology*, II, pp. 114-116. In these and other ways, Tillich's thought could form a useful direction enabling Torrance to heal the breach in the needed "field relation" in order to effect real knowledge of God.

109. Anderson, *Historical Transcendence*, pp. 213-214.

110. Ibid., p. 220.

111. John Calvin, *Institutes of the Christian Religion*, 2 vols., ed. by John T. McNeil, translated by Ford Lewis Battles (Philadelphia: The Westminster Press, 1960)., IV, vii, 2.

112. Ibid., IV, viii, 2-3.

113. Ibid., I, viii, 4.

114. Ibid., IV, viii, 6.

115. Ibid., IV, viii, 9.

116. Ibid.

117. Ibid., IV, viii, 10.

118. Ibid., IV, viii, 9.

119. Ibid., IV, viii, 11. Cf., IV, viii, 13, on the vital relation of the spirit and the Word in Calvin's thought, " . . . inasmuch as the church is governed by the Spirit of God, it can proceed safely without the "Word" (says "papist" dogma), but Calvin responds by saying that "If we grant . . . that the church cannot in matters necessary to salvation then here is what we mean by it: the statement is true insofar as the church, having forsaken all its own wisdom, allows itself to be taught by the Holy Spirit through God's Word. This, then, is the difference. Our opponents locate the authority of the church outside God's Word; but we insist that it be attached to the Word, and do not allow it to be separated from it." Cf., also IV, x, 14, and Ronald S. Wallace, *Calvin's Doctrine of Word and Sacrament* (Grand Rapids: Wm. B. Eerdmans Publishing Company, 1957), p. 100.

120. Ibid., IV, ii, 4.

121. Ibid.

122. Wallace, *Word and Sacrament*, p. 101.

123. John Calvin, *Commentaries on the Twelve Minor Prophets*, vol. IV, translated by John Owen (Grand Rapids: Wm. B. Eerdmans Publishing Company, 1950), p. 368. Cf., also John Calvin *Opera Selecta*, vol. 1, ed. by W. Niesel and P. Barth (Munich: 1926-1952), 1:465, cited in Bouwsma; cf., also John Calvin, *The Epistles of Paul the Apostle to the Galatians, Ephesians, Philippians and Colossians*, translated by T.H.L. Parker (Grand Rapids: Wm. B. Eerdmans Publishing Company, 1965), pp. 179-180; and Calvin Institutes, IV, x, 7, 9-22, 23, 26 and 30.

124. Calvin, *Institutes*, IV, xi, 1.

125. Ibid.

126. Ibid.

127. Ibid.

128. John Calvin, *Commentaries on the Prophet Ezekiel*, translated by Thomas Myers (Grand Rapids: Wm. B. Eerdmans Publishing Company, 1948), pp. 306-307.

129. Bouwsma, p. 50.

130. Ibid., pp. 220f.

131. Calvin, *Institutes*, IV, xi, 1.

132. Ibid., cf., Bouwsma, pp. 215, 218-219; *Institutes*, IV, vii, 21.

133. Ibid., IV, xi, 2.

134. Ibid., IV, xi, 8.

135. Cf., discussion in Parker, p. 58.

136. Ibid., cf. *Opera Selecta*, 1:235ff.

137. Ibid., p. 59.

138. Bouwsma, p. 44.

139. Note Calvin's exposition on the question and issue of the Incarnation as it relates to this question in his commentary on I John chapter one. Cf. Calvin's statement about Christ's person and purpose in *The Gospel According to John*, vol. II, translated by T.H.L. Parker (Grand Rapids: Wm. B. Eerdmans Publishing Company, 1959), p. 78. Cf. also John Calvin, *The Epistle of Paul the Apostle to the Hebrews and the First and Second Epistles of St. Peter*, translated by William B. Johnston (Grand Rapids: Wm. B. Eerdmans Publishing Company, 1963), p. 6; and *Institutes*, I, i, 1.

140. Calvin, *Institutes*, IV, viii, 1.

141. Ibid., IV, viii, 4.

142. Ibid.

143. Ibid., IV, viii, 7.

144. Ibid., IV, x, 2.

145. Ibid.

146. Ibid., IV, x, 7.

147. Note here Calvin's Christological and cosmological discussion stating to this larger issue in his commentary on Ephesians 1:20-23. Cf. also *Institutes*, IV, x, 14.

148. Ibid., IV, X, 17.

149. Ibid.

150. Ibid., IV, x, 23.

151. Ibid., IV, x, 32. Cf. Eberhard Jüngel's brief but helpful discussion regarding Calvin's point against Osiander that Christ, in all of his relatedness to us, is "the *event* of fellowship with Christ constituted by his *coming*." In his work, *God as the Mystery of the World: On the Foundation of the Theology of the Crucified One in the Dispute between Theism and Atheism*, translated by Darrell L. Guder (Grand Rapids: Wm. B. Eerdmans Publishing Company, 1983), p. 296.

152. Ibid., IV, xi, 1.

153. Ibid., IV, xi, 5.

154. Calvin, *Gospel of John*, vol. 1, p. 139.

155. Ibid., vol. 2, p. 53, cf. also *Institutes*, IV, xi, 8 and 14.

156. Wallace, *Word and Sacrament*, pp. 99-101. Cf. Ronald Wallace, *Calvin's Doctrine of the Christian Life* (Tyler, TX: Geneva Divinity School Press, reprint 1982), pp. 206-218.

157. John Calvin, *Commentary on the Book of the Prophet Isaiah*, vol. 1, translated by William Pringle (Grand Rapids, Wm. B. Eerdmans Publishing Company, 1958), pp. 381-382. It must be carefully noted that for Calvin the relationship between Word and Spirit is vital for a number of reasons, not least among which is stability in contrast to what Calvin perceives among the "Anabaptists." Cf. Calvin, *Institutes*, IV, viii, 13. See Timothy George's fine discussion of this aspect of Calvin's theology in his *Theology of the Reformers* (Nashville: Broadman Press, 1988), pp. 192-199.

158. Torrance, *KBET*, pp. 118-119.

159. Paul Ricoeur, *Essays on Biblical Interpretation*, ed. by Lewis Mudge (Philadelphia: Fortress Press, 1980), p. 80.

160. G. Ernest Wright, "Archeology, History and Theology," *Harvard Divinity Bulletin*, 28 (April, 1964) pp. 88-89f. Cf. G. Ernest Wright, *The Old Testament and Theology* (New York: Harper and Row Publishers, 1969), pp. 19, 21f., 49, against the Barthian understanding of history, interpretation and Scripture.

161. Abraham J. Heschel, *God in Search of Man* (London: Jason Aronson, Inc., 1987), pp. 200, 204, 239, and Arthur A. Cohen, *The Natural and Supernatural Jew: An Historical and Theological Introduction* (New York: Pantheon Books, 1963), pp. 301, 304.

162. George Lindbeck, *The Nature of Doctrine: Religion and Theology in a Postliberal Age* (Philadelphia: Westminster Press, 1984), pp. 33-36, 121-128. Lindbeck says helpfully that "the question raised in reference to Nicaea and Chalcedon is not how they can be interpreted in modern categories, but rather how contemporary Christians can do as well or better in maximizing the Jesus Christ of the biblical narratives as the way to the one God of whom the Bible speaks." Ibid., p. 107.

163. Torrance, *TRst*, p. 138.

164. Anderson, *Historical Transcendence*, p. 213-214. Cf. E. L. Mascall's criticism of Torrance's lack of use of Scripture or perception of its relation to and connection to Church tradition, E.L. Mascall, *Theology and the Gospel of Christ* (London: SPCK, 1977), p. 47. Here Mascall says, " . . . he has a less than adequate discussion of the nature of Scripture and its relation to Church tradition." Here too, contra Torrance and Barth, Pannenberg is correct in saying that revelation of God in Christ and the apostolic message belong together for only thereby does reconciliation reach its goal. Cf. David Ford's important discussion in *Barth and God's Story: Biblical Narrative and Theological Method of Karl Barth* (Bern: Peter Lang, 1981), 165-185, and Robert W. Jenson, *Alpha and Omega: A Study in the Theology of Karl Barth* (New York: Thomas Nelson, 1963), pp. 162ff., as they discuss the Barthian tendency toward a *Bildungsroman* Christ.

165. Ibid. Cf. James Barr's many criticisms of Torrance's misuse and loss of the Scripture principle in his fine work *The Semantics of Biblical Language* (Oxford: Oxford University Press, 1961). Cf. Wolfhart Pannenberg's important discussion on the role of historical and theological interpretive processes in relation to the Word in Jesus Christ within the whole complex of the revelation of God within the space-time domain, *Systematic Theology*, translated by Geoffrey W. Bromiley, (Grand Rapids: Wm. B. Eerdmans Publishing Company, 1991), pp. 194-257. Within Pannenberg's analysis of the Barthian understanding of the Word of God as revelation and revelation as the revelation of God himself, he brings careful criticism to the "thin" and even unbiblical Barthian position which overlooks the fact that in Scripture God himself is rarely the content of his revelation.

166. *CD* I/1, p. 321; I/2, pp. 802, 816, 862ff.

167. Hans Frei, *The Eclipse of Biblical Narrative* (New Haven: Yale University Press, 1974), p. 58.

168. Ibid., p. viii.

169. Hans Frei, "The Literal Reading of Biblical Narrative in the Christian Tradition: Does it Stretch or Will it Break?" in Frank McConnel, ed., *The Bible and Narrative Tradition* (Oxford: Oxford University Press, 1986), p. 62. *cf.* Paul Ricoeur, *The Conflict of Interpretation: Essays in Hermeneutics* (Evanston: Northwestern University Press, 1974), p. 290; and Thiemann, *Revelation,* pp. 2, 4, 31, 72, 109.

170. Thiemann, pp. 95-96. Cf. p. 85.

171. Frei, *Eclipse*, p. 2.

172. Personal Interview with Thomas F. Torrance, January, 1989.

173. Emil Brunner, *Revelation and Reason*, translated by Olive Wyon (Philadelphia: Westminster Press, 1946), p. 122, note 9. Cf. David Kelsey, *The Uses of Scripture in Recent Theology* (Philadelphia: Fortress Press, 1975), p. 1f., and Carl Braaten, *History and Hermeneutics* (Philadelphia: Westminster Press, 1966), p. 25, and Nicholas Woltersdorff, "How God Speaks," *Reformed Journal* (September 1969), pp. 17f., and "On God Speaking," *Reformed Journal* (1971), pp. 8ff.

Chapter 8

Conclusion

Torrance's Task: Overcoming Theological Dualism
By Restored Theo-logical Science
Grounded In The Trinity

The body of the preceding discussion has presented Thomas Forsyth Torrance as one who writes and works out of an active concern to deal correctively with what he perceives to be the injurious "dualist" disintegration of thought and culture, particularly as it has obscured the objective knowlhdge of God in Christ. He beliepes such problems are rooted in the modern re-entrenchment of "disjunctive," or "dualist" thinking arising from such influential thinkers as René Descartes, Immanuel Kant (epistemology), and Isaac Newton (cosmology). The consequent loss of the "classical attitude of mind," with its emphases upon objectivity (versus objectivism), critical realism, emphasis on relation and thus dynamic/kinetic thinking in submission to the disclosure of the being of the proper object, i.e., to know it as it is, has led "theologically" to the "eclipse" or obscuring of the Truth of God by the intrusion of the human subject (e.g., Schleiermacher, Bultmann). As a result, true theo-logical science out of the objectively given Word of God out of God in Jesus Christ is reckoned by Torrance to have "retreated" into the obscurantism of subjectivism and existentialism, having dualistically lost sight of its proper Object, God's self-disclosure in Jesus Christ.

The problem with what Torrance refers to as "dualism," or "disjunctive thinking," is that one way or another it is falsely assumed that what was thought to be interactively related is actually understood to be disjoined, creating inaccessibility and the necessity of some formulation of "truth" that arises not out of the inherent order, harmony and intelligibility of the proper object but out of the knowing subject, and then this is objectivistically "foisted" or "projected" upon the object. Descartes is said to have disjoined subject from object, Newton disjoined God as the inertial "container" and absolute time and space from relative time and space and all that occurs therein. Kant is said to have disjoined the phenomenal from the noumenal (as unknowable by "pure reason") and transferred Newton's inertial absolute from the mind of God (*divinum sensorium*) to the mind of the subject by his *a priori* categories of the mind. As such thinking began to increasingly influence theology, it too lost sight of its proper Object, believing God to be "deistically" separated from the world and that knowledge of God as he is in himself is not possible. Therefore theology turned inward to the subject's feelings of dependence or its existential alienation from itself and need for "decision" and "authenticity." Such "dualism" is understood to have led to the desperate intrusion of the human subject in place of the object, thus cutting off, or eclipsing, the redemptive knowledge of God.

Therefore, like those who are historically paradigmatic for Torrance, i.e., the Nicene Fathers and St. Athanasius against "Greek dualism," and Calvin (and the Reformers) against "medieval dualism," he wants to restore theology to needed, rigorous scientific thinking after its own Object, the self-revelation of God in Jesus Christ. From a basis in God's actual interaction with the world or the totality of reality (cosmos) in "creation out of nothing," providence, and especially incarnation-redemption, Torrance is endeavoring to reestablish the bases for real theo-logical thinking and speaking/expression which has God as its true basis and God as its true reference. Indeed, God is the only truth of theology, even as all scientific truth lies not in thought or statement but in the object to which each must faithfully and obediently refer. Torrance is at work then re-building the "meta-scientific" bases for scientific theology in theological objectivity, theological realism, unitary thinking out of God's actual, factual, historical relation to the world and to humanity in the world in Jesus Christ, in whom God effects redemptive transformation (cf. Torrance's emphasis on the "triadic relation" "God-world-man" and/or "God-man-world").

My discussion has also unfolded and explained the formative, epistemological and methodological significance of the "modern revolution" in the physical sciences, especially physics, for Torrance's own theological science. From within Torrance's own Scottish realist and Reformed way of thinking about reality, the actuality of real, objective knowledge, and the contingency of the world, J. Clerk Maxwell is found to be a physicist whose work forced the breakthrough out of "static" modes of thought in order to develop faithful, dynamic or kinetic ways of thinking after the actual nature of objective reality without clamping "alien" frameworks upon it. Because of his "ultimate beliefs" (foundations) in the contingent reality and graspability of the world external to the knower and in the objective reality of truth, all in relation to God the Creator, Maxwell began to apprehend the crucial role of relations (onto-relations) in the process of coming to the truth of being with regard to any particular object. The object's relations are constitutive to what it is. By means of Maxwell's work, especially "field theory," Torrance has explained how Albert Einstein was enabled to develop the special and general theories of relativity, and also to open understanding to the unexpected nature of reality in quantum theory. Against Kant and all who would deny knowledge of the *Ding an sich*, Einstein found that the world discloses itself and is knowable out of itself if one would inquire properly and follow what it "speaks" of itself. Einstein too is found to work with ultimate beliefs about the intelligibility of the external world and truth, and his subsequent discoveries of such led him to "awe" and "wonder" at the "mysterious" rationality inherent in the contingent, finite but unbounded universe. Thus he spoke of the "religious" nature of such realizations and of an ultimate Rationality or "God" upon which such must depend. Einstein's general and special theories of relativity are said by Torrance to be prime exemplars of the truly scientific "disclosure model" or theory which arises out of believing, faithful, and obedient response "level by level" to the proper object. Such a "faithful" or "obedient" disclosure model then serves the object's ongoing disclosure for further penetration and refinement by being made "transparent" media for such. Einstein is also held to be responsible for overturning Newton's cosmological dualism by emphasizing that the finite universe is unbounded and open up to the ultimate Rationality upon which it depends. Torrance's own meta-theological formulations, and especially his Christocentric-Trinitarian formulation, is itself meant to be such a scientific theo-logical disclosure model (cf. chapter five). But Einstein's thought is said to have lacked real understanding of the crucial role of persons, or the personal, in all real knowing. He remained trapped in "impersonal" modes of thought. Torrance was then found to point to Michael Polanyi as the scientist-philosopher who essentially completed the modern restoration to the "classical attitude of mind," to objectivity and realist epistemology by clarifying further the role of belief and by uncovering the necessary role of persons as persons in the knowing, subject-object, relation. In all true knowing it is persons who know. The role of the personal or the person in the knowing relation is heightened when persons are the object of inquiry and understood as such. But this is said to be dramatically heightened before the self-disclosure of God who, in our scientific theological inquiry, is said to bring about an epistemological reversal by "questioning us down to the roots of our being." The restoration of such emphases is said by Torrance to have restored and clarified the true nature of knowledge and the knowing relation as truly objective, realist and unitary, and to have re-opened the necessary relation, the "complementarity," between theological science and the physical sciences.

As a result of the modern "revolution" or "restoration" of the "classical attitude of mind" in epistemology and cosmology, Torrance has been shown to be ready to use and to interpret such objectivity, realism and rigorous scientific methodology as "prescribed" by the proper object, i.e., *a posteriori* ("mode of rationality") by the proper object. This is applied *mutatis mutandis* to the theological task. Out of the triadic "God-world-man" relation established by God by creation and incarnation-redemption, theology as science also works with ultimate beliefs. To Torrance belief in God is finally basic to all real rationality. But with Maxwell, et al., belief in God as Creator and Redeemer relates directly to belief in the inherent and unified rationality, knowability and contingency of the world, which, while knowable out of itself, is not self-explanatory and points beyond itself to the Creator, the uncreated Rationality of God. But then God's active, dynamic, lordly, sovereign, interactive relatedness for, to and in the world, which by creation and redemption is "open up" to God, is basic and central to Torrance's entire theo-logical understanding and expression. Torrance finds then that the restoration to true scientific thinking out of the thing itself is of great help to the process of restoring theology from its modern subjectivism and retreat into existentialism and irrationalism, calling it to "repentant" thinking out of itself and toward its own proper Object, the Word made flesh, the self-revelation of God in Christ (cf. "the epistemological implications of justification by Grace)." As the "new" physics has shown the need for epistemology to follow ontology (*a posteriori* from the actuality of knowledge). This means that human inquiry is called to know the object out of itself, and thus that there is no singular "scientific method" which is "forced" upon all objects of inquiry. But then all truly scientific knowing or discovery is common only in needing to submit/assent to the truth of the proper object as it "impresses" itself on thought. Likewise theological science must submit to the Truth of the Supreme Being of God in his Word. It must know God out of the real relations he has established with the world and with existing human beings, the "field" grounded in divine creation and above all in Jesus Christ. This is why Torrance has been shown here to regard the Nicene *homoousion* doctrine to be a first order theological truth and "disclosure model." It is said to express the fact that "God is toward us in Jesus Christ as he is in himself from all eternity." He believes this to be the central truth of the gospel message, central to the knowledge of the truth of God, and to the reality of redemption. Thus in and from Jesus Christ one can know God truly and in "realist" terms (though finitely). From that necessarily historical place of objective disclosure, from that one in whom God has objectified himself to be known, a person can move from the initial "tacit" knowledge of God in Christ, "level by level up," following the logic of Grace, the economy of God's self-giving to be known, to the very Being of God. Thus the restoration of realist science, onto-relations, the rediscovery of contingency, the stratification (levels) of truth, the intrinsic rationality and intelligibility of the proper object/Object, and thus the recognition of "correspondence" (or "correlation") of thought to the inherent "coherence" in the proper object and the real referential (signitive) relation of language (as "transparent") to being are found to be and are expressed as being of critical importance to Torrance's own scientific theological task out from the concrete "level" of divine disclosure in the incarnate Word of God. All that we have shown of Torrance's "meta-scientific" or "meta-theological" formulations and conclusions, as both "clearing the way" of dualist, disjunctive assumptions and in healing and restoring the setting, the "classical attitude of mind," in which theology as science is to be done, has been to uncover the way whereby Torrance believes he can give positive theological expression to his Christocentric-Trinitarian "disclosure model."

The basis, the center and the goal of Torrance's theo-logical science has been shown to be his understanding of the redemptive knowledge of God out of God. This is objective, realist knowledge of God as he is in himself in the way God has given himself to be known in space-time, in and through and in relation to the created intelligibilities of the world by existing human beings. In "theologically" following out the epistemological, cosmological and methodological implications which Torrance has found in post-Einsteinian physics, our discussion then traced out and laid open his unitary, interrelated process of scientific theological thinking after the objective self-giving of God, level by level "up," from the concrete, historical disclosure and presencing of God (Torrance's emphasis upon the absolute criticality of the Incarnation of the Word of God, Jesus) "up" to the economic level of God's self-objectification to and for the world and humanity *ad extra*, and completed the process at the final or "ontological" level of God's own "Supreme Being" *ad intra*. Herein I unfolded and examined more fully, and at last explicitly, the nature, meaning and epistemologico-theological implications of Torrance's Christocentricity. In Jesus Christ, in the human being Jesus of Nazareth, Torrance follows his mentor Karl Barth in emphasizing first and ever that Jesus is the place, the "scandalously" particular place, of God's objective manifestness in the world. The Word, which is of the very Being of God, "Light of Light," "true God of true God," became flesh, truly human and historical, in order to fully and finally reveal God in himself and to effect the reconciling and redemptive knowledge of God, the transformation of human beings, and the creation as well, from the "inside out." By the incarnation, the Truth, Reality and uncreated Rationality of God's own transcendent Being is "objectified," it is "the given" to be known, and thereby our humanity is said to be "bent back" in real obedience to God. He is the Truth of God to us, and he is also the obedient, worshiping human being unto God--the Mediator.

It is then from Christ, but ever in Christ (for Torrance often emphasizes that the incarnation is never left behind in the knowledge of God), the "concrete level," from which "theological science must begin as it "assents" to the "impress" of the Truth of God in the way it has historically taken. From within the matrix of the penetrating Word the triadic (and "asymmetrical") God-world-human relation is grounded and thus to be known and thought after "unitarily" in covenanted (not necessary) correspondence to the freely given Truth of God. It is at this crucial juncture, as Torrance thinks with and from Christ to the "economic level," that the "epistemological relevance" of the Holy Spirit is said to play such a crucial role. By the Spirit, the limited human range and capacity is "lifted up" or "expanded" to be able to grasp truly, though finitely, the Truth of God which "outruns all forms of our understanding." The creative work of the Spirit is said to open the mind, taking it beyond all creaturely limits until it is made "appropriate" to the divine object. Thus Torrance maintains that the Spirit actualizes the self-giving of God in Christ by enabling human beings to receive and apprehend the self-knowledge of God as in-fleshed in Christ. Given the economy of God's self-revelation in the world and the fact that "God is Spirit," there is no knowledge of God apart from the Spirit. Thus by the Spirit the human knower is given and is enabled to receive God as self-objectified in Christ. Torrance consistently emphasizes that this occurs by "faith" as the "appropriate mode of knowing" before the revelation of God in Christ.

This knowing relation, this faith-knowing, intuitive apprehension or believing as "tacit," or "non-formal" knowing, is said to be initially an "encounter," a Word-event occurring in the "moment." Torrance formulates his understanding of the dynamism of this "meeting" after the thought of Soren Kierkegaard's understanding of "contemporaneity" and "trans-historical" relation of the believer to original revelation, and also within the Barthian tradition. In the Word-event or encounter in the "moment," and by the enablement of the Spirit, the human knower (or particularly the "scientific theologian") continuously submits thinking to the Truth of God, God himself, as self-given from the Father, through the Son and in the Spirit, in the "mystical" apprehension of the Truth and in repentant "unknowing" through the Son and by the Spirit to the Father, and thus to the ontological Trinity. Torrance refers to the Trinity as "the ground and grammar of theology," and the doctrine of the Trinity to simply be *theologia*. Indeed he esteems the Trinity the basis of all truth, rationality, knowledge. As the physical sciences seek the truth of being, theological science thinks after the Truth of God, the way taken by God for us in Christ and by the Spirit, into the Truth of and the relations within the Supreme Being of God. This is Torrance's *telos*, the goal and end, the knowledge of God as he is in himself and in his own "perichoretic" relations within himself as Father, Son and Holy Spirit from all eternity. Hence, we see again the epistemological and methodological centrality of the Nicene *homoousion* ("the epistemological linchpin" of all theology) for all of Torrance's Christocentric-Trinitarian theology, i.e., that God is toward us in Jesus Christ as he is in himself from all eternity.

Torrance Against Himself: The Kierkegaardian-Barthian Disjunction at the Heart of Torrance's Theology

Our critical examination has presented, then, Thomas Torrance's understanding and formulation of a unitary theology, realist knowledge of God out of God in and from Jesus Christ, the "way God has taken" in the world. His emphasis in restoring true, theo-logical science has consistently been that God is not "cut off" or deistically disjoined from the world and from direct and real knowability as he is (i.e., "dualism"), but within the "field" of relations rooted in divine creation (*creatio ex nihilo*) and in incarnation-redemption preeminently, that God is directly and immediately knowable in Jesus Christ "through" the space-time, created intelligibilities of this world, the bearers of rationality in the world. These, as "media" of God's truth and within such, are "transparent" to the objective Word of God's own being, the Word made flesh. It is also for this reason, given the actual space-time coordinates of creation and redemption, that theological science can never subjectivistically retreat from the natural sciences.   Each of the sciences works within the same contingent intelligibilities of the world and must be faithful to the differing "modes of rationality" arising from the differences in the being or nature of the proper objects which each seeks to know, yet they all represent one basic way of knowing. The "asymmetrical," "triadic," interactive God-world-human relation, known and epistemologically centered emphatically in Jesus Christ, is considered the only proper way of engaging in thought and expression as truly appropriate to theology's proper Object who ever remains lordly Subject over all human knowing of him.

Because of this Christocentric-Trinitarian pattern, as "prescribed" by the "Being and Act" of God in Jesus Christ, as Torrance's own scientific theo-logical agenda, certain requirements arise for Torrance if his theology is to be complete or if it is to be all that Torrance clearly intends. Here the Nicene *homoousion* is, again, so important to Torrance as it is understood to unfold the basis of realist knowledge of God in Christ and how theology as truly that can be faithful to the nature of God's redemptive movement, not clamping down an "alien" formulation which would only obscure knowledge of God. Thus it is necessary that God be known out of God as God has given himself to be known in the only place and way in which human beings could apprehend such disclosure. God then must objectify himself, give himself to be known, though, as Torrance ever emphasizes in order to distinguish God from mere determinate objects over which humanity often seeks "technological" control, God is known objectively as that above mentioned lordly, transcendent Subject who, in being known, enacts the "epistemological reversal" (or "inversion"). But it is also necessary for Torrance's theo-logical science that God's objective self-disclosure, God's Word as consubstantial with God, be truly historical. There can be no indirectness here, no remaining aloofness, no "transcendentalizing," for the Word must be truly flesh. The Word must not merely come to but must partake and participate in the world and in the human as human (without ceasing to be God). There can be no (as Torrance accuses Adolf Harnack) "liberal fear of physicality" in the last analysis. Indeed the Word of God and out of God, who is by nature "eloquent" Being, must come as human word, not merely as lightning through word, but Word as word. Word of God, while not ceasing to remain *homoousios to patri*, must truly partake of the historical in the full trinitarian and economic way of God if redemption, in Torrance's own terms, and the person of Christ himself, is not to be finally lost or "arianized" by a latent dualism. This is absolutely necessary for Torrance's theo-logical purpose.

Our critical analysis then pointed out that in the question of the Word's real historicity, the eternal *Logos* of God as truly participator or partaker of the historical and human, of the Word's manifestness as human word, Torrance's thorough rooting in the Kierkegaardian-Barthian "transcendentalizing" of the Word has left him with "disjunctive" thinking of his own which de-historicizes the Word of Grace. Torrance consistently maintains the principle, in whatever the context, of maintaining the divine difference to the extent that what is creaturely, contingent and human cannot be God's self-presencing but only that "instrument" through which the divine "encounters" the human. God has not partaken of the space-time existence wherein human beings know the pain and death of estrangement. Torrance's desire for a "duality" or "asymmetrical God-world relatedness" has been shown to actually be dualistic. Torrance seems clearly to want such completion but the philosophico-theological principles with which he works negates his purposes in the end. As with his modern mentors, Kierkegaard and Barth, the Word of God to the existing human, the "god in time," comes to one only indirectly, only as the wholly other and the different as such. Like lightning it comes to the individual, encountering one in the trans-historical "moment," in its own "time," the time of redemption. Therein one is made partaker of that "time of revelation" by being made "contemporaneous" with the Word who cannot be true partaker of our time. In the "moment" the person is brought to "mystical," non-discursive, yet somehow cognitive and conceptual encounter on the higher "level" of the divine as the Word "jumps" the gulf without participating in the creaturely while negating all historical distinction. The individual is "lifted" by the Spirit to the place of knowledge and relation. While Kierkegaard's "theo-logic" as "dynamic" or "kinetic" and not static has opened possibilities for Torrance's Barthian theological concerns against what he understands to be the lineage of "theological dualism," Torrance's own latent dualism has not allowed him to fulfill his intent, i.e., restoring the realist knowledge of God as he is in himself as self-disclosed in Jesus Christ and by the Spirit. Revelation remains totally contingent to humanity as an Act of God, having no ontological existence itself, and thus God seems to finally be removed from the sphere of the historical into non-objectivity for us.

For Torrance's own theo-logical purpose in Christ and as ultimately grounded in the ontological Trinity, God's revelation must be both transcendent and historical (i.e., truly mediated, covenantal). Given his own rooting within the heritage of Reformed theology one possible and appropriate way of completion or terminus for Torrance is found to be reflected in the thought and method of John Calvin, and to an extent in aspects of Barth. We have described the necessity for Torrance to theologically reflect real divine historicity. Indeed this is true in its "once-for-all" aspect and ongoingly in the continuing "field" of human redemption by the Spirit. It must become central to Torrance's thinking regarding the "logic of Grace" or the "logic of the incarnation," as the kenotic movement of God in Christ, that the transcendence of God, the Godness of God is most fully revealed as manifested in and as the not-God, especially and most poignantly when the eternal Son, *homoousion* with the Father, was under the judgment of the Cross. In the kenotic movement of Grace in Jesus Christ the word of man *was* the Word of God. This is the rationale which must be allowed to expose the rationale of the historical, prophetic-apostolic scriptures. While Torrance wants to separate the authority of scripture from its historicity and creatureliness, again reflecting the same problematic principle, only the opposite role would effect for Torrance that which he requires for his own theological fulfillment. Divine transcendence is revealed as such in its very historicity and humanness. Thus, for Torrance's own goal within the Reformed (and Patristic) tradition after Calvin, the historical scriptures ought to be in some real sense an aspect of God's participatory self-revelation and the fully historical pole of God's transcendence in the divine presencing economically by the Holy Spirit. It is in this way that Torrance can overcome his latent "dualism" in a way which will complete his purposes while being consistent with them. As a result we have proposed a Hebraic threefold model, i.e., Being-Act-interpretation, interpretation-Act-Being, as more effective in completing Torrance's own emphasis on the knowledge of God out of God's own economic trinitarian movement for us than his twofold Being-Act, Act-Being form.

Such conclusions led to examination of corrective possibilities for Torrance's theology, in the logic of the incarnation, to be found in the recent insights on the theological role of the text of scripture, e.g., in Paul Ricoeur and especially, because of his Reformed and Barthian relation to Torrance, the insights of Hans Frei, though these are not without difficulties of their own.

BIBLIOGRAPHY

Books by Thomas F. Torrance

Torrance, Thomas F. ed. *Belief in Science and in Christian Life: The Relevance of Michael Polanyi's Thought for Christian Faith and Life*. Edinburgh: The Handsel Press, 1980.

_____. *Calvin's Doctrine of Man*. London: Lutterworth, 1949.

_____. *The Christian Frame of Mind*. 2nd ed. Colorado Springs: Helmers and Howard, 1989.

_____. *Christian Theology and Scientific Culture*. Oxford: Oxford University Press, 1980.

_____. *Divine and Contingent Order*. Oxford: Oxford University Press, 1981.

_____. *The Doctrine of Grace in the Apostolic Fathers*. Grand Rapids: Wm. B. Eerdmans Publishing Co., 1958.

_____. *God and Rationality*. Oxford: Oxford University Press, 1971.

_____. *The Ground and Grammar of Theology*. Charlottesville, VA.: The University Press of Virginia, 1981.

_____. *The Hermeneutics of John Calvin*. Edinburgh: Scottish Academic Press, 1988.

_____. *Karl Barth: Biblical and Evangelical Theologian*. Edinburgh: T. and T. Clark, 1990.

_____. *Karl Barth: An Introduction to His Early Theology*, 1910-1931. London: SCM Press, Ltd., 1962.

_____. *Kingdom and Church: A Study in the Theology of the Reformation*. London: Oliver and Boyd, 1956.

_____. *The Mediator*. Grand Rapids: Wm. B. Eerdmans Publishing Co., 1975.

_____. *Reality and Evangelical Theology*. Philadelphia: Westminster Publishing Co., 1982.

_____. *Reality and Scientific Theology*. Edinburgh: Scottish Academic Press, 1981.

_____. *The School of Faith: The Catechisms of the Reformed Church*. London: James Clark and Co., Ltd., 1959.

_____. *Space, Time and Incarnation*. Oxford: Oxford University Press, 1969.

_____. *Space, Time and Resurrection*. Grand Rapids: Wm. B. Eerdmans Publishing Company, 1976.

_____. *Theology in Reconciliation: Essays Towards Evangelical and Catholic Unity in East and West*. Grand Rapids: Wm. B. Eerdmans Publishing Company, 1975.

_____. *Theology in Reconstruction*. Grand Rapids: Wm. B. Eerdmans Publishing Company, 1965.

_____. *Theological Science*. Oxford: Oxford University Press, 1969.

_____. *Transformation and Convergence in the Frame of Knowledge*. Grand Rapids: Wm. B. Eerdmans Publishing Company, 1984.

_____. *The Trinitarian Faith: The Evangelical Theology of the Ancient Catholic Church*. Edinburgh: T. and T. Clark, 1988.

Articles by Thomas F. Torrance

_____. "The Deposit of the Faith," *Scottish Journal of Theology.* 36 (1983) 1-28.

_____. "The Doctrine of the Holy Trinity according to St. Athanasius." *Angelican Theological Review.* LXXI: 4, 395-405.

_____. "Hermeneutics According to F. D. E. Schleiermacher," *Scottish Journal of Theology.* 21 (1968) 257-67.

_____. "Justification: Its Radical Nature and Place in Reformed Doctrine and Life," *Scottish Journal of Theology.* 22 (1969) 225-46.

_____. "Karl Barth," *Scottish Journal of Theology.* 22 (1969) 1-9.

_____. "Karl Barth and the Latin Heresy," *Scottish Journal of Theology.* 39 (1986) 461-82.

_____. "Karl Barth and Patristic Theology," *Theology Beyond Christendom: Essays on the Centenary of the Birth of Karl Barth* May 10, 1886, ed. John Thompson. Allison Park, PA.: Pickwick Press, 1986.

_____. "My Interaction with Karl Barth," *How Karl Barth Changed My Mind.* Grand Rapids: Wm. B. Eerdmans Publishing Company, 1986.

_____. "The Place of Christology in Biblical and Dogmatic Theology," *Essays in Christology for Karl Barth*, ed. T. H. L. Parker. London: Lutterworth Press, 1956, 11-37.

_____. "The Place of Word and Truth in Theological Inquiry According to St. Anselm," *Studia Medievalia et Mariologica, P. Carolo Balic OFM Septvagesium Explendi Annum Dicta*, ed. P. Zavalloni. Rome:" Antonianum, 1971, 131-60.

_____. "Scientific Hermeneutics According to St. Thomas Aquinas," *Journal of Theological Studies.* 13 (1962) 259-89.

_____. "Theological Realism," *The Philosophical Frontiers of Christian Theology*: Essays Presented to D. M. MacKinnon. Cambridge: Cambridge University Press, 1982, 169-96.

_____. "Toward Ecumenical Consensus on the Trinity," *Theologische Zeitschrift*. 31 (1975) 337-50.

_____. Ultimate Beliefs and the Scientific Revolution," *Cross Currents*. Summer (1980) 129-149.

Other Books

Anselm. *Monologion*. Trans. J. Hopkins and H. Richardson. New York: Mellen, 1975.

_____. *Proslogion*. Trans. M. J. Charlesworth. Notre Dame: Notre Dame University Press, 1979.

Anderson, Ray S. *Historical Transcendence and the Reality of God: A Christological Critique*. Grand Rapids: Wm. B. Eerdmans, 1975.

Athanasius. *Contra Gentes* and *De Incarnatione*. Trans. Robert W. Thomson. Oxford: Clarendon Press, 1971.

Augustine. "On the Trinity." *Augustine: Later Works*. Ed. by John Burnaby. Philadelphia: The Westminster Press, 1965.

Avis, Paul D. L. *The Church in the Theology of the Reformers*. Atlanta: John Knox Press, 1981.

Baillie, John. *Our Knowledge of God*. London: Oxford University Press, 1939.

Balthasar, Hans Urs von. *The Theology of Karl Barth*. Translated by John Drury. New York: Holt, Rinehart and Winston, 1971.

Barth, Karl. Anselm: *Fides Quaerens Intellectum: Anselm's Proof of the Existence of God in the Context of His Theological Scheme*. Translated by Ian W. Robertson. London: SCM Press, Ltd. 1960.

_____. *Church Dogmatics*, I/1. *The Doctrine of the Word of God*. Translated by Geoffrey W. Bromiley. Edinburgh: T. and T. Clark, 1963.

_____. *Church Dogmatics*, I/2. *Doctrine of the Word of God*. Translated by G. T. Thomson and Harold Knight. Edinburgh: T. and T. Clark, 1956.

_____. *Church Dogmatics*, II/1. *The Doctrine of God*. Translated by T. H. L. Parker, W. B. Johnston, Harold Knight, J. L. M. Haire. Edinburgh: T. and T. Clark, 1957.

_____. *Church Dogmatics*, II/2. *The Doctrine of God*. Translated by Geoffrey W. Bromiley, J. C. Campbell, Iain Wilson, J. Strathearn McNab, Harold Knight, R. A. Stewart. Edinburgh: T. and T. Clark, 1957.

_____. *Church Dogmatics*, III/2. *The Doctrine of Creation*. Translated by Harold Knight, Geoffrey W. Bromiley, J. K. S. Reid, R. H. Fuller. Edinburgh: T. and T. Clark, 1960.

_____. *The Epistle to the Romans*. Translated by Edwyn C. Hoskyns. Oxford: Oxford University Press, 1968.

_____. *The Word of God and the Word of Man*. Translated by Douglas Horton. Grand Rapids: Zondervan Publishing House, 1935.

Bauman, Michael. Roundtable Talks: *Conversations with European Theologians*. Grand Rapids: Baker Book House, 1991.

Bonhoeffer, Dietrich. *Christology*. Trans. John Bowden. London: Collins Publishing, 1971.

_____. *Creation and Fall*. London: SCM Press, 1959.

Bouwsma, William J. *John Calvin: A Sixteenth Century Portrait*. New York: Oxford University Press, 1988.

Braaten, Carl. *History and Hermeneutics*. Philadelphia: Westminster Press, 1966.

Brunner, Emil. *Revelation and Reason*. Translated by Olive Wyon. Philadelphia: The Westminster Press, 1946.

_____. *Truth as Encounter*. Translated by Amandus W. Loos and David Cairns. Philadelphia: Westminster Press, 1964.

Buber, Martin. *Eclipse of God*. New York: Harper and Row, (1952) 1957.

_____. *I and Thou*. Translated by Walter Kaufmann. Edinburgh: T. and T. Clark, 1970.

Bultmann, Rudolf. *Jesus Christ and Mythology*. New York: MacMillan Publishing Company, 1966.

_____. *Theology of the New Testament*. 2 vols. Trans. Kendrick Grobel. New York: Charles Scribner's Sons, 1955.

Calvin, John. *Commentary on the Gospel According to John*. Calvin's Commentaries translated by William Pringle. Grand Rapids: Wm. B. Eerdmans Publishing Company, 1956.

_____. *Epistle to the Hebrews*. Calvin's Commentaries translated by John Owen. Grand Rapids: Wm. B. Eerdmans Publishing Company, 1949.

_____. *The Epistles of Paul the Apostle to the Romans and to the Thessalonians*. Calvin's Commentaries translated by Ross Mackenzie. Grand Rapids: Wm. B. Eerdmans Publishing Company, 1973.

_____. *The Epistles of Timothy, Titus and Philemon*. Calvin's Commentaries translated by William Pringle. Grand Rapids: Wm. B. Eerdmans Publishing Company, 1948.

_____. *The Institutes of the Christian Religion*. 2 vols. Edited by John T. McNeil and translated by Ford Lewis Battles. Philadelphia: The Westminster Press, 1960.

_____. *Selected Words of John Calvin*. 2 vols. Edited by Henry Beveridge and Jules Bonnet. Grand Rapids: Baker Book House, 1844. Reprinted 1983.

Carnell, Edward John. *The Burden of Soren Kierkegaard*. Grand Rapids: Wm. B. Eerdmans Publishing Company, 1965.

Clayton, Philip. *Explanation from Physics to Theology: An Essay in Rationality and Religion*. New Haven: Yale University Press, 1989.

Cobb, John B. *A Christian Natural Theology: Based on the Thought of Alfred North Whitehead*. Philadelphia: The Westminster Press, 1965.

Collins, James. *The Mind of Kierkegaard*. London: Secker and Warburg, 1954.

Cullman, Oscar. *Christ and Time*. Translated by Floyd V. Filson. Philadelphia: The Westminster Press, 1963.

Davies, Paul. *God and the New Physics*. London: Dent Publishing, Ltd., 1983.

Dicenso, James J. *Hermeneutico and the Disclosure of Truth: A Study in the Work of Heidegger, Gadamer and Riceour*. Charlottesville: University Press of Virginia, 1990.

Dowey, Edward A. *The Knowledge of God in Calvin's Theology*. New York: Columbia University Press, 1952.

Einstein, Albert. *Out of My Later Years*. New York: Philosophical Library, 1950.

_____. *The World as I See It*. New York: Covici Publishing Company, 1934.

_____. *Relativity: The Special and the General Theory*. Translated by Robert W. Lawson. New York: Crown Publishers, 1956.

Evans, C. Stephen. *Existentialism: The Philosophy of Despair and the Quest for Hope*. Grand Rapids: Zondervan Publishing House, 1984.

_____. *Kierkegaard's Fragments and Postscript: The Religious Philosophy of Johannes Climacus*. Atlantic Highlands, N.J.: Humanities Press, 1983.

_____. *Subjectivity and Religious Belief: An Historical, Critical Study*. Washington, D.C.: University Press of America, 1982.

Ferreira, M. Jamie. *Skepticism and Reasonable Doubt: The British Naturalist Tradition in Wilkins, Hume, Reid, and Newman*. Oxford: Oxford University Press.

_____. *Transforming Vision*. Oxford: Oxford University Press, 1991.

Feuerbach, Ludwig. *The Essence of Christianity*. New York: Harper and Row, Publishers, 1958.

Florovsky, Georges. *Creation and Redemption.* Belmont, MA: Nordland Press, 1976.

Ford, David. *Barth and God's Story: Biblical Narrative and the Theological Method of Karl Barth in the "Church Dogmatics".* Frankfurt: Peter Lang, 1981.

Forstman, H. Jackson. *Word and Spirit: Calvin's Doctrine of Biblical Authority.* Stanford, CA: Stanford University Press, 1962.

Frei, Hans W. *The Eclipse of Biblical Narrative: A Study in Eighteenth and Nineteenth Century Hermeneutics.* New Haven: Yale University Press, 1974.

Gadamer, Hans-Georg. *Truth and Method.* Edited by G. barden and J. Cumming. New York: Crossroads Publishing, 1976.

Gray, Bryan. *Theology as Science: An Examination of the Theological Methodology of Thomas F. Torrance.* Doctorate in sacred theology thesis, Katholieke University te Leuven, 1975.

Grillmeier, Aloys. *Christ in the Christian Tradition.* 2 vols. Translated by John Bowden. Atlanta: John Knox Press, 1965ff.

Gunton, Colin E. *Becoming and Being: The Doctrine of God in Charles Hartshorne and Karl Barth.* Oxford: Oxford University Press, 1978.

_____. *The Promise of Trinitarian Theology.* Edinburgh: T. and T. Clark, 1992.

_____. *Yesterday and Today: A Study in Continuities in Christology.* Grand Rapids: Wm. B. Eerdmans Publishing Company, 1985.

Hackett, Stuart C. *The Reconstruction of the Christian Revelation Claim: A Philosophical and Critical Apologetic.* Grand Rapids: Baker Book House, 1984.

Hanson, R. P. C. *The Search for the Christian Doctrine of God: The Arian Controversy.* Edinburgh: T. and T. Clark, 1988.

Hebblethwaite, Brian and Stewart Sutherland, eds. *The Philosophical Frontiers of Christian Theology: Essays Presented to D. M. MacKinnon.* Cambridge: Cambridge University Press, 1982.

Heidegger, Martin. *The Basic Problems of Phenomenology.* Translated by Albert Hofstadter. Bloomington: Indiana University Press, 1976.

_____. *Basic Writings.* Edited by David F. Krell. New York: Harper and Row, Publishers, 1977.

_____. *Being and Time.* Translated by John Macquarrie and Edward Robinson. New York: Harper and Row, Publishers, 1962.

Henry, Carl F. H. *God, Revelation and Authority.* Vol 3. Waco, TX: Word Publishing Company, 1980.

Heschel, Abraham J. *God in Search of Man.* London: Jason Aronson, Inc., 1987.

Hume, David. *A Treatise on Human Nature.* Edited by L. A. Selby-Biggs. Oxford: Clarendon Press, 1978.

Hunsinger, George. *How to Read Karl Barth: The Shape of His Theology.* Oxford: Oxford University Press, 1991.

Jaki, Stanley. *The Road of Science and the Ways of God.* Chicago: The University of Chicago Press, 1978.

Jenson, Robert W. *Alpha and Omega: A Study in the Theology of Karl Barth.* New York: Thomas Nelson and Sons, 1963.

_____. *The Triume Identity: God According to the Gospel.* Philadelphia: Fortress Press, 1982.

Jüngel, Eberhard. *The Doctrine of the Trinity: God's Being Is in Becoming.* Grand Rapids: Wm. B. Eerdmans Publishing Company, 1976.

_____. *God as the Mystery of the World: On the Foundation of the Theology of the Crucified One in the Dispute Between Theism and Atheism.* Translated by Darrell L. Girder. Grand Rapids: Wm. B. Eerdmans Publishing Company, 1983.

Kant, Immanuel. *Critique of Pure Reason.* Translated by Norman Kemp Smith. New York: St. Martin's Press, 1965.

_____. *Religion Within the Limits of Reason Alone.* Translated by Theodore Green and Hoyt Hudson. New York: Harper and Row, Publishers, 1960.

Kantzer, Kenneth. "Calvin's Doctrine of the Knowledge of God and the Word of God." Unpublished doctoral dissertation, Harvard University, 1950.

Kelsey, David. *The Uses of Scripture in Recent Theology.* Philadelphia: Fortress Press, 1975.

Kierkegaard, Soren. *The Concept of Irony.* Translated by Lee M. Capel. Bloomington: Indiana University Press, 1968.

_____. *Concluding Unscientific Postscript.* Translated by David F. Swenson. Princeton, NJ: Princeton University Press, 1941.

_____. *Fear and Trembling.* Translated by Howard V. Hong and Edna H. Hong. Princeton, NJ: Princeton University Press, 1983.

_____. *Philsophical Fragments.* Translated by Howard V. Hong and Edna H. Hong. Princeton, NJ: Princeton University Press, 1985.

_____. *Training in Christianity and the Edifying Discourse Which Accompanied It.* Princeton, NJ: Princeton University Press, 1967.

Kuhn, Thomas S. *The Essential Tension: Selected Studies in Scientific Tradition and Change.* Chicago: The University of Chicago Press, 1977.

Lindbeck, George A. *The Nature of Doctrine: Religion and Theology in a Postliberal Age.* London: SPCK, 1984.

Lonergan, Bernard J. F. *Method in Theology.* New York: Herder Publishing, 1972.

_____. *The Way to Nicea.* Translated by Conn O'Donovan. Philadelphia: The Westminster Press, 1976.

Lowrie, Walter. *Kierkegaard.* London: Oxford University Press, 1938.

Macquarrie, John. *An Existentialist Theology: A Comparison Between Martin Heidegger and Rudolf Bultmann.* New York: Harper and Row, Publishers, 1965.

_____. God-Talk: An Examination of the Language and Logic of Theology. New York: Seabury Press, 1979.

Mascall, E. L. *Christian Theology and Natural Science: Some Questions on Their Relations.* London: Longman's Publishing, 1956.

_____. *The Openness of Being: Natural Theology Today.* London: Darton Publishing, 1971.

_____. *The Triune God: An Ecumenical Study.* Allison Park, PA: Pickwick Press, 1986.

McBrien, Richard P. *Catholicism.* (Study Edition), 2 vols. in 1. Minneapolis: Winston Press, 1981.

McGrath, Alister. *The Making of Modern German Christology.* Oxford: Basil Blackwell, 1986.

Moltmann, Jürgen. *The Trinity and the Kingdom.* New York: Harper and Row, Publishers, 1981.

Newton, Sir Isaac. *Mathematical Principles of Natural Philosophy and His System of the World.* Berkeley: University of California Press, 1947.

Niebuhr, Richard R. *Resurrection and Historical Reason: A Study of Theological Method.* New York: Charles Scribner's Son, 1957.

Ozment, Stephen. *The Age of Reform, 1250-1550.* New Haven, Conn.: Yale University Press, 1980.

Pannenberg, Wolfhart. *Systematic Theology.* Vol. 1. Translated by Geoffrey W. Bromiley. Grand Rapids: Wm. B. Eerdmans Publishing Company, 1991.

Partee, Charles. *Calvin and Classical Philosophy.* Leiden: E. J. Brill, 1977.

Paul, Iain. *Science and Theology in Einstein's Perspective.* Edinburgh: Scottish Academic Press, 1986.

Peacocke, A. R. *Creation and the World of Science*. Oxford: Oxford University Press, 1979.

_____. *Intimations of Reality: Critical Realism in Science and Religion*. Notre Dame: Notre Dame University Press, 1984.

Pelikan, Jaroslav. *The Christian Tradition: A History of the Development of Doctrine*. 5 vols. Chicago: University of Chicago Press, 1984-89.

Plantinga, Alvin. *God and Other Minds*. Itaca, NY: Cornell University Press, 1977.

Plantinga, Alvin and Nicholas Waltersdorff. *Faith and Rationality*. Notre Dame: University of Notre Dame Press, 1983.

Polanyi, Michael. *The Tacit Dimension*. Magnolia, MA: Smith, 1983.

_____. *Knowing and Being*. Chicago: University of Chicago Press, 1969.

_____. *Personal Knowledge: Towards a Post-Critical Philosophy*. Chicago: University of Chicago Press, 1958.

_____. *Science, Faith and Society*. Chicago: University of Chicago Press, 1964.

Polkinghorne, John. *One World: The Interaction of Science and Theology*. Princeton: Princeton University Press, 1986.

Popper, Karl. *Objective Knowledge: An Evolutionary Approach*. Oxford: Clarendon Press, 1979.

_____. *Truth, Rationality, and the Growth of Scientific Knowledge*. Frankfurt A. M.: Klostermann, 1979.

Rahner, Karl. *Foundations of Christian Faith*. New York: Crossroad Press, 1978.

Richardson, Kurt Anders. "Trinitarian Reality: The Interrelation of Created and Uncreated Being in the Thought of Thomas Forsyth Torrance." Unpublished D. Theol thesis, University of Basel, 1991.

Schacht, Richard. *Classical Modern Philosophers: Descartes to Kant*. London: Routledge Press, 1984.

Scharlemann, Robert P. *The Being of God: Theology and the Experience of Truth*. New York: Seabury Press, 1981.

_____. *The Reason of Following: Christology and the Ecstatic I*. Chicago: The University of Chicago Press, 1991.

_____. *Reflections and Inscriptions: Essays in Philosophical Theology*. Charlottesville, VA: The University Press of Virginia, 1989.

Scotus, John Duns. *God and Creation: The Quodlibetal Questions*. Translated by Felix Alluntis and Allan B. Wolter. Princeton: Princeton University Press, 1975.

Smith, Peter. *Realism and the Progress of Science*. Cambridge: Cambridge University Press, 1981.

Stamps, Robert J. "The Sacrament of the Word Made Flesh: The Eucharistic Theology of Thomas F. Torrance." Unpublished Ph.D. thesis, University of Nottingham, 1986.

Sansom, Dennis L. "Scientific Theology: An Examination of the Methodology of Thomas Forsyth Torrance." Unpublished Ph.D. thesis, Southwestern Baptist Theological Seminary, 1981.

Sponheim, Paul. *Kierkegaard on Christ and Christian Coherence*. New York: Harper and Row, Publishers, 1968.

Swinburne, Richard. *The Coherence of Theism*. Oxford: Oxford University Press, 1981.

_____. *The Existence of God*. Oxford: Oxford University Press, 1979.

_____. *Faith and Reason*. Oxford: Clarendon Press, 1981.

_____. *Revelation*. Oxford: Oxford University Press, 1992.

Sykes, S. W., ed. *Karl Barth: Studies of His Theological Method*. Oxford: Clarendon Press, 1979.

Thielicke, Helmut. *The Evangelical Faith.* Translated by Geoffrey W. Bromiley. 3 vols. Grand Rapids: Wm. B. Eerdmans Publishing Company, 1977.

Thiemann, Ronald. *Revelation and Theology: The Gospel as Narrated Promise.* Notre Dame: Notre Dame University Press, 1985.

Thiselton, Anthony C. *The Two Horizons: New Testament Hermeneutics and Philosophical Description with Special Reference to Heidegger, Bultmann, Gadamer, and Wittgenstein.* Grand Rapids: Wm. B. Eerdmans, 1980.

Thompson, John. *Christ in Perspective: Christological Perspectives in the Theology of Karl Barth.* Grand Rapids: Wm. B. Eerdmans, 1978.

Thulstuys, Niels. *Commentary on Kierkegaard's Concluding Unsaint-Postscript.* Princeton, NJ: Princeton University Press, 1984.

Tillich, Paul. *Systematic Theology.* Vol. 1. Chicago: The University of Chicago Press, 1951.

Trook, Douglas A. "The Unified Christocentric Field: Toward a Time Eternity Relativity Model for Theology in the An-/Enhypostatic Theology of Thomas F. Torrance." Unpublished Ph.D. thesis, Drew University, 1985.

Van Buren, Paul. *Christ in Our Place.* Grand Rapids: Wm. B. Eerdman's Publishing Company, 1957.

Wallace, Ronald S. *Calvin's Doctrine of the Christian Life.* Tyler, TX: Geneva Divinity School Press, 1959, Reprint 1982.

_____. *Calvin's Doctrine of the Word and Sacrament.* Grand Rapids: Wm. B. Eerdman's Publishing Company, 1957.

Welch, Claude. *In His Name: The Doctrine of the Trinity in Contemporary Theology.* New York: Charles Scribner's Sons, 1952.

Wendel, Francois. *Calvin: Origins and Development of His Religious Thought.* Translated by Philip Mairet. Durham, NC: Labyrinth Press, 1987.

Wittgenstein, Ludwig. *The Blue and Brown Books*. New York: Harper and Row, Publishers, 1958.

_____. *Philosophical Investigations*. Transalted by G. E. M. Anscombe. New York: MacMillan Publishing, 1968.

_____. *Tractatus Logico-Philosophicus*. Translated by D. F. Pears and B. F. McGuiness. London: Routledge, 1961.

Wright, G. Ernest. *The Old Testament and Theology*. New York: Harper and Row, Publishers, 1969.

Other Articles

Avis, Paul. "Does Natural Theology Exist?" *Theology 87 (1984)*: 431-37.

Baltasar, Hans Urs von. "God Is His Own Exegete." *Communio* 13 (1986): 280-87.

Barth, Karl. "How My Mind Has Changed." *The Christian Century*, Jan. 20 (1960): 72-76.

Florovsky, Georges. "The Concept of Creation in St. Athanasius." *Studia Patristica* (1962).

Gill, Jerry H. "Faith Is as Faith Does." Kierkegaard's Fear and/Trembling: Critical Appraisals. Robert L. Perkins, Ed. University, Alabama: University of Alabama Press, 1981.

Gray, Bryan J. "Towards Better Ways of Reading the Bible." *Scottish Journal of Theology* 33 (1980): 301-315.

Gunton, Colin. "Barth, the Trinity, and Human Freedom." *Theology Today* 43 (1986): 317-33.

_____. "Augustine, the Trinity and the Theological Crisis of the West." *Scottish Journal of Theology* 43 (1990): 33-58.

Hardy, Daniel W. "Thomas F. Torrance." *The Modern Theologians: An Introduction to Christian Theology in the Twentieth Century*. Vol. 1. Edited by David F. Ford. New York: Basil Blackwell, 1989, 70-99.

Hesselink, I. John. "A Pilgrimage in the School of Christ--An Interview with T. F. Torrance." *Reformed Review* 38 (1984): 49-64.

Howe, Günther. "Parallelen zwishen der Theologie Karl Barths und der heutigen Physik." *Antwort*. Zurich: Evangelischer Verlag, 1956, 409-22.

Jüngel, Eberhard. "Karl Barth." In *Theologische Real-Enzyklopaedie*, edited by G. Krause and G. Müller. Berlin: deGruyter, 1980, 251-68.

Klinefelter, Donald S. "God and Rationality: A Critique of the Theology of Thomas F. Torrance." *The Journal of Religion* 53 (1973): 117-35.

Kroner, Richard. "Introduction." *On Christianity: Early Theological Writings* by G. W. F. Hegel. Translated by T. M. Knox. Chicago: Chicago University Press, 1948.

Kruger, C. Baxter. "The Doctrine of the Knowledge of God in the Theology of T. F. Torrance: Sharing in the Son's Communion with the Father in the Spirit." *Scottish Journal of Theology* 43 (1985): 366-89.

Langford, Thomas A. "T. F. Torrance's *Theological Science*: A Reaction." *Scottish Journal of Theology* 25 (1972): 155-70.

McGrath, Alister E. "Justification: Barth, Trent, and Küng." *Scottish Journal of Theology* 34 (1981): 517-29.

_____. "Review of *The Hermeneutics of John Calvin*." *The Evangelical Quarterly* 62 (1990): 191f.

Molnar, Paul D. "The Function of the Immanent Trinity in the Theology of Karl Barth: Implications for Today." *Scottish Journal of Theology* 42 (1990): 367-99.

Muller, Richard. "The Place and Importance of Karl Barth in the Twentieth Century: A Review Essay." *Westminster Theological Journal* 50 (1988): 127-56.

Palma, Robert J. "Thomas Torrance's Reformed Theology." *Reformed Review* 38 (1984): 23-29.

Plantinga, Alvin C. "The Reformed Objection to Natural Theology." *Christian Scholar's Review* 11 (1981): 187-98.

Scharlemann, Robert P. "Hegel and Theology Today." *Dialog* 23 (1984): 257-62.

INDEX

Abelard, Peter, 15.

Alexander of Alexandria, 13.

Analogia gratiae/analogia fidei, 148, 157ff., 247, 259, 292.

Anderson, Ray S., 250, 256ff., 270f., 279, 322.

Anselm, 15ff., 19, 67, 95, 120, 124, 148, 196ff., 275, 291, 315, 320, 335ff.

Arianism, 14f., 109f., 175, 190, 208, 279, 339.

Aristotelianism, 2, 18, 268f., 290f.

Asymmetry (triadic God-world-human relation), 18, 50ff., 58ff., 69, 82, 106, 150, 153ff., 157, 162ff., 168, 170, 177, 180ff., 185, 190, 193ff., 200, 203, 242ff., 246, 279, 286ff., 292, 299, 318ff., 321, 330, 332, 339, 355, 357, 359ff.

Athanasius, 2, 14f., 19, 24, 60, 79, 183, 187, 216, 250, 270, 289f., 292, 320, 355

Atonement, 156ff., 165ff., 173ff., 180ff., 183.

Augustine, 9ff., 14, 26, 31, 131, 153, 219, 289f., 292.

Bacon, Francis, 55, 79.

Baillie, John, 11, 82.

Barr, James, 352n.

Barth, Karl, vi, 1, 10ff., 23ff., 56ff., 60, 67f., 82, 89, 109, 146, 149, 156, 158, 168, 179f., 183, 188, 194, 197ff., 201, 217, 221f., 244, 255, 257ff., 262, 265, 267, 270f., 272ff., 275, 277ff., 280, 286, 288ff., 291ff., 294f., 300, 306f., 309ff., 313ff., 317ff., 320f., 322, 331ff., 334ff., 337ff., 358ff., 360ff.

Bi-polarity, 7f., 149, 176, 242, 263, 272f.

Boethius, 17.

Bohr, Niels, 200.

Bonhoeffer, Dietrich, 255, 271, 301, 332.

Brunner, Emil, 11, 175, 179, 188, 197, 275, 278, 292, 339.

Buber, Martin, 4, 30, 47f., 54, 58, 164, 167.

Bultmann, Rudolf, 26, 48ff., 53, 56, 69, 135, 150f., 161, 208, 210, 221, 242, 271, 297, 315, 319, 322, 331, 335,, 338, 354.

Butler, Joseph, 56, 104.

Printed in Great Britain
by Amazon

41920621R00225